12:00
18:00
Albany
Moose
L. Nippigon
NADA
NESOTA
Lake Superior
MAINE
Augusta
Montpelier
Mohawk Reservation
NEW HAMPSHIRE
VER- MONT
Concord
Lake Ontario
MASSACHUSETTS
NEW YORK
Boston
Albany
Hartford
Providence
RHODE ISLAND
CONNECTICUT
WISCONSIN
Lake Huron
MICHIGAN
Lake Michigan
Plymouth
Madison
Lansing
Detroit
L. Erie
IOWA
Moines
Chicago
New York
NEW JERSEY
Trenton
Cleveland
PENNSYLVANIA
Reading
Philadelphia
Harrisburg
Pittsburgh
Dover
DELAWARE
Annapolis
Washington D.C.
MARYLAND
INDIANA
OHIO
AMERICA
Columbus
Indianapolis
Springfield
ILLINOIS
MISSOURI
WEST VIRGINIA
Cincinnati
St. Louis
Charleston
Richmond
Jefferson City
Frankfort
Ohio
VIRGINIA
KENTUCKY
Springfield
Appalachian Mountains
Raleigh
Nashville
Tennessee
NORTH CAROLINA
TENNESSEE
ARKANSAS
Memphis
Mississippi
SOUTH CAROLINA
Columbia
Atlanta
MISSISSIPPI
ALABAMA
LOUISIANA
Jackson
Montgomery
GEORGIA
Baton Rouge
Tallahassee
New Orleans
Seminole Reservation
FLORIDA
Atlantic Ocean
Gulf of Mexico
Miami
Nassau
BAHAMAS
Havana
CUBA
HAITI
Port-au-Prince
W0109499
Heights in m
0 – 200
200 – 500
500 – 1000
1000 – 2000
> 2000
12:00 Times in zones
18:00 Times in Germany
more than 1 Mio.
less than 1 Mio.
Washington D.C. national capital
Austin capital of state
250
500

Herausgegeben von
Prof. Dr. Torben Schmidt, Leuphana Universität Lüneburg, Mitglied THE ENGLISH ACADEMY

Erarbeitet von
Denise Arrandale (Neumünster), Michael Biermann (Hamburg), Hannelore Debus (Mörfelden-Walldorf), Phil Mothershaw-Rogalla (Volkmarsen-Külte), Susanne Quandt (Bremen), Dr. Ivo Steininger (Wetzlar)

sowie
Otfried Börner (Hamburg), Ingrid Preedy (Dortmund), Jürgen Wrobel (Oberursel)

Fachliche Beratung
Rolf-Olaf Geisler (Oberhausen), Dr. David Gerlach (Marburg), Dr. Sandra Götz (Gießen), Sascha Mohr (Wiesbaden), Semra Siyli (Hamburg), Kathleen Unterspann (Halstenbek)

Für Klasse 8 an Gesamtschulen und anderen integrierenden Schulformen

Zusatzmaterialien zum vorliegenden Schülerbuch

Materialien für Schülerinnen und Schüler

- Workbook mit Audio-CD 978-3-425-14614-0
- Workbook mit Lernsoftware und Audio-CD 978-3-425-14624-9
- Klassenarbeitstrainer 978-3-425-14694-2
- Lernsoftware Einzelplatzlizenz 978-3-425-14654-6
- Vocab-App (Android-Version) WEB-425-14664
- Vocab-App (iOS-Version) WEB-425-13970
- Inklusions- und Fördermaterialien mit Audio-CD 978-3-425-14674-4
- Zoom-App www.zoom-app.de
- BiBox Schüler-Einzellizenz WEB-425-30007

Fördert individuell – passt zum Schulbuch

Optimal für den Einsatz im Unterricht mit Notting Hill Gate! Stärken erkennen, Defizite beheben. Online-Lernstandsdiagnose und Auswertung auf Basis der aktuellen Bildungsstandards. Individuell zusammengestellte Fördermaterialien.

www.diesterweg.de/diagnose

Online-Diagnose

Materialien für Lehrkräfte

- Lehrerfassung zum Schülerband 978-3-425-13996-8
- Teacher's Manual 978-3-425-14904-2
- Vorschläge für Lernerfolgskontrollen mit CD-ROM 978-3-425-14944-8
- Workbook mit Lösungen und Audio-CD 978-3-425-14914-1
- Audio-CD für Lehrkräfte 978-3-425-14934-9
- DVD für Lehrkräfte 978-3-425-14824-3
- Kopiervorlagen 978-3-425-14954-7
- Module für projektorientierten Unterricht Klasse 7-10 978-3-425-14073-5
- BiBox – Digitale Unterrichtsmaterialien
  Einzellizenz WEB-425-14994
  Kollegiumslizenz WEB-425-14998
  DVD-ROM-Version 978-3-425-14886-1
- Lernsoftware Schullizenz 978-3-425-14984-4

westermann GRUPPE

Druck A[1] / Jahr 2018
Alle Drucke der Serie A sind im Unterricht parallel verwendbar.

Redaktion: Doris Bos, Jutta Eckardt-Scheurig, Amy Frances Koerner, Dr. Katja Nandorf und Daniel Walker sowie Esther Morrison und Stevan Veljkovic
Vokabelanhang: Doris Bos
Illustrationen: Ulf Marckwort, Kassel
Umschlaggestaltung: blum design und kommunikation GmbH, Hamburg
Umschlagfoto: Dirk Schmidt/dsphotos.de
Layoutkonzeption: tiff.any GmbH, Berlin
Druck und Bindung: westermann druck GmbH, Braunschweig

ISBN 978-3-425-**14604**-1

MOBILIZED
at&t
FOR 7 AVE
SOUTH OF
W 45 ST
USE B'WAY
TARGET
DISCOVER CARD
ONE WAY
W 50 ST
TDK
John
Travolt
ONE WAY
WORK
AREA
AHEAD
FOR 7 AVE
SOUTH OF
W 45 ST
USE B'WAY
BIKE
ROUTE
AHEAD
TAVERN
AERO NYC

Q Quiz – What do you

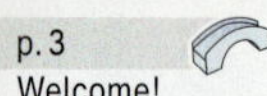
p. 3
Welcome!

In this book you will find out lots about the USA. What do you already know about the country? Try to answer the questions. The correct letters make a sentence.

1 In the USA there are ...
- B 5 states.
- A 25 states.
- W 50 states.

2 The capital of the USA is ...
- P New York City.
- A Frankfort.
- E Washington, D.C.

3 The first president of the USA was ...
- L Arnold Schwarzenegger.
- A George Washington.
- N John F. Kennedy.

4 A ranger works ...
- I at a cinema.
- R in a national park.
- Q in Hollywood.

5 The most important American film award is ...
- J the Lucas.
- T the Leonardo.
- E the Oscar.

6 An important American holiday in November is ...
- G Thanksgiving.
- B Independence Day.
- M Pancake Day.

7 The Statue of Liberty is in ...
- O New York City.
- U Los Angeles.
- E San Francisco.

8 The very first people who came to America were from ...
- S Africa.
- I Asia.
- C Australia.

9 Martin Luther King ...
- W was a US president.
- N won the Nobel Peace Prize.
- R was the first African American to win an Oscar.

10 **In New York City there are …**

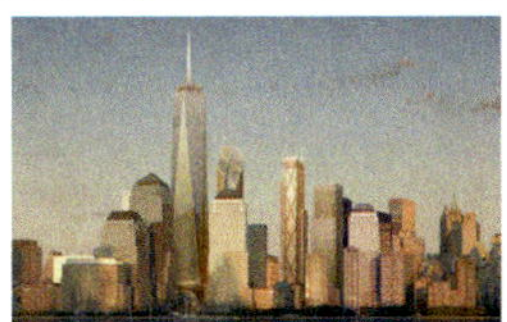

- F 2 million people.
- I 5 million people.
- G more than 8.5 million people.

11 **The colours of the US flag are …**

- T red, white and blue.
- E red, white and black.
- H red, black and yellow.

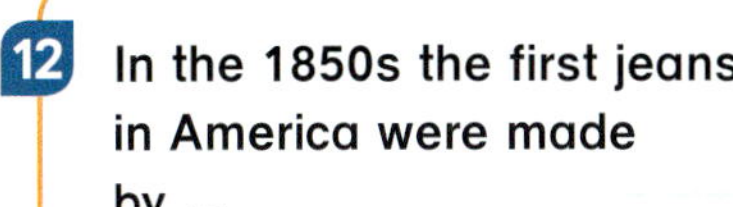

12 **In the 1850s the first jeans in America were made by …**

- A Billy Jean.
- D Johnny Blue.
- O Levi Strauss.

13 **'Moccasins', 'anorak' and 'kayak' are words from …**

- T Native American languages.
- L African American languages.
- R European languages.

14 **The letter 'B' in 'NBA' stands for …**

- P badminton.
- O breakfast.
- H basketball.

15 **Cheerleaders …**

- E shout, dance and do stunts at games.
- O play American football at school.
- N bake cakes.

16 **The first hamburger was sold in …**

- V 1465.
- J 1605.
- U 1885.

17 **'NYPD' is short for …**

- D New York Peace Dealer.
- S New York City Police Department.
- Z New York Popular Disco.

18 **The Super Bowl can be won in …**

- A American football.
- G mini golf.
- K cooking.

Your sentence:

1 2 3 4 5 6 7 8 9 10 11 12 13 14 15 16 17 18

Inhalt

R = *revision*

Inhalt

Die Angebote in *Notting Hill Gate* sind nicht linear abzuarbeiten.
Die Auswahl richtet sich nach den Schwerpunkten des schulinternen Curriculums.

R = *revision*

In diesem Buch gibt es folgende Symbole:

A1 Diese Aufgabe gehört zum **Basisweg**.

A7 Diese Aufgabe gehört nicht zum Basisweg und ist **fakultativ**.

A8 Choose
Suche dir eine Aufgabe aus. Ihr könnt alleine arbeiten, zu zweit oder in einer Gruppe. Ihr könnt euch auch eine eigene Aufgabe ausdenken.

A9 Target task
Zielaufgabe der Sequenz

Diese Aufgabe eignet sich auch für Schülerinnen und Schüler mit **Förderbedarf**. Sie kann im Sinne eines inklusiven Unterrichts mit der ganzen Lerngruppe bearbeitet werden.

 leichte Aufgabe

 mittelschwere Aufgabe

 schwierige Aufgabe

 Diese Aufgabe eignet sich für die **kooperative Arbeit** in der Klasse mit allen Schülerinnen und Schülern.

 Zu dieser Aufgabe gibt es einen Videoclip.

CD 1/1 — Der Hörtext ist auf der **Audio-CD** für Lehrkräfte (CD 1, Track 1).

CD 1 — Der Hörtext ist auf der **MP3-Audio-CD** für Schülerinnen und Schüler (Track 1).

DVD 1 — Der Videoclip ist auf der **DVD** für Lehrkräfte (Clip 1).

WB p. 5 A1, A2 — Hierzu gibt es im ***Workbook*** weitere Übungen.

p. 4 A1 — Hierzu gibt es Übungen in den **Inklusions- und Fördermaterialien**.

LiF p. 178 1 — Hierzu gibt es eine Erklärung im Grammatikteil ***Language in Focus***.

how to p. 148 talk — Hierzu gibt es eine Erklärung in den ***How to …***-Seiten.

wordbank food p. 164 — In den ***Wordbanks*** befinden sich die wichtigsten Wörter zu einem Thema.

Ein ***model text*** ist eine Vorlage für deinen eigenen Text.

Tipp
britisches Englisch: Mr/Mrs
amerikanisches Englisch: Mr./Mrs.

Hier bekommst du kleine **Tipps** und Hilfen.

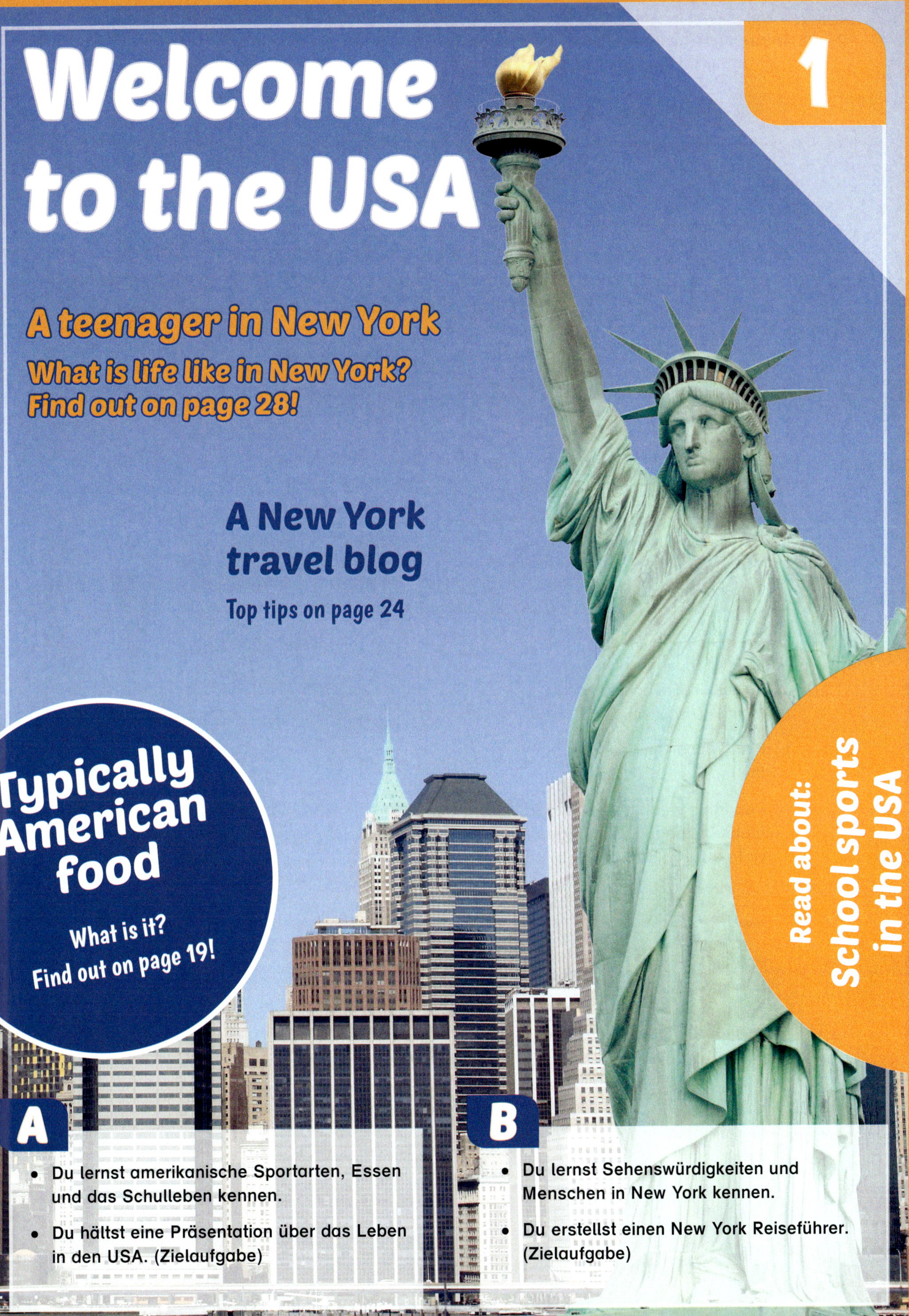

1
Welcome to the USA
A teenager in New York
What is life like in New York? Find out on page 28!
A New York travel blog
Top tips on page 24
Typically American food
What is it? Find out on page 19!
Read about: School sports in the USA
A
Du lernst amerikanische Sportarten, Essen und das Schulleben kennen.
Du hältst eine Präsentation über das Leben in den USA. (Zielaufgabe)
B
Du lernst Sehenswürdigkeiten und Menschen in New York kennen.
Du erstellst einen New York Reiseführer. (Zielaufgabe)

A1 Welcome to the USA

What comes to mind when you think of the USA? Collect ideas and talk about them.

p. 4 A1

Look at the map at the front of the book. Talk about it with a partner.

On the map I can see ...

There is ... in the west.

There are ...

Do you know what ... is?

I find ... interesting.

...

in the west
in the north
in the east
in the south
in the centre

WB p. 5 A1, A2

A2 Back in the USA

Look at the picture. What things tell you that Bill is back in the USA?

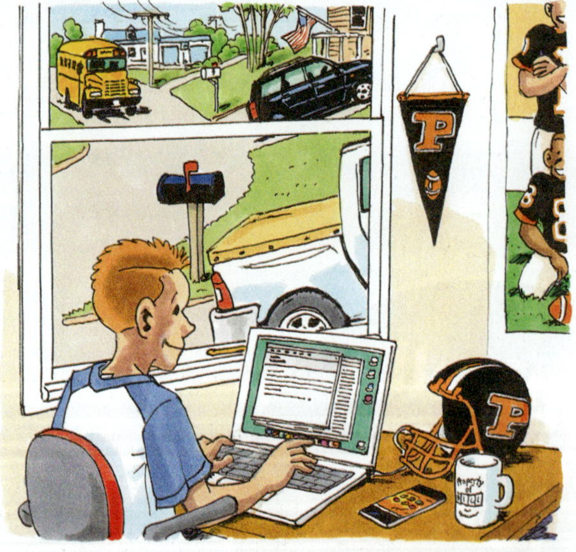

p. 5 A2, A3

Bill, who was at a secondary school in London when his family stayed there for six months, is back home in Plymouth, Wisconsin.

a) **Find Wisconsin and Plymouth on the map.**

how to read p. 149

b) **Read this email from Bill to Ellie, a friend in London. What does Bill write about his American friends?**

CD 1/1 2

Subject: Hello from Wisconsin!

Hi Ellie!
How are you?
So I'm back at Plymouth High again and wondering how you're all doing. Luckily, I'm back in my old grade with all my friends. (I keep on saying 'form' instead of 'grade' and they're all like: "Have you forgotten how to speak like an American?!") I told them how much I enjoyed myself in London.
Email me as soon as you can and tell me what's going on with you guys.
Miss you!
Bill

c) **Read at least the first of these emails from Bill. Collect information about his high school. Take notes about Bill's new schedule. Compare with a partner.**

Subject: Plymouth High Calling

Dear Ellie,
Plymouth High calling!
So, I've got my new schedule which is really different from your 'timetables'.
Every day is the same: English first period, computer science second period, math third and fourth period, social studies (that's a little like geography) before lunch and Spanish afterwards. In the afternoons I have study hall which means another period at school for homework and studying.
At your school every day was different – that was awesome! But I don't miss the uniform! When I showed the other students here the pictures of me in my uniform, they laughed themselves silly!
By the way, good luck on your math test on Wednesday. I'm sure you'll be fine, just believe in yourself!
Talk to you later,
Bill

Subject: Bad luck

Hi Jake,
Thanks for emailing me the soccer team score. Gee, the goal in the last minute was bad luck!
Prepare yourself for another shock! I made it into the football team (American football to you guys!), the Panthers, so my soccer career is over for a while.
Say hi for me to Mr. Giles. He's an awesome coach. He believed in us, and helped us believe in ourselves. That's what team spirit is all about! You'll make it next Saturday!
Bill

Tipp
britisches Englisch: Mr/Mrs
amerikanisches Englisch: Mr./Mrs.

d) ☆ **What would you like to ask Bill? Write down at least four questions.**

☾ **What would you like to ask Bill? Write down four questions. Work with a partner and answer each other's questions.**

☼ **Reply to one of Bill's emails.**

What's your favourite ...?
Who is your ...?
Do you ... ?
...

Dear Bill,
How are you? I ...
...
Speak to you soon, Ellie

how to write an email p. 155

WB p. 6 A3, A4

A3 Language detective

a) Look at the emails in A2 again. Find sentences with words from the box.

LiF p. 178 1

b) What do you notice? Can you find a pattern?

myself • yourself • himself • herself • ourselves • yourselves • themselves

c) Complete the sentences with the words from the box.

1. "I really enjoyed ??? in London," Bill said.
2. Bill says that his friends laughed ??? silly.
3. "Mr Giles is an awesome coach. He made us believe in ???."
4. Mr Giles said to his team, "Enjoy ???, guys! Football's a great game!"
5. "Prepare ??? for a shock, Jake!"
6. Ellie enjoyed ??? at the farewell party.
7. Jake is preparing ??? for the soccer game.

WB p. 7 A5, A6

CD 4

d) Listen to the CD and check your sentences.

A4 Activities at Bill's school

Look at the after-school activities. What do you find interesting?

p. 7 A4, A5

a) Copy the table and fill it in. Compare with a partner.

What?	Where?	When?	Who?
baseball			

After-school activities

Baseball
We are looking for student athletes in grades 9–12 who want to represent their team, school and community. Training takes place Monday 3–4 on the baseball diamond. Contact Mr. Jones.

Chess Club
Chess Club brings together students to play and enjoy chess. Chess can teach you life skills such as discipline and sportsmanship. Club meets Tuesday 3:30–4:30 in room 213. Contact Mrs. Hogan.

Cooking Club
Come and take part in a variety of events such as a cake competition and food science projects. Club meets Thursday 3–4 in the school kitchen. Contact Mrs. Wigand.

Game Development Club
This club is for students interested in the creation of video games. All students who are interested in making video games are welcome. Club meets Friday 2:30–3:30 in the computer room. Contact Mr. Carulli.

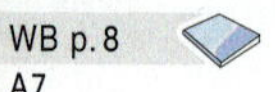

WB p. 8 A7

b) Do you have the same or similar clubs at your school? Talk to a partner.

A5 American football

a) What do you know about American football? Do you know any teams? Talk in class.

b) Watch the video clip. What do you think about the sport? Talk in class.

DVD 1

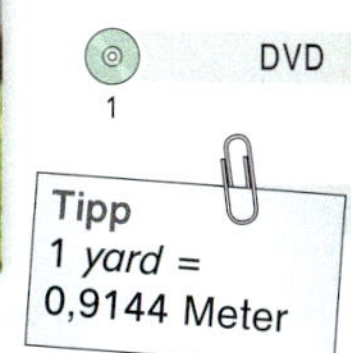

Tipp
1 *yard* =
0,9144 Meter

c) Watch the video clip again. Find out if the statements are right or wrong.

1. The rules are similar to hockey.
2. A match takes sixty minutes.
3. There are twelve players in each team.
4. The field is one hundred yards long.
5. A touchdown is worth one point.
6. The Super Bowl is an international game.

how to p. 151 watch a video

Tell a partner in German what you found out about American Football.

A6 School sports

a) Read this flyer. Look up words you don't know.

p. 9 A6

American school sports

Sports are important in American school life. School teams play baseball, basketball, American football and many other sports against teams from other schools. Cheerleaders often support their team with chants, dances and stunts. These four sports are also very popular:

1. **FIELD HOCKEY** is played on a field. The players try to score goals using a hockey stick to hit the ball.
2. **SOFTBALL** is a form of baseball that is played on a smaller field, and with a bigger, softer ball.
3. **WRESTLING** is a competition in which two people try to pin each other to the ground.
4. **LACROSSE** is a game played on a field. Players can catch, throw or carry the ball, using a long stick with a net on the end.

b) Match the photos and the descriptions.

c) What do you think about the sports? Talk to a partner.

I think ... is exciting.
... is very ...
... sounds ...
...

A

C

B

D

wordbank sports p. 165

d) Listen to two cheerleaders. Tell a partner in German what they say about their sport.

CD 1/2

WB p. 9 A8

LAND & LEUTE 1

DVD 2

Die USA – ein Land der Kontraste

Die USA sind ein riesiges Land mit vielen Einwohnern. Washington, D.C. ist die Hauptstadt. Circa 324 Millionen Menschen leben in 50 Bundesstaaten.

Kalifornien beispielsweise, das an der Westküste der USA liegt, ist mit mehr als 39 Millionen Einwohnern einer der am dichtesten bevölkerten Bundesstaaten. Die Hauptstadt ist Sacramento und die größte Stadt Los Angeles.

Hollywood, ein Stadtteil von Los Angeles, ist vor allem für seine Filmindustrie berühmt.

Die Gegend südlich von San Francisco wird „Silicon Valley“ genannt. Größere Computer- und Informationstechnologiefirmen sind dort ansässig. Wenn du im Internet danach suchst, wirst du überrascht sein, wie viele weltbekannte Firmen dort ihren Hauptsitz haben.

Ein Grund für Kaliforniens Spitznamen „The Golden State“ geht zurück auf die Zeit um 1849, als der „Goldrausch“ zahlreiche Siedler zum Goldsuchen nach Kalifornien lockte.

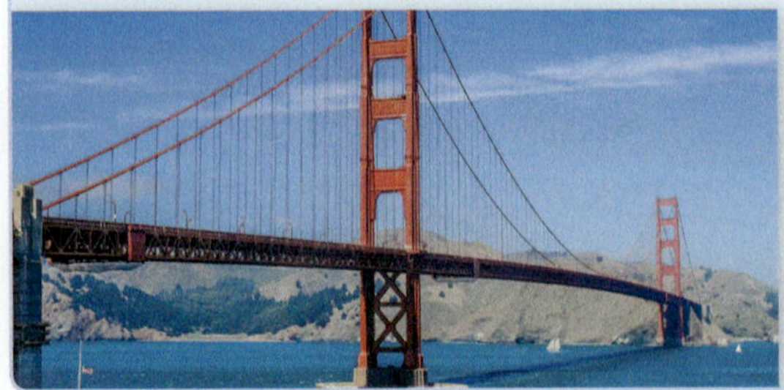

Viele bekannte Sport-Teams kommen aus Kalifornien, z. B. die San Francisco 49ers (American Football) und die Los Angeles Lakers (Basketball).

Der Staat **Wisconsin** hat 5,7 Millionen Einwohner. Die Hauptstadt ist Madison, die größte Stadt ist jedoch Milwaukee, der Hauptsitz der Harley-Davidson Motor Company, die bekannt für ihre Motorräder ist. Wisconsin, das im Norden der USA liegt, ist einer der größten Produzenten von Molkereiprodukten.

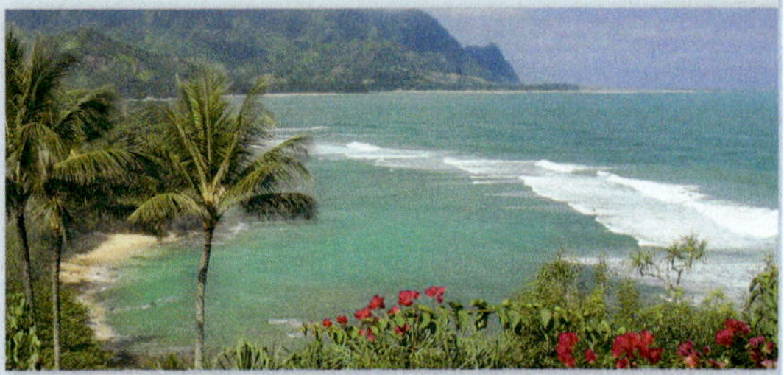

Hawaii ist der einzige Bundesstaat der USA, der nicht Teil des nordamerikanischen Kontinents ist. Er ist der jüngste der 50 Staaten, hat 1,4 Millionen Einwohner und besteht aus mehr als 130 Inseln im Nordpazifik. Die Hauptstadt ist Honolulu. Hawaiis Spitzname ist „The Aloha State“ – „Aloha“ ist in der hawaiianischen Sprache ein Ausdruck für Zuneigung und Respekt. Wegen der einzigartigen Landschaft kommen sehr viele Touristen nach Hawaii, weshalb es nicht verwundert, dass der Tourismus ein wichtiger Wirtschaftszweig ist. In Bezug auf Sport ist Hawaii vor allem für das Surfen bekannt.

Sport spielt in den USA generell eine wichtige Rolle. Erfolgreiche Teams der beliebtesten Sportarten spielen in sogenannten *major leagues*: *the National Football League (NFL)*, *Major League Baseball (MLB)* und *the National Basketball Association (NBA)*.

Suche die erwähnten Bundesstaaten auf der Karte vorne im Buch.

A7 Typically American?

What American food do you know? Collect ideas.

p. 10 A7
CD 1/3 6

a) Look at the pictures and listen to these Americans talking about American food.

1 *For Thanksgiving we usually have turkey and pumpkin pie.*

2 *A burger and French fries. Yeah, that's totally American. American fast food.*

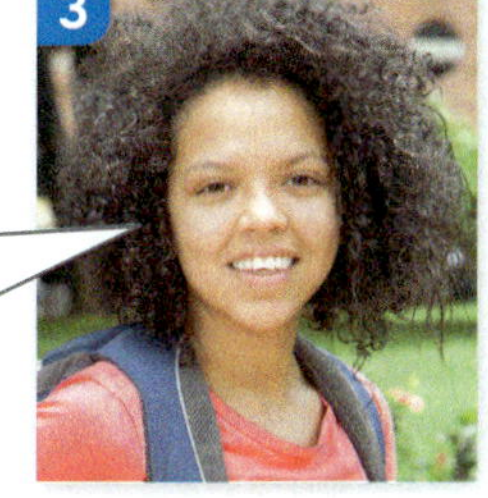

3 *I love salads. I buy organic food at the local farmers' market.*

4 *I like traditional dishes like meat loaf and apple pie. They were brought to America by the first English settlers, I think.*

5 *I love sauerkraut on my hot dog! A lot of people I know like it that way. But sauerkraut is German, right?*

6 *I live in Arizona and I love Tex-Mex food. You know, chili con carne, burritos and stuff like that.*

7 *I don't think there is one typically American dish. People from many different backgrounds live here. My family is from Italy and Ireland. A typical meal for us – and for lots of other Americans – is pasta with some kind of sauce.*

b) Read what the people say. Make a list of the different dishes. Pasta with sauce, ...

c) Which of the dishes do you sometimes eat? Talk to a partner.

I sometimes eat ...

wordbank food p. 164

d) What do you think? Is there a dish that is typically American?

In my opinion ...

WB p. 10 A9

A8 How much USA is in your life?

p. 11 A8

a) Is there anything in your life that is from the USA? Talk to a partner.

I listen to ...
I often watch ...
...
I sometimes wear ...
I like to eat ...

b) How much USA is in your life? Make a word web.

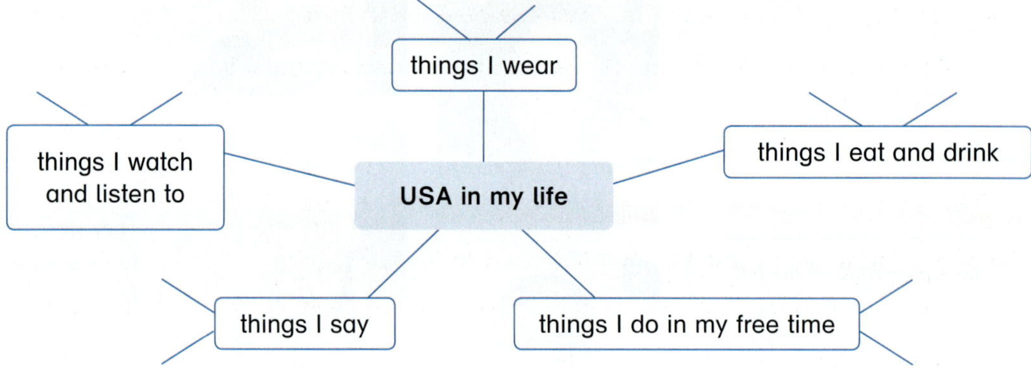

how to p. 160 discuss

c) Compare your word webs in class. How much USA is in your lives? Discuss.

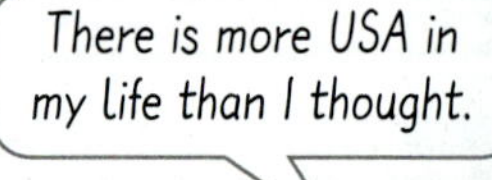

There is more USA in my life than I thought.

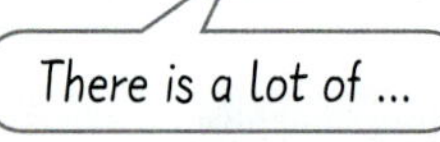

There is a lot of ...

There is not so much ...

WB p. 10 A10

A9 The American Dream

p. 12 A9

a) Have you heard of 'The American Dream'? What is it?

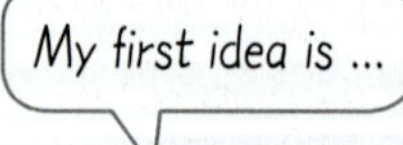

My first idea is ...

b) Read the definition.

The American Dream is the idea that anyone in the USA can become rich and successful if they just work hard enough. The idea dates back to the beginning of the United States. The Declaration of Independence, written in 1776, says that "all men are created equal" with the right to "life, liberty and the pursuit of happiness".

The Statue of Liberty is a symbol of the American Dream.

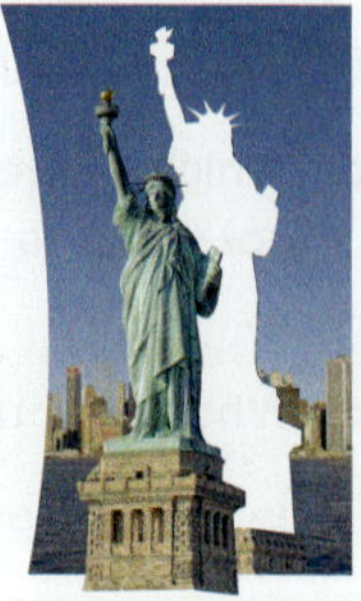

c) Now read what some people have said about the American Dream.

> "I have spent my life judging the distance between American reality and the American Dream."
> *Bruce Springsteen*

> "For many Americans, the American Dream has become a nightmare."
> *Bernie Sanders*

> "To realize the American Dream, the most important thing to understand is that it belongs to everybody. It's a human dream. If you understand this and work very hard, it is possible."
> *Cristina Saralegui*

> "No person can maximize the American Dream on the minimum wage."
> *Benjamin Todd Jealous*

d) ☆ Talk to a partner in German about what the American Dream means and what people think about it today.

☾ What is the American Dream? Take notes and talk to a partner.

☼ What is the American Dream? What do people think about it today? Take notes and talk to a partner.

A10 Target task: The USA – country, people and culture 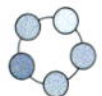

You are going to give a presentation about life in the USA.

p. 13 A10
WB p. 11 A11, A12

1. Get into small groups and decide on a topic and a product. For example you can ...

- make a fact file about a US state. You can use the license plate of the state as a starting point and add information about the capital, inhabitants and geography.
- make a poster or computer presentation on school sports in the USA. Think about the rules and the teams.
- plan a menu for an American restaurant or collect recipes for popular American dishes.

Florida

Geography
Capital City: Tallahassee
Largest City: Jacksonville
Area: 170,304 km²
Longest River: St. Johns River

Florida is the third largest state in the USA with over **20 million inhabitants**.

Its nickname is 'The Sunshine State', but Florida often has severe weather conditions like lightning strikes and hurricanes.

MYFLORIDA.COM 06-11
458 YFD
SUNSHINE STATE

Tourism
The city of Orlando is called the **Theme Park Capital of the World. More than 62 million tourists** visit the parks each year. The most famous ones are Walt Disney World and Universal Orlando Resort.

History
Florida was one of the first areas in North America where Europeans lived. It was discovered in 1513 by Juan Ponce de León, who named it **La Florida**. This is Spanish and means **abundance of flowers**.

model text

wordbank
food p. 164
sports p. 165
American English p. 173

2. In your group, decide who does what.
3. Research your topics and collect information and pictures.
4. Prepare your presentation.
5. Give your presentation in class. Give each other feedback.

how to p. 154 give feedback

Practice matters

P1 Explain

Explain what you have to do.

1. Look at the map at the front of the book.
2. Copy the table and fill it in.
3. Complete the sentences with the words from the box.
4. Look up words you don't know.
5. Research your topics and collect information and pictures.

P2 Reflexive or not?

LiF p. 178 1

a) Decide whether you need a word from the green box or the yellow box to complete the sentences. Write the sentences down.

1. "Can I help ??? with the cake, Mum?" – "No, thanks, I can do it ???."
2. Do you sometimes talk to ????
3. I met Jessica yesterday. When I saw ???, she was looking at ??? in a shop window.
4. The boy was very angry at ???. Perhaps his teacher should talk to ???.
5. Yesterday I was talking loudly to ??? and people started to look at ???.

green box	yellow box
me	myself
me	myself
you	yourself
him	himself
her	herself

CD 8

b) Listen to the CD and check your sentences.

Complete the sentences with words from the box.

6. Our teacher talked to ??? yesterday. He told ??? that we have to believe in ???.
7. The pupils don't need any help. Look at ??? – they are doing their homework by ???.

themselves • us • them • us • ourselves

CD 9

Listen to the CD and check your sentences.

P3 Not reflexive

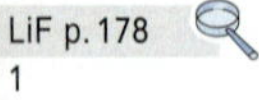
LiF p. 178 1

a) Look up the verbs in brackets in your German-English dictionary. Then complete the sentences.

1. I ??? whether it is going to rain this afternoon. *(sich fragen)*
2. You have to ??? – do you want pizza or pasta tonight? *(sich entscheiden)*
3. Do you always ??? your parents' birthdays? *(sich erinnern an)*
4. Don't ???! Everything is going to be fine! *(sich Sorgen machen)*
5. It is important to ??? if you want to stay healthy. *(sich fit halten)*
6. When you find it difficult to ???, you should take a walk. *(sich konzentrieren)*

1. I wonder whether it is going to rain this afternoon.

CD 10

b) Listen to the CD and check your sentences.

P4 American school words

a) Unscramble the words and write them down.

scheledu | mhta | dgrae | cslioa sutidse | ytusd lalh

b) Listen to the CD. Check your words and repeat them.

CD 11

Write sentences with the words to show what they mean.

P5 The USA

a) Unscramble the sentences.

1. The – USA – huge – country. – a – is
2. is – the USA. – Washington, D.C. – of – the capital
3. California's – Los Angeles. – city is – largest
4. is – San Francisco. – near – Silicon Valley
5. Sports – life. – of – American – are an – important part
6. for – Hawaii – known – surfing. – is

b) Listen to the CD and check your sentences.

CD 12

P6 Stand up paddleboarding

An English exchange student at your school who doesn't speak much German found this article in a German magazine.

Tell him or her in your own words what the article says.

how to mediate p. 150

Das Stehpaddeln ist eine Wassersportart, bei der man auf einer Art Surfbrett steht und ein Paddel zur Fortbewegung benutzt. Man kann es ohne Wind und Wellen betreiben.
Auf Hawaii war Stehpaddeln lange der Sport des Königs. Später stellten sich Surflehrer auf Hawaii mit einem Paddel auf ihre Bretter, um schneller zu guten Surfgebieten zu gelangen oder ihre Surfschüler besser sehen zu können.
Das Stehpaddeln wird weltweit immer beliebter und es finden viele Wettkämpfe statt.

P7 Sound check: how to say the letters 'ea'

a) Listen to the words and repeat them.

CD 13

b) Make two lists. Write the words in the correct list.

healthy • head • east • cheap • clean • heavy • beach • bread

c) Listen to the CD and check your lists.

CD 14

/e/	/iː/
healthy	east

B1 A glimpse of New York 

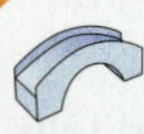

What do you know about New York? Collect ideas.

p. 15 B1

DVD 3

Watch the video clip. What is your first impression of New York?

I think New York looks really ...

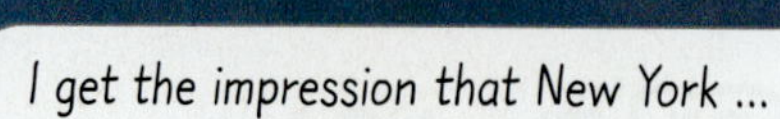
I get the impression that New York ...

B2 Alex's travel blog

how to p. 149 read

Read the blog entries. Make a list of the sights and places Alex writes about.

p. 15 B2

CD 1/4 15

www.blogs.com/alexstravels

Posted by Alex, Wednesday, April 20, New York

I arrived here yesterday. What an amazing city! Today, Cheryl, a friend from New York, took me on a tour of Manhattan.

We started with the Statue of Liberty and Ellis Island. It was amazing to see the Statue of Liberty up close. I haven't seen anything like it before. Does anybody know anything about the history of it?

But the real highlight was Ellis Island, where immigrants to the USA arrived. It's now a museum. We read lots of immigrants' stories. Some immigrants weren't allowed to enter the country, for example if they couldn't read and write or had severe physical problems. They couldn't go anywhere and were sent home on the next ship. Only the fit ones were allowed to stay.

We then took a cab – a yellow one, of course! – across the Brooklyn Bridge. We looked at some designer shops on 5th Avenue and then went for dinner. Did anybody tell you that New York is expensive? They weren't joking! I paid 11 dollars for a burger – and that was the cheapest one in the restaurant! That's a lot more than the burgers from my little town in Michigan.

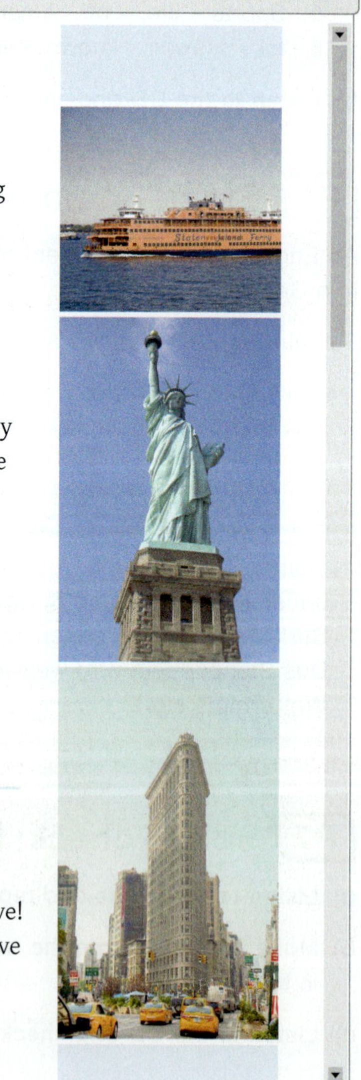

Comment posted by Serena: Wasn't the Statue of Liberty a present from the French people to the US?

Comment posted by Peter: $11 for a burger?! Wow! That's expensive!

Comment posted by Sandy: I don't care about the prices, I'd still love to go!

www.blogs.com/alexstravels  

Posted by Alex, Thursday, April 21, New York

There are a lot of skyscrapers in New York, but the newest and tallest one is One World Trade Center, which we visited today. The elevator took less than 60 seconds to get to the top. The view from up there was awesome! It really is something you shouldn't miss here!

After that, we went to the Empire State Building. The elevator's not quite as fast as the one in One World Trade Center, but I didn't complain – it was still better than walking up 102 floors! There is a race up the steps each year – can you imagine running up 1,860 steps? No thanks!

We don't have any big plans for this evening yet. Maybe we'll get hot dogs somewhere downtown or in Central Park. The hot dogs here are bigger and better than the ones at home – and don't let anybody tell you anything different!

Tomorrow we're going to the Flatiron Building, where they filmed 'Spiderman'. Has anybody seen the movie? What did you think of it?

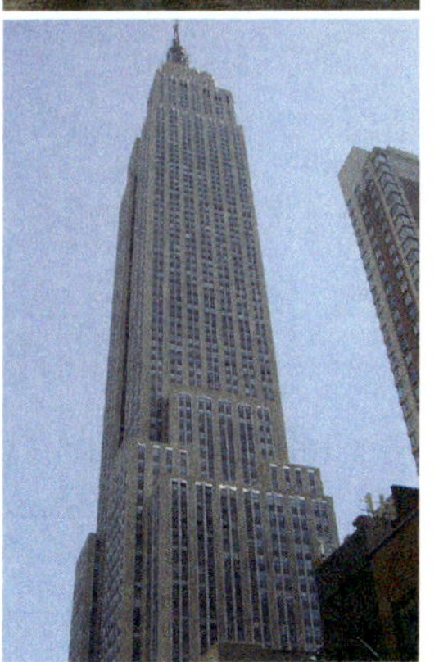

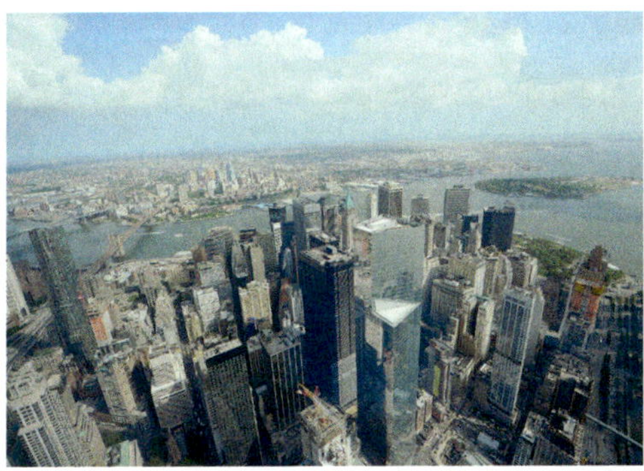

Comment posted by Hannah: The view from the top of One World Trade Center looks amazing! I'm so jealous!

Comment posted by Mark: Is that what New Yorkers usually have for dinner? Hot dogs?

 WB p. 12 B1

B3 Two days in New York

p. 17 B3

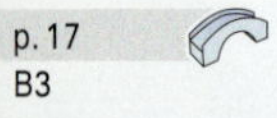

a) Look at the maps at the back of the book. Find some of the places from Alex's blog.

wordbank places p. 167

b) Which of the sights would you like to see and which of the activities would you like to do? Make a top 5 list.

c) Write down the answers to at least four of these questions.

1. Who took Alex on the tour of New York?
2. How did Alex get to the Statue of Liberty?
3. Why couldn't some immigrants enter the USA after they had arrived at Ellis Island?
4. What did Alex see on 5th Avenue?
5. What are the taxis called in New York?
6. What is the tallest skyscraper in New York called?

d) Read the blog and the comments again.

☆ Write a short blog comment on one sight.

Wow, that looks ... ! What ... ?

☾ What did Alex do each day? Write down his activities in order.

Wednesday: 1. went on a ferry. 2. ...

☼ Collect facts about at least two sights. Write a short text about one of them.

The Empire State Building has got ... There are ...

WB p. 13 B2

B4 Language detective

a) Look at these sentences from Alex's blog. What do the words 'one' and 'ones' stand for in these sentences? Find more examples.

We then took a cab – a yellow one, of course!
The hot dogs here are bigger and better than the ones at home.

LiF p. 178 2

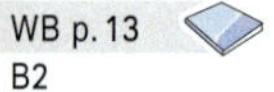

b) Can you say when to use 'one' and when to use 'ones'? Talk about it with a partner in German. Check with the LiF.

c) Copy the sentences and complete them with 'one' or 'ones'.

1. Lots of immigrants came to the USA. Only the fit ??? were allowed to stay.
2. Has anyone seen my camera? It's the ??? with the red case.
3. The hot dogs I ate in New York were bigger than the ??? I normally eat at home.
4. There were so many buses and I didn't know which was the right ??? to take to Chinatown.
5. "Which is your new bag, Alex?" – "It's the ??? with the 'Big Apple' sticker on it."

1. Lots of immigrants came to the USA. Only the fit ones were allowed to stay.

CD 16

d) Listen to the CD and check your sentences.

WB p. 13 B3, B4

LAND & LEUTE 2

The Big Apple

New York City, oder auch *the Big Apple*, wie es oft genannt wird, ist mit über 8,5 Millionen Einwohnern die bevölkerungsreichste Stadt der USA.

Menschen aus der ganzen Welt leben hier, besonders Einwanderer aus der Karibik, aus Mittel- und Südamerika, Europa und Asien. Mit ungefähr 2 Millionen Juden gilt New York als die größte „jüdische Stadt" der Welt. New Yorks *Chinatown* ist eine der größten chinesischen Gemeinden der USA.

Die Stadt New York besteht aus fünf verschiedenen Stadtteilen, den *boroughs*: Manhattan, Brooklyn, die Bronx, Staten Island und Queens. Manhattan mit seinen berühmten Wolkenkratzern ist der bekannteste, aber auch der flächenmäßig kleinste Stadtteil New Yorks. Brooklyn, das auch für seine kulturelle Vielfalt bekannt ist, ist der bevölkerungsreichste Stadtteil. Die Bronx hatte früher eine hohe Verbrechensrate, aber diese ist inzwischen stark gesunken. Der Stadtteil ist auch bekannt für seinen Zoo, der als einer der besten in den USA gilt. Staten Island, der ländliche Teil New Yorks, ist wegen seiner zahlreichen Seen, Wälder und Parks sehr beliebt. Queens, New Yorks flächenmäßig größter Stadtteil, ist einer der vielfältigsten Orte der Welt. Man sagt, dass dort 138 verschiedene Sprachen gesprochen werden.

Von 1973 bis 2001 waren die Zwillingstürme des World Trade Center eine der wichtigsten Sehenswürdigkeiten in Manhattan. Am 11. September 2001 brachten Terroristen die Türme mit entführten Passagierflugzeugen zum Einsturz. Fast 3000 Menschen verloren ihr Leben. Auf dem Gelände des ehemaligen World Trade Center (auch Ground Zero genannt) wurde das neue One World Trade Center gebaut. Es ist der höchste Wolkenkratzer in der westlichen Welt.

New York ist auch berühmt für seine lebhafte Kulturszene. Es gibt tausende Theater, Kunstgalerien, Museen, Musicals, Konzerte und viele andere kulturelle Ereignisse. New York ist auch der Schauplatz vieler Filme und TV-Serien.

Finde mehr über ein Theaterstück, Musical oder ein anderes kulturelles Ereignis in New York heraus.

WB p. 14
B5

B5 Boroughs and people

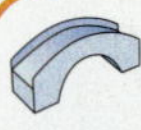

Read the first line of each text. Who lives in the Bronx, Manhattan, Staten Island and Brooklyn? Find the boroughs on the map at the back of the book.

CD 1/5 19

p. 19 B4, B5

a) Listen to what these young people say about their boroughs and read along. Do you think they are happy where they live?

Bilal Hinawy, 19

Our apartment is in the north of Manhattan, in the part called Harlem. It's not a bad place to live. We're from Lebanon, but we've been living in New York for eight years.

My dad has an old hot dog truck. On bad days he hardly sells anything. He works six days a week. I help him on Saturdays. Then we drive to MetLife Stadium, park the truck in the parking lot and sell hot dogs before and after the game. Somebody told me that the stadium is fantastic. I'm a big Jets fan, but I've never been inside the stadium.

Brooklyn is the best – I grew up around here. I go to high school in downtown Manhattan, but I'm glad to get back here in the evening. It's not as loud and there are lots of parks and beaches.

Brooklyn also has lots of cool little shops with clothes and the latest sneakers. To me, Brooklyn's special – there's no other neighborhood like it. I wouldn't live anywhere else.

My family and I live in a nice apartment on the 7th floor – luckily there is an elevator. The apartment is big, only the washroom is really tiny.

Marian Jones, 15

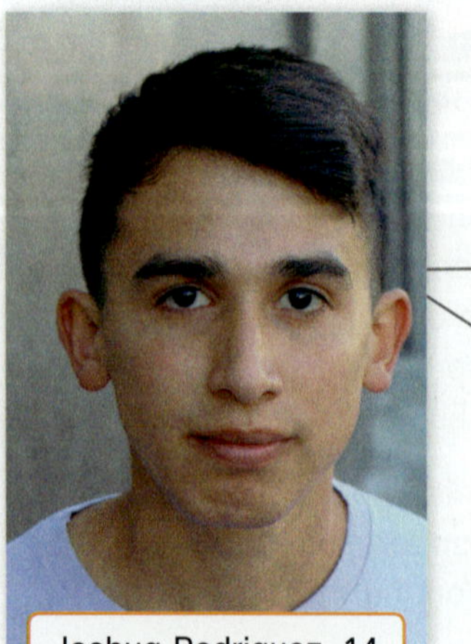

Joshua Rodriguez, 14

I'm from the Bronx. It's a busy place with lots of street art. People mostly come from South America, but my family is from the Caribbean.

Lots of people who work in Manhattan live in my borough. In the 70's and 80's it had a bad reputation because of its high crime rate, but now it's a good place to be. Hip hop, my favorite kind of music, started here. Many people have hip hop ringtones on their cellphones.

Oh yeah, and we have the best baseball team in the world – the Yankees. At home we only speak Spanish. My mom came from Puerto Rico when she was young.

I think Staten Island is the best. I don't know of anybody from Staten Island who doesn't like it here. It's not as loud and busy as Manhattan or Brooklyn, and there are lots of lakes and parks. But I love to shop in Brooklyn because it is really cool.

Some people think that living on Staten Island can be boring because it's so quiet. But it's near Manhattan with all its great clubs. You can get there by ferry – there's always something to do there.

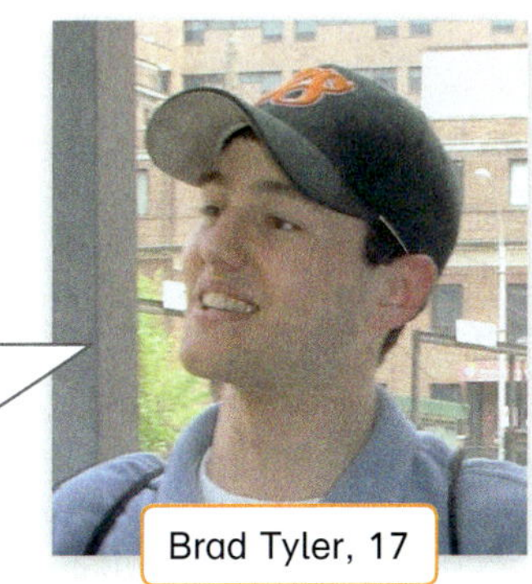

Brad Tyler, 17

b) Find the American words for these British English words in the texts.

flat • lorry • car park • city centre • trainers • neighbourhood • lift • toilet • mobile phone • favourite • mum

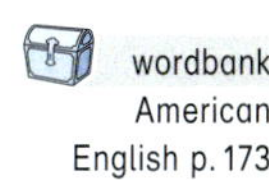

wordbank American English p. 173

c) Find phrases or chunks that show how the people feel about their borough. Write them down.

How do you feel about where you live? You can use the phrases and chunks from c).

WB p. 15 B6-B8

B6 Language detective

a) Find all the sentences in B5 with 'somebody', 'something', 'somewhere', 'anybody', 'anything' or 'anywhere' in them. Write them in two lists: 'some-' and 'any-'.

b) What do you notice? Check with the LiF.

LiF p. 179 3

c) Complete the following sentences.

1. Do you know ??? who has been to the USA? *(somebody/anybody)*
2. No, but I know ??? who is going this summer. *(somebody/anybody)*
3. I have been ??? in the USA but I can't remember where. *(somewhere/anywhere)*
4. I would like to go ??? where there is a beach. *(somewhere/anywhere)*
5. Does ??? know where Staten Island is? *(somebody/anybody)*
   I can't find it ??? on the map. *(somewhere/anywhere)*

WB p. 16 B9

d) Listen to the CD and check your sentences.

CD 21

B7 Choose

1. **Make a word web about New York.**
2. **Create a New York quiz for a partner. Swap and do the quizzes.**
3. **Find out about a TV show set in New York. Tell the class about it.**

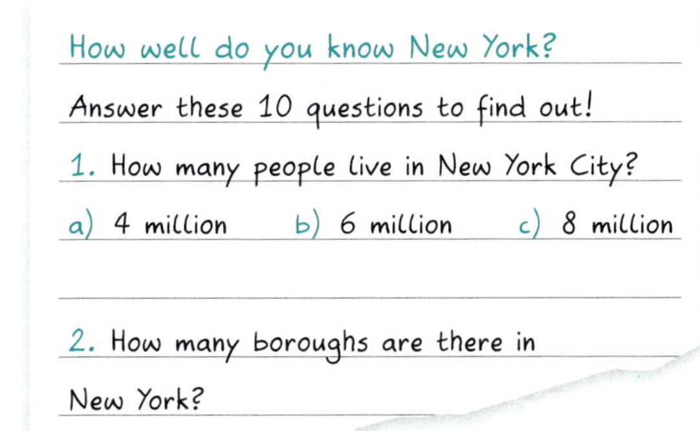

How well do you know New York?
Answer these 10 questions to find out!
1. How many people live in New York City?
a) 4 million b) 6 million c) 8 million
2. How many boroughs are there in
New York?
a) five b) fo

p. 21 B6

B8 Empire State of Mind

CD 1/6

p. 22 B7

a) Listen to this song about New York. What do you think about the music?

I think it sounds really ...

The singer's voice is ...

The music makes me feel ...

...

Grew up in a town that is famous as a place of movie scenes
Noise is always loud, there are sirens all around and the streets are mean
If I can make it here, I can make it anywhere, that's what they say
Seeing my face in lights or my name on marquees found down on Broadway
Even if it ain't all it seems, I got a pocket full of dreams

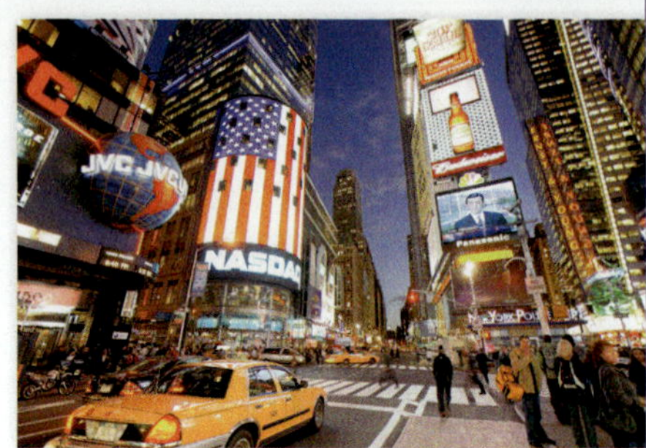

Chorus:
Baby, I'm from New York
Concrete jungle where dreams are made of
There's nothing you can't do
Now you're in New York
These streets will make you feel brand-new
Big lights will inspire you
Hear it for New York, New York, New York!

On the avenue, there ain't never a curfew, ladies work so hard
Such a melting pot, on the corner selling rock, preachers pray to God
Hail a gypsy cab, takes me down from Harlem to the Brooklyn Bridge
Someone sleeps tonight with a hunger for more than an empty fridge
I'm gonna make it by any means, I got a pocket full of dreams

Chorus

One hand in the air for the big city,
Street lights, big dreams, all looking pretty
No place in the world that can compare
Put your lighters in the air, everybody say yeah, yeah, yeah, yeah

In New York
Concrete jungle where dreams are made of
There's nothing you can't do
Now you're in New York
These streets will make you feel brand-new
Big lights will inspire you
Hear it for New York!

Music and lyrics: Carter, Shawn/Hunte, Angela/Keyes, Bert/Keys, Alicia/Robinson, Sylvia/Sewell, Janet/Shuckburgh, Alexander

b) Now read the lyrics. How do you feel about New York when you read them?

The lyrics make me feel ...

I feel that New York is ...

...

WB p. 17 B10

Find words and expressions in the lyrics that describe the city and the people.

B9 Tourists in Manhattan

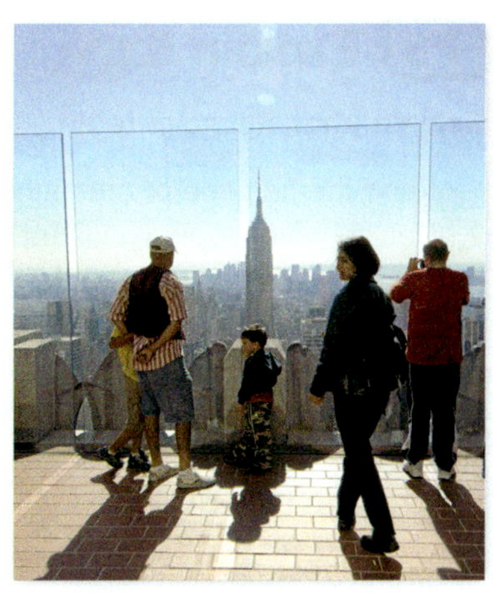

CD 1/8

how to p. 148 listen

a) Listen to an interview with two tourists in New York. Take notes.

☆ Where is Lindsay from? What is her first impression?

☾ Where are Lindsay and Pierre from? What are their first impressions?

☼ Where are Lindsay and Pierre from? What are their first impressions? What information does the reporter give them?

b) Compare your notes with a partner.

B10 Target task: New York in your pocket

p. 23 B8

You are going to make a New York travel guide.

1. Collect ideas in class. Think about:
   - sights
   - places to eat and drink
   - activities to do when it rains
   - things to do under $10
   - …
2. Collect ideas on how to present the information. Think about:
   - fact files
   - restaurant reviews
   - top ten lists
   - photos
   - …

   Think about a cover and a title, too.
3. Decide which topic you want to work on.
4. Get into small groups with classmates who want to work on the same topic.
5. In your group, decide who does what. Think about research, writing texts, finding or drawing pictures, …
6. Prepare your page together and present it to the class.
7. Put your pages together to make a brochure. Show your brochure or guide to other classes.

10 Things to do in New York

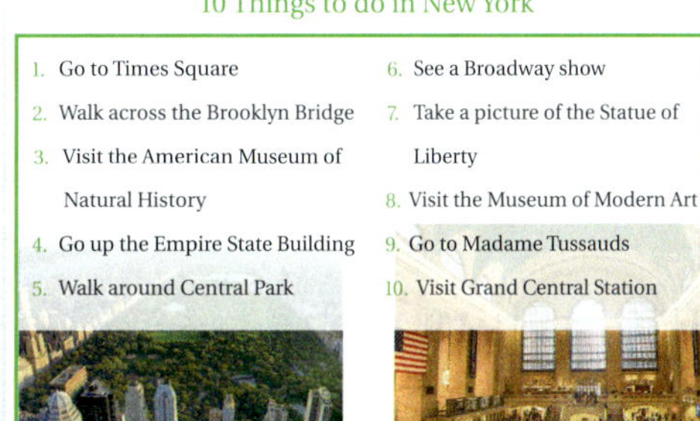
1. Go to Times Square
2. Walk across the Brooklyn Bridge
3. Visit the American Museum of Natural History
4. Go up the Empire State Building
5. Walk around Central Park
6. See a Broadway show
7. Take a picture of the Statue of Liberty
8. Visit the Museum of Modern Art
9. Go to Madame Tussauds
10. Visit Grand Central Station

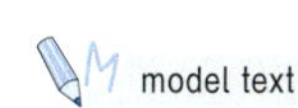
model text

wordbank places p. 167

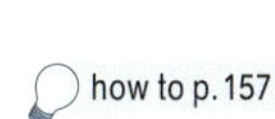

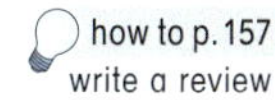
how to p. 157 write a review

Activities for a Rainy Day in New York

American Museum of Natural History

Learn about history and science in the American Museum of Natural History.

Museum of Modern Art

If you like art, this is the place for you. They have all sorts of pictures, including photographs and paintings.

Grand Central Station

This is one of the busiest train stations in the USA but it's not just about trains. The building is beautiful and you can also shop and have dinner there.

Madame Tussauds

Take a picture of your favourite famous person at Madame Tussauds. The people are made of wax, but they look very real!

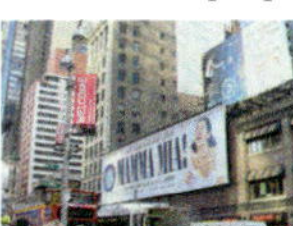

Broadway Show

There is a big selection of musicals and plays on Broadway. Everyone can find something they will enjoy.

P8 Explain

Explain what you have to do.

Ich soll ...

Wir sollen ...

...

1. Read the first line of each text.
2. Decide which topic you want to work on.
3. Find the American words for these British English words in the texts.
4. Think about a cover and a title, too.
5. Copy the sentences and complete them with 'one' or 'ones'.

P9 Don't say it again!

LiF p. 178 2

a) Copy these sentences and replace the marked word in each sentence with 'one' or 'ones'.

1. Has anybody seen my sneakers? They are the red and white sneakers.
2. This bus is more comfortable than the bus we usually take.
3. One of these postcards must be the postcard from my sister.
4. These verbs are a bit difficult. Those verbs are easy.
5. This hamburger is much tastier than the hamburger I had in Brooklyn.
6. I would like to buy that shirt. You know, the pink shirt.

1. Has anybody seen my sneakers? They are the red and white ones.

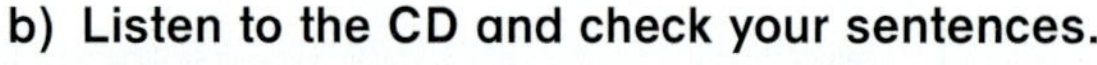

CD 23

b) Listen to the CD and check your sentences.

P10 Which ones?

LiF p. 178 2

a) Complete the sentences with 'one' or 'ones'.

1. I like skyscrapers, especially the ??? in New York.
2. What is your favourite film? – I love the Harry Potter films, especially the third ???.
3. Has anyone seen my jacket? I'm looking for the blue ??? I was wearing yesterday.
4. The sandwiches in this café are more delicious than the ??? in our cafeteria.
5. Which of the ferries is the ??? that goes to Staten Island?
6. Which is your new bike? – It's the green ???.

1. I like skyscrapers, especially the ones in New York.

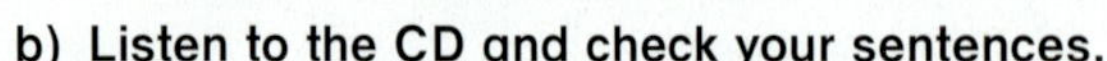

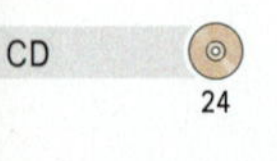

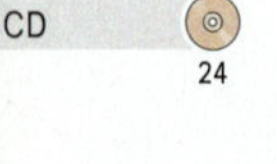

CD 24

b) Listen to the CD and check your sentences.

P11 My neighbourhood

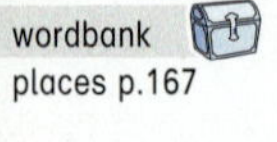

wordbank places p. 167

Make a word web with 'my neighbourhood' in the middle.

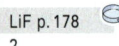

Practice matters

P12 New York

a) Look at the maps at the back of the book and complete the sentences.

1. Times Square is on the corner of … Street and …
2. Rockefeller Center is on …
3. The Brooklyn Bridge goes across the …
4. Coney Island is part of …
5. New York's airports are in …
6. The park in the middle of Manhattan is called …

b) Listen to the CD and check your sentences. CD 25

Write down similar sentences for a partner. Take turns.

P13 Any ideas?

a) Complete the sentences with the words from the box.

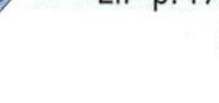
LiF p. 179 3

1. Are there ??? interesting things we haven't seen yet?
2. Alex saw ??? really famous sights in New York.
3. Marian loves it in Brooklyn. She wouldn't want to live ??? else.
4. Brooklyn is a great place. I don't know ??? who doesn't love it.
5. I know ??? who lives in Queens and he loves it there.
6. Do you know ??? about the Statue of Liberty?
7. I'd like to go ??? warm on holiday next year.
8. In Manhattan, there is always ??? to do on weekends.

some • any • anything • anywhere • somebody • somewhere • anybody • something

1. Are there any interesting things we haven't seen yet?

b) Listen to the CD and check your sentences.  CD 26

P14 Check the accent

Listen to these five little scenes. For each scene, say which of the two people is American and which is British. CD 27

P15 Different Englishes

a) Find the matching pairs and write them down.

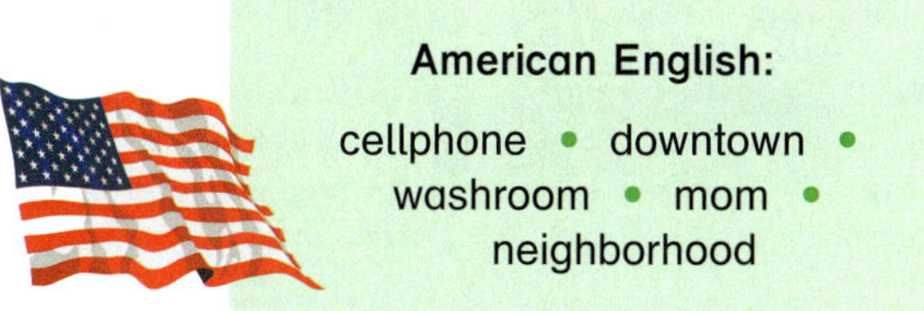

American English:
cellphone • downtown • washroom • mom • neighborhood

British English:
neighbourhood • toilet • mum • mobile phone • city centre

wordbank American English p.173

b) Listen to the CD and check your pairs.  CD 28

Optional

O Street art

street art

Street art is visual art created in public locations. The term became popular in the early 1980s. Today, there are many different forms of street art, such as graffiti, poster or sticker art, street installation, sculpture, and video projection. Artists who choose to work on the streets often want to communicate directly with the public.

Street art at 5Pointz, New York

One of the first street artists in New York was Richard Hambleton. He was born in Vancouver, Canada, in 1954. Although Hambleton's work is often compared to graffiti, he himself describes his work as 'public art'. Along with Keith Haring and Jean-Michel Basquiat, he was part of a successful group of street artists that came out of the New York City art scene in the 1980s.

A popular British street artist is Banksy. His street art can be seen in many countries all around the world, including Australia, Japan and the USA.

Shadow person by Richard Hambleton

Street art in Oxfordshire, UK

Street art by Banksy in London

Find out more about the street artists and their work. Present your findings to the class.

Challenges

2

Find out about the lives of children all over the world and their challenges

We asked a group of teenagers in the USA:

What has been your biggest challenge?

Find out what they said on page 39

Stress with schoolwork?

Take a look at Youth Helpline's advice on page 42

Read about: Land diving on Vanuatu

A

- Du findest etwas über Teenager und ihre größten Herausforderungen heraus.
- Du erstellst eine Zeitschrift für Teenager über Herausforderungen, die Teenager zu bewältigen haben. (Zielaufgabe)

B

- Du erfährst von verschiedenen Herausforderungen, denen Kinder in der Welt gegenüberstehen.
- Du hältst einen Vortrag darüber, wie Kinder in verschiedenen Ländern der Erde leben. (Zielaufgabe)

A1 A proud moment

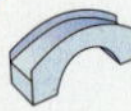 One of you talks about a picture. The others guess which one it is.

p. 24 A1

a) **Look at the pictures and find the matching phrases in the box. There are two more phrases than you need.**

- getting a good mark in a test
- winning a race
- going out with a popular boy or girl in school
- winning a football match
- saying 'no' to smoking
- baking somebody a birthday cake
- helping an elderly person

b) **Which of the situations in a) would you be proud of? Write them down.**

I would be proud of getting a good mark in a test. ...

LiF p.180 4R

c) **Talk to a partner about being proud.**

A2 Something to be proud of?

p. 25 A2

a) **Look at the situations in the box. Are they things to be proud of? Talk to a partner.**

- making a lot of money
- having lots of friends
- being attractive
- making or repairing something
- doing a bungee jump
- spraying a piece of graffiti
- speaking different languages
- standing up to a bully
- owning a fast car
- raising money for charity
- …

... is something to be proud of.

I wouldn't be proud of that.

I'm not sure that's something to be proud of.

In my opinion ...

building your own house

climbing a mountain

fighting for an idea

having a big family

buying a new car

graduating from high school

b) **Write about someone who was proud of something.**

I know someone who did a bungee jump and raised 150 euros for charity. He was really scared, but he did it. He was really proud. I also think that's something to be proud of.

model text

WB p. 25 A1, A2

A3 Choose

1. **Take a selfie or photo that has something to do with pride and write a caption. Show your photos in the classroom and comment on the other photos.**
2. **Interview someone from a different generation or someone from a different cultural background. What do they feel proud of in their lives? Report to the class.**
3. **Choose one of the people in the pictures in A1 or A2 and write a diary entry for them.**

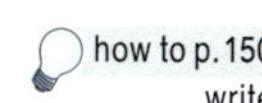
how to p. 150 write

A4 Proud

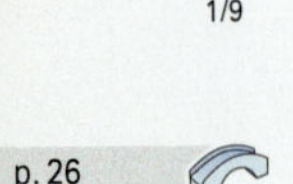

CD 1/9

p. 26 A3

a) Listen to the song. Do you like it? Do you think the music matches the topic?

I look into the window of my mind
Reflections of the fears I know I've left behind
I step out of the ordinary
I can feel my soul ascending
I'm on my way – can't stop me now
And you can do the same, yeah

Chorus:
What have you done today to make you feel proud?
It's never too late to try
What have you done today to make you feel proud?
You could be so many people
If you make that break for freedom
What have you done today to make you feel proud?

Still so many answers I don't know (there are so many answers)
Realize that to question is how we'll grow (to question is to grow)
So I step out of the ordinary
I can feel my soul ascending
I'm on my way – can't stop me now
You can do the same, yeah

Chorus

Yeah
We need a change – yeah
Do it today – yeah
I can feel my spirit rising
Change – yeah
We need a change – yeah
So do it today – yeah
'Cause I can see a clear horizon

What have you done today to make you feel proud? (yeah, let me hear you)
So what have you done today to make you feel proud? (yeah)
'Cause you could be so many people
If you make that break for freedom
So what have you done today to make you feel proud?
What have you done today to make you feel proud? (Yeah, let me hear you)
What have you done today?
What have you done today?
…

Music and lyrics: Heather Small and Peter John Vettese

b) Copy your three favourite phrases from the song. Compare with a partner.

c) ☆ Think of someone who 'steps out of the ordinary'. Write a few different examples.

Someone who 'steps out of the ordinary' is for example someone who was a couch potato but then starts to train for a marathon.
Or someone who doesn't travel much but …

☾ **Choose one phrase from the song. Write down everything it makes you think of.**

☼ **Choose your favourite phrase from the song. Write it down and explain why you like it.**

d) What have you done today to make you feel proud?

A5 What has been your biggest challenge?

p. 27 A4

CD 1/10 31

WB p. 26 A3

a) Work with a partner. Look at the photos and the boxes below. Is it possible to tell who faced which challenge?

b) Listen to the teenagers talking about their biggest challenges. Who talks about what? Take notes.

I think …'s biggest challenge might be …

Speaking in front of the class could be …'s biggest challenge.

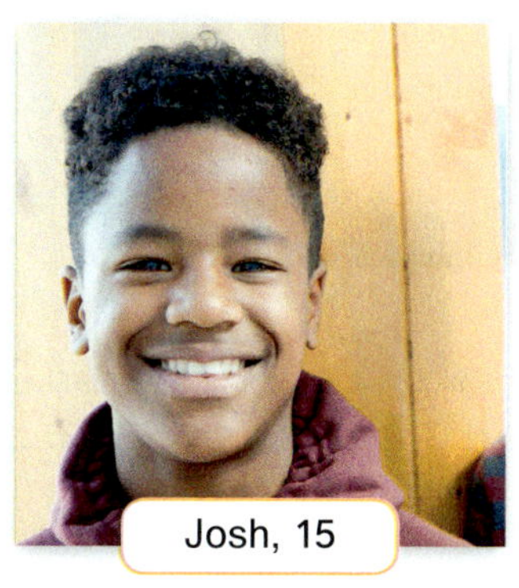

Josh, 15

Aaron, 17

Alex, 16

Briana, 16

Akash, 15

Julia, 18

1 quitting smoking	4 learning to ride a bike
2 breaking up with a boyfriend	5 dealing with an unfair teacher
3 speaking in front of class	6 adapting to a new country

c) Which one do you think is the hardest or the easiest challenge? Why do you think so?

d) ☆ Write a list of challenges **you** have faced. Which one was the biggest? Talk to a partner.

☾ What has been **your** biggest challenge? What was it like? Make notes and talk to a partner.

☼ What has been **your** biggest challenge? What was it like? How did you feel? How did you cope with it? Make notes and write a short text. Share it with a partner.

wordbank feelings p.166

A6 Two interviews

In Tom's interview, he talks about coming out as gay.

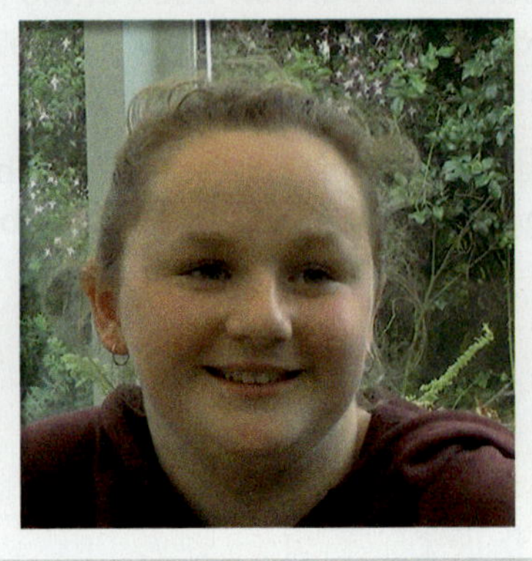

In Zoe's interview, she talks about being bullied.

come out as gay • deal with something • be yourself • accept something • support someone • LGBTQ (Lesbian, Gay, Bisexual, Transgender, Queer/ Questioning) • to adopt a child

spread rumours • say mean things to someone's face • make rude jokes • feel isolated • isolation • hurt someone • feel worthless

DVD 4, 5

a) As a class, choose the person that you would like to find out more about. Watch the video clip. What do you find out about his or her challenge?

how to p.151 watch a video

b) What do you think about what you watched? Talk in small groups.

I found it interesting that ...
...

c) Watch the video clip again and take notes on the questions in the box.

d) Answer the questions in the box.

1. The person in the video clip is called ...

2. ...

Use your notes to write about the challenge in the video clip.

Use your notes to write about the challenge in the video clip. Add some more information.

1. What is the person's name?
2. What was the person's challenge?
3. When did it all start?
4. How did the person feel?
5. Who or what helped the person?
6. What is the situation like now?

A7 Gabrielle's biggest challenge

Look at the picture, title and headings of the report on the next page. What do you think it is about?

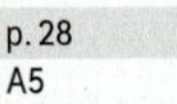

p. 28 A5

a) Read Gabrielle's report and find out if you were right.

Butt out – I quit

Why I started

I started at 13. Some of my friends started smoking and they asked me to join them. I wanted to fit in and they seemed cool – I felt some peer pressure. It made me feel different somehow.

Why I stopped

After a while I started to feel stressed when I couldn't smoke. I had no energy. Even walking made me feel tired. My parents were angry and told me to stop. They said I smelled of smoke all the time.

How I did it

I tried nicotine gum instead of cigarettes. But it didn't work. Then I tried smoking less – 20 cigarettes in the first week, then 10 in the next week. It was difficult – I got angry quickly when I couldn't smoke. But finally, I put out my last butt.

The hardest part

The first weeks were the hardest. At first I had headaches. I wanted something in my mouth so I wouldn't smoke. I ate more. Gaining weight and not feeling well made things very difficult. But after a few weeks, I started feeling better. My skin and hair look better now.

My message to you

It's hard, but you can do it. Different things work for different people. It's important to find out what works for you. I advise you not to do it alone. My family and friends helped me a lot. Lots of kids think smoking won't hurt them. But it can ruin your life. So stop now – while you're still young and healthy.

CD 1/11 32

b) **Read the report again. Why did Gabrielle start smoking? What helped her to stop?**

c) **What do you think about Gabrielle's report? Which part did you find interesting?**

I think the part where she ... was very interesting.

WB p. 27 A4

A8 Health warnings

a) **Read the health warnings from some American cigarette packets. Talk in class about what they mean in German.**

cigarette smoke contains carbon monoxide • smoking causes lung cancer • smoking causes heart disease • smoking causes emphysema • smoking may complicate pregnancy • smoking by pregnant women may result in fetal injury and premature birth • smoking by pregnant women may result in low birth weight

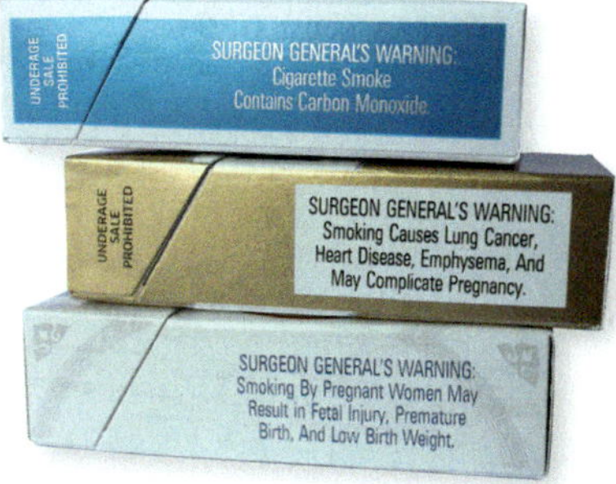

b) **What health warnings are there on cigarette packets in Germany or other countries? Are they similar?**

What do you think about health warnings on cigarette packets? Do they have an effect on you? Talk in class.

wordbank health p.165

A9 Just be smoke-free

p. 30 A6

a) Read this flyer about how to stop smoking. Which piece of advice do you find most useful?

Breaking the habit
It is not easy to quit smoking.
Breaking the habit is the hardest thing.
Here are some things you can do to help you quit:
Go to non-smoking places with your friends.
Spend a few days away from your friends who smoke.
Don't go to places where you normally smoke.
If your family smokes, ask them not to smoke around you.
Exercise! It will make you feel better, and keep you healthy.
Plan lots of fun activities. Keep yourself busy.
Buy lots of carrots, celery and other healthy foods so you can munch instead of smoke.

b) What does it tell you to do to break the habit?

The flyer tells you to ... | *The flyer tells you not to ...* | *One tip is to ...* | *It says it is a good idea to ...* | *It advises you not to ...*

wordbank health p. 165

how to p. 160 discuss

c) What do **you** think about smoking? Make notes with a partner and discuss in class.

WB p. 28 A5

A10 Youth Helpline

p. 31 A7

Steven is having problems with a big homework project but he is afraid to tell his teacher about it. He sends a text message to Youth Helpline.

a) Read the reply that Steven gets. Copy three pieces of advice.

Don't panic, ...

LiF p. 180 5
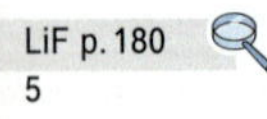

b) Work with a partner. Take turns to tell each other the advice Youth Helpline gives Steven.

They tell Steven not to ... | *They also advise him to ...*

WB p. 28 A6–A8

What other advice would **you** give Steven? Tell a partner.

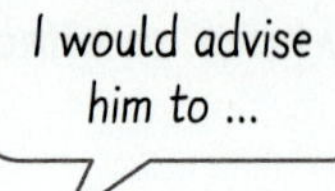

I would tell him not to ...

Hi! Thanks for writing to us! Firstly, don't panic! And don't hide your stress from everyone – it will only make things worse. Talk to your classmates about the project, maybe they can help you. Don't leave the project until the day before the deadline. Talk to your teachers, if possible. They will understand and will try to help you!

Reply to this text message if you want some more advice, or if you want to talk to one of us, call us on

A11 Target task: Challenges

As a class, you are going to design and create a teen magazine on challenges. Look at some teen magazines for ideas.

p. 32 A8

1. **Discuss the following points and make notes:**
   - What do you want to have in your magazine? Think about:
     - an interview
     - an article
     - a photo story
     - a fact file
     - a comic
     - illustrations
   - What do you want to write about? Here are some ideas:
     - a typical teen challenge
     - your personal challenge
     - a famous person's challenge
     - someone who could not face a challenge or did not complete it
     - community, health or global challenges
2. **Use your notes to plan your magazine in more detail. Write a list of the contents on the board. Don't forget to think about a cover and a table of contents.**
3. **Decide who wants to work on which topic and get into small groups.**
4. **In your group, collect ideas on how to present your topic. Decide on the best one and plan what you need to do.**
5. **Work on your part of the magazine and present it.**
6. **Give each other feedback.**
7. **Edit your work.**
8. **As a class, put the magazine together. You could even publish a print or digital edition.**

how to p. 152 work on a project

PERSONAL CHALLENGES!

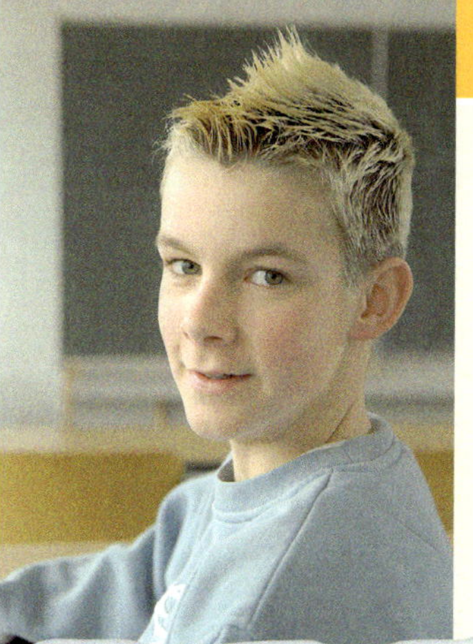

Joshua: reading buddy

I am going to become a school reading buddy. My dad told me to apply because he thinks I will be good at it. I help my little sister with her reading at home. She has just started reading and she loves it.

It will be a challenge for me, because I will work with pupils who really need help with reading. Many of them don't enjoy it like my sister does.

I'm looking forward to it because I think it will be

Practice matters

P1 Explain

Explain what you have to do.

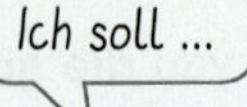

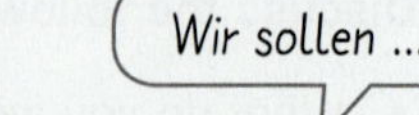

...

1. Show your photos in the classroom and comment on the other photos.
2. Report to the class.
3. Read the health warnings from cigarette packets.
4. Take turns to tell each other the advice.
5. Use your notes to plan your magazine in more detail.

P2 Being proud

LiF p. 180 4R

a) Match the words and phrases and write them down.

raising saying helping getting	'no' to smoking someone cross the road a good mark in a test money for charity

winning climbing looking fighting	after somebody who is ill a football match for an idea a mountain

CD  39

b) Listen to the CD and check your phrases.

P3 Teen challenges

LiF p. 180 4R

What are typical challenges that teenagers face? Write down your ideas. You can use the verbs in the box.

> speaking • breaking up • learning • quitting • ...

speaking in front of the class, ...

P4 Working with words

a) Read A7 about Gabrielle's challenge again. Write down these words and phrases in English.

> ich höre auf • Gruppenzwang • müde • ich roch nach Rauch • schwierig • meine letzte Kippe • ich aß mehr • ich fing an, mich besser zu fühlen • gesund

CD  40

b) Listen to the CD and check your words and phrases.

☼ **Choose at least four words or phrases and explain what they mean.**

tired: When somebody is tired, he or she does not have a lot of energy and needs ...

P5 In the classroom

a) Report what the teacher told her class to do and what not to do.

She told them to use a dictionary.
She told them not to leave …
…

LiF p. 180 5

Don't leave the classroom.
Use a dictionary.
Don't talk when I'm talking.
Work quietly.
Don't play on your cellphones.
Use a black pen.
Choose a text.

b) Listen to the CD and check your sentences.

CD 41

P6 Listen to the advice

Listen to the teacher talking to a group of pupils about how to quit smoking. Report the advice to a friend. You can use the phrases in the box.

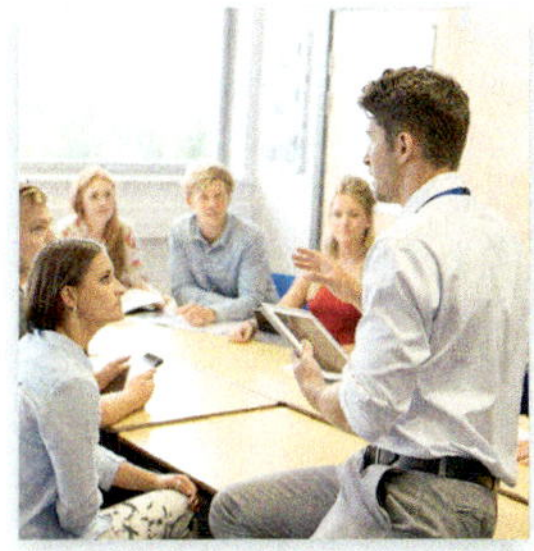

CD 42

LiF p. 180 5

The teacher told the pupils to …

He advised them to …

He advised them not to …

He told the pupils not to …

- find a new way to school
- go past the places where you normally get cigarettes from
- spend time with people who are smoking
- do sports as often as possible
- be too hard to yourself

P7 Sound check

a) Listen to the CD and repeat the words in the box.

CD 43

challenges • horizon • nicotine • elderly • attractive • reflection • personal • charity • cigarette • graduate

b) Listen again. Is the stress on the first, the second or the third syllable? Write three lists.

first syllable	second syllable	third syllable
challenges	…	…
…		

c) Listen to the CD and check your lists.

CD 44

B1 Your life

Choose one day of the week. What do you do in the morning, in the afternoon and in the evening?

On Mondays I …

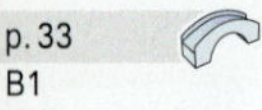

p. 33 B1

Work with a partner. Describe your everyday life. Think about:

- When do you usually get up, have breakfast and leave the house?
- What do you do in your free time? What are your hobbies, sports, clubs, friends, …?
- What jobs do you have to do at home?
- How do you get to school?
- Have you got a room of your own?
- …

I usually … | *I often …* | *I never have to …* | *I've got …* | *…* | *In my free time I sometimes …* | *I have to …*

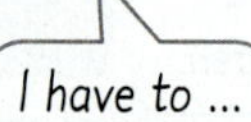

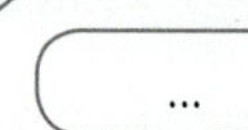

B2 Growing up

Read the first lines of the texts. How old are the children? Where are they from?

p. 34 B2

CD 1/12 45

how to read p. 149

a) Read at least the first two profiles. What does each child say about his or her life?

Miriam

I'm Miriam, I'm 12 years old and I come from a small village in Ghana in Africa. I have been going to school since I was eight years old. I love school, but I can only go for another two years until I'm 14. My parents say I will then be old enough to look after the house and children.

My older sister is 15. She has to stay at home and look after my younger brothers and sisters.

My mother works in our peanut fields. My father goes to the market in the next village to sell the peanuts. When we harvest our peanuts, I have to work in the fields all day. I have been helping in the fields for a few years. I always collect water in the mornings. It takes an hour to walk to school, but I like school more than working in the fields.

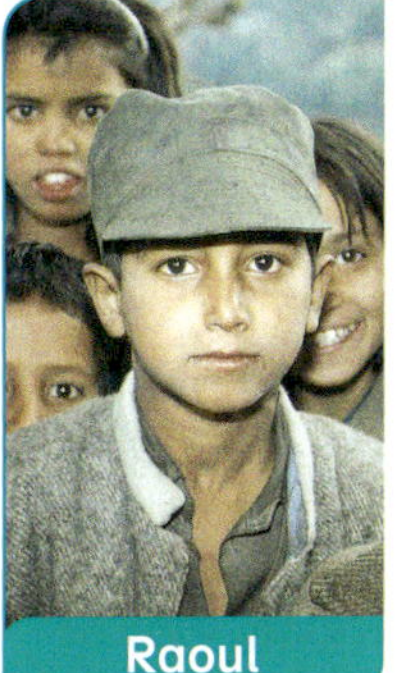

Raoul

I'm Raoul and I'm 13 years old. I'm a shoe shine boy in Mexico City. I live with my two brothers and three sisters in a small house outside the city centre. Our parents died in an accident three years ago.

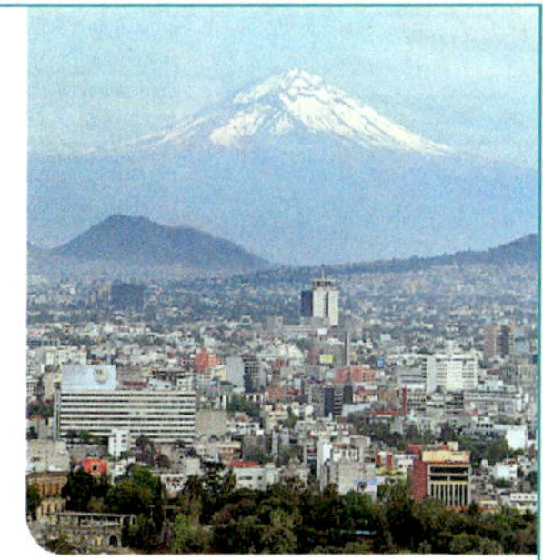

I get up at six every morning, but I don't have any breakfast. I leave the house and get on a bus into town. I don't have any money so I hang on to the back of the bus. When we are in the city, I jump off. I clean shoes all morning. I have been doing that since I was nine years old. Sometimes I earn about 100 pesos but that is not much to buy food for six people.

After that I go to school for three hours. I have been going to the local school for two years. I do my homework in the evening. We have no electricity so when it gets dark I just go to bed. My sisters share a bed. My brothers and I sleep on the floor.

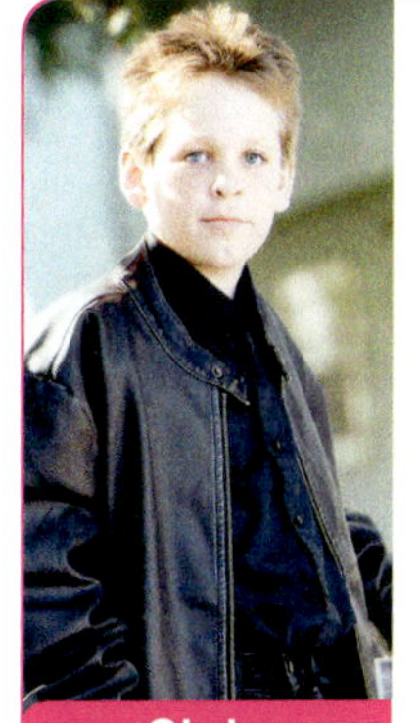

Chris

I'm Chris, I'm 12 years old and I've got two brothers, Thomas and Oliver. We live with our parents in a trailer park in the state of New York.

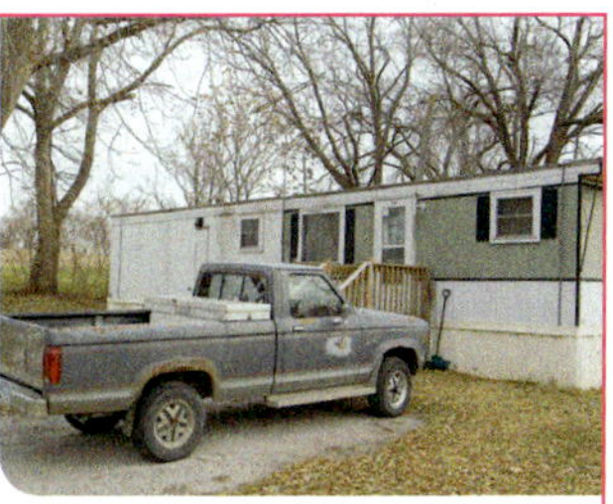

After school, I eat and then I do my homework or go out to collect aluminum cans. I get cash for them at the local store. I've been collecting cans since I can remember!

In the summer the trailer gets really hot and in the winter the floors are really cold. We have got AC but it's too expensive to run.

Life in the park is not that bad. We've got a football field and two playgrounds. My friends from the park and I have been using the football field a lot this year. A few of the residents have been leaving a lot of trash around, so the park is sometimes really dirty. I never invite any of my school friends home because I don't want them to see how poor we are.

b) Work in groups of three. Each person chooses a text and reads it in more detail. Collect information in the table in your workbook.

WB p. 30 B1

c) Tell your group about the information you collected. Complete your table with information about the other children.

He has got ...

She usually goes ...

d) In your group, compare the children's lives to your lives. What is the same? What is different?

WB p. 31 B2, B3

Raoul has to do homework. I have to do homework, too.

Miriam has to collect water, I don't.

Chris ...

B3 Different lives

p. 36 B3

☆ **Read about Miriam and Raoul again and write down the answers to these questions.**

1. How much longer can Miriam go to school?
2. What does her older sister do?
3. What does she do in the mornings?
4. How long does it take her to walk to school?
5. Where does Raoul live?
6. Who does he live with?
7. How does he get to the city centre?
8. Why does he go to bed when it gets dark?

☾ **Read about all the children again and write down the answers to these questions. Why …**

1. … has Miriam only got two more years of school?
2. … does Miriam's father go to the market?
3. … does Raoul have to hang on to the back of the bus?
4. … does Raoul try to earn more than 100 pesos a day?
5. … does Chris collect cans?
6. … does Chris's family not use the AC?

☼ **Read about all the children again and write down the answers to these questions.**

1. Which of the children work? What do they do?
2. Who do you think has got the most responsibility? Explain.
3. What do you think are each of the children's biggest challenges?

B4 Language detective

a) Look at these two sentences from Miriam's profile. What do you notice about the verb after 'have been'?

I have been going to school since I was eight years old.

I have been helping in the fields for a few years.

LiF p. 181 6

b) Find more examples in the profiles. Write them down. When do you use these sentences? Share your ideas with a partner.

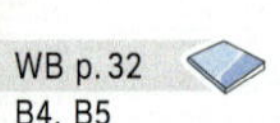
WB p. 32 B4, B5

☼ **What about you? Write sentences about yourself or someone you know.**

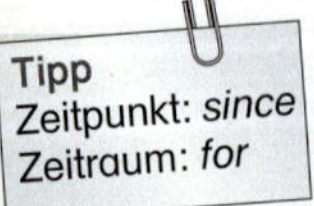

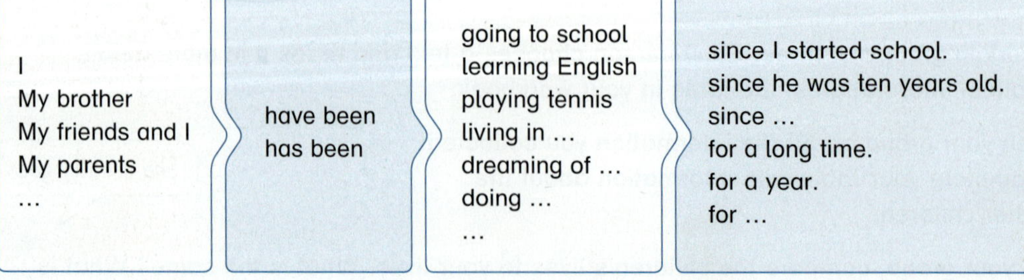

I
My brother
My friends and I
My parents
…
have been
has been
going to school
learning English
playing tennis
living in …
dreaming of …
doing …
…
since I started school.
since he was ten years old.
since …
for a long time.
for a year.
for …

I have been going to school since I was six years old.

B5 Choose

1. The children in B2 live on different continents. Who comes from which continent? What do you know about these continents?
Work in groups. Choose a continent and make a poster.

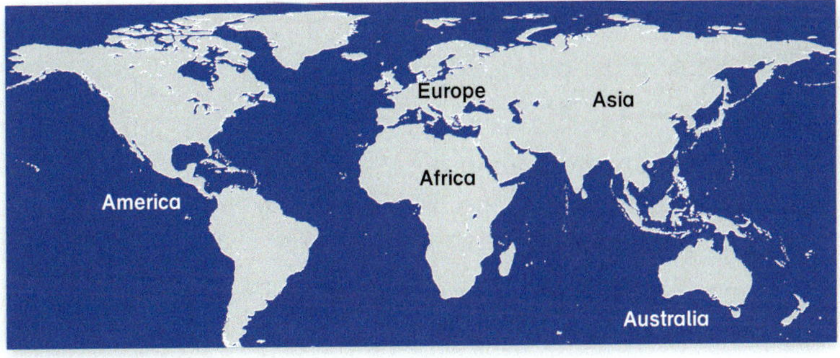

2. Choose one of the countries in B2: Ghana, Mexico or the USA. Find a map and pictures. Find out more about the country and about the people who live there. Make a fact file.

how to p. 152 research online

Fact sheet
Name of the country: Ghana
Capital: ...
Population: ...
...

3. Write a diary entry for one of the children. What did he or she do? How did he or she feel?

Dear diary,
today I ... I felt ...

B6 A difficult challenge in Malawi

Look at the photo. What can you see? What do you think it is?

CD 1/13 48

Listen to the reporter talking about how William Kamkwamba, a young boy from Malawi in Africa, used wind to produce electricity for his village.

How did William get the idea?

Listen again and complete the sentences.

1. William wanted to get …
2. He went to the library to …
3. When he read a report about a windmill, he …
4. Finally he managed to …
5. Later he also brought …
6. William wrote …
7. He went … and …

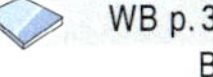
WB p. 33 B6

B7 Growing up on Vanuatu

Look at the photo. What can you see?

p. 37 B4

WB p. 34 B7

a) Tamal is a boy from Vanuatu. Read what he says about land diving. What is it and why do people do it?

We do land diving on Vanuatu to test our courage and show that we are no longer little boys but have become men. We dive off platforms on tall wooden towers.

Land diving has been practised for centuries. It takes about thirty men one month to build a tower. Trees are cut to build the body, a site is cleared for the tower and all rocks are removed from the soil. The centre of the tower is made from one tree and the scaffolding is made of poles that stabilise it.

Platforms come out about two metres from the front of the tower. The lowest platform is 10 metres high and the highest platform is near the top. When we dive off our platform, the platform bends downwards and absorbs some of the force from falling.

There are vines tied to our ankles when we dive. The vines are chosen by a village elder to match each diver's weight. The vines have to be very elastic so that they do not break easily. That's why we only do land diving in the months of April, May and June following the wet season. Last year, the vines were chosen by my grandfather and the tower was built in May so we could dive in June.

There is no other safety equipment, but the soil below is turned over and softened before each dive. The night before we dive, we sleep beneath the tower to keep evil spirits away. When we dive, we try to touch the soil with our shoulders. That is what makes a good dive. If we have lots of good dives, we will be respected by others.

LiF p. 182 7R

b) Write down what is done to prepare for land diving.

c) What do you think about land diving? Talk to a partner.

First, a tower is built.
Trees are ...

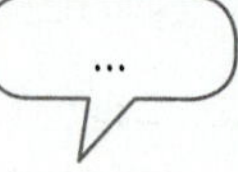

It sounds really ...

I don't think I would ...

I don't understand how ...

...

WB p. 35 B8

Do you know similar tests of courage from other cultures? Tell the class about them.

B8 Children's rights and responsibilities

The United Nations Convention on the Rights of the Child tells everyone the rights of children and young people under the age of 18.

a) **Read about the rights of children.**

b) **Talk to a partner about the rights in German. What do you think they mean?**

Rights

- Children have the right to be adequately fed …
- Children have the right to be educated …
- Children have the right to make mistakes …
- Children have the right to play and relax …

c) **But children also have responsibilities. Read and talk about them.**

Responsibilities

- … and the responsibility to learn from their mistakes.
- … and the responsibility to let others join in their games.
- … and the responsibility not to waste food.
- … and the responsibility to learn as best they can.

d) **Work with a partner. Match the responsibilities with the rights and write down the sentences.**

Children have the right to be adequately fed and the responsibility not to waste food.
Children …

WB p. 35 B9, B10

Choose the statement that you think is the most important. Tell your partner which one you have chosen and why.

I think … is the most important because …

B9 Target task: Different worlds

You are going to give a three-minute computer presentation with the title 'Different worlds'.

p. 39 B5

1. **Get into groups of three or four. Choose a country where you think children live completely differently from you.**
2. **Do some research. You can find ideas in the box.**
3. **Work on your presentation. It should contain five slides and last three minutes. Concentrate on the most important information.**
4. **Decide who presents which part. Think of a question you can ask the class at the end of your presentation.**

You could find out about:

- what the country is like
- challenges that the children in the country face (poverty, getting to school, living in a war zone, …)
- the rights and responsibilities of children in the country
- a day in the life of a child in the country

how to present p. 153

5. **Give your presentation and listen to the other presentations. Take notes and answer the other groups' questions.**

P8 Explain

Explain what you have to do.

1. Read at least the first two profiles.
2. Collect information in the table in your workbook.
3. Find more examples in the profiles.
4. Choose the statement that you think is the most important.
5. Share your ideas with a partner.

P9 What have they been doing?

LiF p. 181 6

a) Unscramble the sentences.

1. harvesting – Miriam – since this morning. – peanuts – has been
2. have been – for five hours. – Miriam's parents – working – in the fields –
3. cleaning – has been – all morning. – Raoul – shoes
4. Raoul's brother – doing – for half an hour. – has been – his homework
5. in the trailer park – living – have been – Chris and his family – for many years.
6. has been – football – playing – Chris – since 10 o'clock.

1. Miriam has been harvesting peanuts since this morning.

CD 50

b) Listen to the CD and check your sentences.

P10 Life in a trailer park

LiF p. 182 7R

a) Look at B2 again and read about Chris. Match the sentence parts.

1. The cans
2. The AC
3. A lot of trash
4. The trailer park
5. Chris's school friends

a. are never invited to his home.
b. are returned at the local store.
c. is not looked after very well.
d. is never used.
e. is left around.

CD 51

b) Listen to the CD and check your sentences.

P11 What has been done today?

LiF p. 182 7R

a) Complete the sentences with chunks from the box.

1. The peanuts …
2. The peanuts … at the market.
3. The homework … by Raoul.
4. Water …
5. The shoes …
6. Lunch …

have been sold has been prepared have been cleaned has been collected have been harvested has been done

1. The peanuts have been harvested.

CD 52

b) Listen to the CD and check your sentences.

P12 When will that be done?

a) **Answer the questions using the information in brackets. Write down your answers.**

LiF p. 182 7R

1. When will the cans be collected? (this afternoon)
2. When will a new school be built near the park? (soon)
3. When will the building be finished? (next summer)
4. When will the football field be used? (after school)
5. When will Chris be given the money for his cans? (tomorrow)

1. The cans will be collected this afternoon.

b) **Listen to the CD and check your answers.**

CD 53

P13 Rights and responsibilities

a) **Complete the sentences using the phrases in the box.**

LiF p. 182 7R

1. Children have the responsibility to listen to others and they have the right to …
2. Children have the responsibility not to waste their food and they have the right to …
3. Children have the responsibility to learn as much as they can and they have the right to …
4. Children have the responsibility to respect others and they have the right to …

be respected be heard be educated be fed

b) **Listen to the CD and check your sentences.**

CD 54

P14 William's windmills

a) **Listen to the report about William Kamkwamba and his invention again. Take notes on the following points:**

CD 1/13 48

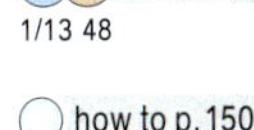

how to mediate p. 150

- where William comes from
- why he wasn't allowed to go to school
- where and how he got the idea of building a windmill
- what the windmills were used for
- how he became famous

b) **Use your notes to give a short summary of the report to a partner in German.**

P15 My life

a) **Listen to the podcast about Lena, who was interviewed for a German youth magazine. Take notes.**

CD 55

how to mediate p. 150

b) **Tell a partner the most important facts in English.**

Optional

O Anti-smoking adverts

1

A TIP FROM A
FORMER SMOKER
ALLOW EXTRA TIME TO PUT ON YOUR LEGS.
Brandon, Age 31, Diagnosed at 18
North Dakota
Smoking causes immediate damage to your body. For Brandon, it caused Buerger's disease, which cut off blood flow and led to amputation. You can quit. For free help, call 1-800-QUIT-NOW.
CDC
U.S. Department of Health and Human Services
Centers for Disease Control and Prevention
www.smokefree.gov

2

For more information on lung cancer, keep smoking.

How effective do you think these posters are?

Find more anti-smoking adverts online and present them to the class. What do you think of them?

Love and friendship

3

Chat-up lines: funny, romantic, or embarrassing?

Check out page 60!

Write your own love story on page 71!

What is a friend?

Find out on page 56 what young people think!

Read the story of Romeo and Juliet

A

- Du sprichst über Freundschaft und liest Gedichte über Liebe und Freundschaft.
- Du machst einen ‚friendship tree' in der Klasse. (Zielaufgabe)

B

- Du lernst Shakespeares berühmtes Theaterstück ‚Romeo and Juliet' kennen.
- Du schreibst eine moderne Liebesgeschichte. (Zielaufgabe)

A1 What is a friend?

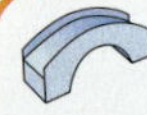

Collect words and phrases about friends and friendship.

p. 40 A1

DVD 6

how to p. 151 watch a video

a) Watch the video clip. Tell a partner which comments you like best.

I really like what ... said.

I like what ... said best.

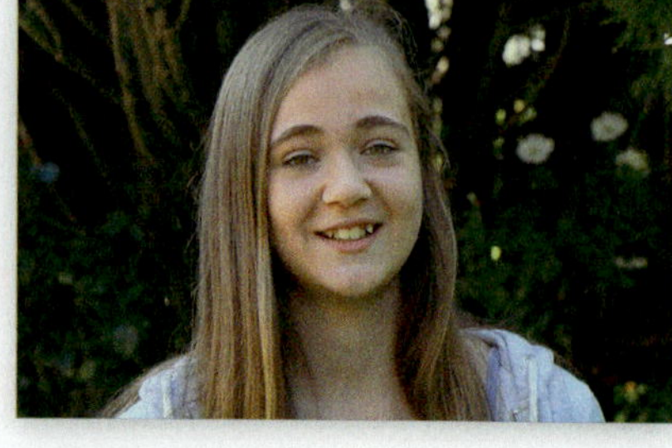

b) What is a friend to you? Talk to a partner about it.

A friend is someone who always helps me.

A friend is someone who never ...

A good friend always ...

WB p. 45 A1, A2

c) Collect your ideas in class.

A2 Friends in a digital world

p. 40 A2

a) Look at the photo. What are the teenagers doing? What is happening?

They are ...

They seem to ...

b) What do you think about the situation?

...

A3 So many friends

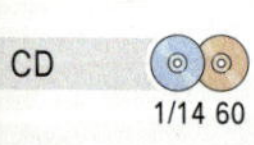

CD 1/14 60

how to p. 148 listen

a) Listen to the CD. Who are the two people? What are they talking about?

b) Work with a partner. Listen again. One of you takes notes on what Carrie says, the other on what Seb says.

c) Share your notes with another pair.

d) Talk in your group. Who do you agree with more, Carrie or Seb?

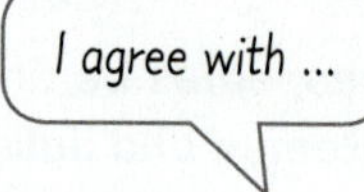

I think ... is right.

WB p. 46 A3

A4 A boy tells his story

a) Read Tim's story.

p. 41 A3, A4

CD 1/15 61

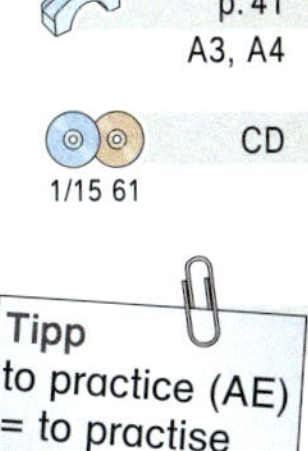

Robbie Miller and Larry O'Grady were my friends. All three of us lived with our mothers. Robbie always cried easily. Larry was tall and clever but a real coward.

We usually spent our free time at my place because my mother worked in a restaurant in the evenings. So we could do whatever we liked. Sometimes we would stand proudly in front of my mother's mirror.

There, we practiced looking cool. We weren't very good at it. So we were nasty to the girls we secretly liked.

But one day things changed. A new girl called Sue came to our class. We all really liked her but none of us would admit it. After two weeks of staring at her, I nervously asked her out on a date. I was surprised when she agreed. I was the happiest guy on earth – but not for long.

She didn't come to our date. When I passed the snack bar round the corner half an hour later, I saw her chatting happily with Robbie. I knew they were talking about me. I guess Robbie and Larry found out about our date. Maybe they told her something bad about me … I went to Larry but he pretended to know nothing …

b) Think up a different title for the story.

c) Split the class into four groups. Each group chooses a different character (Sue, Larry, Robbie or Tim). Write down questions you would like to ask your character.

Why did you …? What did you …? Were you …? …

d) One person in your group takes the role of the character. The others ask him or her the questions. You can find answers together.

> *Robbie, what did you tell Sue about Tim?*

how to p. 148 talk

e) Present some of your questions and answers to the class.

WB p. 47 A4

A5 Good friends?

p. 43 A5

CD 1/16 62

a) Tim is very upset and needs to talk to someone about what happened. Listen to the CD and find out who he calls.

b) Listen again and say what advice the person gives him. What do you think of the advice?

how to p. 148 listen

c) ☆ Imagine you are Tim. Write a text message to Sue or Robbie or both of them.

WB p. 47 A5

☾ Imagine you are Tim. Write down how you feel and why.

☼ Imagine you are Tim. You call Sue or Robbie. With a partner, write down your conversation.

> I was so sad that you … • Why did you …? • I was so shocked when I … • I feel … • Let's talk about … • …

how to p. 150 write

A6 I'll be there for you

Listen to the song. Who do you think it is about?

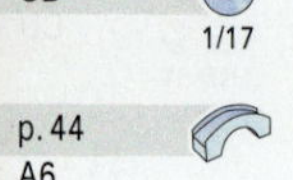

CD 1/17

p. 44 A6

a) Look at the chorus. What is the song about? Write down your ideas and compare with a partner.

So no one told you life was gonna be this way
Your job's a joke, you're broke, your love life's D.O.A.
It's like you're always stuck in second gear
When it hasn't been your day, your week, your month, or even your year, but

Chorus:
I'll be there for you
When the rain starts to pour
I'll be there for you
Like I've been there before
I'll be there for you
'Cause you're there for me too

You're still in bed at ten and work began at eight
You've burned your breakfast, so far things are going great
Your mother warned you there'd be days like these
But she didn't tell you when the world has brought you down to your knees that

Chorus

No one could ever know me
No one could ever see me
Seems you're the only one who knows what it's like to be me
Someone to face the day with, make it through all the rest with
Someone I'll always laugh with
Even at my worst, I'm best with you, yeah!

It's like you're always stuck in second gear
When it hasn't been your day, your week, your month, or even your year

Chorus x 2

Music and lyrics: Phil Solem, Danny Wilde et al.

b) Listen to the song again and read along. Which lines do you like? Why?

I like the line 'Someone I'll always laugh with' because I like to laugh with my friends, too.

What problems are mentioned in the song? Quote from the text and explain.

'Your job's a joke' – your job isn't very good

A7 Love and friendship

a) **Read the poems. Which one do you like better?**

p. 45 A7

CD 1/18 63 1/19 64

1

If friends were flowers,
I would not pick you!
I'd let you grow in the garden
And cultivate you with love and care
So I can keep you as a friend forever!!

Anonymous

2

Love is inclusive, love is for all,
whether you're short or incredibly tall.
Love is for you whether gay or straight,
fifteen years old or a hundred and eight.

Whatever your colour, religion or race,
from London or Paris or outer space,
yes love is for you, whoever you are,
a baker, professor or movie star.

Love for your parents, a sibling, a friend,
love for your partner that knows no end.
Love for your rabbit, your goldfish, your cat,
yes love is inclusive, please don't forget that!

Amy Frances Koerner

b) **Work with a partner. Listen to the poems. Choose one of them and answer the questions for it.**

Poem 1

1. Who is the speaker talking to?
2. Why wouldn't the speaker pick his or her friend if he or she were a flower?

Poem 2

1. What is the poem about?
2. What does 'inclusive' mean in the poem?

c) **Think of a title for the poem you read. Draw or find a picture or symbol to go with it.**

WB p. 48 A6, A7

d) **Practise reading the poem out loud and present it in class.**

A8 Choose

p. 46 A8

wordbank feelings p. 166

1. **Make a word web about friendship.**
2. **Draw a picture or make a collage of the three boys in A4 standing in front of the mirror. Write thought or speech bubbles.**
3. **A friend lets you down. Write to him or her and tell him or her how you feel about it.**
4. **Write your own friendship or love poem.**

A9 Fun with chat-up lines

a) Read the definition of a chat-up line. Do you know any chat-up lines?

chat-up line – something funny that is said by someone to start a conversation with a person he or she finds attractive

b) Work with a partner. Read the chat-up lines. Which ones do you like?

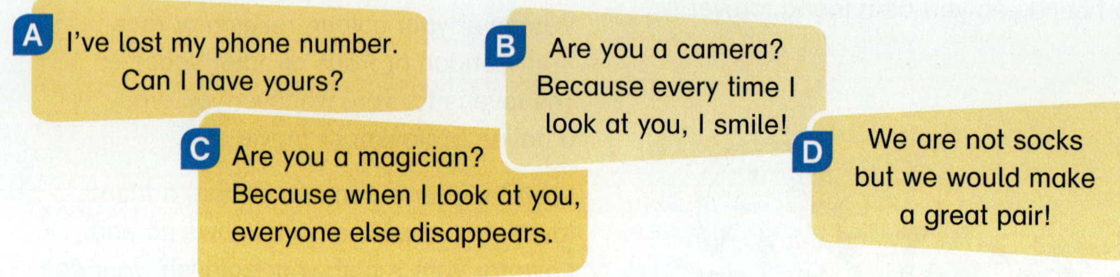

A I've lost my phone number. Can I have yours?
B Are you a camera? Because every time I look at you, I smile!
C Are you a magician? Because when I look at you, everyone else disappears.
D We are not socks but we would make a great pair!

LiF p. 182 8R

c) Unscramble these chat-up lines and write them down.

1. call me anytime. – but you can – People call me Katie,
2. take your picture – Can I – that angels exist? – to show my friends
3. so beautiful, – you made me forget – You're – my chat-up line.

d) What do you think about the chat-up lines in b) and c)? Would you ever use any of them? Why or why not? Talk in small groups.

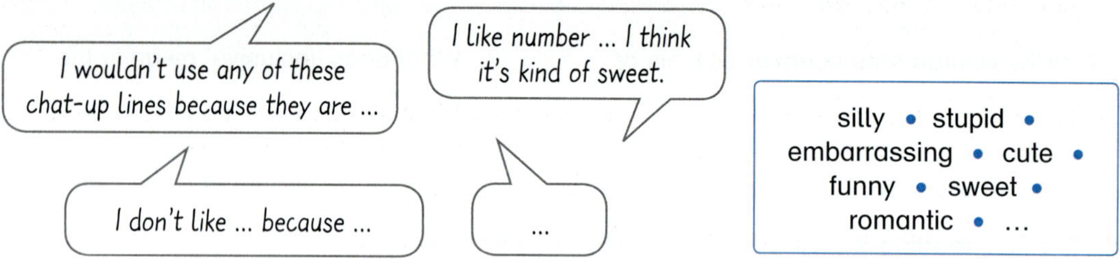

I wouldn't use any of these chat-up lines because they are ...
I like number ... I think it's kind of sweet.
I don't like ... because ...
...
silly • stupid • embarrassing • cute • funny • sweet • romantic • ...

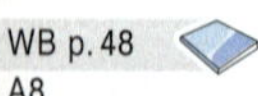
WB p. 48 A8

e) In your groups, write your own chat-up lines. You can find help in your workbook.

f) What can you do if you like someone? Write sentences.

LiF p. 182 8R

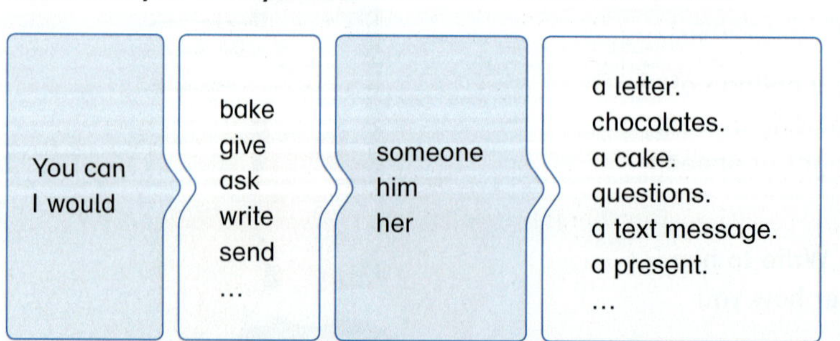

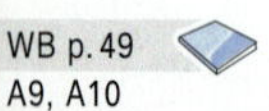
WB p. 49 A9, A10

You can bake him or her a cake.

A10 A film review

a) Read the film review. Would you like to watch the film?

Truly, Madly, Deeply
RELEASE DATE: 1990, UK
RUNNING TIME: 106 min.
CAST: Juliet Stevenson, Alan Rickman
DIRECTOR: Anthony Minghella
AGE: 12

Pianist Nina falls madly in love with Jamie, a cellist. They love making music together. Then Jamie dies and Nina does not know how to go on with her life. She misses him so badly that she can't work properly.

One evening, she hears a cello. She looks behind her and sees Jamie's ghost. They begin to lead their old life together again. Jamie asks her not to tell anyone that he is in her apartment.

When Nina goes back to work, everyone notices how well she looks. She works more cheerfully than before.

But soon Jamie gets bored in the apartment that he cannot leave. Nina meets another man, Mark, who falls in love with her.

What will happen? Will Nina realise that she is more deeply in love with a ghost than a real person? Or will she realise that she loves Mark more passionately than she thought?

Watch this romantic film and find out.

how to p. 156 write a summary

b) Work with a partner and write a short summary of the film.

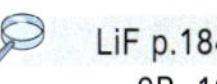

LiF p. 184 9R, 10

c) Be a language detective. Read the text again. Find sentences with adverbs and write them down. Compare with a partner.

The pianist Nina falls madly ...

LiF p. 185 10

WB p. 50 A11, A12

d) Some of the sentences contain comparisons with 'than'. Write them down and mark the comparisons. What do you notice about the adverbs? Talk to your partner.

A11 Target task: A friendship tree

p. 47 A9

You are going to make a friendship tree to show what friends and friendship mean to you.

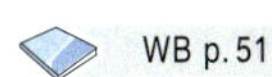

WB p. 51 A13

1. Plan your tree. Decide as a class:
   - how to make the tree
   - what materials to use
   - how big it will be
   - how many branches and leaves it will have
   - where to put it
   - ...

2. Agree on what you would like to hang on the tree. It could be:
   - poems or stories
   - song lyrics
   - slogans or quotes
   - photos or pictures
   - ...

Friendship is...
... when you do everything together.

3. Work on your part of the tree alone, in pairs or in groups.

4. As a class, put together your friendship tree and talk about it.

P1 Explain

Explain what you have to do.

1. Share your notes with another pair.
2. Quote from the text and explain.
3. Practise reading the poem out loud and present it in class.
4. Read the definition of a chat-up line.
5. Agree on what you would like to hang on the tree.

Wir sollen ...

P2 Words for love and relationships

a) Match these phrases from Tim's story in A4 with the German phrases. Write them down.

stare at someone • ask someone out on a date • secretly like someone • talk about someone

jemanden heimlich mögen • jemanden anstarren • jemanden fragen, ob er/sie mit einem ausgehen will • über jemanden reden

stare at someone = jemanden anstarren

CD 68

b) Listen to the CD and check your answers.

c) Write sentences. In each sentence, use one of the phrases.

Hannah stared at the new boy in her class.

P3 Sound check: how to say the letter 's'

a) Look at the song 'I'll be there for you' in A6. Find the word that rhymes with 'these'.

CD 69

b) Listen to the CD. In which of the words does the 's' sound the same as in 'these'?

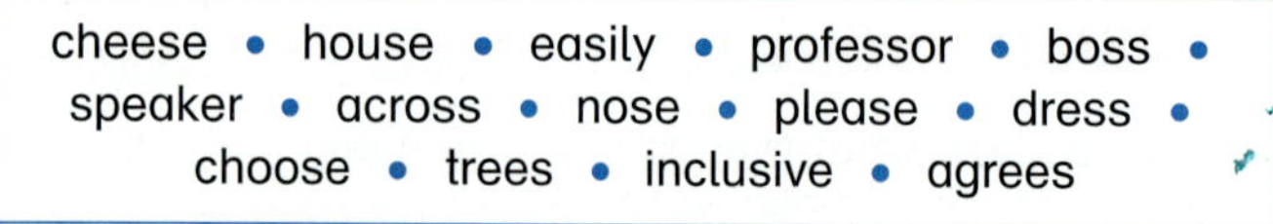
cheese • house • easily • professor • boss • speaker • across • nose • please • dress • choose • trees • inclusive • agrees

c) Copy the table and write the words into two lists.

CD 70

d) Listen to the CD and check your lists.

/z/	/s/
cheese	house
...	...

Practice matters

P4 Find the word

a) Look at the sentences and complete them with words from the box.

shocked • mirror • whether • explain • pretend • chat

1. I can't decide ??? I should eat pizza or pasta.
2. I like to ??? to my brother. He always gives me good advice.
3. When you tell someone something that helps them understand, you ??? it.
4. You always ??? to listen but I know you don't care!
5. I was so ??? when she was nasty to me.
6. When you want to put on some make-up, you should look in a ???.

b) Listen to the CD and check your sentences.

CD 71

P5 Give me your answer!

a) Unscramble the following sentences and write them down.

LiF p. 182 8R

1. to give her – I wanted – a present.
2. beautiful poems. – writes me – My girlfriend
3. a CD – My boyfriend – for his birthday. – loves music – so I gave him
4. asked us – questions. – Our English teacher – lots of
5. some flowers. – to my grandparents' house – When I go – take them – I often

b) Compare your sentences with a partner.

P6 Comparisons

a) Use the adverbs in the box to complete the sentences. Write them down.

LiF p. 185 10

more openly • faster • more healthily • better • more carefully • more beautifully

1. My girlfriend eats ??? than I do – I just love fast food!
2. I think I fell in love ??? than my boyfriend did – it took him a while!
3. I can talk to my friends ??? than to my parents.
4. If I do my homework with my friends, I do it ??? than if I do it alone.
5. My boyfriend loves to draw – he can draw ??? than anyone else I know.
6. My best friend works really hard at school – she does her homework ??? than I do.

1. My girlfriend eats more healthily than I do - I just love fast food!

b) Compare with a partner.

B1 Romeo and Juliet

 **What do you need for a good love story? Collect ideas.**

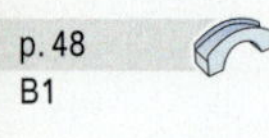
p. 48 B1

a) 'Romeo and Juliet' is a very famous love story. It was written over 400 years ago. Do you know anything about it? Talk to a partner.

CD 1/20 72

b) Read this version of 'Romeo and Juliet'. Is it a happy or a sad story?

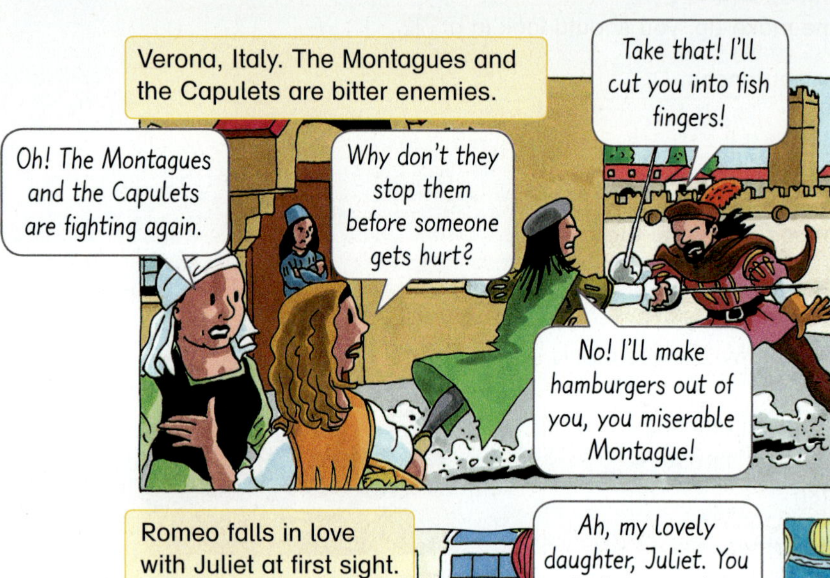

Verona, Italy. The Montagues and the Capulets are bitter enemies.
Oh! The Montagues and the Capulets are fighting again.
Why don't they stop them before someone gets hurt?
Take that! I'll cut you into fish fingers!
No! I'll make hamburgers out of you, you miserable Montague!

A party at the Capulets' palace. Romeo Montague arrives in disguise.
I hope nobody recognises me ...

Romeo falls in love with Juliet at first sight.
Wow, who's that beautiful girl over there? I must get to know her.
Ah, my lovely daughter, Juliet. You don't look a day over 13.
Oh, Dad, I am 13!
You look beautiful tonight, Juliet.

Some time later.

Romeo! Romeo!

I'm here in the garden, waiting for you. Come down.

No, you come up. My father might hear us in the garden.

You must have wings to climb this wall.
I do. The wings of love, my Juliet!

Juliet! Juliet!
You must leave now. It's too dangerous!
Marry me tomorrow.
Yes, yes!

Oh, Romeo. Come back to me, no matter what.
The next day the lovers get married in secret. But Romeo must leave Verona because of a fight. They have to say goodbye.
I promise, my love, my rose.

You must marry Count Paris, Juliet. I say you must.

No, no, Father. That man is old enough to be my grandfather.

At Friar Laurence's house.
I'll help you, Juliet. Drink this. Then you will die and I'll write to Romeo ...
Die? Are you crazy, Friar?

No, of course you won't really die. You'll just be asleep. But your parents and Count Paris will think you're dead. Romeo will come and wake you up and you can leave together.

It's a great idea. Now, drink it.
OK ... Here goes!

Oh, my lovely Juliet, my rose.
But Romeo doesn't receive the friar's letter and when he finds Juliet, he thinks she's dead. – He drinks poison.

Juliet wakes up – and finds Romeo dead. She kills herself, too.

Capulet and Montague find the lovers.
Yeah, you're right. Let's get someone to write a book about them and make a film.
Montague, let's be friends. This must never happen again.

WB p. 52 B1, B2

B2 Who is it?

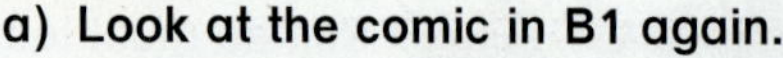

p. 50 B2, B3

how to p. 159 work with literary texts

a) Look at the comic in B1 again.

- ☆ Make a list of the characters. Add one sentence about each of them. 1. Juliet: She is …
- ☾ Write down the names of the characters and what they do in the story.
- ☼ Write about the characters and what they do in the story. What are their relationships to each other?

b) Talk about the characters with a partner.

LiF p. 186 11R

c) Write down who says what. 1. Romeo. 2. …

1 I hope nobody recognises me …
2 You must leave now.
3 You must marry Count Paris.
4 I'll help you.
5 This must never happen again.

d) Unscramble the sentences and write them down.

1. Romeo says that – nobody – he hopes – recognises him.
2. Juliet – must leave – says that – now. – Romeo
3. she – says that – must marry – Juliet's father – Count Paris.
4. he will – Friar Laurence – her. – help – says that
5. Juliet's father – must never happen – this – says that – again.

WB p. 53 B3

LAND & LEUTE 3

DVD 7

Shakespeare

Der englische Dichter, Schriftsteller und Schauspieler William Shakespeare wird als der größte Schriftsteller in der englischen Sprache und als berühmtester Bühnenautor der Welt angesehen.

Er wurde in Stratford-upon-Avon geboren und dort am 26. April 1564 getauft. Sein genaues Geburtsdatum ist unbekannt.

1582 heiratete Shakespeare Anne Hathaway, und sie bekamen drei Kinder: 1583 eine Tochter und 1585 Zwillinge.

Wann er nach London zog, ist nicht bekannt, aber 1592 wurde Shakespeares erstes Stück dort rezensiert, also muss er zu dieser Zeit bereits einige Zeit in London verbracht haben. Er war sowohl als Schriftsteller als auch als Schauspieler erfolgreich. Circa 1613 zog er zurück nach Stratford und starb dort am 23. April 1616.

Shakespeare schrieb viele Gedichte, Sonette und ungefähr 38 Theaterstücke. Die bekanntesten Tragödien heißen *Romeo and Juliet*, *Hamlet* und *Macbeth*, und zu seinen beliebtesten Komödien zählen *Much Ado About Nothing* und *The Merchant of Venice*.

Shakespeares Stücke sind immer noch auf der ganzen Welt beliebt, weil die Themen immer noch von Bedeutung sind.

Heute kann man in vielen Ländern Shakespeare-Produktionen sehen.

Im *Globe Theatre* in London kann man wie früher Produktionen im Freien ansehen.

Finde heraus, welche Theaterstücke von Shakespeare zurzeit in deiner Umgebung zu sehen sind.

B3 A famous play

a) Read this summary of the play from a theatre guide. What information is new to you?

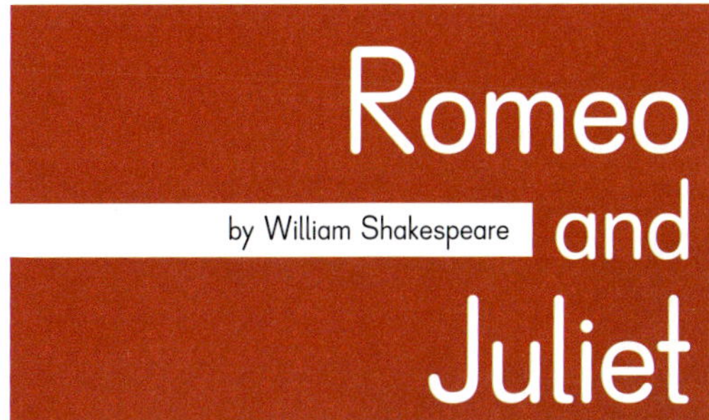

In Verona, two families, the Montagues and the Capulets, are fighting. One evening Romeo, a Montague, disguises himself and goes to a ball at the Capulets' house.

There, Romeo sees Juliet and falls in love with her. Later, he visits Juliet and tells her he loves her. They get married in secret the next day.

Tybalt, Juliet's cousin, is angry that Romeo was at the ball, and he wants to fight Romeo. Romeo does not want to fight but Mercutio, his best friend, takes up Tybalt's challenge and is killed by Tybalt.

Romeo then kills Tybalt. The Prince of Verona bans Romeo from the city. Romeo can only spend one night with his wife.

Meanwhile, the Capulets want Juliet to marry Count Paris. With the help of Friar Laurence, Juliet makes a plan to stop the marriage. She takes a drug that makes her seem dead. Really, she is only asleep. Friar Laurence sends a letter to Romeo so that he can rescue her and they can run away together.

The letter arrives too late. Romeo hears that Juliet has died. He rushes to her and kills himself. Juliet wakes up and finds Romeo dead so she kills herself, too.

When they find out what has happened, the Montagues and Capulets stop fighting.

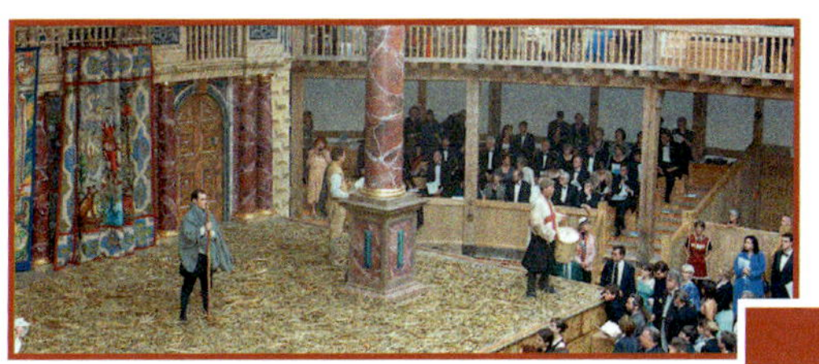

b) Romeo and Juliet both die tragically. Explain how it came to that.

First, ... Then ... After that ... In the end ...

WB p. 53 B4, B5

B4 Dramatic reading

p. 51 B4
CD 1/20 72

a) Look at B1 again. Listen to the CD and read along.

b) Practise how to say the sentences from the comic.

c) In groups, practise acting out the scenes.

- Think about the situations the characters are in.
- Think about how the characters feel.
- Think about how the characters speak. Do they speak quietly? Are they out of breath? Are they crying?

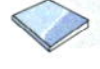
WB p. 55 B6

B5 The Prince's questions

a) After the death of Romeo and Juliet, the Prince of Verona asks Juliet's parents a lot of questions. Read his questions.

LiF p. 186
12

b) Juliet's parents do not know the answers so they talk to her nurse and tell her what the prince wants to know. Write down what they say.

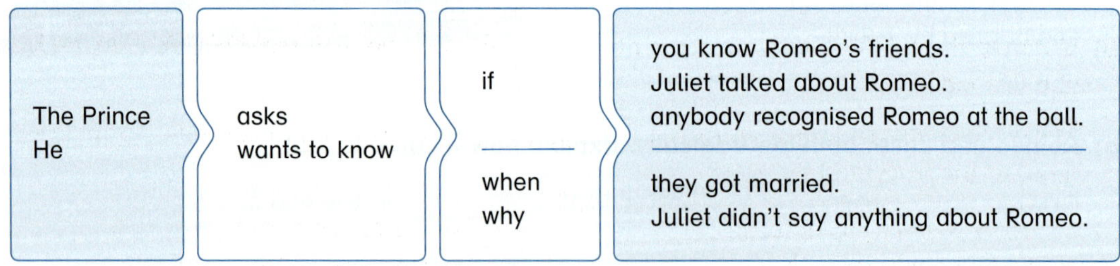

The Prince He	asks wants to know	if	you know Romeo's friends. Juliet talked about Romeo. anybody recognised Romeo at the ball.
		when why	they got married. Juliet didn't say anything about Romeo.

WB p. 56
B7, B8

The Prince has even more questions that Juliet's parents cannot answer. Report the questions.

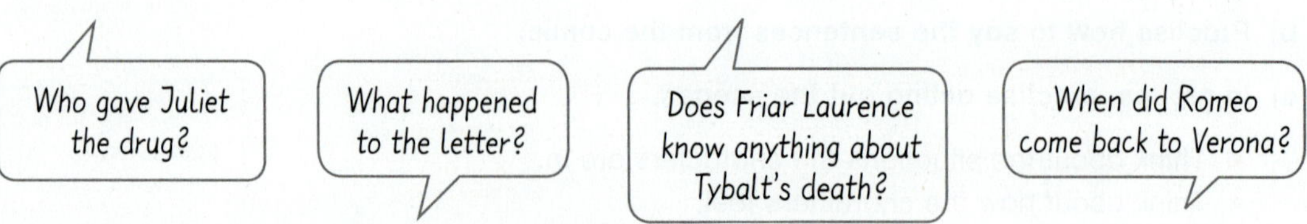

Who gave Juliet the drug?
What happened to the letter?
Does Friar Laurence know anything about Tybalt's death?
When did Romeo come back to Verona?

The Prince wants to know who … He asks …

B6 Film reviews

How do you decide if you want to watch a film? Collect ideas.

a) Skim the information about the three films. What do they have in common?

how to p. 149 read

Romeo and Juliet

RELEASE DATE: 2013, UK/USA
RUNNING TIME: 113 min.
CAST: Hailee Steinfeld, Douglas Booth
DIRECTOR: Carlo Carlei
AGE: PG
GENRE: Romance, Drama

The film *Romeo and Juliet* came to cinemas in October 2013. The dialogue has been changed a bit from what Shakespeare originally wrote, which I think is a shame. …

West Side Story

RELEASE DATE: 1961, USA
RUNNING TIME: 152 min.
CAST: Natalie Wood, Richard Beymer
DIRECTORS: Jerome Robbins, Robert Wise
AGE: PG
GENRE: Crime, Drama, Musical

West Side Story came out in October 1961. It is a modern version of Shakespeare's *Romeo and Juliet*. It uses none of Shakespeare's language …

Shakespeare in Love

RELEASE DATE: 1998, USA
RUNNING TIME: 123 min.
CAST: Gwyneth Paltrow, Joseph Fiennes
DIRECTOR: John Madden
AGE: 15
GENRE: Comedy, Drama, History

The film Shakespeare in Love came out in 1998. It is set in England in 1593 and follows part of Shakespeare's life. At the beginning of the film, Shakespeare is trying to write a new play …

b) Listen to the full film reviews. Which film does the reviewer like most? Which film does she like least?

CD 1/21 75 1/22 76 1/23 77

c) Which film would you like to see? Listen to the review again and take notes on at least three of the following topics:

WB p. 57 B9

- where the film takes place
- when the film takes place
- what happens
- what the reviewer likes
- what the reviewer does not like
- …

d) Get into groups with other people who chose the same review. Use your notes to talk about it.

Tipp
Schau dir im Internet Filmposter und Trailer an.

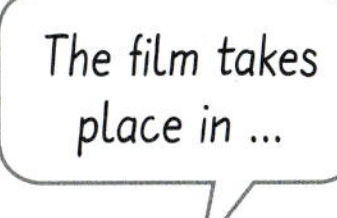

First … and then …

The reviewer likes …

The reviewer doesn't like …

Talk about a film you have seen or write a short film review.

how to p. 157 write a review

B7 Choose

p. 52
B5

1. Find a partner. Choose a scene from the comic version of 'Romeo and Juliet'. Make a freeze-frame of your scene. Other pairs have to guess which scene it is.
2. Write a dialogue between Romeo and Juliet when they first meet. You can act it out.
3. Find out more about the Globe theatre.

B8 A scene from Romeo and Juliet

CD 1/24 78
1/25 79

a) Listen to this scene at the Capulets' party in Shakespearean and modern English and read along. What do you think of the Shakespearean English?

SHAKESPEARE'S ORIGINAL TEXT

NURSE
Madam, your mother craves a word with you.

JULIET *moves away*

ROMEO
What is her mother?

NURSE
Marry, bachelor,
Her mother is the lady of the house,
And a good lady, and a wise and virtuous.
I nursed her daughter, that you talked withal.
I tell you, he that can lay hold of her
Shall have the chinks.

ROMEO
(aside) Is she a Capulet?
O dear account! My life is my foe's debt.

MODERN TEXT

NURSE
Madam, your mother wants to talk to you.

JULIET *moves away*

ROMEO
Who is her mother?

NURSE
Indeed, young man, her mother is the lady of the house. She is a good, wise and virtuous lady. I nursed her daughter, whom you were just talking to. Let me tell you, the man, who marries her will become very wealthy.

ROMEO
(to himself) Is she a Capulet? Oh, this is a heavy price to pay! My life is in the hands of my enemy.

b) Work with a partner. Look at both versions of the text and find the answers to these questions. Make notes.

1. How did Shakespeare express 'wants to talk'?
2. How did he express 'young man'?
3. How did he express 'my enemy'?

WB p. 58
B10
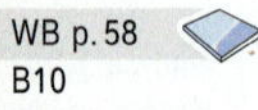

c) Work with a partner. Choose the modern or the Shakespearean version and practise reading it out loud.

B9 Target task: A modern love story

Work with a partner or in a small group. Create your own modern love story. You could:

- write a short story
- write a short play
- draw a cartoon
- shoot a short film

p. 53 B6

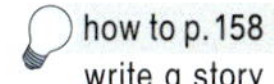
how to p. 158 write a story

Step 1: Characters

1. Start with the first main character. Think about:
   - what his or her name is
   - how old he or she is
   - what he or she looks like
   - …

2. Do the same for the other main character.
3. Are there any other characters? What is their relationship to the main characters?

Step 2: Place

- Where do the characters live?
- Where does the story take place?

Step 3: Plan what happens in your story

1. Think of an interesting beginning to your story. Where and when do the characters meet?
2. What happens to the characters? Think of something interesting.
3. What happens next? Think of something really exciting.
4. Explain the exciting part of your story. Why did it happen?
5. How does the story end? Is it a happy or a sad ending? Or do you want to leave that open?

Present your story to your class or other classes.

Practice matters

P7 Explain

Explain what you have to do.

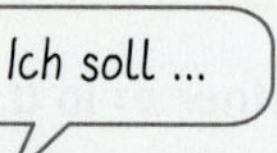

Ich soll ...

Wir sollen ...

...

1. Make a list of the characters.
2. Read this summary of the play from a theatre guide.
3. Report the questions.
4. Get into groups with other people who chose the same review.
5. Practise how to say the sentences from the comic.

P8 This is what he said ...

LiF p. 186
11R

a) Juliet's nurse wants to know why Juliet is unhappy. Juliet tells her what her father says. Write down what she says.

You must marry Count Paris.
Your mother agrees!
You are our daughter and you have to do what we say.
I will wait until tomorrow for your answer.
You will get married soon.
If you don't marry Count Paris, then you're not my daughter anymore.

He says that I must marry Count Paris.
He says that he ...

CD  80

b) Listen to the CD and check your sentences.

P9 Adjectives for characters

how to p. 159
work with literary texts

Look at the list of characters and the box of adjectives. Describe the characters and how they feel.

1. Juliet
2. Romeo
3. Juliet's father
4. Friar Laurence

beautiful • old • young • angry • sad • helpful • happy • unhappy • friendly • lonely • frightened • ...

1. Juliet is young and beautiful. When she meets Romeo she feels ...

Practice matters

P10 Sound check

a) Listen to the words in the box and repeat them.

CD 81

characters • relationship • situation • enemy • challenge • marriage • dramatic • review • recognise • costume • reviewer

b) Copy the words. Listen again. Underline the syllables that are stressed.

c) Now read the words out loud. Ask a partner to check your pronunciation.

P11 Nosy friend

a) You get an email from an American friend. She has lots of questions about your new boyfriend or girlfriend. Read her questions.

- What's your boyfriend's or girlfriend's name?
- Is he or she good-looking?
- What colour are his or her eyes?
- Where did you go on your first date?
- Has he or she met your friends?
- Can you send me a photo?

b) You tell your boyfriend or girlfriend what your friend wants to know. Write sentences.

LiF p. 186 12

She wants to know what your name is.
She wants to know if you ...
...

P12 West Side Story

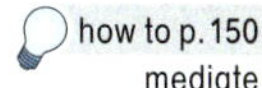
how to p. 150 mediate

A local English theatre group is performing a play at your school and you want to see it. You have a flyer that tells you what the play is about, when it will be performed and how much the tickets cost. Tell your family in German what it says on the flyer.

West Side Story

Two rival gangs are at war with each other in New York City. Tony is a Jet who wants to leave the gang, and Maria is the sister of The Sharks' leader. Both should be enemies, but when they meet, they fall in love and risk their lives.

12th and 13th April,
7:30 pm,
No admission fee

Optional

O Hannah and Zach

I normally hated taking the bus home after school. It took ages and it was always so hot and full. But that one day, I was so happy I was on that bus.

That one day, I got on, showed my bus pass, found a seat and then looked up ... to see a boy from school staring at me.

He was tall with dark brown, curly hair. That hair framed a face with big, dark eyes and – as he saw me looking at him – the most beautiful smile I had ever seen.

The bus stopped and people got off. It pulled away again. As more and more people got off the bus, it got quite empty, but still he was staring at me. Saying nothing, just staring as if he couldn't stop.

I, in return, couldn't look anywhere but at him, either. I felt like I knew him, like I'd always known him.

At some point we got to my stop. I got up and moved towards the door and so did he. He was getting off, too. The bus stopped suddenly, and I nearly fell – but he caught my arm just in time.

As I stepped off the bus, I found that I was shivering, even though it wasn't cold outside. Excitement bubbled up inside me as I said, "Hi, my name's Hannah. Thanks for ... you know ..." Suddenly shy, I couldn't meet his eye.

Not taking his eyes off me once, he said, "Hi, I'm Zach. And you're welcome. See you around ... Hannah."

Smiling, he walked away. I just stood there, watching him until he was out of sight ...

Imagine you are Hannah or Zach. What do you tell your friends about the bus ride? Make notes.

Read the rest of the story on pages 142 to 143 from line 38 onwards. Tell the class in German what happens.

The world of work

4

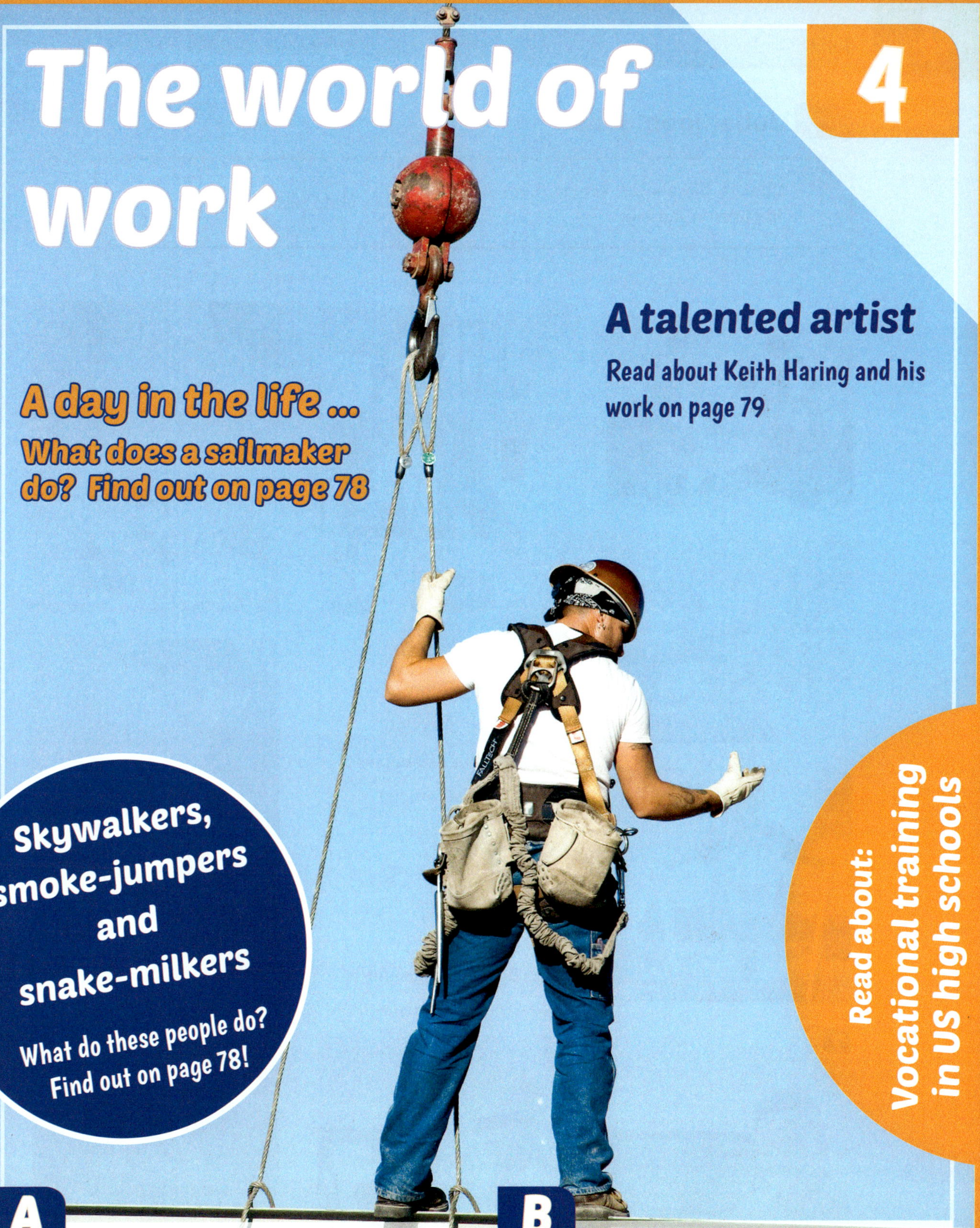

A talented artist

Read about Keith Haring and his work on page 79

A day in the life ...

What does a sailmaker do? Find out on page 78

Skywalkers, smoke-jumpers and snake-milkers

What do these people do? Find out on page 78!

Read about: Vocational training in US high schools

A

- Du sprichst über die Talente von Personen und über ungewöhnliche Berufe.
- Du erstellst einen Beitrag für eine Klassenausstellung über interessante Berufe. (Zielaufgabe)

B

- Du beschäftigst dich mit verschiedenen Berufen und damit, was du nach der Schule machen möchtest.
- Du nimmst ein telefonisches Bewerbungsgespräch auf. (Zielaufgabe)

A1 Jobs, jobs, jobs

p. 54 A1

CD 2/1

Look at the photos. Match them with the jobs in the box.

I think photo number ... shows ...

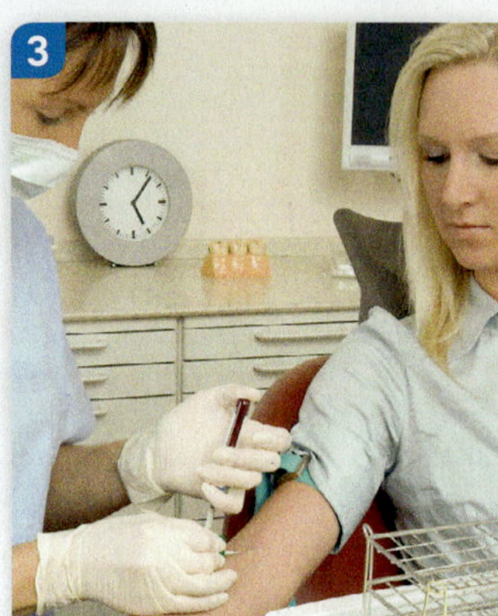

secretary
flight attendant
software developer
physiotherapist
engineer
social worker
plumber
lifeguard
doctor's assistant

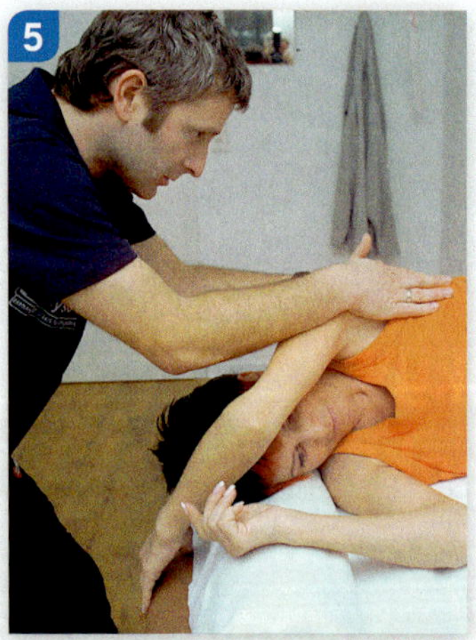

a) Write down what the people do in these jobs.

develops machines or buildings • looks after passengers on a plane • works in an office • installs and repairs heating and water systems • supports people with problems • does exercises with people who have medical problems • makes sure people are safe when swimming • creates computer programs • looks after patients in the doctor's office • …

A flight attendant looks after passengers on a plane. …

b) What do the people say about their jobs? Listen and take notes. Compare your notes with a partner.

c) What do **you** think about the jobs? Talk to a partner.

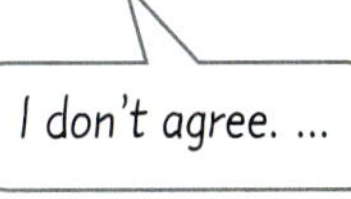

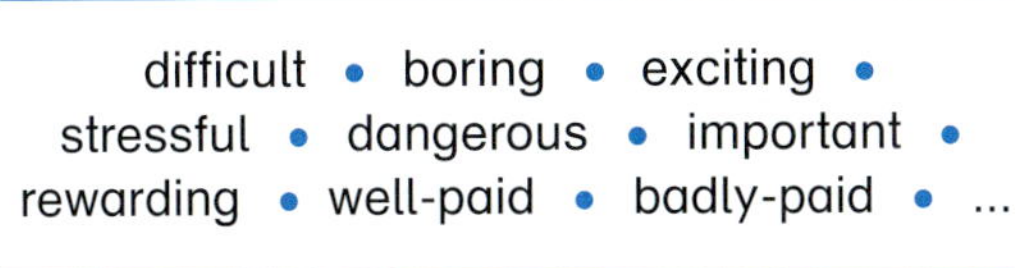

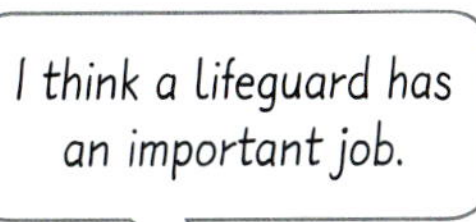

I agree. …

…

A2 A job game

a) Work with one or two partners. Close your books and write down all the jobs you know. You have three minutes.

b) Compare your lists with the other groups. You get one point for each job that the other groups do not have and an extra point if you can give information about the jobs.

p. 56 A2

A3 A job for you?

a) Look at your list of jobs from A2 and the jobs in A1 again. What is necessary to do these jobs? Match the sentence parts.

LiF p. 187 13R

1. If I become a baker,
2. If I want to become a doctor's assistant,
3. If I become a flight attendant,
4. If I become a secretary,
5. If I become a plumber,

a. I will have to do an apprenticeship at a doctor's office.
b. I will have to work in an office.
c. I will have to get up early.
d. I will have to install and repair heating and water systems.
e. I will have to travel a lot.

Think of more sentences and write them down.

b) Compare your sentences with a partner.

c) Talk about the jobs with your partner.

I hate getting up early, so being a baker is not for me.

I love to travel, so being a flight attendant would be a good job for me.

A4 Simon the sailmaker

a) **Watch the interview with Simon. What did you find interesting? Talk to a partner.**

b) **Watch the video clip again and take notes on at least four of the following questions.**

1. What does Simon do in his job?
2. How do you make a sail?
3. How did Simon become a sailmaker?
4. What is the best part of his job?
5. What skills does he need to be a sailmaker?
6. Which words does he use to sum up his job?

Would you like to have a job like this? Give reasons.

A5 Exciting jobs

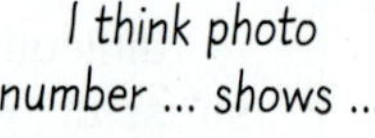
I think photo number ... shows ...

What can you see in the photos? What do they have to do with jobs?

p. 57 A3

CD 2/3

a) **Listen and find out ...**

1. ... where skywalkers work.
2. ... what smoke-jumpers are.
3. ... what smoke-jumpers do.
4. ... what snake-milkers do.

b) **Which of the jobs would or wouldn't you like to do? Give reasons.**

I'd like to work as a/an ... because ...

I'd love to be ...

I wouldn't like to work as a/an ... because ...

A6 An unusual job

p. 58 A4

Amanda is a violinist from Georgia, USA. She specialises in repairing violin bows.

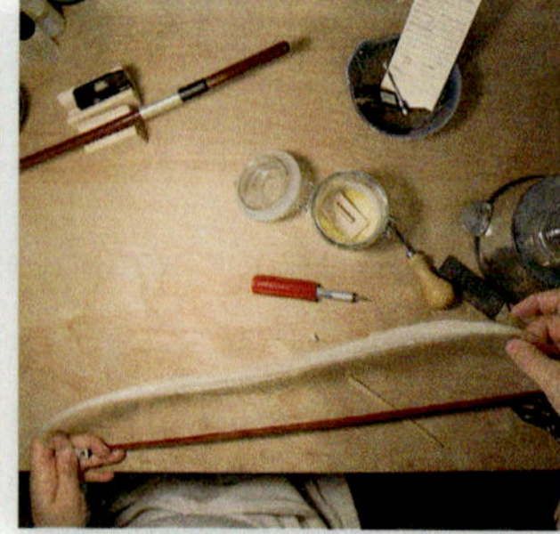

CD 2/4 86

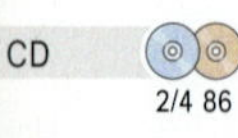

Listen to what Amanda says about how she turned her talent into a profession. You can find help in your workbook. Talk to a partner in German.

WB p. 69 A6

Amanda says: **"My hands have been my most important tool for as long as I can remember." Talk to a partner about this quotation.**

I think she means that ...

As I understand it, Amanda ...

A7 Keith Haring

Look at the works of art. What do you see in them?

p. 59 A5

CD 2/5 87

how to p. 149 read

Listen and read along. Who was Keith Haring?

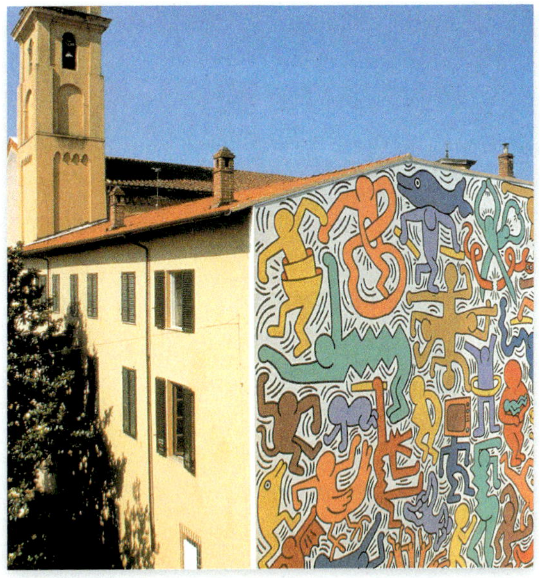

Keith Haring was born in Reading, Pennsylvania, in 1958. As a child, Haring could already draw extremely well. At the age of 18, he started studying at art school in Pennsylvania. He then went to an academy in New York. In New York Haring discovered that he was also a very good sculptor and performance artist – and there he also found his own style.

One day in the subway Haring saw a black panel for advertisements. He bought a box of white chalk, went back down and did a drawing like a cartoon on the black paper.

After that, he started looking out for these black spaces. Whenever he saw one, he did a drawing on it.

Then Haring realized that people liked his drawings. Nobody tried to rub them out. He found out that drawing in front of people allowed him to communicate with them. His images became more and more popular with New Yorkers. So he started making buttons with his images on them and sold them in the subway.

In 1986 Keith Haring opened his Pop Shop in New York. There he sold T-shirts, baseball caps and posters showing his images. He wanted everyone to be able to buy products with his images on them. He also found that he was good at working with children. In some schools teachers allowed Haring and the children to make large wall paintings together.

Keith Haring died in 1990 at the age of 31 of AIDS. In 2008 a documentary about Haring and his art was released. Today many people remember him as a great artist and friend.

WB p. 70 A7

A8 A talented artist

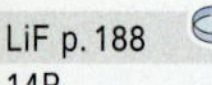
LiF p. 188
14R

a) Unscramble the sentences and write them down.

1. so well that – out of his talent. – a profession – Haring could draw – he made
2. was able to – He – sell buttons – in the subway. – with his images
3. to buy – He wanted – his work. – to be able – everyone
4. school children – work with Haring. – were allowed to – Some
5. find – was able to – Haring – in New York. – his own style
6. had to buy chalk– before he was able to – Haring – start drawing – in the subway.

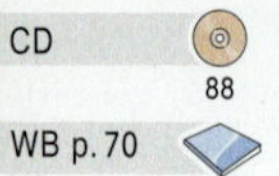
CD 88
WB p. 70
A8

b) Listen to the CD and check your sentences.

A9 Keith Haring's talent

a) Complete the sentences. You can find the information in the text.

1. As a child, Keith Haring …
2. He started studying …
3. In New York he …
4. In the subway …
5. In 1986, Haring …
6. At the age of 31, he …

b) ☆ Write down what Keith Haring was good at.

☾ Read the text again and take notes on important moments in Keith Haring's life.

☼ Complete the following sentences. The information is not in the text, so you need to think for yourself.

1. I think Keith Haring used chalk for his pictures because …
2. I think people did not try to rub out Haring's pictures because …
3. I think he worked with children because …

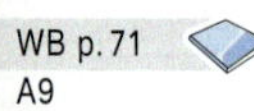
WB p. 71
A9

c) Why do you think Haring was so successful? Talk in class.

A10 Discover your talent

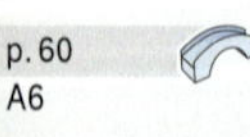
p. 60
A6

Keith Haring's talent was discovered when he was very young. Sometimes it is not that obvious and it takes some time to find out what you are good at.

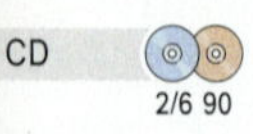
CD 2/6 90

a) Listen to Emma talking to her guidance counselor, Mr. Lemkey, at school. What are they talking about?

b) Listen again and read along. Answer the questions.

1. What is Emma's problem? How do you think she feels?
2. How does Mr. Lemkey help her?
3. How do you think Emma feels at the end?

Mr. Lemkey: Hello Emma. Please take a seat. So, have you chosen an elective yet?

Emma: No. Honestly, I don't know what to do. I'm not very good at school right now.

Mr. Lemkey: OK. Why do you say that?

Emma: Um, well I guess … I just don't seem to be very good at math or languages at the moment. If my brother didn't help me, I would fail in math.

Mr. Lemkey: Hmm, well, you could choose a completely different elective if you wanted to.

Emma: I could? Oh! Like what?

Mr. Lemkey: Well, what about basketball? Lots of students collect credit points for that.

Emma: If I was fitter, I would take that course. But I broke my leg last year and I'm not fit enough yet to do hours of training again. What else could I choose?

Mr. Lemkey: Well, is there anything you're really good at – that you really enjoy?

Emma: I'm not sure. Well … I guess … my friends say I'm really good at drawing …

Mr. Lemkey: Great! Do you enjoy drawing?

Emma: Yes, I've always loved it. Mom says if she had the money, she would send me to art school in the summer.

Mr. Lemkey: Then I think I've got just the thing. Mrs. Miller is offering a course in graphic design. It's right after lunch, in room 204. What about that?

Emma: That's a great idea! Thank you! That's what I'll do, it sounds perfect.

c) **Practise and act out the dialogue between Emma and Mr. Lemkey.**

how to p. 148 talk

A11 Language detective

a) **Find the sentences with 'if' in the dialogue in A10 and write them down.**

b) **Compare your sentences with the sentences in A3. What do you notice? Can you find a pattern?**

c) **Check with the LiF.**

LiF p. 190 15

d) **Write sentences.**

If	Emma Emma's mother Emma's brother I …	chose graphic design, worked harder at school, had more money, didn't help her, was Emma, …	she would I would …	get better results. be happier. send Emma to art school fail in math. choose graphic design. …

If Emma chose graphic design, she would be happier.
If I was Emma, I would …
…

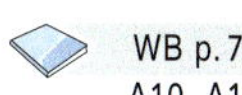

WB p. 72 A10, A11

LAND & LEUTE 4

DVD 9

Berufsbildung in Schulen in den USA

In vielen amerikanischen Highschools können sich die Schülerinnen und Schüler in berufsbildenden Kursen auf das Arbeitsleben vorbereiten. Im Klassenzimmer lernen sie zunächst etwas über verschiedene Bereiche des Arbeitslebens, um anschließend ihr Wissen in der Praxis anzuwenden.
Normalerweise erhalten sie für ihre Arbeit kein Geld, dafür können sie verschiedene Arbeiten unter realen Bedingungen ausprobieren und feststellen, was ihnen am besten gefällt. Arbeitsstätten können zum Beispiel Autowerkstätten, Bauernhöfe, Büros, Küchen, Krankenhäuser und Altenheime sein.

In diesen Bereichen, die oft an den Schulen selbst vorhanden sind, bekommen die Jugendlichen eine Ahnung davon, wie das Berufsleben wirklich aussieht und wie man Probleme, die dort eventuell auftreten können, bewältigen kann.

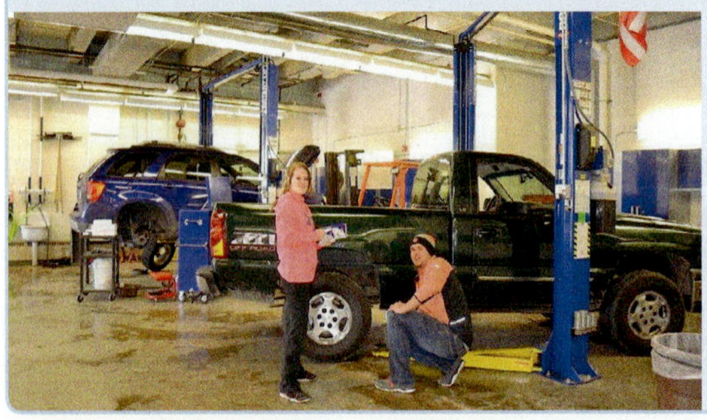

Einer der beliebtesten Bereiche der Berufsbildung an Schulen in den USA ist die kaufmännische Berufsbildung *(business and office work)*, dicht gefolgt von Handel und Industrie *(trade and industry)* sowie Kommunikation *(communications)*. Landwirtschaft *(agriculture)* ist ein Bereich, der in großen Agrarstaaten gern gewählt wird.
Es stehen auch manchmal Fächer wie Kochen, Frühkindliche Erziehung und Betreuung, Marketing, Metallverarbeitung, Unfallreparatur sowie Automobiltechnologie auf dem Programm.

Welche berufsbildenden Kurse hättest du gerne?

A12 Choose

p. 61 A7

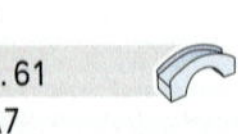

1. **Make a jobs and talents word web.**

jobs and talents — engineer — good at maths

how to p. 161 use a dictionary

2. **Make a job quiz for a partner. Use a dictionary for help.**

   1. You look after passengers on a plane. What's your job?
   2. You make sure people are safe at a swimming pool. What's your job?
   3. ...

wordbank jobs p. 168

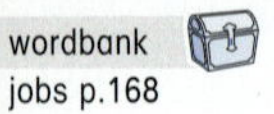

3. **Do a class survey of talents in your class.**
4. **What does it mean to have 'talent'? Find a definition. Explain it to your classmates.**

A13 What are you good at?

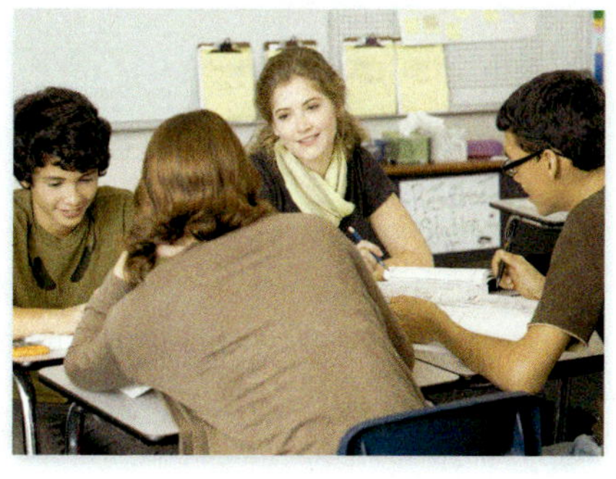

how to p. 163 work together

a) Work in groups of four. Prepare a placemat. Write the things you are good at in your section of the placemat. Think about:

- subjects (PE, art, maths, ...)
- interests and hobbies
- jobs you do at home
- special skills like being patient, well-organised, ...
- ...

b) Turn the placemat and read what the others have written. Talk to the other members of your group about what you think they are good at.

c) Add the others' ideas to your section of the placemat.

A14 Target task: Talents and jobs

p. 62 A8

WB p. 73 A12

Make a class display about jobs you and your class think are interesting.

You could think about jobs that you have read about in this Theme. You can also present someone who turned his or her talent into a profession.

1. Get together in small groups. Decide on a job or person you would like to present.
2. Collect information about the job or about the person. Try and find pictures, too.
3. Decide who does what.
4. Create your part of the display.
5. Present your part of the display.

how to p. 161 use a dictionary

model text

Flight attendant

A job profile

What do flight attendants do?

- Discuss flight details with pilot
- Inspect emergency equipment
- Demonstrate use of safety and emergency equipment
- Make sure passengers have seat belts fastened
- Serve drinks, meals and snacks
- Take care of passengers
- Check if plane is clean

Qualifications needed:

- High school diploma
- Work experience in customer service
- Language skills
- Be in good health
- Be able to swim
- Good vision

Tips: The display will be effective if you ...

- keep information short and precise.
- use paragraphs and underline headings.
- use different colours.
- use pictures and photos.

Practice matters

P1 Explain

Explain what you have to do.

1. Compare your notes with a partner.
2. Give reasons.
3. Practise and act out the dialogue.
4. Talk to the other members of your group.
5. Do a class survey of talents in your class.

P2 Dream jobs

a) Look at the list of people and their dream jobs. Write sentences. Put 'a' or 'an' in the right place.

1. John: teacher	3. Max: musician	5. Tim: software developer
2. Bev: artist	4. Sonia: engineer	6. Claire: social worker

John would like to become a teacher.

CD 95 **b) Listen to the CD and check your sentences.**

Think about how you would say the sentences in German. What do you notice?

P3 Sound check: how to say the letter 'g'

engineer • designer • gardener • well-organised • original • guess • fight • image • lifeguard • teenager • dialogue • right

CD 96 **a) Listen to the CD and repeat the words.**

b) Copy the lists and fill in the words. The third list is for words with a silent 'g'.

/dʒ/	/g/	/-/
engineer	gardener	designer

CD 97 **c) Listen to the CD and check your lists.**

P4 What might happen in the future ...?

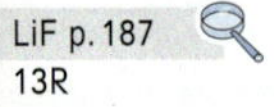
LiF p. 187 13R

a) Complete the sentences. Use the simple present in the if-clause and the will-future in the main clause.

1. If Jean ??? *(become)* a nurse, she ??? *(be able to)* help many people.
2. If Arne ??? *(move)* to California, he ??? *(learn)* English quickly.
3. If Anna ??? *(go) to New York, she* ??? *(look) for a job there.*
4. If Richard ??? *(miss)* his bus, he ??? *(be)* late for work.
5. If you ??? *(become)* a sailmaker, you ??? *(spend)* a lot of time on boats.
6. If Janet ??? *(work)* as a flight attendant, she ??? *(travel)* a lot.

1. If Jean becomes a nurse, she will be able to help many people.

CD 98 **b) Listen to the CD and check your sentences.**

P5 If only ...

Look at the pictures and write down what the people would do.

LiF p. 190
15

1

If Emma's parents ??? *(agree)*, she ...

2

If Alex ??? *(be)* fitter, he ...

3

If the boys ??? *(have)* time, they ...

4

If Gemma ??? *(find)* a nice dress, she ...

5

If Claire ??? *(live)* near the sea, she ...

go to the cinema
try it on
play football
go to a concert
go surfing

If Emma's parents agreed, she would go to a concert.

P6 Choosing an elective

Read Jack's email to his older cousin about choosing an elective at school. Complete it using the modal verbs from the box. There is more than one solution.

would • could • should • wouldn't • couldn't • shouldn't

LiF p. 188
14R

Hi Malcolm,
How are you? I need some advice ...
You see, I don't know which elective to choose. I ??? choose a sport, like soccer, but I ??? be very good because I hurt my foot last week.
Spanish ??? also be possible, but I ??? even order food in Spanish in Columbia last year, so I probably ??? choose Spanish.
I think I ??? choose either computer sciences or marketing. Computer sciences ??? be interesting because I love working with computers, but then it ??? be interesting learning about marketing, too. What ??? you do in my situation?
Thanks for your help,
Jack

B1 My future job?

Think of a job and mime it. Your classmates guess what it is.

I think you're a ...

p. 64
B1

a) **What is important to you for your future job? Look at the pictures and the questions in the speech bubbles. Talk to a partner and make notes.**

Would you like to work with people, animals, your hands, computers, ... ?

Would you like to work indoors or outdoors?

Would you like to work alone or in a team?

What skills would you like to use at work (language skills, maths, social skills, ...)?

b) **Work with your partner. Using your answers from a), collect and write down ideas for jobs that each of you could do.**

how to p. 163
work together

c) **Mill around and share your ideas with your classmates.**

What could be a good job for you?

A good job for me would be a ... because ...

B2 The job for you

p. 65
B2
CD
2/7 99
WB p. 74
B1
how to p. 150
mediate

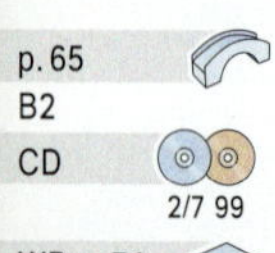

'The job for you' is a radio programme which gives young people information about jobs.

a) **Listen to what Angie says about her job. What do you remember?**

b) **Listen to Angie again. Imagine your younger sister wants to be a hotel receptionist. Her English is not as good as yours. Tell her the most important facts from the radio programme in German.**

B3 Nick's work experience

Look at the pictures. Where do you think Nick is doing his work experience?

p. 66 B3
WB p. 74 B2

a) Read about Nick's work experience. What does he complain about?

What a day! My first day of real work experience in what I thought would be my dream job – working in a sports shop!

I thought I would show people how to skateboard or demonstrate how to play darts. But it wasn't anything like that – just a day of disasters and boring tasks.

My boss for the week, Mr. Cameron, said that he was not happy with me when I arrived late. He told me I had to be there on time.

Then he sent me off with a long list of jobs, like taking old cardboard boxes down to the basement, putting shoelaces in trainers and sweeping the floors. Boring!

3

I was so bored that I fell asleep during my lunch break and went over my hour for lunch. Mr. Cameron told me I would have to work late to make up the time and sent me to the cash register – but no customers came.

I was just pulling out my phone to text my friends, when Mr. Cameron appeared from nowhere. He said that I was at work and I couldn't sit around playing with my phone.

4

When I got home at 6, I lay down on my bed, fell asleep and missed dinner.

Now I can't sleep. I feel as if I've been sweeping that storeroom and carrying cardboard boxes my whole life!

b) What do you think went wrong?

c) Work with a partner and write down tips for pupils starting work experience.

WB p. 75 B3, B4

B4 A telephone call

CD 2/8 100

a) Read what Mr. Cameron told Nick. Then listen to what Nick told his sister Melanie on the phone and read along.

What Mr. Cameron told Nick:

Nick and Melanie's telephone conversation:

Nick: Hi, Melanie. I just got home.
Melanie: Hi, how was your first day?
Nick: Ugh, actually, it was awful.
Melanie: Really? Why?
Nick: Well, I was late and Mr. Cameron said that he was not happy with me. He told me that I had to be there on time.
Melanie: Hmm, OK …
Nick: And then I fell asleep at lunch and he said that I would have to work late to make up the time. And then, Mr. Cameron …

LiF p. 191 16

b) Be a language detective. Look at what Mr. Cameron told Nick and what Nick tells Melanie. What do you notice? Talk about it with a partner. Check with the LiF.

c) Look at some more things Mr. Cameron said. Write down what Nick tells Melanie.

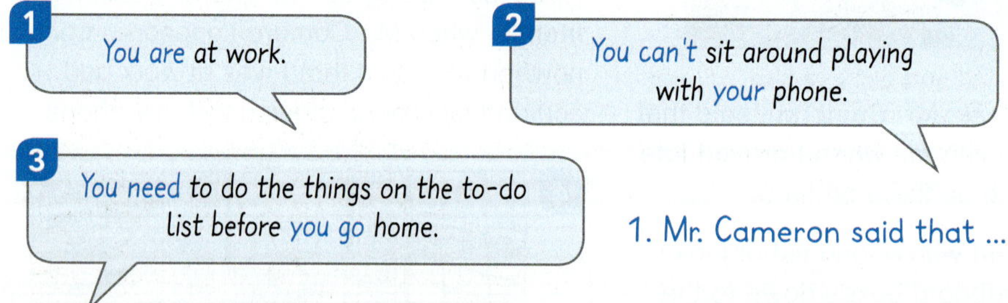

1
You are at work.
2
You can't sit around playing with your phone.
3
You need to do the things on the to-do list before you go home.

1. Mr. Cameron said that …

WB p. 76 B5–B7

CD 2/9 101

d) Listen to the rest of the conversation and check your sentences.

B5 Choose

1. **Make a list of work places in your area where you or your classmates could try to get work experience.**

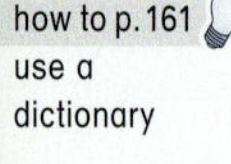
how to p. 161 use a dictionary

2. **Do you have any work experience? What did you have to do? Could it become a part-time job or even a permanent full-time job after school? Write a short text. Use a dictionary.**
3. **How could Nick and Melanie's conversation continue? What advice could she give Nick? Write a dialogue.**

B6 Everybody has skills

a) **Read this American magazine article. What is it about? Talk about it with a partner in German.**

p. 67 B4

how to p. 149 read

Have you ever thought about what it takes to apply for a job or work placement? When employers want to hire people, they look for two kinds of skills: soft skills and hard skills. Everybody has soft and hard skills – but what exactly are they?!

Hard skills

Hard skills (also called job skills) are skills that help you do special jobs. Examples are:

- cooking
- typing
- repairing cars
- computer programming

People learn hard skills at school, on the job or from life experience. You can even try and teach yourself skills like using a special computer program.

Soft skills

Soft skills are also called people or personal skills. Examples are:

- politeness
- reliability
- good communication
- ability to work in a team

How you talk, listen and present yourself are also soft skills. They are really important when you talk to an employer on the phone or in an interview.

Recognising your hard and soft skills

If you play a team sport, you've probably got good teamwork skills.
Are you good at presentations? Your communication skills are likely to be great!
Do you babysit for neighbors? For that you have to be reliable and responsible.
Think about it for a moment – what hard and soft skills have you got?

Improving your skills

To practice soft skills, talk to friends and family and ask them for feedback. What can you do better?
To practice or learn hard skills, take a course – or buy a book and teach yourself!
When you apply for a job, don't just list these skills in your résumé – make sure you give examples. Good luck!

> **Tipp**
> résumé (AE) = CV (BE)

b) **Collect hard and soft skills in the article and make two lists.**

c) **Read the text again and write down the answers to the questions.**

1. How can you learn hard skills?
2. When are soft skills really important?
3. How and where can you learn soft skills?
4. How could you improve your skills?

WB p. 77 B8

B7 A soft skill check

p. 68 B5

a) **Read and answer the questions to find out if you have good soft skills! Write down the letters that you choose for each question.**

1. You're late for school.
a) You enter the classroom, don't say anything and sit down.
b) You enter the classroom and say good morning to everyone.
c) You apologize to the teacher.

2. You start group work in class.
a) You choose a group with good classmates so you don't have to work so hard.
b) You choose classmates that you know you can work well with.
c) You ask your teacher for an individual task.

3. Your class has to tidy the playground every day for a week.
a) You wait and hope that others will volunteer.
b) You say that you will do it.
c) You say you won't do it.

4. Your teacher wants to explain something to the whole class.
a) You listen carefully and ask specific questions.
b) You talk to your neighbor and don't listen at all.
c) You look out of the window.

5. Your group work is due tomorrow. Some of you haven't done the work.
a) You help the others in order to get a good group result.
b) You work all night long on your own and on your partners' work.
c) You do your own part of the presentation.

b) **Work out how many points you scored. Look at page 93 and check your result.**

c) **What soft skills are the situations about?**

organisational skills • ability to work in a team • politeness • being on time • listening skills • taking initiative • …

Situation number one is about politeness and …

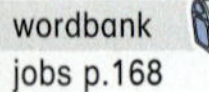

wordbank jobs p. 168

d) **Which skills do *you* need to work on? How could you improve them?**

I need to work on being on time. I could …

Group work is a problem for me. I could …

I need to improve …

…

WB p. 78 B9, B10

B8 A phone interview

Joe wants to do a work placement in a department store. He has a phone interview with the staff manager.

p. 69 B6

a) Listen to the CD and match the questions and answers.

CD 2/10 102

1. When are you available?
2. Why are you interested in a placement?
3. Do you already have some work experience?
4. When will you be finished at school?
5. Which subjects are you good at?

a. I'm really good at sports, but I also like English.
b. I'm available for three weeks in September.
c. I'd like to gain some experience working with customers.
d. I'll be done with school in three years' time.
e. Well, I once helped out for a day in my aunt's shop, but other than that, no.

b) Write down what Joe said. Remember the rules for reported speech.

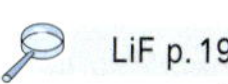
LiF p. 191 16

Joe said that he was available for three weeks in September. He answered that ...

c) What would you answer the staff manager? Make notes.

B9 Target task: A work experience interview

p. 70 B7

WB p. 79 B11

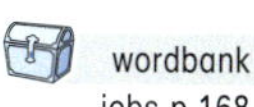
wordbank jobs p. 168

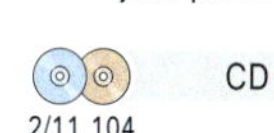
CD 2/11 104

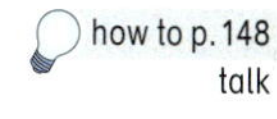
how to talk p. 148

1. **You are going to apply for work experience for example at a supermarket. Think of the hard skills and the soft skills you need for the job. Make notes.**
2. **Why are you the right person for the job? Look at B6 and B7 for help.**
3. **Listen to the CD. You will hear interview questions for a two week placement. How would you answer the questions? Make notes.**
4. **Practise the interview several times.**
5. **Record the interview.**
6. **Play it to a small group of classmates. Do your classmates think you will get the work placement? Why? Why not? Take turns.**
7. **Present the best interview from your group in class.**

P7 Explain

Explain what you have to do.

1. Using your answers from a), collect and write down ideas for jobs that each of you could do.
2. Imagine your younger sister wants to be a hotel receptionist.
3. Work out how many points you scored.
4. Remember the rules for reported speech.
5. Record the interview.

Ich soll ...
Wir sollen ...
...

P8 Talking about jobs

LiF p. 191 16

a) Report what these people said.

1. Betty: "I work with children."
2. Mrs Black: "I teach maths."
3. Robert: "My job at the supermarket is boring."
4. Johnny: "I like my job."
5. Jenny and Pete: "Our mum is a gardener."
6. Faisal: "I want to become a software developer in the future."

1. Betty said that she worked with children.

CD 105

b) Listen to the CD and check your sentences.

P9 Positive feedback

LiF p. 191 16

a) After the first week of her work experience at a travel agency, Lisa's boss, Mrs Michael, gives her feedback. Write down what Lisa tells her mum about it in the evening.

You are a very friendly person.
Politeness is very important.
You can work well with other people.
You are really good at typing.
You know a lot about other countries.
You are always on time.

1. Mrs Michael said that I was a very friendly person. 2. She said that I could ...

CD 106

b) Listen to the CD and check your sentences.

What hard and soft skills does Mrs Michael mention?

P10 A job interview

a) **Look at Aidan's CV. He wants to do a work placement as a car mechanic. Work with a partner and make notes for a telephone interview: one of you is the employer, the other is Aidan.**

Aidan Bradley

21 Pratt Street, London NW1 0LY
Home: 020 23412 – Mobile: 0760 45234 – Email: aidb@mail.co.uk

Date of birth:	3 March 2003	
Place of birth:	Birmingham, UK	
Work experience:	Summer job with Lucky Motors, Garage Services, London	
Education:	2013 – now	Haverstock School, London
	2008 – 2013	Fleet Primary School, London
Languages:	English, Spanish	
Hobbies:	basketball, music, cars	

Why are you interested in the placement?	I like ... that is why ...
What did you do in your summer job?	I helped ...
What do you ...?	...
What is ...?	...
When ...?	...
Where ...?	...
How long ...?	...
Which ...?	...
...	...

b) **Present your job interview in class.**

B7 Soft skill check results

	a	b	c
1	1 points	2 points	3 points
2	2 points	3 points	1 points
3	2 points	3 points	1 points
4	3 points	1 points	2 points
5	3 points	2 points	1 points

12–15: You have very good soft skills. You are a very responsible and patient person who can communicate and work well with other people.
8–11: There's room to improve your soft skills, but you are a good team player.
5–7: You should work on your soft skills!

Optional

O Jobs for him, jobs for her?

Once upon a time, if there was a fire, you called a fireman. If you were in trouble, you hoped a policeman would walk past. And on your birthday, you might have waited for the postman.

Look at those job titles again. Clearly back then, women couldn't put out fires, fight crimes or deliver letters! There were also 'female jobs' such as a nurse or secretary, even if not all of them have female job titles, such as housewife!

Today, we speak of a male or female firefighter, a policeman or policewoman and a postman or postwoman. You may also have your hair cut by a male hairdresser or be treated by a male nurse.

So in the 21st century, can men and women really do any job they want to?

Read the text and look at the pictures. Can men and women do any job they want today? Or are some jobs still 'male' or 'female' jobs? Talk in groups.

I think most jobs today are ...

I don't think men and women ...

Looking at the pictures, I would say ...

I know a man who is a ...

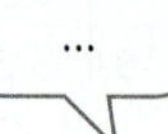

Away from home

Immigration country USA

Read on to find out more

Hurricane
atrina took
away my
home'

Find out on page 108

Away from home, away from school

Read about Hassan and Muzoon on page 109

Read about:
The Irish potato famine

A

- Du findest etwas über die Vielfalt in den USA und die Auswanderung aus Irland in die USA heraus.
- Du machst eine Ausstellung in der Klasse über Einwanderung in die USA. (Zielaufgabe)

B

- Du erfährst einiges über Menschen, die ihre Heimat verlassen mussten.
- Du drückst deine persönliche Reaktion auf einen der Texte oder eins der Fotos in diesem Theme aus. (Zielaufgabe)

A1 The kids in school with me

CD  2/12 110

Listen to the poem and read along. Who is in the class?

When I studied my A-B-C's
And learned arithmetic,
I also learned in public school
What makes America tick:
The kid in front
And the kid behind
And the kid across the aisle,
The Italian kid
And the Polish kid
And the girl with the Irish smile,
The colored kid
And the Spanish kid
And the Russian kid my size,
The Jewish kid
And the Grecian kid
And the girl with the Chinese eyes –
We were a regular Noah's ark,
Every race beneath the sun
But our motto for graduation was:
One for All and All for One!
The kid in front
And the kid behind
And the kid across from me –
Just American kids together
The kids in school with me.

Langston Hughes (1902–1967)

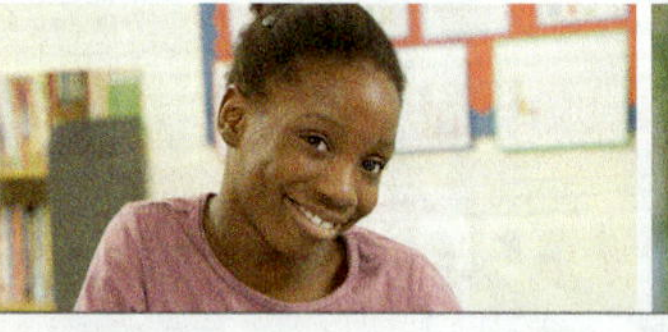
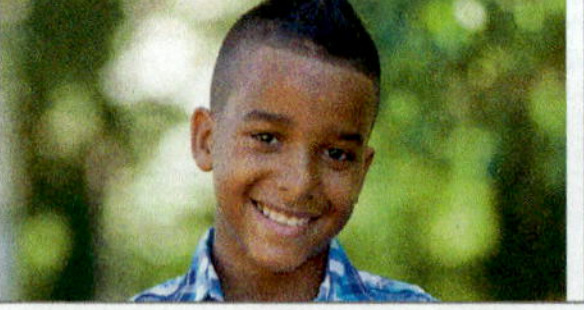

INFO BUBBLE

Langston Hughes was an African American writer. He was born in 1902 in Missouri, USA. His work shows that he was proud of his identity and culture. Some of the phrases he uses, such as 'colored kid' or 'Chinese eyes', are no longer used today because they are considered racist.

p. 72 A1

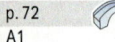

a) **What is the poem about? Talk to a partner.**

b) **Choose one of the quotes. What do you think it means? You can talk in German.**

What makes America tick | We were a regular Noah's ark

c) **How diverse is your class? Talk about it.**

We've got classmates from … | *In our class there are …* | *We all …*

In his poem Hughes criticises the idea of categorising people according to nationality or appearance. To him they are all Americans. Write down the two lines in the poem that reflect his opinion.

LAND & LEUTE 5

Die USA – ein Einwanderungsland

Tausende von Jahren wurde der nordamerikanische Kontinent nur von den amerikanischen Ureinwohnern *(Native Americans)* bewohnt. Heute könnte man die Vereinigten Staaten allerdings als ‚Nation von Immigranten' oder auch ‚Schmelztiegel der Kulturen' *(melting pot)* bezeichnen.

Die Mehrheit der Immigranten im 17. Jahrhundert kam aus England, Irland, Schottland, Deutschland und den Niederlanden. Viele von ihnen kamen, um ihre Religion frei ausüben zu können.

Viele Afrikaner wurden in die USA gebracht, um als Sklaven zu arbeiten. Im 18. Jahrhundert waren 20 Prozent der Bevölkerung afrikanischen Ursprungs.

Bereits ab 1815 wanderten viele Iren in die USA aus. Als 1845 eine Krankheit die Kartoffelernte zerstörte und mehr als eine Million Menschen verhungerten, wanderte mindestens eine weitere Million Iren aus.

In den 80er Jahren des 19. Jahrhunderts gingen viele Deutsche in die USA. Die deutschen Einwanderer hofften auf bessere Lebensbedingungen.

Am 1. Januar 1892 wurde die Einwanderungsstelle auf Ellis Island in New York eröffnet. Zwischen 1892 und dem Jahr der Schließung 1954 durchliefen mehr als 12 Millionen Einwanderer Ellis Island. Einige wurden zurückgeschickt, zum Beispiel, wenn sie ernsthaft krank waren oder einen Eintrag im Strafregister hatten. Ellis Island wurde bekannt als die ‚Insel der Tränen' *(Island of Tears)*.

Heute ist das Land immer noch für Einwanderer attraktiv. Allerdings muss man jetzt eine *Green Card* besitzen, um dauerhaft in den USA leben und arbeiten zu können.

Aus welchen Gründen verlassen heutzutage Menschen ihre Heimat?

DVD 10

A2 Leaving Ireland

a) Read about Ireland in the 19th century.

p. 73 A2

Ireland is a very beautiful island, but it was once called "Isle of hunger – isle of pain". This was because of the potato famine from 1845 to 1852.

A disease destroyed the potatoes. That was a disaster, because most poor people grew potatoes to eat. More than one million people starved to death and many more got sick.

As a result, many people left Ireland and emigrated to the United States or Canada. At that time, the journey across the Atlantic Ocean could take over a month. The ships were overcrowded and there was little food. Many people got sick and died.

The potato famine was one of the worst events in Irish history.

WB p. 87 A1, A2

b) Tell a partner the most important facts in German. Take turns.

how to p. 150 mediate

A3 The city of Chicago

Listen to the song. Find out where Chicago and Donegal are.

**a) Listen again and read along.
What is the song about?**

In the city of Chicago
As the evening shadows fall
There are people dreaming
Of the hills of Donegal.

Eighteen forty seven
Was the year it all began
Deadly pains of hunger
Drove a million from the land.
They journeyed not for glory
Their motive wasn't greed
A voyage of survival
Across the stormy sea.

To the city of Chigaco …

Some of them knew fortune
And some of them knew fame
More of them knew hardship
Died upon the plain.
They spread throughout the nation
They rode the railroad cars
Brought their songs and music
To ease their lonely hearts.

To the city of Chigaco …

Music and lyrics: Luka Bloom

b) What do some people in Chicago dream of?

c) How did songs and music help the people of Donegal in the USA?

A4 The story of Annie Moore

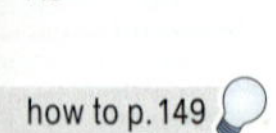
p. 74
A3

how to p. 149
read

a) Read about Annie Moore. What do you learn about her and her family?

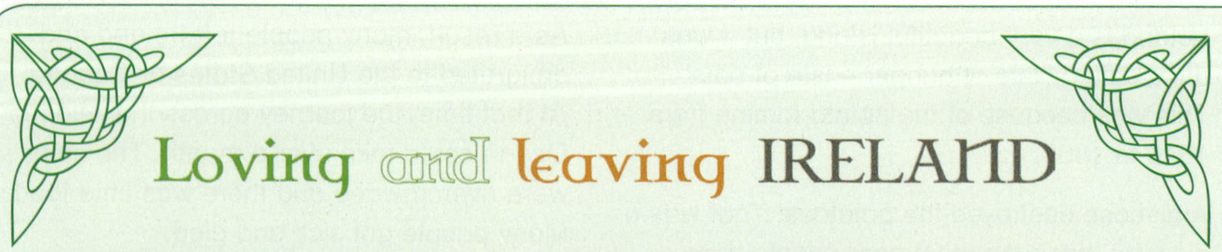

Loving and leaving IRELAND

It was December 1891. Annie Moore and her younger brothers were waiting nervously to board the ship that would take them from Ireland to New York.

Annie was sad to leave her Irish home. But she was also excited to see her parents again. It would be wonderful to have the whole family together. Her parents had gone to

America two years earlier with her older brother. After they had arrived in America they found a place to live and jobs in New York. Life was better there than it had been in Ireland.

After everyone had boarded the ship, Annie and her brothers' voyage began. They travelled in the hold of the ship – a big space that was crowded, cold and dirty. They had to share it with lots of people. The food was bad and many people got sick. They were on the ship for 12 days and Annie hated it.

On January 1st, 1892, the ship reached New York. Annie was very happy that the trip was almost over. The captain announced that the ship would dock at Ellis Island.

Annie was the first person to leave the ship. She got ten dollars as a gift because she was the first immigrant on Ellis Island. She couldn't believe it. She had never seen so much money! And that's how Annie's life in America began.

Today a statue of Annie stands on Ellis Island, which is now a museum. There is also a statue of Annie and her brothers in Cobh, Ireland, where they began their voyage.

b) Choose a title for each of the six paragraphs.

Statues of Annie • Arrival in New York • Mixed feelings • Leaving Ireland • The voyage • First immigrant on Ellis Island

c) Answer at least four of these questions.

1. When did Annie board the ship?
2. What was Annie excited about?
3. What was it like on the ship?

Answer all the questions.

4. What happened on January 1st, 1892?
5. Why did Annie get ten dollars?
6. What is Ellis Island today?

Answer questions 1 to 6 above. Then write four more questions about Annie's story. Swap with a partner and answer the questions.

WB p. 88 A3, A4

A5 Language detective

LiF p. 192
17
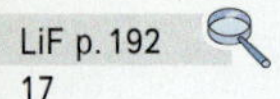

a) **Have a look at this sentence. What do you notice? Check with the LiF.**

After they <u>had arrived</u> in America, they <u>found</u> a place to live.

b) **Find more examples in A4. Copy the sentences and underline the past perfect form.**

c) **Match the sentence parts and write them down.**

1. Before Annie went to America
2. Before Annie left Ireland
3. When they finally arrived in New York
4. Annie received ten dollars

a. they had been on the ship for 12 days.
b. after she had left the ship.
c. she had lived in Ireland for 15 years.
d. she had said goodbye to her friends.

WB p. 89
A5, A6
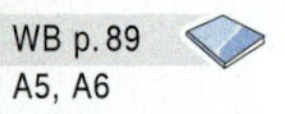

d) **Underline the part of each sentence that tells you what happened first.**

A6 Choose

p. 75
A4

1. **Find out more about Ellis Island. Make a fact file.**
2. **Write thought bubbles for Annie when she leaves Ireland or when she arrives in New York. Think about her feelings, hopes, fears, …**

   I wonder what … is like.

3. **Imagine how Annie felt when she left Ireland and when she arrived in New York. Use adjectives from the box to write about her.**

   I think Annie was sad to leave her friends. She was probably …

   nervous • excited • frightened • sad • upset • worried • …

how to p. 148
talk

4. **Imagine what it was like when Annie said goodbye to her best friend or when she met her parents in New York. Write a dialogue and act it out.**

A7 Immigration country USA

p. 76
A5
CD 2/14

a) **Look at the bar chart and listen to the description of the situation in 1850 and 2000.**

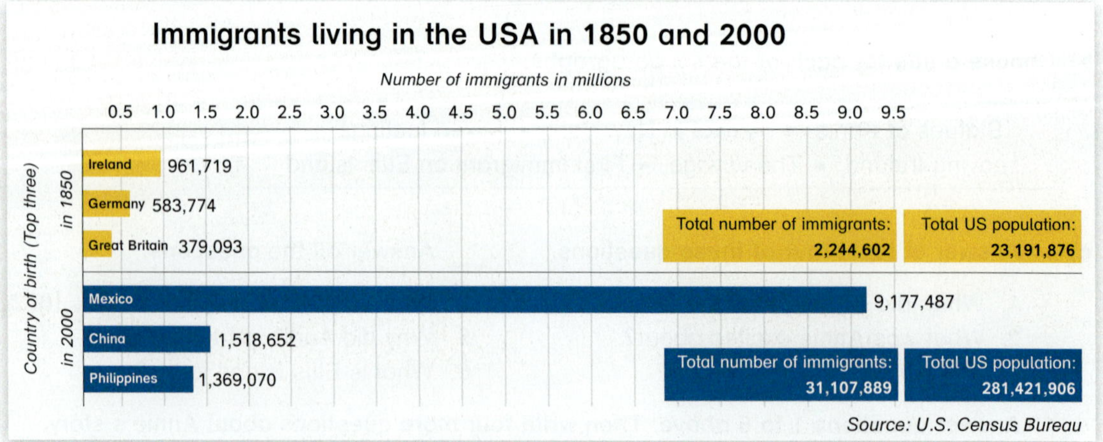

b) Listen again. Then use these phrases to talk about the bar chart in class.

the total number of … • most of the … • the total amount • compare • more • most • …

In 1850, most immigrants living in the USA were born in …

When you compare the top half of the bar chart …

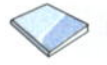
how to p. 162 work with statistics

WB p. 91 A7, A8

Write about the bar chart. Use the phrases from b).

A8 Across the border

a) Look at the photos. What do they show? Where do you think this could be? Talk in class.

p. 78 A6

1
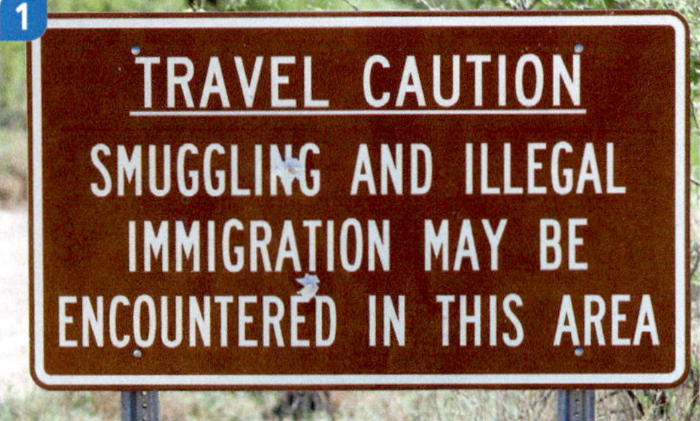

Picture … shows …

I think the people are …

I think this is in …

…

2

3

4

5

b) How do the photos make you feel? Make notes and talk to a partner.

Picture … makes me feel …

A9 The border to the USA

p. 79 A7

a) Look at the photos and the titles. Then skim the text.

how to p. 149 read

The Mexico-United States border

The Mexico-United States border runs from California in the west to Texas in the east. Around half a million people illegally cross the border and get into the USA each year.

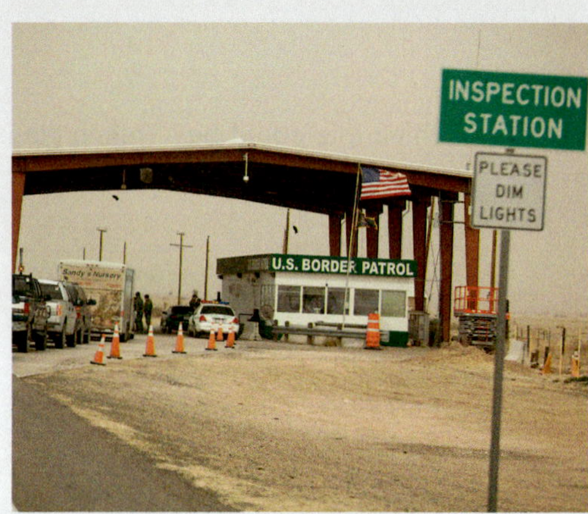

Reasons for leaving Mexico

Mexico has a lot of problems: poverty, crime, drugs and violence. Many Mexicans want to leave because of this. Most of them believe that life is better in the USA.

The deadly border

Illegal immigrants try to avoid the US Border Patrol by walking through the desert. But this is dangerous. Many immigrants die of thirst or heat exhaustion on the way. Over 2,000 people died like this in Arizona from 2001 to 2014.

Deportees

But a lot of people make it across the border. Some of them get caught immediately and are sent back. Others get caught after they have lived in the USA for some time. They are also sent back. These people are called 'deportees'. Many of them try to get back into the USA again, because their families live there.

Life for illegal immigrants in the US

There are more illegal immigrants in the USA from Mexico than from any other country.

Life is hard for them. They live in fear. Without the right papers it is very hard or even impossible to get a job. For many illegal immigrants the fight for a better life just goes on – but on the other side of the border.

b) Read the text with a partner. Write down key phrases for each paragraph.

c) Read the questions below. Together with your partner, find as many answers as you can.

1. Where is the border?
2. Why do people leave Mexico?
3. Why is the border deadly?
4. What is a deportee?
5. Why is life hard for illegal immigrants?

WB p. 92 A9, A10

 **Use your answers to write a summary.**

A10 Rosa's story

a) **Read the first paragraph. Which of the photos in A8 fit the situation?**

b) **Read the rest of the story.
How do Rosa and the others feel?**

nervous • scared • excited • worried • sad • upset • …

CD 2/15 120

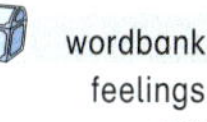
wordbank feelings p. 166

Rosa listened nervously as the coyote told them what would happen. He had planned everything perfectly. That evening they were going to cross into the United States from Mexico. Rosa felt pangs of fear in her stomach.

The coyote put everyone in groups. Weak people with strong people. Men with women. Young with old. He told them where to meet and told them not to take much with them. There were thieves out there. If they caught you they would take all your things. Or they would hurt or kill you. Rosa felt the pangs of fear get stronger.

That night, Rosa and her group met once more. It was a dark night so they couldn't see much. Finally the coyote gave the signal. The group ran across the valley. They ran as fast as they could. Rosa turned and looked back, then followed the others into some bushes.

They ran on and on and then suddenly the people in front stopped. Rosa stopped, too. No one moved. They heard voices. They all lay down, quickly. Lying there, Rosa looked around the group, seeing only eyes. Frightened eyes.

She breathed really quietly. It wasn't easy. The voices were getting louder. From the darkness, the coyote whispered one word. 'Thieves!'

Tipp
Der Begriff „coyote" wird für Schlepper verwendet, die Menschen über die Grenze schmuggeln.

c) **Talk to a partner. What do you think happens next?**

I think the voices …

Maybe they …

d) **Now listen to the end of the story. Does Rosa make it across the border?**

CD 2/16

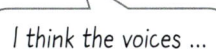

A11 Target task: The USA, a country of immigrants

Make a class display about immigration in the USA.

p. 80 A8

1. **Decide as a class what you want to include in your display. Think about …**
   - charts and maps
   - photos with captions
   - articles, stories, poems, …
   - fact files
   - timelines
   - …
2. **Think about the number of immigrants, their homelands, journeys, languages …**
3. **Decide as a class who does what.**
4. **Research your topic and work on your product with a partner or in a small group.**
5. **Put your product on the wall to make your class display. Present it.**

how to p. 153 present

Practice matters

P1 Explain

Explain what you have to do.

Ich soll ...

Wir sollen ...

...

1. Write down the two lines in the poem that reflect his opinion.
2. Skim the text.
3. Underline the part of each sentence that tells you what happened first.
4. Use these phrases to talk about the bar chart in class.
5. Research your topic and work on your product with a partner or in a small group.

P2 Where are they from?

a) Read the names of the countries. What are the nationalities? Look at A1 for help.

1. USA
2. Italy
3. Poland
4. Spain
5. Russia
6. China

1. USA – American

b) Write at least five more pairs. You can use a dictionary.

P3 Scrambled facts

a) Unscramble the facts about the Irish potato famine and write them down.

1. was – in Irish history. – most terrible events – The potato famine – one of the
2. The famine – ended – started – in 1852. – in 1845 and
3. poor people – to eat. – grew – Most – potatoes
4. More than – starved – people – one million – to death.
5. emigrated – United States. – Many people left – Ireland and – to the

1. The potato famine was one of the ...

CD 121

b) Listen to the CD and check your sentences.

P4 Sound check: how to say the letters 'ou'

CD 122

a) Listen to the CD and repeat the words in the box.

young • enough • out • country • about • announce • found

b) Copy the table. Write the words from the box into two lists.

/ʌ/	/aʊ/
young	out
...	...

CD 123

c) Listen to the CD and check your lists.

P5 The right little word

a) Copy the sentences and fill in the missing words.

1. Annie was waiting to board the ship that would take her ??? Ireland ??? New York.
2. She had never been ??? of the country before.
3. Her parents had gone to America two years earlier ??? her older brother.
4. Now they lived and worked ??? New York.
5. Annie was ??? the ship for 12 days.
6. When she got to Ellis Island, her new life ??? America began.

1. Annie was waiting to board the ship that would take her from Ireland to New York.

b) Listen to the CD and check your sentences.

124 CD

P6 Going to New York

a) Use the words in brackets to join the two actions. Change the tense of the verb in the first action.

LiF p. 192 17

1. My mum got a new job in New York. We moved to the USA. (after)
2. We arrived in New York. We went to our new house. (when)
3. Dad made us sandwiches. We all ate lunch on the floor. (when)
4. Everyone finished eating. I went to my new room. (when)
5. I went to my new room. I wrote a letter to my best friend back home. (after)
6. I finished the letter to my friend. I was sad. (when)

1. After my mum had got a job in New York, we moved to the USA.

b) Listen to the CD and check your sentences.

125 CD

P7 After I had ...

a) Make sentences and copy them. There is more than one solution.

LiF p. 192 17

1. After I had done all my homework,
2. After my mum had made a salad,
3. When my brother had got up,
4. After we had had dinner,
5. When my best friend had arrived,
6. When everyone had finished eating,

a. I helped my dad tidy the kitchen.
b. we all played a game together.
c. I fell asleep.
d. we had lunch in the garden.
e. we watched a film and ate pizza.
f. we went swimming together.

1. After I had done all my homework, I fell asleep.

b) Compare your ideas with a partner. Did you write down the same sentences?

B1 Away from home

Have you ever been away from home? What was it like?

p. 81 B1

a) Work in groups. Think of reasons why people could be away from home. Make notes.

b) Talk about your ideas in class.

away from home
- school exchange
- job abroad
- ...

B2 Leaving home

p. 82 B2

a) Why do you think the people in the photos are leaving their homes? Talk in class.

1

2

war • a flood • poverty • an earthquake • the political situation • a natural disaster • ...

I think the people in photo ... are leaving because of ...

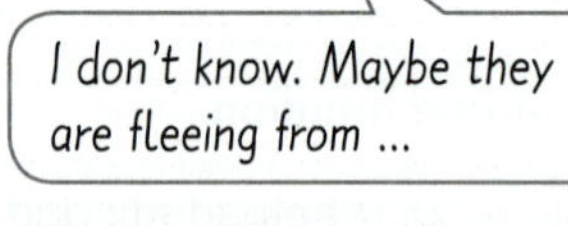

I don't know. Maybe they are fleeing from ...

...

3

CD 2/17 126

b) Listen to the news reports. Match them to the photos.

News report number one matches photo ...

how to p. 148 listen

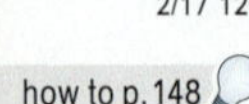

c) Choose one of the situations. Listen again and take notes.

WB p. 93 B1

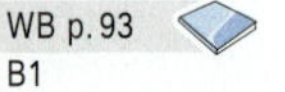

d) Write about the situation.

Photo number ... shows ... The people have to leave because ... There are ...

B3 People on the move

a) **Look at the title. What do you think it means?**

I think "people on the move" are people who ...

b) **Now skim the text and find out if you were right.**

p. 83 B3

how to read p. 149

More than 230 million people live outside the country they were born in.

Why do so many people **leave** their homes?

There are many reasons why people leave their homes. Some people **choose** to move. Other people **have** to leave.

MIGRATION
IS NOT A CRIME

Why do some people **choose** to move?

Some people try to start a new life somewhere else because they want to find better work or a higher standard of living. Some want a better future for their children. These are called '**pull factors**' – they 'pull' people to a new place.

Why do some people **have** to leave their homes?

Wars or natural disasters can destroy lives and houses. That makes it unsafe or impossible to stay at home. Some people flee because they are persecuted due to their race, religion, nationality or political opinions. Others leave to escape extreme poverty. These are called '**push factors**' – they 'push' people to leave a place.

c) **Scan the text for reasons for migration. Take notes. Compare with a partner.**

find better work, ...

d) **With your partner, sort the reasons for migration into two lists: 'push factors' and 'pull factors'.**

pull factors	push factors
better work	...

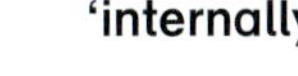

Read the definitions and look up the words 'migrant', 'refugee', 'asylum seeker' and 'internally displaced person'. Explain the terms to a partner in German. Take turns.

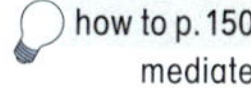
how to mediate p. 150

Who is a migrant?

Migrants move around within their own country, or from one country to another, usually to find work. Some choose to move, others have to leave because of economic or other sorts of problems.

Who is a refugee?

Refugees have fled their own country because it is not safe. Their own government does not protect them and so they have to leave. Refugees are protected by international law.

Who is an asylum seeker?

Asylum seekers have fled their country in fear for their lives. They hope to get refugee status.

Who is an internally displaced person?

Internally displaced people have been forced to leave their homes, but have stayed within their own country.

WB p. 94 B2, B3

B4 Displaced by Hurricane Katrina

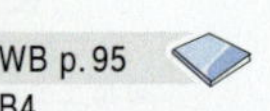
WB p. 95
B4

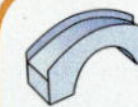
Look at the photos. What can you see? What do you think happened?

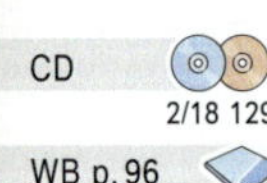
p. 84
B4
CD 2/18 129
WB p. 96
B5

a) Listen to Jeremiah, who was eight years old when his family was displaced by Hurricane Katrina. What is your first reaction to his story? Collect your thoughts on the board.

b) What happened to him and his family? Take notes.

First ... Then ... Days later ... In Houston ... At school ... Now ...

c) What do you think the hardest part was for Jeremiah? Write down your opinion.

I think ... was the hardest part for Jeremiah.

the evacuation • staying at stadium • being airlifted in helicopter • staying at trailer park • neighborhood was flooded • house was destroyed

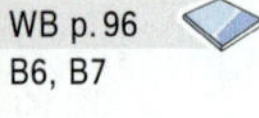
WB p. 96
B6, B7

Find out more about Hurricane Katrina. Report to the class.

B5 The right to learn

All children have the right to go to school and learn. But for some children that is not so easy.

p. 85
B5

Read about Hassan. What can you find out about him and his family?

Hassan is ... His father was ... His mother works ...

Read about Hassan or Muzoon. What can you find out about his or her hopes for the future? Write it down.

Read both texts. Compare Hassan and Muzoon's lives. What is the same? What is different?

Hassan fled from Syria. ...
Now he lives ...
In the future he wants to ...

Muzoon ...
Now she ..
...

Hassan – at work six days a week

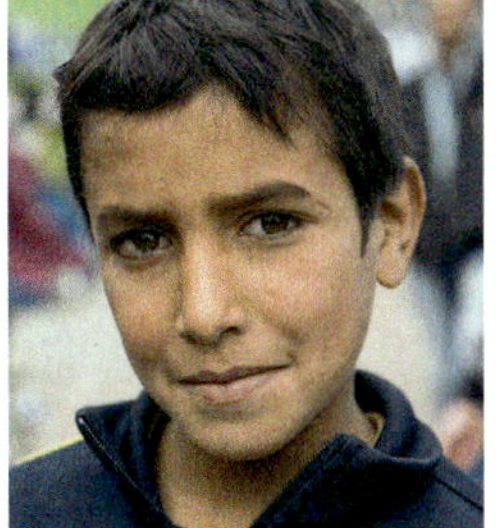

Hassan is a Syrian refugee living in Turkey. He and his family fled from Syria when his father was killed.

Work

Hassan would love to go to school, but he can't. Instead, he goes to work. 12 hours a day, six days a week, Hassan sits at a sewing machine and makes shoes. He can make hundreds of pairs of shoes every day but he earns less than the price of one pair of shoes for a day's work.

Family

Hassan's mother works as a housekeeper but she doesn't earn much money either. She can only pay rent and feed the family because Hassan and his brothers work.

Hassan's dream

Hassan has now been out of school for three years, and his dream of becoming an engineer seems less and less likely.

Muzoon Almellehan – campaigning for education

Muzoon Almellehan was 13 years old when she and her family fled from Syria. They went to a refugee camp called Zaatari, in Jordan.

At the refugee camp

Not all children in the camp went to school, but Muzoon did. The classes were large and the teachers had different accents.
But education was really important to Muzoon so she kept going to school. She tried to get others to do the same. She walked around the camp and told families that school was more important for their daughters than getting married.

England and the future

In 2015, Muzoon's family emigrated to Newcastle, England. There, Muzoon started at a local senior school. She still fights for girls' education In the future, she wants to go to university and become a journalist. Then she wants to return to Syria and help rebuild the country.

WB p. 97
B8, B9

B6 Choose

1. **Collect words that have to do with migration. Make a poster for your classroom.**

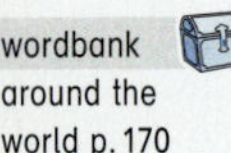
wordbank around the world p. 170

2. **Take a map of the world. Label countries that are currently in the news because of refugees or migrants. Display and explain the map in class.**
3. **Write a letter from Hassan to his family back home in Syria.**

Dear ...,
Today I ...

B7 Dreams and goals

CD 2/19 131 2/20 132

a) **Listen to the poems and read along. Which one do you like better?**

Growing strong

I no longer have blisters.
I don't have to run.
I am free
Like a chicken hatching out of an egg.
I have broken the shells
That were made out of fear.

I am now a warrior,
one full of happiness,
happiness that explodes out of me
like blazing hot sunrays.

Instead of crying, I am laughing.
Instead of starving, I am feasting.
I am growing.
I am better.

The future I have strived for
Is here.
Now, my goal
Is to keep
GROWING STRONG.

Eyonna, 13

I've arrived

Finally
the large gray ship
Crammed full of people just like me
Smelling of sweaty men and women
docks in America
and I disembark to meet my sponsor.

I'm led to a small eatery
and asked what I would like on my pizza.
I do not even know what pizza is,
but after it is explained to me
I begin to get a sense of how very different
my life will be now.

I have more choices on what toppings to
put on my food
than all the choices I had combined
back in Afghanistan

I wish I could have chosen to
have my mom with me.

Kiam, 13

b) **Work with a partner. Choose one of the poems and answer the questions.**

- What was life like for the speaker in her old home?
- How does she describe herself now?

- Being in America, what is different for the speaker?
- What does the speaker wish?

WB p. 98 B10

B8 Hope for the future

p. 86 B6

People flee their homes because they are scared and afraid. But they also have hopes for the future.

a) What hopes might they have? Talk in class.

Maybe they hope to ... | ...

find a good job • live without fear • start a new life • go back to school • learn a new language • make new friends • live in peace • ...

Children in a camp for Syrian refugees near the Turkish border

A refugee and his son, Greece

School for children from refugee and migrant families, Bolton, UK

b) Choose one of the people from the photos. What do you think his or her hopes for the future are? Are they similar to your hopes? Write about it.

My name is ... I come from ... I hope to ...

B9 Target task: A personal response

p. 87 B7

In this Theme you have seen photos and read texts about migration. What do you think about them? There are lots of ways to express yourself. You can:

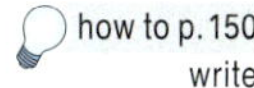
how to p. 150 write

- write about how a text, photo or topic makes you feel
- write a poem, story or text about one of the situations (fiction or non-fiction)
- write a letter to one of the people
- try to imagine how you would feel in one of these situations and write about it
- draw or find pictures about migration and write captions
- ...

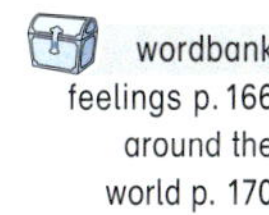
wordbank feelings p. 166 around the world p. 170

You can share your products in class if you want to – maybe in a gallery walk.

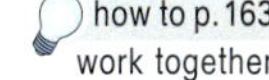
how to p. 163 work together

Practice matters

P8 Explain

Explain what you have to do.

Ich soll ...

...

Wir sollen ...

1. Scan the text for reasons for migration.
2. With your partner, sort the reasons for migration into two lists.
3. Explain the terms to a partner in German.
4. Write down your opinion.
5. Label countries that are currently in the news because of refugees or migrants.

P9 Sound check: how to say the letter 's'

CD 133

a) Listen to the CD and repeat the plural nouns.

migrants • wars • camps • reports • disasters • floods • journalists • problems • maps

b) Copy the lists and fill in the words.

CD 134

c) Listen to the CD and check your lists.

/s/	/z/
migrants	wars

P10 Nouns and verbs

a) Read the nouns in the box. Use a dictionary to find the verbs that go with them.

migration • definition • education • graduation • creation

b) Write down the word pairs.

CD 135

c) Listen to the CD and check your word pairs.

P11 Leaving home

a) Look at the family in the photo. Think about the following questions:

- Why do you think they are leaving their home? (Because of war, an earthquake, a hurricane, … ?)
- How do you think they feel? (Scared, excited, nervous, worried, happy, …?)
- What do you think their hopes are? (To find safety, find work, make friends, …?)

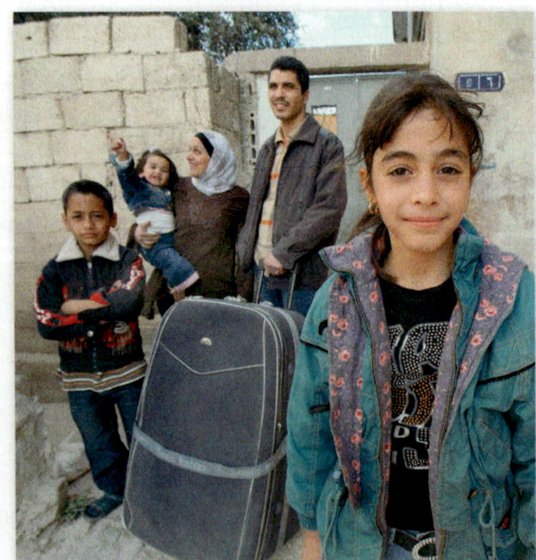

b) Make notes about your ideas.

c) Share your ideas with a partner. Are they similar?

Practice matters

P12 Definitions

a) Match the words with the definitions.

1. Hurricane:
2. Poverty:
3. Refugee:
4. Earthquake:
5. Flood:

Someone who has fled their country because it is not safe and who is protected by international law.

A natural disaster in which the ground suddenly moves.

When someone doesn't have enough money to live.

A storm with very strong winds and lots of rain.

A large amount of water that covers an area of land.

1. Hurricane: A storm with very strong winds and lots of rain.

b) Work with a partner and check your definitions.

P13 Who, what, where, why?

a) Choose the right question word or words and write questions.

Who	is Hassan's job?
What	campaigns for girls' education?
When	does Hassan live?
How much	do some people have to leave their homes?
Why	does Hassan earn for a day's work?
Where	did Muzoon and her family flee Syria?

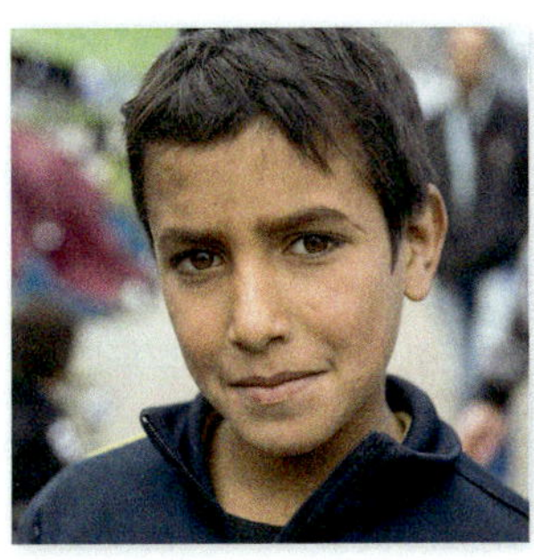

Who campaigns for girls' education?

b) Listen to the CD and check your questions.

CD 136

c) Work with a partner. Look at page 109 and find the answers to the questions. Write them down next to the question.

Who campaigns for girls' education? – Muzoon

d) Compare in class.

Optional

O Never give up on your dream

Girls living in refugee camps are often expected to stay at home for their safety and to help their families. This means they don't go to school. Many of these girls have experienced war and have had to leave their homes. Despite this, they have dreams like anyone else.

An organisation called the 'International Rescue Committee' helped a group of Syrian girls living in Jordan to visualise their ambitions, with a programme called 'Vision not Victim'. They wanted to help the girls not to give up on their dreams.

The girls created action plans and drew pictures of their ambition. Every girl directed her own photo shoot. The photos show the girls doing their dream jobs. Many of the girls also met people already doing those jobs.

Read what two of the girls, Amani and Fatima, have written as their future selves.

Amani, aged 10

Vision: future pilot

"I love planes. Even before I had ever been on a plane, I knew I wanted to be a pilot. Flying is adventurous and exciting.

When I was younger, my brother always told me that a girl can't be a pilot, but I knew deep down this is what I wanted to do. I finished my studies and found a way to get to flight school.

Now, not only do I get to live my dream, but I also get to help people travel, to see the world, and discover new places."

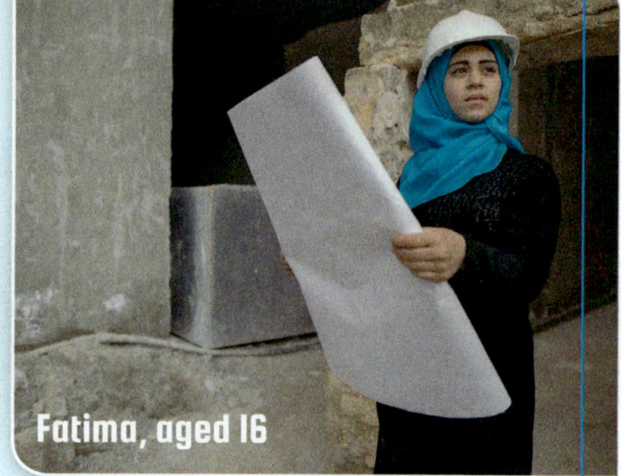

Fatima, aged 16

Vision: future architect

"I've always wanted to be an architect. Yet, when I was young people told me that this is not something a woman could achieve, and they encouraged me to pursue a more 'feminine' profession.

But I dreamt constantly of making beautiful homes for families, and designing buildings that bring people joy. Now that I've reached my vision, I hope I am a model for other girls – showing them that you should never give up on your dream – no matter what others say."

What do the two girls have in common?

What do you think about the programme? Talk to a partner or make notes.

6

Projects: Going green

How green are you?
Take the quiz on page 116!

Topic A
Green cities

Topic B
A plastic planet

Topic C
Toxic fashion

Intro
Steps
Topic A
Topic B
Topic C
YOU
Help

With a handy navigation bar!

Choose a topic and do your own project!
Find tips on pages 132 and 133!

Going green

p. 88
WB p. 107

How green are you? Do the quiz with a partner and write down your answers.

How green are you?

1. Do you switch off your TV or computer when you aren't using it?

A. Always.
B. Sometimes.
C. Not very often.

2. When you brush your teeth, do you let the water run?

A. No!
B. Sometimes.
C. Yes.

3. How do you get to school?

A. I walk or cycle.
B. I take the bus.
C. We always drive.

4. Do you grow your own food at home?

A. Yes, lots of it!
B. Yes, some.
C. No, we don't.

5. How many times do you reuse a plastic bag from the supermarket?

A. I never use plastic bags.
B. Once or twice, maybe.
C. I don't reuse them at all!

6. How much of your household waste do you recycle?

A. As much as we can.
B. We recycle some of it.
C. None of it.

Share your answers in class. What can you say about the results?

I got five As and one B. I think that means I'm very green.

It's good that most of us …

What was your answer for question …?

Mostly As: You are an eco hero!
Mostly Bs: You are an eco friend!
Mostly Cs: You are an eco monster!

wordbank environment p.171

p. 89

Look at the photos. Do they show a green world? What comes to mind? Make notes. Use a dictionary.

Talk about your ideas with a partner or in a small group.

Talk in class. What is a green world? Collect all your ideas. Compare your ideas with the definition at the bottom of the page.

Intro
Steps
Topic

Topic
Topic

YOU

Help

DEFINITION: A GREEN WORLD

A green world is a clean world. People do not use toxic chemicals to produce food and clothing. People use bikes and electric cars, so that traffic doesn't pollute the air. There is a lot of green space for free time activities and people are aware of their ecological footprint and the environment.

Project steps

1 Choose a topic

p. 90

Look through the three topics in this Theme:

Green cities *p. 120–123*

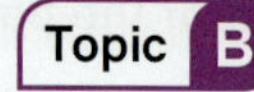

A plastic planet *p. 124–127*

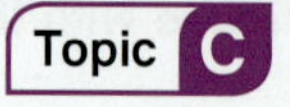

Toxic fashion *p. 128–131*

DVD 11–13

Watch the video clip for each topic. Then decide which one you want to find out more about. Get into a group with classmates who want to do the same topic as you.

2 Get into your topic

Look at the first page of your topic. Do the activities together in your group.

3 Explore your topic

On the second and third pages there are pictures, facts and figures, newspaper articles, podcasts, and much more, for example:

How to build a green city

Tips from the world's greenest cities!

Urban gardening in NYC – The 'edible' city

You don't all have to read every text! Split up your group so that different people explore different texts.

Webcode DSW-14604-601

If you want to find out even more, go to www.diesterweg.de/webcodes and type in the webcode of your topic. You will find a list of links to useful websites. You can also search for other useful websites yourself.

how to p. 152 research online

As a group, start a wordbank now for your topic. Add to it during the project.

Inform other group members about what you found out.

4 Spotlight on ...

On the fourth page you will find a text called 'Spotlight on ...'. This text goes into a bit more detail than the others. Read the text as a group, take notes and talk about it. There are also links to websites to find out more information.

5 Get ready to share

You and your group now know quite a lot about your topic. It is time to share your knowledge with your class.

Prepare a presentation. You could make a poster, a computer presentation, a fact file, ... Decide on the aspects you want to focus on. Be prepared for questions and feedback from the other groups.

If as a class you want to go further and carry out your own projects, do step 6.
If not, go straight to step 7.

Steps

6 Over to you!

Each group can now plan their own project based on their topic. If you prefer one of the other topics, you can change groups at this point.

Each group would need to:

- identify a problem
- research it
- think of a solution
- put their plan into action
- present their project to the class.

All the details for this part of the project are on pages 132 and 133.

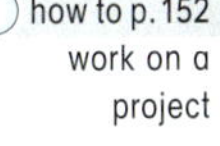

how to work on a project p. 152

7 Reflection

After the project is over, you have a chance to think about how it went and reflect on the work you have done.

You can find a questionnaire to help you with this in your workbook.

how to give feedback p. 154

WB p. 114

On pages 134–136 you will find useful words and phrases for each topic. These pages can be helpful to you during or after your project.

Topic A Green cities

p. 91
A1

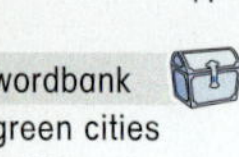

DVD
11

wordbank
green cities
p. 171

What makes a green city? Look at the photos and talk about them with a partner.

In a green city, there is/are ...

In a green city, people ...

use • have • travel • create • grow • go • try • ...

public transport

local food market

green space

vertical garden

bike lane

rooftop farm

Share your ideas in your group.
What do you think is most important? Make notes.

p. 92
A2

Five Green Cities

1. **Reykjavik**, Iceland ➜ The city wants to use no fossil fuels at all by 2050.
2. **San Francisco**, USA ➜ It was the first US city to ban plastic bags.
3. **Malmö**, Sweden ➜ They make their city buildings as energy-efficient as possible.
4. **Vancouver**, Canada ➜ By 2050 the city wants to use only renewable energy.
5. **Portland**, USA ➜ This is the city in the US where most people go to work by bike.

'GREEN CARPET'

EPISODE 1:
Eco-citizens

It's not easy to go green at home, but you can do it!
In our first episode, John O'Hara has many tips on how to make your home as green as possible.

CD
2/21 142

NYC *Green* News

PAGE 2
Monday, August 31

OUR CITY – GREENEST CITY!
Our city is the biggest and also the greenest city in the US!

We New Yorkers consume less gasoline and less electricity than the rest of the country. Only 54% of people in our city have a car.

I think that's because we live in a very compact city. It's easy to get around by public transport, bike, or on foot.

Most of us live in apartment buildings. Apartment buildings are very energy-efficient. All of this means that New Yorkers have some of the smallest carbon footprints in the whole of the country!

That's great, but if you want to do more, check out the Eco-Watch page on our website. There are more ideas to make your carbon footprint smaller!

Urban gardening in NYC – The 'edible' city

Today there are about 700 urban farms and gardens in New York City. They are on the ground and on rooftops!

These urban farms and gardens grow fresh and local food right in the city! They are good for the environment and they look nice!

These urban farms and gardens help people to live a better life because they work together for a better world. People create a community where they care about each other.

ONE WAY
MTA
The New York of the future?

How to build a green city

Tips from the world's greenest cities!

1. Build energy-efficient 'green' buildings.
2. Use renewable energy resources.
3. Spend money on public transport.
4. Try to reduce waste and use less water.
5. Make sure people have access to affordable, healthy food.
6. Make sure the city government sets a good example.

Webcode DSW-14604-601

how to research online p. 152

Want to find out more? Use the webcode or do your own research online. Here are some ideas for search terms.

- green cities
- vertical gardens
- urban gardening
- the world's most eco-friendly cities
- how to build a green city
- green city market

City Farm Chicago

You can see empty, unused plots of land in lots of cities all over the world. Most people just ignore them, but one organization in Chicago sees these plots of land in a different way.

There are about 80,000 unused plots in the city of Chicago and the organization 'City Farm Chicago' turns these unused plots into farms.

On just a single acre, City Farm Chicago can set up a farm that produces 20,000 pounds of food and creates three or four full-time jobs for people in the local neighborhood.

City Farm Chicago also makes compost from food waste and sells organic food at farm stands, farmers' markets and to restaurants.

City Farm Chicago can use the plots of land for free. But they must collect $30,000 per acre to put up fencing, lay the soil and start planting.

When the city needs the land back, the farm has to move. So the organization looks for land that is free for at least two or three years.

City Farm Chicago offers tours of the farms and asks people to volunteer. By doing that they are also educating people on farming and sustainability.

This fantastic project shows what can happen when the people all work together to make a neighborhood nicer for all who live and work there.

p. 93
A3, A4

Topic

Webcode
DSW-14604-601

Topic B A plastic planet

p. 95 B1
DVD 12
wordbank a plastic planet p. 172

Look at the photos and talk about them with a partner. What problems do they show?

wildlife • drop litter • irresponsible • dangerous • plastic bags • plastic pollution • plastic packaging • …

Now talk about these photos. Do you think they show solutions to the problems?

The earth is a plastic planet. Do you agree? Talk in your group and make notes.

p. 96
B2, B3

Plastic – it's all around us

It's in our homes, our offices, our cars, our gardens, our playgrounds. We buy food in plastic packaging, we buy drinks in plastic bottles, we use plastic bags to carry our shopping, we buy plastic toys for our kids, and much more.

Plastics have had a big positive effect on our lives. They have helped us to produce, package and transport goods more easily and more cheaply.

But: plastics are also a threat to our planet. The big problem is that plastics don't biodegrade. Instead, they just break down into smaller and smaller pieces.

Just imagine: most of the plastic that was ever made still exists in some form!

Fantastic – no plastic!

Since 2002, people in Ireland have had to pay for plastic bags at supermarkets. The result is that most people now bring their own shopping bags or buy reusable ones, which is much better for the environment.

Lots of other countries have done the same, but Zanzibar has gone even further. There, plastic bags were banned in 2006. Now, when you travel to the country, you are not allowed to take any plastic bags with you. Zanzibar is a plastic bag-free zone!

EPISODE 2:
Plastic Planet Earth

Plastic bag litter has a very bad effect on ocean wildlife. It kills tens of thousands of whales, birds, seals and turtles every year. They often mistake plastic bags for food.
To discuss this problem this week we have in the studio Dr Karen Gilmour, a marine biologist from the Australian Institute of Marine Science.

CD
2/22 144

Reducing pollution – and saving energy!

Recycling is also a very good way to save energy! Did you know that …

- one recycled plastic bottle would save enough energy to power a 60-watt light bulb for 3 hours?
- one recycled can would save enough energy to power a TV for 3 hours?
- one recycled glass bottle would save enough energy to power a computer for 25 minutes?
- 70 % less energy is needed to recycle paper compared with making it from raw materials?

Plastic facts and figures

- If we don't take action immediately, by **2050** there will be about **40 billion tons of plastic** on Earth – enough to wrap the planet six times over.
- From water bottles to the microbeads in our shampoo, we send **millions of tons** of plastic into the ocean every year. A lot of it ends up in our food.
- On average, a plastic bag is used for **12 minutes**, but it will be in the environment for **100 years**.

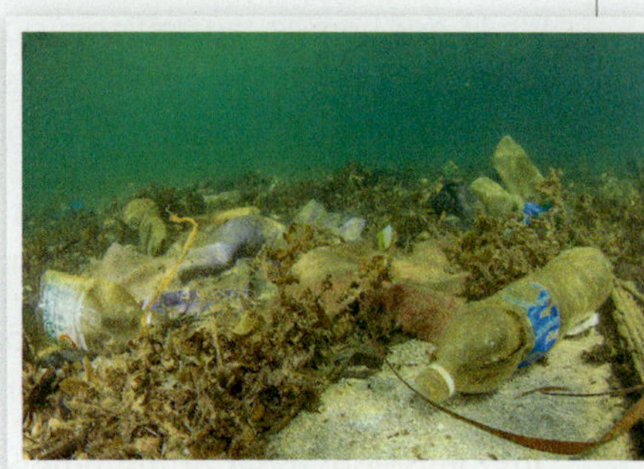

Here are ten easy ways ...

... to help keep plastics out of our oceans:

1. Use reusable shopping bags, preferably made of cotton or other natural materials.
2. Use returnable glass bottles instead of plastic ones or cans.
3. Avoid products with lots of packaging.
4. Take your own cup, knife, fork and spoon with you to cafés or coffee shops, so you don't have to use plastic ones.
5. Buy products made from recycled plastic, recycled paper or other recycled materials.
6. Replace plastic sandwich bags and bottles with reusable lunchboxes and bottles.
7. Find new uses for old things rather than just throwing them away.
8. Don't buy more new things than necessary and if something is broken, try to repair it.
9. Volunteer at a beach clean-up or join an environmental organization to find out what you can do in your local area.
10. Talk to your family and friends about why it is important to stop using plastic.

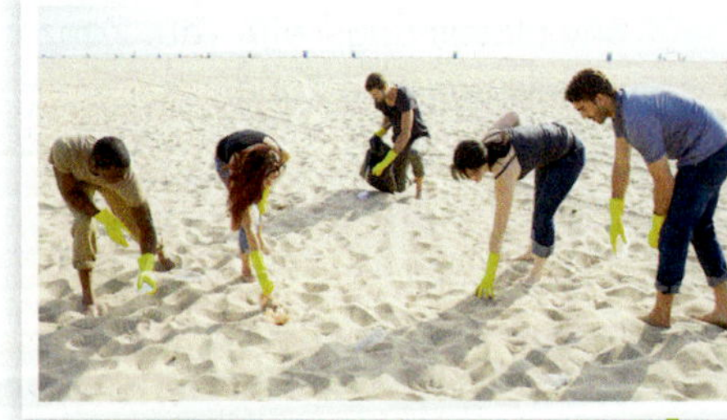

Webcode DSW-14604-602

Want to find out more? Use the webcode or do your own research online. Here are some ideas for search terms.

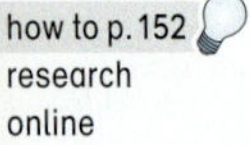

how to research online p. 152

- plastic pollution
- recycling plastic
- the majestic plastic bag
- plastic bottle recycling ideas
- beach clean-up
- plastic bag ban

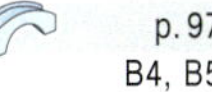
p. 97
B4, B5

Preserve Gimme 5

Bottle caps are one of the most frequently found forms of trash in the world's oceans and on beaches.

They are made from materials that are very recyclable, but they are difficult to recycle because they are so small. They are often too small for recycling machines and literally 'fall through the cracks'.

One organization in America noticed this problem and has found its own unique solution. Preserve Gimme 5, with schools in Massachusetts and Florida, is helping to make sure that plastic caps are recycled properly. The organization recommends two ways to recycle caps:

Caps-On:

Keep caps on recyclable plastic bottles before throwing them into recycling bins. This makes them easier to recycle.

Save the Caps with Gimme 5:

Preserve Gimme 5 organizes collection bins in supermarkets and schools for plastic caps without a recyclable 'carrier', such as glass bottles and toothpaste tubes.
They take the caps and use them to make new products, such as toothbrushes and razors.

Topic B

Webcode
DSW-14604-602

Topic C Toxic fashion

p. 99 C1
DVD 13
wordbank toxic fashion p. 172

What is there to think about when you need new clothes? Look at the pictures and talk to a partner.

Where do you buy them? • How much do they cost? • Where were they made? • Who made them? • What are they made of? • Do they contain toxic chemicals? • …

Share your ideas in your group. What do you think is most important to think about when you buy new clothes? What makes fashion toxic?

SPEAK OUT! THIS WEEK: ECO-FRIENDLY CLOTHING

This week's 'Speak out!' column was written by Megan Hall, 15, from Boston.

I wear eco-friendly, chemical-free clothes. And you can do it too!

The easiest thing? Buy **fewer clothes**!

But when you buy clothes, think about buying them from a **second-hand shop**, or going to a '**swap shop**' event – that's where people take clothes they would like to swap with other people.

I love going 'shopping' in my own closet! I love **restyling** my clothes into new ones: putting new buttons on old shirts, dying shirts a new color with an eco-friendly dye, things like that.

I made a cute purse out of an old jeans pocket. Look at the photo! Invite your friends and it's even more fun! Have a restyling party!

You could also buy clothes made from **recycled material**. Clothes made out of **organic cotton**, **bamboo** or **hemp** are also very eco-friendly.

Check out the label next time you want to buy something. Avoid Polyester! Let's all be **detox trendsetters**, not **detox losers**.

This way we can put a lot of pressure on fashion brands to '**go green**' too.

Topic C

p. 100 C2

All about organic cotton!

People wear T-shirts all over the world. Most T-shirts are made of cotton.

Cotton has been used to make textiles for over 5,000 years. Cotton is made from the cotton plant.

Over 300 million people work in cotton production and over 50 million are cotton farmers.

Conventional cotton growing

- Very toxic chemicals are used.
- Farmers have to buy expensive chemicals and fertilizers.
- Thousands of cotton farmers die each year because they use toxic chemicals.
- Farmers don't earn enough money from their cotton to make a decent living.

Organic cotton growing

- Alternative methods, such as picking bugs by hand, are used instead of chemicals.
- Farmers don't have to buy expensive chemicals and fertilizers.
- Farmers and their families can lead healthier and longer lives.
- Farmers get more money for their cotton in addition to selling other products.

FIVE QUESTIONS ON ... TOXIC FASHION

Are you wearing toxic fashion?
To find out, look at the label in the clothes that you are wearing.

Where were your clothes made?
There is a good chance that you will find the names of Asian countries such as China, Indonesia, Bangladesh or India.

Why are so many clothes made in Asia?
Over the last 20 years, American and European clothing brands have moved their clothes production to these countries.

Why did the clothing brands choose Asia?
They can pay the workers there very low wages, so they can make more profit.
They produce enough clothing in Asia to reach the moon and back every day.

What does that mean for the workers, us and the environment?
It means that many workers work very hard but earn so little money that they often can't afford two meals a day.
Because of the toxic chemicals drinking water becomes toxic.
Some of the toxic chemicals are still in the clothes when we buy them.
The clothes come a long way which is bad for the environment because of the use of planes and ships.

Not exactly eco-friendly, is it?

p. 100
C3

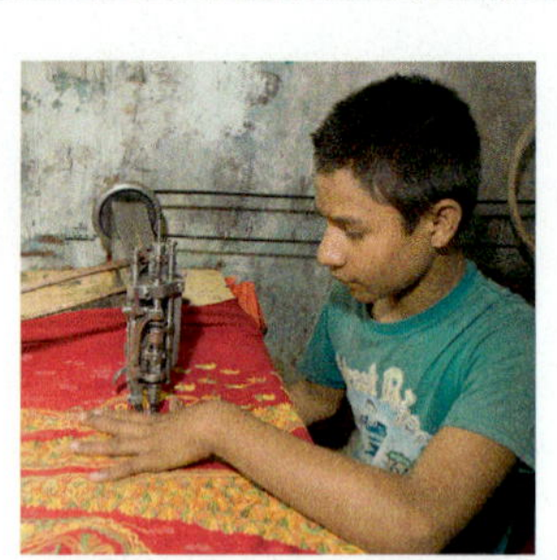

EPISODE 3:
Child labor and toxic fashion

What has the topic 'fast fashion' got to do with child labor? Joining us today is UNICEF's Carl Johnson to discuss this worldwide problem.

CD
2/23 145

Wash and wear!

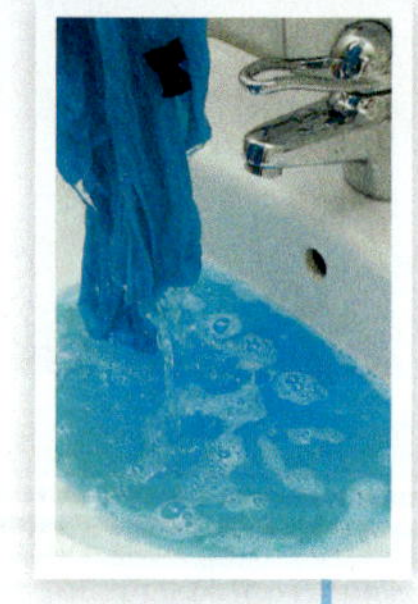

Do you need to wash your new clothes before wearing them?

Definitely YES! But why?

Clothes may contain toxic chemicals such as synthetic dyes and formaldehyde which can lead to allergic reactions and illnesses.

So, to be on the safe side:
Wash your new clothes at least twice before you wear them.

Webcode
DSW-14604-603

Want to find out more? Use the webcode or do your own research online. Here are some ideas for search terms.

how to p. 152
research online

- toxic fashion
- organic cotton
- Greenpeace
- restyling old clothes
- child labour in fashion industry
- chemicals in clothes

Maya's Ideas

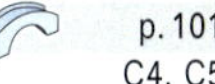
p. 101
C4, C5

Eco-friendly clothing is 'in'. But how can you be really sure that your clothes are 100% eco-friendly?

In 2008, when she was 8, Maya Penn thought of a solution to this problem. She founded her own company: 'Maya's Ideas'. She started making and selling eco-friendly clothing.

Maya uses only 100% organic cotton, hemp and bamboo and recycled materials for her clothing and accessories. She makes bags, scarves, T-shirts, hair accessories and even organic artwork.

Maya supports recycling and reusing materials which don't use up any of the earth's natural resources.

She doesn't use leather, silk or new wool. She always uses old fabrics or organic cottons.

Maya donates 10-20% of her profits to local and global charities and environmental organizations, and she has also started a separate non-profit organization called 'Maya's Ideas 4 The Planet'.

Maya sees herself as an environmentalist. She is doing everything she can to make the planet a good place for people and animals.

Webcode DSW-14604-603

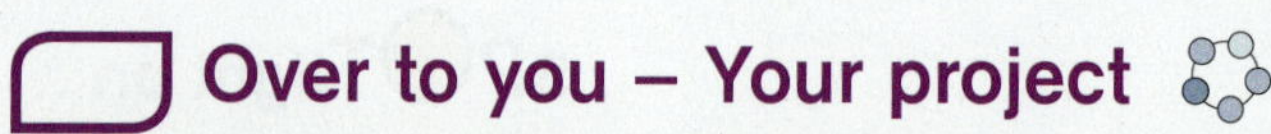

Over to you – Your project

wordbank
green cities p. 171
a plastic planet p.172
toxic fashion p.172

WB
A1, A2
B1, B2
C1-C3

1. In your group, discuss issues from your topic that affect your school, home or community.

A *I think it's a shame that our school doesn't have a vegetable garden.*

B *Have you noticed that our school cafeteria only uses plastic knives and forks?*

C *I think there's an eco-friendly clothes shop in town, but it never has many customers.*

2. Agree on one problem that you want to investigate and work on for your project.

I think we should ...

It would be fantastic if we could ...

For me, the most important thing is ...

Why don't we ...?

3. Research the problem. Discuss and decide:

- Who do you need to talk to?
- What do you need to find out?
- How will you collect the information? (a survey, an interview, the Internet, ...)

Make a plan and carry out your research.

4. Talk about your findings and discuss possible solutions to your problem. Which ones would be most practical and effective? Decide on the best solution.

5. Create an action plan for your solution. Here is an example:

Problem:
There is a small space in the school playground that is empty.

Our solution:
We want to use the space to make a school vegetable garden.

Why we want to do this:
It will make the playground look prettier and the school can use the vegetables in the cafeteria. Lots of pupils will also learn how to grow vegetables.

Project details:
- What we will need to do: buy seeds, plants and tools; advertise for pupil gardeners; find out which teachers can help us; prepare and plant the garden.
- How much it will cost: seeds and plants: 50 €; tools: 60 €; posters: 20 €. Total: 130 €
- How long the project will take: garden will take about 2 weeks to prepare
- Who will be involved: pupils, at least one teacher and someone from the school cafeteria

6. Now put your plan into action.
Use English where you can!

TAKE ACTION!

To carry out your action plan in your school, home or community, you could:

- Advertise what you are doing (posters, leaflets, school website, local newspaper, ...).
- Present the action plan to people outside your class, such as parents, other classes or the local community.
- Organise some fundraising activities to raise the money you need.
- Find more people who want to help.
- Make an action plan diary and take photos of your progress.

7. Once you have put your plan into action, it is time to prepare a presentation for your class.
Be creative and use your imagination! Your presentation could include:

- a slide show using a video projector or whiteboard
- a short role play
- a video or a podcast
- a live debate
- a poster
- a cartoon or drawing

how to p. 153 present

Prepare your presentation and make sure that:

- you have everything you need
- you have enough time to prepare the presentation
- everyone in your group knows what he or she is responsible for
- you know how much time you will have to present your project
- you practise your presentation

8. Present your project to the class. Listen to the other presentations and take notes.
Talk about the projects in class.

Useful words and phrases

A1 New words

a) **Match the words and phrases in the box to the definitions below.**

urban farm • fossil fuel • rooftop garden • environment • renewable energy • carbon footprint • sustainability • community

- the people living together in a neighbourhood
- a garden situated on the top of a house
- a farm situated in a city or town
- a measure of someone's effect on the environment
- oil or coal
- the world around us
- using or doing something without making life difficult for future generations
- energy that we cannot run out of, such as energy from the sun or water

urban farms: farm situated …

b) **Compare your answers in your group.**

A2 Adjectives and nouns

a) **Match the words to make phrases that have something to do with green cities. There is more than one solution.**

b) **Write statements about green cities using the phrases.**

In New York, there is a lot of energy-efficient housing.

compact	vegetables
green	gardening
energy-efficient	food
small	metropolis
urban	housing
healthy	communities
sustainable	carbon footprint
public	transport
local	cities

A3 Discussion

how to p. 160 discuss

Talk about making your community a greener place and reducing your carbon footprint. Work with a partner or in a small group.

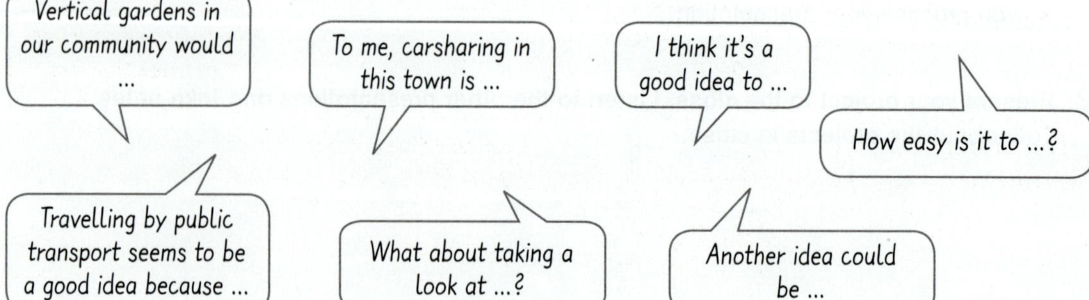

Vertical gardens in our community would …
To me, carsharing in this town is …
I think it's a good idea to …
How easy is it to …?
Travelling by public transport seems to be a good idea because …
What about taking a look at …?
Another idea could be …

Useful words and phrases

B1 Defining the principles

a) Match the words in the box to the definitions below.

reduce • reuse • recycle • raw materials • biodegrade

find new uses for old products

try to avoid producing waste as much as possible

when something rots without harming the environment

use the waste material to produce new products

a substance found in nature that has not been changed

reduce: try to avoid ...

b) Compare your answers in your group.

B2 Plastic word pairs

a) Match the words to make phrases that have something to do with 'A plastic planet'. There is more than one solution.

b) Write statements about 'A plastic planet' using the phrases.

Recyclable packaging is better for the environment.

recyclable	litter
toxic	bin
plastic bag	wildlife
reusable	packaging
recycling	plastic bottles
beach	pollution
ocean	kitchen utensils
plastic	shopping bags
reused	clean-up

Help

B3 Discussion

Talk about the problem of plastic and what you can do about it. Work with a partner or in a small group.

how to discuss p. 160

The best solution to the problem of plastic pollution is ...

The idea of recycling bottle caps is ...

How realistic is the idea of ...?

If you ask me, banning plastic bags is ...

I really don't think it's a good idea to ...

We could volunteer/ write to/organise ...

What environmental organisations are there in ...?

Useful words and phrases

C1 New words

a) **Match the words and phrases in the box to the definitions below.**

pesticides • herbicides • fertilisers • sweatshop • toxic dyes • harmful chemicals • synthetic dye • formaldehyde

chemicals that cause damage, e.g. hurt someone

chemical substances used to kill insects

toxic colours

substance used to make soil better

chemical substances used to destroy weeds

a chemical often used to keep clothing looking new

a non-natural substance used to dye material

a factory where people work very hard in bad conditions and earn very little money

pesticides: chemical substances used to …

b) **Check your answers in your group.**

C2 Verbs and nouns

a) **Match the words to make phrases that have something to do with toxic fashion. There is more than one solution.**

b) **Write statements about toxic fashion using the phrases.**

Toxic chemicals are found in many new clothes.

grow	ideas
keep	profit
rely on	clothes
make	toxic chemicals
swap	ideas
detox	less clothes
avoid	fashion
buy	cotton
share	animals

C3 Discussion

how to p. 160 discuss

Talk about the problem of toxic fashion and what you can do about it. Work with a partner or in a small group.

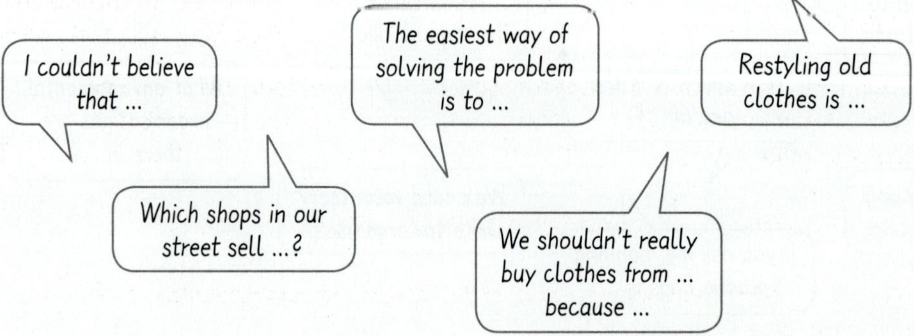

I couldn't believe that …
The easiest way of solving the problem is to …
Restyling old clothes is …
Which shops in our street sell … ?
We shouldn't really buy clothes from … because …

BS1 How a great city started

Tipp
Du sagst ‚sixteen oh nine'.

Before 1609 Manhattan is the home of the Lenape tribe. In 1609, the English explorer Henry Hudson arrives on the island.

1624–26 Dutch explorers arrive on the island. They buy the island from the Lenape tribe.

1664 The English arrive. They give the place a new name – New York. About 2,000 people live there.

1775–1783 The Revolutionary War begins. In 1783, the British lose the war and leave New York. The USA is now independent.

1785–1790 New York is the capital of the 13 states of the USA. The city grows. About 60,000 people live there. In 1800, Washington, D.C. becomes the capital of the USA.

1886 The French give the USA the Statue of Liberty, a symbol of freedom.

1892 Ellis Island is opened. This is where all immigrants to the USA first arrive.

1898 The five boroughs Manhattan, Brooklyn, the Bronx, Queens and Richmond (now Staten Island) become Greater New York. More than 3.5 million people live there.

1902 The first skyscraper, later known as the Flatiron Building, is opened on Manhattan Island.

1931 Almost 7 million people live in New York. The Empire State Building is opened.

Broadway, New York, 1895

1960 7.8 million people from all over the world live in New York. It is a big city with a lot of problems. In the 1980s, people start to leave New York and move to other cities.

2001 The World Trade Center, opened in 1973, is destroyed by terrorists.

2017 More than 8.5 million people live in New York. It remains one of the most important cities in the world.

BS2 The story of the first Thanksgiving

Thanksgiving is one of the most popular holidays in the USA. It is celebrated on the fourth Thursday in November. Many families spend the day together and celebrate with a traditional meal.

The entire family often helps with the cooking. The meal usually includes roast turkey, cranberry sauce, potatoes and pumpkin pie.

Before they eat, people usually pause to give thanks, often in prayer, for the good things in their lives. For example, they might give thanks that they could be together to celebrate Thanksgiving or that their family and friends are healthy.

Thanksgiving has a long history. The first Thanksgiving was celebrated in 1621.

On 16 September 1620, the Pilgrim Fathers left England and sailed to America on a ship called the Mayflower. They hoped to find a new home and religious freedom there. On November 21, the Pilgrims arrived in what is now the state of Massachusetts, America.

That winter was very cold and the Pilgrims did not know how to find food in their new country. Many died from the cold and from disease. A tribe of Native Americans also lived in the same area. They were friendly, but the Pilgrims were scared of them. Finally, in March 1621, two Native American men called Samoset and Squanto decided to help the new settlers.

They showed the Pilgrims how to hunt, catch fish, grow food and build houses. Squanto stayed with them. Thanks to him, the Pilgrims learned how to grow food.

In November 1621, the Pilgrims invited the Native Americans to celebrate their first harvest with them. Many Native American chiefs came with their families. They brought food with them, too. They ate many of the same foods that people eat today. They ate, sang and celebrated for three days – and that was the first Thanksgiving.

BS3 Scott's expedition

Captain Robert Falcon Scott was a British explorer. He led two expeditions to the Antarctic. The second, the *Terra Nova Expedition,* was his famous attempt to be the first person to reach the South Pole.

He set off on this second expedition on 15 June 1910. As well as actually reaching the Pole, he also wanted to do some scientific research there. Scott had made it as far as Australia when he found out that a famous Norwegian explorer called Roald Amundsen was also trying to reach the South Pole.

By 4 January 1911, Scott's ship, the *Terra Nova*, had reached Antarctica. They set up a base camp and on 1 November 1911, after many months of planning, Scott and his men finally set off for the South Pole – 13 days after Amundsen.

Scott's team included 16 men, two dog teams and ten ponies. As they progressed, the team got smaller. They travelled on foot and pulled their sledge. On 17 January 1912, Scott and just four other men rearched the Pole.

When they arrived, they found that Amundsen had got there first. He had arrived on 16 December 1911, a whole month before Scott.

Extremely disappointed, they started the 800-mile journey back to base camp. After 700 miles there was some very bad weather. They did not have a lot of food and they were suffering from frostbite. One of Scott's men became very ill and weak. One night, he bravely walked out to his death. He wanted to give the others a chance.

But, in the end, they all lost the battle against the terrible weather. Their frozen bodies were later found in their tent – only eleven miles from a food depot which would have saved them.

Scott's diary was found near his body. It tells of how he managed to do so many of the things he wanted to do. It tells of the courage of five men in extreme conditions. "Had we lived," Scott wrote as his last words, "I would have had a story to tell of the bravery and courage of my friends. These notes and our dead bodies must tell the story."

If you want to read more about Captain Scott's life, take a look at the book 'Scott's Last Expedition' by A. Huxley.

BS4 Eating insects

Next time you have a dinner party, why not serve your guests spicy grasshoppers? Enjoy a creamy mealworm soup and then let them try chocolate-covered caterpillars? Sounds delicious, right? Well, I'm not so sure.

To most of us, the idea of eating insects is shocking, but millions of people all over the world eat insects every day. And these insects are delicious – at least, that is what the insect cookbooks say!

About 1,500 species of insects can be eaten. You can eat them live, fried, ground, roasted, grilled, marinated or dipped into chocolate! So what do these insects actually taste like?

If you like dessert, try ants – they taste sweet and nutty. Wasps taste like pine nuts and – it's really true – stink bugs taste like apples. Boiled butterflies can taste like chicken. Crickets taste like whatever you cook them in. Cricket curry, anyone?

How about an alternative barbecue? Grilled tarantula spiders with marinated wasps? It would certainly be healthier than most normal barbecues because there are a lot of vitamins and minerals in insects.

Another good reason to add insects to your menu is that they are easy to keep – even in a small flat – and easy to kill. How many insects have you already killed in your lifetime? Most probably you have not only killed quite a lot of insects, but you have also eaten a lot of them too – in bread, fruit or vegetables.

So why wait? If you are feeling really brave, you could even eat the insects while they are still alive. Food that crawls off your plate – if only your horrible vegetables did that when your mum wasn't looking, too!

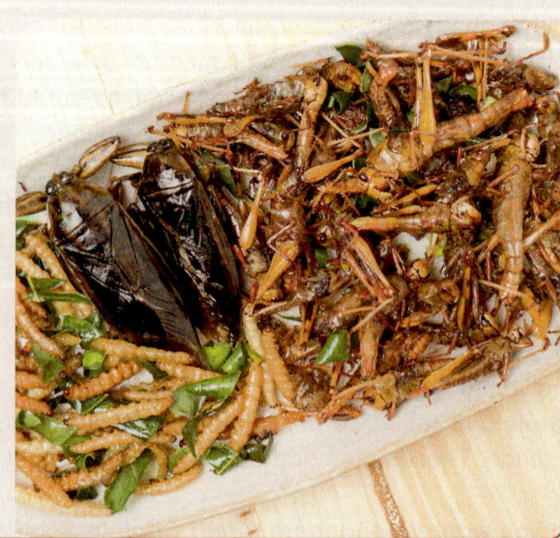

BS5 Burger queen

Burger queen

Like a pizza with no topping
like baked beans with no toast
like fish without fingers
like Sunday without roast

Like a burger with no ketchup
like milk that's had no shake
like steak pie without the kidney
it's more than I can take

Like Popeye without spinach
like kraut that isn't sauer
like bread without butter
like a cauli with no flower

Like Mac without Donald
like chips without the fish
like ham that's lost its burger
or a wishbone without a wish

Like trifle without sherry
like lamb with no mint sauce
like gin without tonic
like a meal with no first course

What is cheese without biscuits?
What are strawberries with no cream?
Won't you share my chicken nuggets
and be my burger queen?

BS6 Hannah and Zach

Hannah and Zach meet for the first time …

I normally hated taking the bus home after school. It took ages and it was always so hot and full. But that one day, I was so happy I was on that bus. That one day, I got on, showed my bus pass, found a seat and then looked up … to see a boy from school staring at me.

He was tall with dark brown, curly hair. That hair framed a face with big, dark eyes and – as he saw me looking at him – the most beautiful smile I had ever seen.

The bus stopped and people got off. It pulled away again. As more and more people got off the bus, it got quite empty, but still he was staring at me. Saying nothing, just staring as if he couldn't stop.

I, in return, couldn't look anywhere but at him, either. I felt like I knew him, like I'd always known him.

At some point we got to my stop. I got up and moved towards the door and so did he. He was getting off, too. The bus stopped suddenly, and I nearly fell – but he caught my arm just in time.

As I stepped off the bus, I found that I was shivering, even though it wasn't cold outside. Excitement bubbled up inside me as I said, "Hi, my name's Hannah. Thanks for … you know …" Suddenly shy, I couldn't meet his eye.

Not taking his eyes off me once, he said, "Hi, I'm Zach. And you're welcome. See you around … Hannah."

Smiling, he walked away. I just stood there, watching him until he was out of sight …

Zach's brother is worried …

"Zach, what's up? You're always alone nowadays, and you look so sad. What's going on?" Zach looked at his brother. "Aaron, I don't know what to do. There's this girl. Hannah. She's amazing. She's funny, smart, beautiful …"

"Doesn't sound like much of a problem, Zach!" laughed Aaron. Zach didn't laugh, though, he just dropped his head lower and said, so quietly that Aaron could barely hear him,

"She's white, Aaron. She's white and all my friends … they think it's weird that I like a white girl. Love a white girl. I think I love her, Aaron."

Aaron put his arm around his brother. "Zach, I've never seen you care about a girl this much. If your friends are really your friends, they will just want to see you happy. And you know what? If they don't, then they're not worth worrying about. Think about it – do you want to lose this girl?"

Hannah and Zach go on their first date …

I came out of class. Another class that I hadn't really listened to. All I could think about was Zach. At least I hadn't lost my appetite. They say that happens when you're in love. In love. Oh my god, did I just think that? I shook my head as I hurried towards the cafeteria.

I was in such a rush that I almost didn't see him, standing in front of a window in the corridor. As I walked up to him, he turned and saw me. "Hannah … hey!" he said. He looked around us, then, finally, he looked me in the eye. I felt my world stand still. "It's lunchtime," I said. "I'm hungry. Do you wanna come get some lunch with me?" I usually met my friends for lunch, but they would understand …

Zach smiled and nodded and we walked towards the cafeteria together. In the queue, two of his friends came up to us.

"Come on, Zach, we're meeting the others for lunch," one of them said. The other stared at me. "Come on, man, what're you hanging around with her for?" he asked Zach. I looked at my feet and felt my cheeks go red.

Zach was quiet. Really quiet. Then he looked at his friends and said to me, "Come on, Hannah. Let's go."

Taking my arm he led me away from them. "Let's go to the park. I'm sick of this place. Sick of them," he said.

We walked out of school and went to Central Park, picking up a burger on the way.

We chatted, about school and exams and, finally, he told me about the problem with his friends. As he was talking, almost without noticing, he took my hand. The tingling started in my fingers and spread all the way down to my toes.

A few months later, Zach's friends still haven't accepted Hannah …

"Zach, I think we need to work this out. I know you love me, but you miss your friends – I can see that," I said to him one day.

"I know. But I'm still angry at them. Why can't they see how much you mean to me? Why does it even matter to them that you're white?"

I looked at him, torn between his love for me and keeping friends he had grown up with. Even if his friends had been like my parents – not exactly enthusiastic but at least accepting – it would have been OK for him. It would have been a start.

I loved him so much, and felt so helpless …

BS7 Unusual jobs

Dog food taster

Dog food tasters taste dog food – yes, really! Pet food companies pay these people to test the quality and nutritional value of their products. But they don't actually eat the dog food – they usually spit it out once they have tasted it.

Professional line stander

Professional line standers do something most people hate: waiting in line. Line standers are particularly busy during big sales and product launches. They stand in line to buy things like new technology or show tickets for people who don't have time or don't want to stand in line themselves. Some of them earn up to $1,000 a week!

Dog surfing instructor

Are you and your dog looking for a new hobby? What you need is a dog surfing instructor. These people can teach you and your dog to surf. Even if you're a couch potato, that doesn't mean your dog can't get on that surfboard – some locations offer lessons just for dogs! As long as your dog isn't scared of water, a dog surfing instructor can teach your dog!

BS8 Bendys – The diner to dine at

Bendys – The diner to dine at

Newsletter

We are very happy to announce our **'Employee of the Month'**. This month it is newcomer Jack Straw. He has only been working with us for three months in our Briarwood Mall branch here in Michigan but has made a great impression. Here are some comments by people who have been working with him since August.

Mike: "Jack's always very friendly. He smiles at the customers and always writes clearly so that the kitchen staff can read the order."

Jane: "And when he brings the customers their food he is always very careful when there are children running around. I don't think he has ever dropped or spilled anything."

Bob, the branch manager: "We are very happy to have Jack here. I have watched how he gives the customers their bill, takes their money and cleans the table when they have left and he is always very polite. He helps older people with their coats and young mothers with their kids. Yes, he deserves to be **'Employee of the Month'**. I hope he stays with us for a long time."

We wanted to know what Jack did before he came to Bendys. Here is what he said.

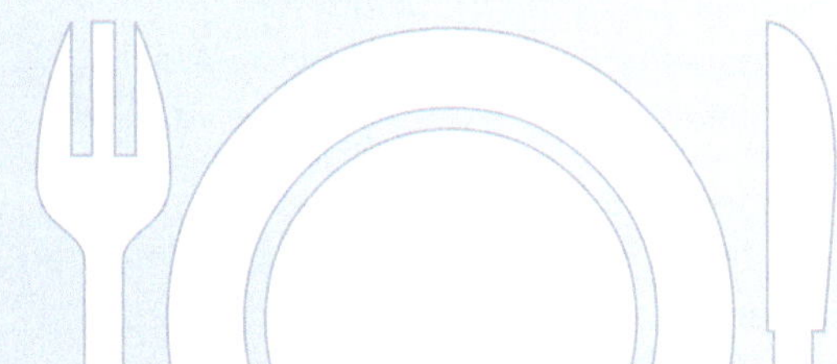

"When I left school two years ago I got a job at the Ford car factory in Detroit. Many of my friends got jobs there. My dad worked there. He told me that my great-grandfather worked there too in 1913 when Henry Ford invented the first assembly line.

Only nine months after I was hired, Ford started to close factories all over the world, and I lost my job. I was out of work for six months but then I saw an ad in a local paper for this job. I applied and got the job. It's better than I thought it would be and it is much better than hanging around or being unemployed like lots of my friends, you know. And here, I mean, the people I work with are just awesome, and so are our customers, as a matter of fact."

Well, Jack. Once again, congratulations on being **'Employee of the Month'**.

BS9 Langston Hughes

Langston Hughes was born on February 1st, 1902, in Joplin, Missouri. He was an African American writer. Hughes first began writing in school, where in the eighth grade he was elected class poet. From then on, writing was what he wanted to do and he continued to write for his school magazine until he left in 1920.

After finishing high school, Hughes went to visit his father in Mexico. He wrote one of his most famous poems on the way – "The Negro Speaks of the Rivers". This poem was published a year later in the National Association for the Advancement of Colored People (NAACP) journal *Crisis*.

Hughes then went to New York to study at Columbia University. He became part of the cultural scene in Harlem, a neighborhood in uptown Manhattan with a large African American population. He didn't stay at Columbia University for long but he kept returning to Harlem for the rest of his life.

Harlem was the centre of the *Harlem Renaissance*, a movement lasting from around 1918 to 1937, which saw an explosion of African American culture. The movement also had a great influence on African American literature. It was at that time that Hughes became very well-known.

In 1926 his first collection of poems, among them the famous poem "I, too", was published as a book, *The Weary Blues*. From there his career as a writer took off.

Throughout his whole career Hughes wrote about the achievements and rights of African Americans. He set up his own magazine, *Fire!!*, to publish the works of African American writers. He also wrote influential essays about the biggest problems African American artists had at the time. Later on in his life, he published biographies of significant African Americans, in books such as *Famous Negro Heroes of America*, and regularly wrote for the African American Newspaper the *Chicago Defender*.

In 1929 he published his semi-autobiographical novel *Not Without Laughter* which was awarded the Harmon Gold Medal for Literature, an award that gave recognition to the work of African American people. Later, towards the end of his life, the NAACP awarded Hughes the Spingarn Medal for distinguished achievement by an African American.

Hughes died in 1967. He was, and remains, one of the most influential African American writers of all time.

Tipp
Im Internet kannst du viele Gedichte von Langston Hughes finden. Suche einmal nach den Gedichten, die in diesem Artikel erwähnt werden.

BS10 Earthkeeper hero

Jack Johnson

My hero is not a war hero, a family member, or a lifesaver. My hero is a musician and earthkeeper. He is someone who loves nature and loves to protect it. He is a special person to me, but lots of people have never heard of him. My hero is Jack Johnson.

Jack has contributed money to the Kokua Festival on Hawaii, the Hurricane Katrina Relief Fund and the Red Cross. He lives on the island of Oahu on the North Shore of Hawaii. Jack's songs raise awareness that Hawaii will only stay green, beautiful and amazing if we take care of the land that we all call our own.

Jack Johnson's tour bus now runs on biodiesel fuel. He tours schools and tells kids about the land and how we should take care of it. He produces singalongs that teach kids while they're having fun.

Jack Johnson raised $65,000 for the Red Cross after Hurricane Katrina. He raised a total of $122,835.05 from touring money. He funds many things like the Kokua Foundation, which sponsors a school program that lets kids plant and farm crops at their school.

I think Jack Johnson is a great hero and definitely a great person. He is a role model, courageous and very smart. I hope my essay helps you understand that we have to do something about our world before it disappears.

Written by
Savannah from Hawaii

Do you remember?

Zu vielen Themen wie etwa zu *How to talk* oder *How to listen* hast du in Klasse 5 bis 7 schon einiges erfahren. Auf den folgenden Seiten findest du Zusammenfassungen wichtiger Punkte:

Remember? – How to talk

- Trau dich zu sprechen und hab keine Angst vor Fehlern!
- Die *classroom phrases* auf Seite 174 und auf dem Einleger können dir bei der Partner- und Gruppenarbeit und beim Klassengespräch helfen.
- Nutze jede Gelegenheit, Englisch zu sprechen. Hör dir zum Beispiel die CD an und lies Texte laut mit.
- Wenn du einen Vortrag, ein Interview oder ein Gespräch vorbereiten willst, mache dir dazu vorher auf Kärtchen Notizen.
- Versuche aber immer, frei zu sprechen. Lies nicht einfach deine Notizen ab.
- Achte auch auf deine Aussprache, Betonung und die Satzmelodie, damit das, was du sagst, lebendig klingt.
- Das Sprechen wird dir leichter fallen, wenn du ein Gespräch oder einen Vortrag vorher gut vorbereitest und übst.
- Achte beim Sprechen auch auf deine Körpersprache, deinen Gesichtsausdruck und deine Gesten.
- Schau deine Zuhörerinnen und Zuhörer beim Sprechen an.

Remember? – How to listen

- Wenn du einem Gesprächspartner zuhörst, schau ihn dabei an.
- Achte im Gespräch auf Körpersprache, Gesichtsausdruck und Gesten.
- Wenn es eine Aufgabe zu einem Hörtext gibt, dann lies dir die Aufgabe vorher genau durch. Überlege, was du zu dem Thema schon weißt.
- Sieh dir Überschrift und Bilder an: Was verraten sie über das Thema?
- Denk beim Hören daran, dass du nicht jedes einzelne Wort verstehen musst.
- Versuche, beim ersten Hören herauszufinden, worum es geht.
- Achte auch auf Geräusche und darauf, wie die Personen sprechen.
- Folgende Fragewörter können dir helfen, das Wichtigste zu verstehen: *Who? What? Where? When? Why?* Du kannst dir hierzu zum Beispiel Notizen in einer Tabelle oder in einem *word web* machen.
- Konzentriere dich beim Notizenmachen auf die wichtigsten Informationen.
- Schreibe Schlüsselwörter *(keywords)* auf und nicht ganze Sätze.

Who?	What?	Where?	When?	Why?
a tourist	talks about his holiday	in New York	...	...

- Beim zweiten Hören kannst du dann weitere Informationen ergänzen.

Remember? – How to read

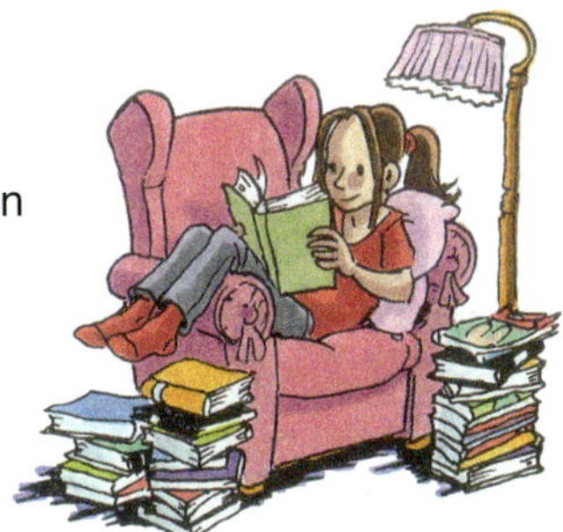

Bevor du liest

- Schau dir Überschriften und Bilder zum Text an, sie verraten oft etwas über den Inhalt.
- Die Art der Gestaltung verrät etwas über die Textsorte: Handelt es sich z. B. um einen Zeitungsartikel, eine Werbeanzeige, eine E-Mail oder einen Blogeintrag?

Während des Lesens

- Überfliege dann zunächst den Text *(skimming)*. Du musst dabei nicht jedes Wort verstehen. Achte auf die Wörter, die du schon kennst. Beim *skimming* kommt es darauf an, sich schnell einen ersten Eindruck zu verschaffen, worum es geht.
- Manchmal möchtest du in einem Text gezielt nach bestimmten Informationen suchen, zum Beispiel nach dem Alter von Personen. Dieses schnelle aber gezielte Suchen nennt man *scanning*. Dabei helfen dir Schlüsselwörter *(keywords)*, also zum Beispiel *age* oder *old*, wenn es um das Alter von Personen geht.
- Achte auch beim detaillierten Lesen auf Schlüsselwörter *(keywords)*.
- Bei einem Text im Workbook oder auf einem Arbeitsblatt kannst du wichtige Wörter und Passagen auch farbig markieren oder unterstreichen.
- Es kann auch hilfreich sein, wenn du dir Zwischenüberschriften für einzelne Abschnitte des Textes überlegst.

Wörter erschließen

- Versuche, beim Lesen unbekannte Wörter aus dem Zusammenhang zu erschließen. Auch Bilder und Illustrationen können eventuell helfen, die Bedeutung unbekannter Wörter zu erraten.
- Manchmal kannst du die Bedeutung von Wörtern auch erschließen, weil sie so ähnlich geschrieben werden wie im Deutschen oder in einer anderen Sprache, die du kennst.
- So kannst du vielleicht in einem Satz wie *Cheerleaders perform spectacular stunts* erkennen, dass *spectacular* ähnlich wie das deutsche Wort spektakulär aussieht, und *stunt* ist dir vielleicht schon bekannt, da der Begriff auch im Deutschen verwendet wird.

Notizen machen

- Die Fragewörter *who*, *what*, *where*, *when* und *why* helfen auch beim Lesen von Texten.
- Du kannst dir hierzu zum Beispiel Notizen in einer Tabelle oder in einem *word web* machen.
- Konzentriere dich beim Notizenmachen auf die wichtigsten Informationen.
- Schreibe Schlüsselwörter *(keywords)* auf und nicht ganze Sätze.

Who?	What?	Where?	When?	Why?
Alex	sights and activities	in New York	...	...

- Lies den Text nicht nur einmal. Beim nochmaligen Lesen wirst du sicher noch mehr Details verstehen und kannst so deine Notizen ergänzen.

Remember? – How to write

- Wenn du einen Text (zum Beispiel eine Geschichte oder einen Zeitungsartikel) schreiben willst, kannst du mit Hilfe von *who, what, where, when* (und eventuell auch *why*) Ideen sammeln und deinen Text planen.
- Überlege dir vorher, wie du deinen Text gliedern möchtest und sammle wichtige Wörter, zum Beispiel in einem *word web*.
- Du kannst auch in den *wordbanks* im Buch oder in einem Wörterbuch nach passenden Wörtern suchen.
- Bei jeder Art von Texten gilt, dass du zunächst einen Entwurf schreiben solltest *(draft)* – entweder handschriftlich oder am Computer.
- Überarbeite und verbessere dann deinen Text *(edit)*. Du kannst auch andere nach ihrer Meinung zu deinem Text und nach Verbesserungsvorschlägen fragen.
- Wenn du deinen Text fertig hast, schreibe ihn ins Reine. Das kannst du handschriftlich oder mithilfe eines Textverarbeitungsprogramms am Computer machen.
- Dein fertiger Text sollte „veröffentlicht" werden *(publish)*. Zeige ihn einem Partner, einer Partnerin oder der Klasse.
- Gelungene Texte kannst du in deinem Portfolio aufbewahren.
- Tipps zum Schreiben findest du auch auf den Seiten *How to write an email* (Seite 155), *How to write a summary* (Seite 156), *How to write a review* (Seite 157) und *How to write a story* (Seite 158).

Remember? – How to mediate

- Bei der Sprachmittlung kommt es darauf an, die wichtigsten Informationen von einer Sprache in eine andere zu übertragen.
- Es kommt dabei nicht darauf an, alles wortgetreu zu übersetzen. Wichtig ist, dass du das Wesentliche auf Deutsch wiedergibst.
- Bilde einfache, kurze Sätze, wenn du den Sinn wiedergibst.
- Schwieriger ist die Sprachmittlung vom Deutschen ins Englische, also wenn du etwas auf Englisch wiedergeben musst.
- Es kann zum Beispiel vorkommen, dass du in deiner Stadt einen englischsprachigen Reisenden triffst, der deine Hilfe beim Lesen eines Fahrplans braucht. Ihm kannst du auf Englisch erklären, wie er zu seinem Ziel kommt.
- Hab keine Angst vor Fehlern. Es kommt darauf an, verstanden zu werden, der andere freut sich auf jeden Fall über deine Hilfe.
- Wenn dir Wörter fehlen, kannst du versuchen, diese zu umschreiben, und Gesten benutzen.

Remember? – How to watch a video clip

Vor dem Sehen

- Gibt es Bilder zu dem Videoclip in deinem Buch oder Workbook? Was ist zu sehen?
- Lies den Titel des Videoclips. Welche Hinweise gibt er auf den Inhalt?
- Worum könnte es in dem Videoclip gehen? Stelle Vermutungen an.

Währenddessen

- Schau dir den Videoclip in Ruhe an. Dabei ist es nicht schlimm, wenn du nicht alles verstehst.
- Konzentriere dich zunächst vor allem auf das, was du siehst:

Who?	Wer ist zu sehen? Um wen geht es?
Where?	Wo findet das Geschehen statt?
When?	Wann findet das Geschehen statt?
What?	Um was geht es? Was passiert?

- Was ist dein erster Eindruck? Mache dir Notizen.
- Konzentriere dich beim zweiten Anschauen stärker auf das, was du hörst. Gibt es Wörter, die immer wieder vorkommen? Notiere sie dir.
- Gibt es eine Aufgabe zu dem Videoclip in deinem Buch oder dem Workbook? Behalte die Frage im Kopf, während du zuschaust. Versuche, gleich danach die Frage zu beantworten.
- Wenn nötig, schau dir dann den Clip ein weiteres Mal an. Überprüfe dabei deine Antworten.

Nach dem Sehen

- Tausche dich mit deinen Klassenkameradinnen und -kameraden aus. Was habt ihr herausgefunden?

Außerdem

- Schau dir an, wie die Personen aussehen und wie sie sich verhalten.
- Achte auf den Gesichtsausdruck und die Gesten der Personen. Ändert sich der Gesichtsausdruck? Wie fühlen sie sich? Wie ist das Verhältnis der Personen zueinander?
- Auch die Musik in einem Videoclip oder Film drückt Stimmungen aus. Ist die Musik lustig oder spannend? Wie fühlst du dich aufgrund der Musik?
- Man kann sich viele Videoclips auch mit Untertiteln ansehen. Es gibt sie auf Englisch und auf Deutsch. Das kann eine große Hilfe sein, denn nach und nach lernt man so besser zu verstehen, was auf Englisch gesagt wird.
- Schau dir doch auch Filme oder Videoclips aus dem Internet auf Englisch an.

Remember? – How to work on a project or target task

Plan it

- Wenn du mit anderen zusammenarbeiten möchtest, dann überlegt gemeinsam, wie euer Endprodukt bzw. eure Präsentation aussehen soll: Poster, Tonaufnahme, Videoaufnahme, Computerpräsentation, ...?
- Überlegt in der Gruppe, welche Informationen, Materialien und Geräte ihr braucht.
- Teilt die Arbeit sinnvoll und gerecht auf.
- Macht einen Zeitplan.

Do it

- Recherchiere Informationen und sammle Material.
- Werte dein gesammeltes Material aus. Entscheide, welche Materialien wichtig sind und welche Ergebnisse du vorstellen möchtest.
- Überlege dir, wie du deine Informationen anschaulich präsentieren kannst. Erstelle dann dein Produkt oder deine Präsentation.

Check it

- Sind alle wichtigen Informationen enthalten? Sind die Texte verständlich? Sind die Bilder groß genug? Gibt es Fehler? Lest eure Texte gegenseitig durch und besprecht sie.
- Überarbeite und verbessere dann nochmal deine Präsentation, wenn nötig.

Present it

- Planst du eine mündliche Präsentation, dann übe vorher mit einem Stichwortzettel (siehe auch *How to present* auf Seite 153).

Remember? – How to research online

- Benutze eine Suchmaschine. Versuche, möglichst genau zu formulieren, wonach du suchst, und zwar auf Englisch.
- Suche auf englischsprachigen Seiten, damit dir der nötige Wortschatz gleich zur Verfügung steht. Bei den Einstellungen der meisten Suchmaschinen kannst du Englisch als Sprache wählen.
- Halte nützliche Informationen fest. Überfliege dafür zunächst einmal die Seiten, die dir interessant erscheinen.
- Wenn du interessante Webseiten gefunden hast, kannst du die Informationen in einem Dokument speichern. Denk daran, auch die Internetadresse festzuhalten, damit du später noch weißt, wo du die Informationen gefunden hast.
- Wenn du Textausschnitte unverändert übernimmst, musst du sie als Zitat kenntlich machen und die Quelle (die Internetadresse) angeben.
- Sei kritisch: Weder inhaltlich noch sprachlich ist alles richtig, was im Internet steht. Überprüfe angegebene Fakten in einer anderen Quelle.
- Einfache und kurze Texte auf Englisch gibt es bei simple.wikipedia.org.

Remember? – How to present

Die Präsentation vorbereiten

- Überlege: Was ist dein Thema? Wie viel Zeit hast du für deinen Vortrag?
- Überlege auch, was deine Zuhörer schon wissen und berücksichtige dies in deiner Präsentation.
- Sammle deine Gedanken und schreibe sie in Stichpunkten auf, zum Beispiel in einem *word web* oder auf Karteikarten.
- Entscheide, in welcher Reihenfolge du die Dinge sagen und wie du anfangen möchtest.

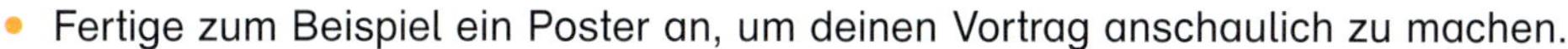

- Fertige zum Beispiel ein Poster an, um deinen Vortrag anschaulich zu machen.
- Übe deinen Vortrag mehrmals, bevor du ihn hältst.

Bei der Präsentation

- Sprich langsam und deutlich.
- Sieh deine Zuhörer an, wenn du sprichst.
- Versuche, frei zu sprechen. Du kannst die wichtigsten Punkte aber von deinen Notizen ablesen.
- Zeige deinen Zuhörern auf deinem Poster, worüber du gerade sprichst.
- Fasse zum Schluss die wichtigsten Punkte noch einmal zusammen.

Nützliche Redewendungen

Für die Einleitung:

- *Hello, everybody. My talk is about …*
- *First of all, I'm going to …*
- *Then I'll talk about …*
- *Finally I'll …*

Etwas Neues einleiten:

- *So let's start with …*
- *OK, my first/next/last point is …*

Auf Hilfsmittel hinweisen:

- *On my poster you can see …*
- *Look at this picture. It shows …*

Wenn du mal den Faden verlierst:

- *Just a moment, please.*
- *Wait a second, please.*

Etwas anders ausdrücken:

- *In other words, …*
- *What I'm saying is …*

Aufmerksamkeit aufrechterhalten:

- *You see?*
- *Do you see what I mean?*
- *Don't you agree?*
- *What do you think?*

Zum Schluss kommen:

- *So, to summarise …*
- *So my main points are …*
- *Thank you for listening.*
- *Have you got any questions?*

Remember? – How to give feedback

- Versuche immer, zuerst etwas Positives zu sagen.
- Formuliere Kritik und Verbesserungsvorschläge vorsichtig, höflich und sachlich.
- Bei Präsentationen kannst du zu verschiedenen Kategorien Feedback geben:

Körpersprache und Augenkontakt

Der/die Präsentierende

- lächelt das Publikum freundlich an
- hält Augenkontakt
- dreht dem Publikum nicht zu lange den Rücken zu

☺ You looked at the audience most of the time.

☹ You turned your back to the audience too much.

Sprache

Der/die Präsentierende

- spricht laut und deutlich
- verwendet kurze, gut verständliche Sätze
- spricht eher frei, liest nicht ab

☺ You spoke loudly and clearly.

☹ You read a lot word-by-word. Maybe you could try to speak more freely next time.

Struktur und Inhalt des Vortrags

Der/die Präsentierende

- führt gut in das Thema ein
- bezieht das Publikum mit ein
- fasst am Schluss noch einmal das Wichtigste zusammen

☺ You introduced your topic very well.

☺ The questions you asked us were very interesting.

☹ You didn't summarise your main points. Maybe you could do that next time.

Die Gestaltung des Materials

Der/die Präsentierende

- hat das Poster/die Seiten/das Handout übersichtlich angelegt
- die Schrift ist gut zu lesen
- hat passende Bilder verwendet

☺ Your poster was easy to read.

☹ I think you packed a little bit too much information on your poster.

E-Mails schreiben

Persönliche und förmliche E-Mails unterscheiden sich in einigen Punkten. Überlege also vorher, wie gut du die Person kennst, der du schreibst, und worum es in der E-Mail geht.

Persönliche E-Mails

- Schreibe in die Betreffzeile kurz und knapp, worum es geht.
- Wähle eine infomelle Anrede wie *Hi, Hello* oder *Dear* (Vorname).
- Im Englischen wird das erste Wort nach der Anrede immer großgeschrieben.
- Vergiss die Abschiedsformel nicht, also in einer persönlichen E-Mail zum Beispiel *Bye for now, See you soon, Talk to you soon* oder *Best wishes.*

Subject: We won the match!

Hi Jake,
How are you? I hope you're doing fine. Guess what! We won the most important match of the season against the Tigers! We had a big party after the match. ☺
How is your soccer career going? Good luck to you and your team.
Bye for now,
Bill

Förmliche E-Mails

- Förmliche E-Mails schreibst du zum Beispiel an Firmen, um eine Information zu erhalten, etwas zu reservieren oder zu bestellen. Die Person, die deine Nachricht liest, kennst du in der Regel nicht oder nicht so gut.
- Auch hier gilt wie bei persönlichen E-Mails: Schreibe in die Betreffzeile kurz und knapp, worum es geht und schreibe das erste Wort nach der Anrede groß.
- Benutze eine höfliche Anrede, z. B. *Dear Mr Ross* (wenn du den Namen der Person kennst) oder *Dear Sir or Madam* (wenn du den Namen der Person nicht kennst).
- Zur höflichen Anrede sollte auch die Abschiedsformel passen: Verwende *Yours sincerely*, wenn du die Person kennst, und *Yours faithfully*, wenn du sie nicht kennst.
- Abkürzungen wie FYI *(for your information)* oder LOL *(laugh out loud)* und auch Emoticons (Smileys und Ähnliches) solltest du in förmlichen E-Mails nicht verwenden.

Subject: Class trip on 15th October

Dear Sir or Madam,
We are planning a class trip to England and would like to visit the Smugglers Adventure Caves with a group of 30 pupils on 15th October. Is it possible to book a visit for that day? We could come at around 11am.
Thank you for your help. We are looking forward to hearing from you soon.
Yours faithfully,
Class 8a

Eine Zusammenfassung schreiben

Wenn du eine Zusammenfassung eines Textes, Buches oder Videoclips schreibst, möchtest du einen generellen Eindruck davon vermitteln, worum es in dem Text, Buch oder Videoclip geht.

1. Bevor du die Zusammenfassung schreibst

- Bevor du eine Zusammenfassung schreibst, musst du die wichtigsten Aussagen und Inhalte des Buches, Textes oder Videoclips herausfinden. In deinem Workbook oder auf einer Kopie kannst du wichtige Stellen in einem Text farbig markieren oder unterstreichen, ansonsten solltest du dir stichwortartig Notizen machen.
- Um den Aufbau eines Buches oder Textes zu erkennen, ist es hilfreich, Stichworte oder Überschriften für die einzelnen Absätze oder Kapitel zu formulieren.
- Außerdem kannst du dir z. B. bei einer Geschichte oder einem Film gezielt Notizen zu folgenden Aspekten machen:
  - *setting*
  - *characters*
  - *time*
  - *action*.

2. Schreibe deinen Text

- Beginne deine Zusammenfassung mit einem Einleitungssatz, in dem du kurz beschreibst, wovon der Text oder Videoclip handelt.

  The book '...' by ... is about ...
  The poem '...' deals with ...
  In the article '...' the author writes about ...
  The video clip shows ...

- Führe nur die wesentlichen Informationen an, lasse alle Beispiele, detaillierten Beschreibungen, direkte Rede oder deine eigene Meinung weg.
- Zitiere nicht aus dem Text oder Videoclip, sondern benutze eigene Formulierungen.
- Benutze *time words* wie *first, then, afterwards, while, ...*
- Achte auf die Zeitform: Die Zusammenfassung steht in der Regel in der einfachen Gegenwart *(simple present)*.

3. Überarbeite deinen Text

- Hast du alle wesentlichen Informationen wiedergegeben?
- Sind sie in der richtigen Reihenfolge angeordnet?
- Stimmen Satzbau, Grammatik und Rechtschreibung?
- Du kannst auch eine Mitschülerin oder einen Mitschüler um Feedback zu deiner Zusammenfassung bitten.

Eine Kritik verfassen

Eine Kritik oder Rezension *(review)* zu schreiben bedeutet, seine Meinung z. B. zu einem Restaurant oder zu einem Film auszudrücken. Die Restaurant- bzw. die Filmkritik soll dem Leser/der Leserin helfen zu entscheiden, ob er/sie in das Restaurant gehen oder den Film ansehen möchte.

Restaurantkritik

Wenn du eine Restaurantkritik schreibst, solltest du erwähnen

- um welche Art von Restaurant es sich handelt
- welche Gerichte serviert werden und welche Qualität sie deiner Meinung nach haben
- wie das Preis-Leistungsverhältnis ist
- wie die Bedienung ist
- wie das Restaurant gestaltet ist, bzw. wie die Atmosphäre dort ist.
- wie du das Restaurant insgesamt einschätzt.

The pizzas are absolutely delicious.

It's good value for money.

The atmosphere is very friendly.

It's a great place to visit.

Filmkritik

Mache dir Notizen, während du dir den Film ansiehst *(who, where, what, when, why)*.
Schreibe nun deine Kritik:

- Nenne den Titel des Films.
- Gib die technischen Daten an (Ort und Jahr, Länge) und erwähne, wer mitspielt *(cast)* und wer Regie geführt hat *(director)*.
- Schreibe, um welche Art von Film es sich handelt *(comedy, drama, thriller, …)*.
- Sage, worum es in dem Film geht, aber verrate nicht zu viel, vor allem nicht das Ende.
- Bleibe sachlich, wenn du deine Meinung äußerst, damit die Leserinnen und Leser sich ihre eigene Meinung bilden können.
- Du kannst in deiner Kritik auch erwähnen, wem du den Film empfehlen würdest.
- Bewerte den Film, zum Beispiel mit 1 – 5 Sternen.

★★★★★	*an absolute must*
★★★★☆	*a very good film*
★★★☆☆	*worth watching*
★★☆☆☆	*a waste of time*
★☆☆☆☆	*a total disaster*

… is an exciting love story.

The film is about …

It can make you dance and sing along! Critics say that the life of teenagers and their problems is shown in a too sugar-coated way. Judge yourself!

I recommend this film for …

Eine Geschichte schreiben

Plane deine Geschichte, bevor du anfängst zu schreiben. Du kannst dich an den Fragewörtern *who, what, where, when* und *why* orientieren und Ideen sammeln. Denke dabei besonders an folgende Dinge:

Die Figuren

- Beginne mit der Hauptfigur oder den Hauptfiguren. Überlege dir Name, Alter, Aussehen, Interessen, Freunde, …
- Überlege dir, wer die Nebenfiguren sein könnten. Wie ist ihre Beziehung zu den Hauptfiguren?

Der Ort

- Überlege dir, wo deine Geschichte spielen soll: In einer Großstadt oder in einem Dorf? In einem anderen Land? Die Geschichte kann auch an mehreren Orten spielen.
- Vielleicht spielt deine Geschichte aber hauptsächlich in einem Gebäude, zum Beispiel in einer Schule oder in einem verwunschenen Schloss.
- Beschreibe den Ort, damit die Leserinnen und Leser ihn sich gut vorstellen können. Überlege zum Beispiel, was man dort sehen, hören, fühlen oder riechen kann.

Die Handlung

- Denke dir eine Handlung aus. Beachte dabei die folgenden fünf Teile einer Geschichte:
- *Exposition* – Überlege dir den Anfang deiner Geschichte. Wie weckst du Interesse? Fällt dir ein spannender erster Satz ein?
- *Rising action* – Hier beginnt die eigentliche Handlung. Denke dir zum Beispiel etwas Spannendes oder Lustiges aus, das passieren könnte.
- *Climax* – Dies ist der spannendste Teil deiner Geschichte. Hier könnte etwas Dramatisches passieren.
- *Falling action* – Nach dem *climax* der Geschichte kannst du zum Beispiel erzählen, wie es zu dem Ereignis kommen konnte oder was danach passiert ist.
- *Resolution* – Wie soll deine Geschichte enden? Entscheidest du dich für ein offenes Ende oder ein *happy ending*?

Der Schreibprozess: *draft – edit – publish*

- Schreibe zunächst einen Entwurf.
- Gib deinen Entwurf jemandem zu lesen und lass dir Feedback geben.
- Überarbeite dann deinen Entwurf.
- Wenn deine Geschichte fertig ist, dann „veröffentliche“ sie – hänge sie zum Beispiel in deiner Klasse aus oder gestalte ein Heft.
- Du kannst deine Geschichte auch in deinem Portfolio aufbewahren.

Figuren in literarischen Texten beschreiben

Wenn du Figuren in literarischen Texten beschreiben willst, kannst du dich an folgenden Aspekten orientieren.

1. Aussehen *(appearance)*

- Wie sieht die Figur aus? Wie ist sie gekleidet?
- Häufig werden Figuren beschrieben, wenn sie das erste Mal erscheinen.

tall, short, of medium height, ...
slim, muscular, skinny, athletic, ...
blond hair, dark hair, ...
wears elegant clothes/casual clothes, ...
...

2. Charakterisierung *(characterization)*

- Manchmal werden Charakterzüge direkt beschrieben, wie in der Geschichte der drei Jungen auf Seite 57:

  "Robbie was a guy who cried easily, a weakness he tried not to show."
  "Larry was tall and clever but also a real coward."

- Um etwas über den Charakter einer literarischen Figur zu erfahren, kannst du dir anschauen, wie sie sich verhält oder handelt und wie sie spricht oder denkt.

a) Verhaltensweisen und Handlungen *(behaviour and actions)*

- Häufig hilft es, zwischen den Zeilen zu lesen, um eine Figur zu verstehen und zu beschreiben.
- Folgende Aspekte können helfen: Wie verhält sich diese Figur? Was tut diese Figur?
  Romeo gets into a fight and has to leave Verona – he is impulsive.
  Juliet does not obey her father – she has a strong will.

b) Sprache und Gedanken *(speech and thoughts)*

- Einen weiteren wichtigen Hinweis für die Charakterisierung einer Figur liefert das, was er/sie sagt und denkt:

  Romeo and Juliet are romantic: "You must have wings to climb this wall." – "I do. The wings of love, my Juliet!"

  Juliet refuses to marry Count Paris: "No, no father. That man is old enough to be my grandfather."

Zusammenfassung

- Wenn du über eine Figur schreibst, berücksichtige folgende Aspekte:
  1. *Appearance*
  2. *Characterization (behaviour and actions, speech and thoughts)*
- In Bezug auf die Charakterisierung einer Figur musst du auch zwischen den Zeilen lesen und deine eigenen Schlussfolgerungen ziehen.

An einer Diskussion teilnehmen

In einer Diskussion tauscht man Meinungen zu einem Thema aus. Oft geht es auch darum, den oder die anderen von der eigenen Ansicht zu überzeugen.

1. Bevor du diskutierst

- Sieh dir das Thema der Diskussion genau an. Wie stehst du zu dem Thema? Mache dir Gedanken über mögliche Argumente.
- Notiere Stichpunkte oder erstelle ein *word web*, damit du nichts Wichtiges vergisst.
- Denke auch an Argumente, die gegen deine Meinung sprechen. Überlege dir Antworten auf diese Argumente.

2. Während der Diskussion

- Schau die Person an, die gerade spricht.
- Höre genau zu, was die anderen Diskussionsteilnehmer sagen.
- Falle niemandem ins Wort.
- Wenn du etwas nicht verstanden hast, frage höflich nach.
- Äußere deine Meinung. Bleibe dabei immer höflich und freundlich.

TIPP **Diskussionsleiter und Feedbackgruppe**

- Bestimmt einen Diskussionsleiter. Er/Sie sollte darauf achten, dass alle Gesprächsteilnehmer zu Wort kommen können, beim Thema bleiben und die vereinbarte Redezeit einhalten.
- Bildet eine neutrale Gruppe, die während der Diskussion Notizen macht und nachher Feedback gibt.

3. Nützliche Redewendungen

Eine Meinung äußern:

- *I think …*
- *I believe …*
- *In my opinion, …*
- *I'm sure …*

Eine Meinung begründen:

- *I think so because …*
- *The reason is …*
- *Well, it's a fact that …*

Jemandem zustimmen:

- *Yes, that's true.*
- *I think you're right.*
- *I agree (with you).*
- *I think so, too.*
- *That's a good point.*

Jemandem widersprechen:

- *I know, but …*
- *Sorry, I don't agree with you.*
- *I disagree.*
- *I don't think so.*

Nachfragen:

- *Could you say that again, please?*
- *Could you repeat that, please?*
- *Do you mean that …?*
- *Can you please explain what you mean?*

Einen abschließenden Satz einleiten:

- *In general, …*
- *All in all, …*

Das richtige englische Wort im Wörterbuch finden

Du brauchst die englische Übersetzung eines deutschen Wortes? Wenn es zum Lernwortschatz aus *Notting Hill Gate* gehört, findest du es im Wörterbuch auf Seite 292–303.
Ansonsten kannst du ein Deutsch-Englisches Wörterbuch benutzen. Du kannst aber auch zunächst einmal versuchen, eine Alternative zu dem gesuchten Wort zu finden.

1. Bevor du zum Wörterbuch greifst

- Überlege, ob du auch ohne Wörterbuch auskommst. Vielleicht kennst du ja ein deutsches Wort mit gleicher oder ähnlicher Bedeutung und kannst den Satz vereinfachen.
- Für ein Projekt zum Thema Berufe erzählt dir dein Onkel zum Beispiel:
  „Ich beschäftige mich meistens mit Computerprogrammen."
  Das kannst du im Englischen folgendermaßen umschreiben, wenn du nicht weißt, was „sich beschäftigen" auf Englisch heißt: *My uncle works a lot with computer programs.*

2. Wörter nachschlagen

- Nimm nicht gleich die erste Übersetzung, wenn du Wörter im Wörterbuch nachschlägst. Für viele deutsche Wörter gibt es verschiedene Übersetzungen. Sieh dir deshalb deinen deutschen Satz genau an, bevor du wählst.
- Du brauchst zum Beispiel die Übersetzung für „Boden", weil du in deinem Praktikumsbetrieb etwas vom Boden holen oder etwas vom Boden aufheben solltest. Hier bedeutet Boden im einen Fall das Lager im Dachgeschoss, im anderen geht es um den Fußboden.
  Im Wörterbuch findest du folgende Einträge:

***m* gibt an, dass das Wort maskulin (männlich) ist.**

Zusätze in Klammern verraten, in welchem Zusammenhang ein Wort gebraucht wird.

Boden *m* **1.** (*Erdoberfläche*) ground; (*Erdreich, lockerer ~*) soil, (*Fuß~*) floor (*Grundbesitz*) land; **2.** (*Dach~*) attic, loft

- Wenn du ein bestimmtes Verb suchst, musst du zunächst die Grundform bilden.
- In deinem Praktikumsbericht möchtest du zum Beispiel sagen, „Ich kam um sieben Uhr in der Firma an." Schlage also das Wort „ankommen" nach.

3. Wörter überprüfen

- Wenn du nicht sicher bist, ob das englische Wort wirklich passt, mache die Gegenprobe und überprüfe es in einem Englisch-Deutschen Wörterbuch. Dort findest du auch die Lautschrift, wenn du Hilfe bei der Aussprache brauchst.
- Bei vielen Online-Wörterbüchern kannst du dir die Aussprache auch vorsprechen lassen.

Wie man mit Statistiken arbeiten kann

Informationen verschiedener Art lassen sich in Statistiken optisch darstellen. Die Art der Darstellung ist abhängig von der Information und natürlich davon, was man veranschaulichen möchte.

Säulen- oder Balkendiagramm *(bar chart)*

Mit Säulen- oder Balkendiagrammen lassen sich übersichtlich Zahlen vergleichen und Veränderungen darstellen.

In 1850, the majority of immigrants living in the USA were born in ...

When you compare the top half of the bar chart ...

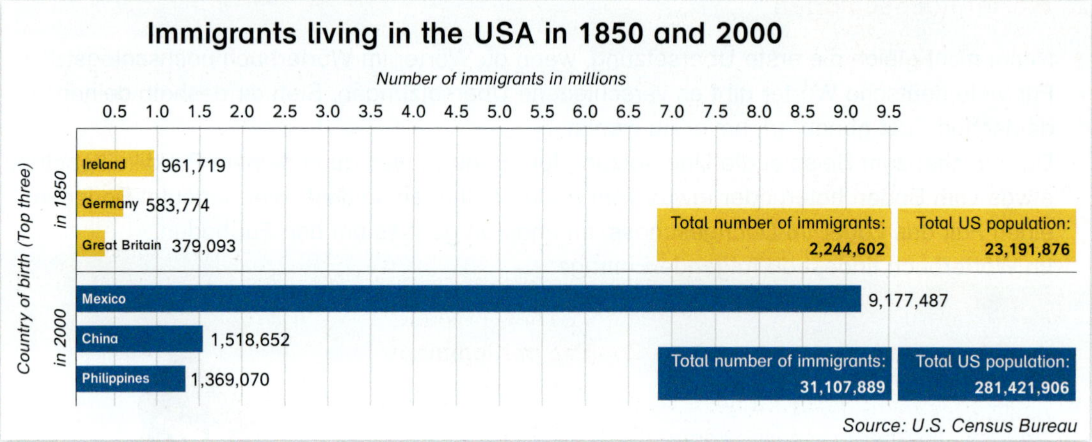

Nützliche Redewendungen:

So kannst du über ein Diagramm sprechen oder schreiben:

- *The bar chart shows ...*
- *In the bar chart you can see ...*
- *When you compare ... and ..., you can see ...*
- *The total number of ... is ...*
- *The total amount ...*
- *The majority of ...*
- *The biggest/smallest group ...*
- *Most of the ...*
- *About half/one third/two thirds/ a quarter/three quarters of ...*
- *There has been a huge increase in the number of ...*
- *Fewer than ...*

Zusammen seid ihr stark!

Milling around

Mit der Methode *milling around* (Umherlaufen) kannst du dich mit deinen Klassenkameraden zu einem Thema austauschen.

1. Gehe durch die Klasse, ohne dass du dabei sprichst.
2. Wenn dein Lehrer/deine Lehrerin ein Zeichen gibt oder „Stop!" sagt, sprich mit der Person, vor der du gerade stehst. Tauscht euch über die Aufgabe aus.
3. Notiere deine Ergebnisse und gehe weiter.

Think – pair – share

Um Ideen zu einem Thema zu sammeln, kannst du in drei Schritten vorgehen:

1. *Think:* Sammle deine Gedanken und Ideen und mache dir Notizen.
2. *Pair:* Tausche dich mit einem Partner/einer Partnerin aus. Ergänze neue Ideen in deiner Liste.
3. *Share:* Teilt dann eure Gedanken und Ideen mit einem anderen Paar. Nun habt ihr schon einige Ideen und Meinungen kennengelernt.

Placemat

Auf einer *placemat* (Tischvorlage, Platzdeckchen) sammelst du mit deinen Gruppenmitgliedern zu einem Thema gleichzeitig Ideen.

1. Alle machen sich auf einem Teil eines großen Bogens Papier Notizen.
2. Dann dreht ihr die *placemat* so lange, bis jede/r alle Beiträge gelesen hat.
3. Einigt euch dann in der Gruppe auf gemeinsame Gedanken und notiert sie in der Mitte des Blattes.
4. Schließlich stellt ein Gruppenmitglied das Ergebnis in der Klasse vor.

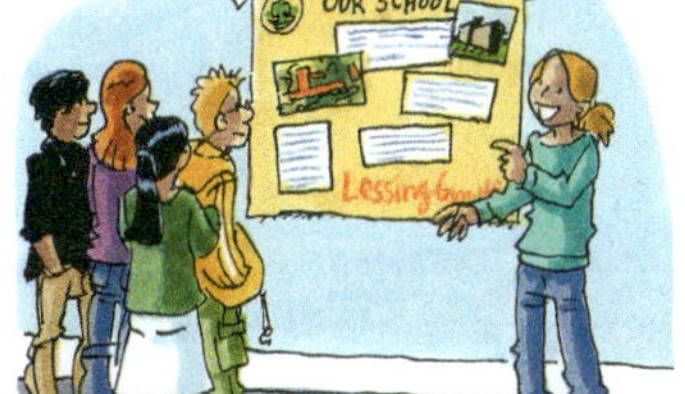

Gallery walk

Wenn ihr alleine oder in verschiedenen Arbeitsgruppen Produkte erstellt habt, könnt ihr einen Rundgang in der Klasse durchführen.

1. Hängt die Produkte im Klassenzimmer auf.
2. Findet euch dann gegebenenfalls in neuen Gruppen zusammen, sodass in jeder Gruppe ein Mitglied jeder Arbeitsgruppe vertreten ist.
3. Geht von Poster zu Poster, und der jeweilige Experte/die jeweilige Expertin erklärt sein/ihr Poster.

Food

a traditional Thanksgiving dinner

roast turkey • potatoes • cranberry sauce • pumpkin pie • apple pie

other food

pasta • bagel • steak • meat loaf • baked potatoes • burritos • chili con carne • French fries • sauerkraut • salad • tofu • hot dog • hamburger

what you do with food

barbecue steaks • cut cucumbers • cook rice • boil potatoes • prepare breakfast • buy organic food • try the soup • have a bagel for lunch

cook dinner for somebody

cut carrots

starter • main course • side dish • dessert • drink • snack

bake a cake

food can be

hot • cold • delicious • tasty • disgusting • mild • spicy • sweet • bitter • vegetarian • traditional

Bananas are healthy.

Milk is an ingredient in ice cream.

For Thanksgiving we usually have turkey and pumpkin pie.

I love sauerkraut on my hot dog!

I love salads. I buy organic food at the local farmers' market.

Sports

(American) football

coach • goal • score a touchdown • field • players • game • Super Bowl

What's the score?

high school sports teams • play against a team • prepare oneself for a game • be supported by cheerleaders • team spirit • discipline • sportsmanship

Our coach made us believe in ourselves!

win • lose

other kinds of sports

baseball • softball • field hockey • wrestling • lacrosse • basketball • cheerleading

indoors • outdoors

Health

start smoking • feel stressed • have no energy • get angry quickly • have headaches • feel peer pressure • ruin your life • cause lung cancer • cause heart disease • result in premature birth

break a habit • quit smoking • go to non-smoking places • exercise • feel better • try nicotine gum • smoke less

Say 'no' to smoking!

Stop now while you're still young and healthy.

It's important to find out what works for you.

It's hard, but you can do it.

cigarette butt

Feelings

positive feelings

excited • fantastic • glad • good • great • happy • proud

negative feelings

angry • awful • bad • bored • frightened • jealous • lonely • nervous • sad • terrible • unhappy • worried

verbs that express feelings

love • like • enjoy • be sorry • miss • laugh • smile • cry • hate

be in love with someone • secretly like someone • ask someone on a date • marry someone

love

boyfriend • girlfriend • partner • lover • hold hands • marriage

I love you.

I miss you.

You look beautiful.

Marry me.

Best friends …

spend time together.
laugh together.
have a good time together.
play video games together.
help each other.
give each other advice.
are always there for each other.

I'll always be there for you!

I love spending time with you.

Places

in the city

airport • cinema • department store • park • restaurant • school • railway station

places can be

beautiful • big • boring • busy • clean • dangerous • dark • dirty • exciting • famous • fantastic • great • interesting • loud • safe • wonderful

the five boroughs of New York

Manhattan
Brooklyn
the Bronx
Staten Island
Queens

nature

beach • field • forest • island • lake • mountain • river • sea • shore

activities

go to the park • go for a walk • go to a museum • go shopping • eat at a restaurant

Let's go for a walk.

You should really see the Statue of Liberty!

talking about sights

… was built in …
… was opened in …
… is the oldest/tallest/longest/biggest/…
… is famous because …
You should really see …
It's in/near …

Jobs

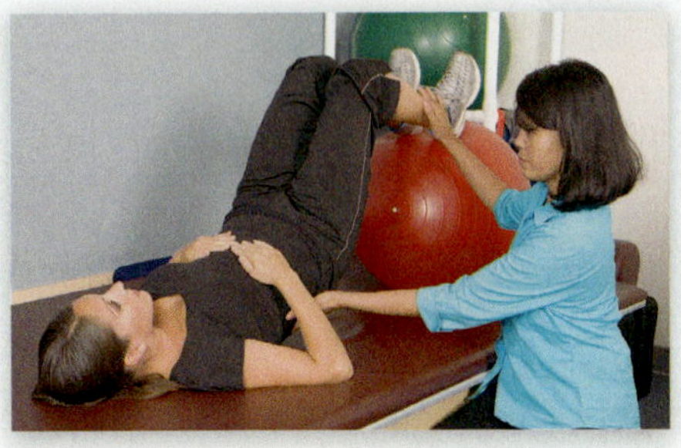

jobs

artist • coach • computer game designer • cook • doctor • doctor's assistant • engineer • firefighter • flight attendant • hairdresser • lorry driver • manager • mechanic • nurse • physiotherapist • pilot • plumber • poet • police officer • secretary • social worker • software developer • staff manager • teacher • vet • waiter/waitress • writer

jobs in entertainment

actor/actress • musician • violinist • pianist • singer • performance artist

outdoor jobs

environmentalist • farmer • lifeguard

unusual jobs

dog food taster • dog surfing instructor • professional line stander • skywalker • smoke-jumper • snake-milker

Wordbank

where people work

in a factory • at a shop • at a department store • in an office • at a school • at a restaurant • on a farm

what people do at work

repair cars • take care of ill people • build houses • design computer games • look after passengers or patients • design gardens • develop machines

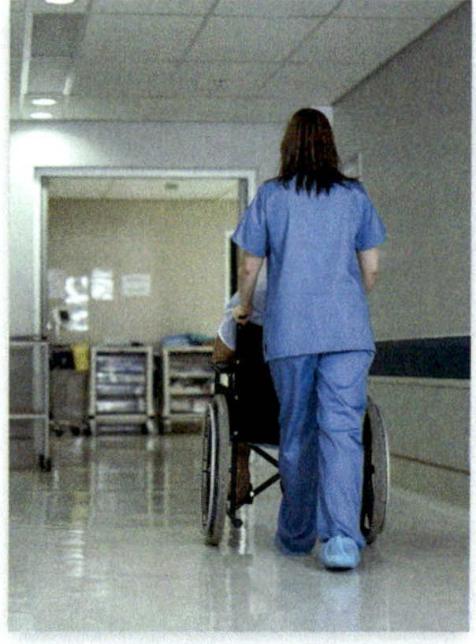

apply for a job • interview • CV (= curriculum vitae) • start a job • be hired • lose one's job • train for a job • be out of work • change jobs

employer • employee • work placement • work experience • apprenticeship

working day • full-time job • weekend job • shift

jobs can be

badly-paid • well-paid • boring • exciting • clean • dirty • easy • difficult • dangerous • stressful • unusual

some people work with

people • customers • computers • animals • their hands • metal • wood

work as a/an … • earn money • make a living • work inside/outside • need qualifications • have a career • work in a team • work alone • work different shifts • be creative

Have you got any experience working with people?

What skills would you like to use at work?

examples of hard skills

computer programming • cooking • school qualifications • repairing cars • typing • speaking different languages

examples of soft skills

communication skills • politeness • reliability • organisational skills • ability to work alone/in a team • taking initiative • being on time

Around the world

continents

Europe
Africa
Asia
Australia
America
Antarctica

countries

Australia • Canada • China • France • Germany • Ghana • Greece • Ireland • Italy • Mexico • Poland • Portugal • Russia • Spain • Sweden • Turkey • UK (United Kingdom) • USA (United States of America)

directions

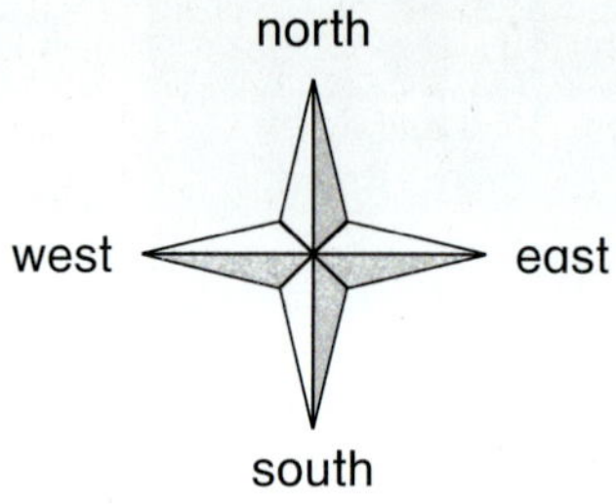

travelling

by plane • by boat • by ship • by ferry • by car • by bus • by train • by motorbike • by bike • on foot • by taxi/cab

leaving home

arrival • emigrate • flight • immigrant • journey • passenger • tourist • travel • trip • voyage

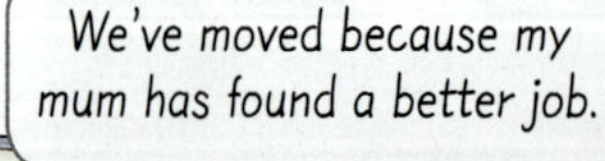

We've moved because my mum has found a better job.

reasons for leaving home

a new job • starting a new life • holiday • fun • problems • no job • war • hunger • hurricane

Environment

what you can do to help the environment

Recycle your rubbish.
Switch off your TV or computer when you're not using it.
Don't let the water run when you brush your teeth.
Grow your own food at home.
Buy eco-friendly clothes.
Walk or cycle to school.
Don't use plastic bags.
Use recyclable bags.
Avoid products with lots of packaging.
Find new uses for old things.
Restyle old clothes.
Volunteer at a beach clean-up.
Join an environmental organization.
Buy products made from recycled materials.
Don't buy CDs and DVDs with cases.

I never use plastic bags!

I sometimes walk to school.

Green cities

public transport • green space • local food market • rooftop farm • vertical garden • carsharing • bike lane • urban gardening • urban farms • energy-efficient buildings

don't use fossil fuels • ban plastic bags • be powered by renewable energy • use renewable energy resources • make your home as green as possible • consume little gasoline and electricity • reduce your carbon footprint • go to work by bike

A plastic planet

plastic can be found in

packaging • bags • litter • bottles • utensils • toys • CD and DVD cases • microbeads • bottle caps

plastic pollution • dangerous • does not biodegrade • a threat to our planet

use reusable shopping bags • use reused plastic bottles • ban plastic bags • use returnable glass bottles • use recycled materials • volunteer at beach clean-ups • join an environmental organization • recycle rubbish

Toxic fashion

toxic chemicals • toxic pesticides • herbicides • synthetic dyes • polyester • formaldehyde • toxic water

clothing label • clothing brands • fabrics • textiles

clothing production • sweatshop • child labour • low wages

buy fewer clothes • restyle old clothes • go to second-hand shops • dye a shirt a new colour • go to swap shops • use eco-friendly dye • organic cotton • bamboo • hemp •

American and British English

apartment	flat
cab	taxi
cellphone	mobile phone
downtown	city centre
elevator	lift
French fries	chips
grade	year/form
high school	secondary school
math	maths
movie	film
on the weekend	at the weekend
parking lot	car park
period	lesson
résumé	CV (= curriculum vitae)
schedule	timetable
sneakers	trainers
soccer	football
store	shop
subway	tube/underground
trash	rubbish
washroom	toilet

aluminum	aluminium
color	colour
favorite	favourite
fertilizer	fertiliser
gray	grey
guidance counselor	guidance counsellor
labor	labour
mom	mum
neighbor	neighbour
neighborhood	neighbourhood
organization	organisation
organize	organise

Working together

Which topic have you chosen?	Welches Thema hast du dir ausgesucht?
Which topic are you going to work on?	An welchem Thema hast du vor zu arbeiten?
Who is going to work on topic A/B/…?	Wer hat vor, an Thema A/B/… zu arbeiten?
I haven't decided yet.	Ich habe mich noch nicht entschieden.
I can't make up my mind.	Ich kann mich nicht entscheiden.
Do you want to work with me?	Willst du mit mir zusammenarbeiten?
Sorry, I haven't got … with me.	Tut mir leid, ich habe … nicht dabei.
Sorry, I forgot to bring …	Tut mir leid, ich habe vergessen … mitzubringen.
I've got a question.	Ich habe eine Frage.
Can you help me, please?	Können Sie/Kannst du mir bitte helfen?
I don't understand this.	Ich verstehe das hier nicht.
What's … in English/German?	Was heißt … auf Englisch/Deutsch?
What does … mean?	Was bedeutet …?
Can you spell that, please?	Kannst du das bitte buchstabieren?
Can you say that again, please?	Kannst du das bitte noch einmal sagen?
Sorry, I don't know.	Tut mir leid, das weiß ich nicht.
What page is it on?	Auf welcher Seite ist das?
Let's do the activities together.	Lass uns die Aktivitäten zusammen machen.
Let's compare …	Lass uns … vergleichen.
What do you think?	Was meinst du?
Whose turn is it?	Wer ist dran?
Are we allowed to use a dictionary?	Dürfen wir ein Wörterbuch benutzen?
Let's look it up in the dictionary.	Lass uns im Wörterbuch nachschlagen.
What else do we need?	Was brauchen wir noch?

Why don't we have a look at this website?

First we have to read up on/investigate the idea about/…	Als Erstes müssen wir uns über … informieren/ die Idee über … untersuchen/…
I think we should first watch/read/explore/…	Ich meine, wir sollten zuerst … anschauen/ lesen/untersuchen/…
Do you know how to use the webcode?	Weißt du, wie man den Webcode benutzt?
Why don't we have a look at the website/on the Internet/…?	Warum schauen wir nicht auf der Website/ im Internet/…?

Classroom phrases

Who wants to keep the word list/take notes/prepare the fact file/...? — Wer will die Wortliste führen/Notizen machen/den Steckbrief vorbereiten/...?
Who is doing the presentation? — Wer übernimmt die Präsentation?
Who is writing down the results? — Wer notiert die Ergebnisse?
What do you think is the biggest problem/the most important fact/...? — Was hältst du für das größte Problem/die wichtigste Tatsache/...?
I think it would be a good idea to ... — Ich finde, es wäre eine gute Idee, wenn wir ...
Can I be the one to call/do the interview with/talk to/...? — Kann ich ... anrufen/das Interview mit ... führen/mit ... sprechen/...?
You're good at ... Why don't you ...? — Du kannst gut ... Warum machst du nicht ...?

You're good at drawing.
Why don't you make a poster?

Let me give you an example. — Lass mich dir ein Beispiel geben.
Well, it's a fact that ... — Es ist nun mal eine Tatsache, dass ...
I think that's a good point. — Ich denke, das ist ein guter Hinweis.
I wouldn't say so. — Das würde ich nicht sagen.
I see what you mean, but ... — Ich verstehe, was du meinst, aber ...
Sorry, I don't agree with you. — Tut mir leid, aber ich stimme dir nicht zu.
I'd rather focus on ... — Ich würde mich lieber auf ... konzentrieren.
We should do some more research on ... — Wir sollten ... besser untersuchen.
I'm sure there's more to it. — Ich glaube, da steckt mehr dahinter.
Only two of us seem to think that it's best to ... — Nur zwei von uns scheinen der Ansicht zu sein, dass es am besten ist, wenn wir ...

I agree with your idea/suggestion/... — Ich stimme deiner Idee/deinem Vorschlag/... zu.
You could make your text more interesting if you ... — Du könntest deinen Text interessanter machen, wenn du ...
I would use a different word here. — Ich würde hier ein anderes Wort verwenden.
We are running out of time. — Uns läuft die Zeit davon.
Well done! — Gut gemacht!

You could make your text more interesting if you used more adjectives.

Deutscher Begriff	Englischer Begriff mit Aussprache	Beispiele	LiF
Adjektiv (Eigenschaftswort)	adjective /ˈædʒɪktɪv/	green, expensive, boring	9R, 10
Adverb der Art und Weise	adverb of manner /ˌædvɜːb‿əv ˈmænə/	quickly, happily, fast, well	9R, 10
Bedingungssatz	conditional clause /kənˈdɪʃənl ˌklɔːz/	If you miss the bus, you will be late.	13R, 15
direkte Rede	direct speech /dɪˌrekt ˈspiːtʃ/	"Close the door, please!"	16
einfache Gegenwart (Präsens)	simple present /ˌsɪmpl ˈpreznt/	Bill lives in the USA.	7R, 13R, 16
einfache Vergangenheit (Präteritum)	simple past /ˌsɪmpl ˈpɑːst/	It was warm and sunny.	14R, 15, 16, 17
Entscheidungsfrage (Ja/Nein-Frage)	yes/no-question /jesˈnəʊ ˌkwestʃn/	Are you from New York?	6
Frage mit Fragewort	wh-question /ˌdʌbljuː ˈeɪtʃ ˌkwestʃn/	What's your name?	6
Futur mit *will*	will-future /ˈwɪl ˌfjuːtʃə/	I'll find a good job.	13R, 16
Gerundium	gerund /ˈdʒerənd/	Dancing can be fun.	4R
Grundform des Verbs (Infinitiv)	infinitive /ɪnˈfɪnətɪv/	be, go, like	5, 14R, 15
Hauptsatz	main clause /ˈmeɪn klɔːz/	If you miss the bus, you will be late.	13R, 15
Imperativ (Befehlsform)	imperative /ɪmˈperətɪv/	Close the door, please!	5, 13R
Indirekter Befehlssatz	reported command /rɪˌpɔːtɪd kəˈmɑːnd/	Mr Cameron told Nick to be on time.	5
Indirekte Rede	reported speech /rɪˌpɔːtɪd ˈspiːtʃ/	Romeo tells Juliet that she looks beautiful.	11R, 16
Indirekter Fragesatz	reported question /rɪˌpɔːtɪd ˈkwestʃn/	The prince asks if Juliet talked about Romeo.	12
Komparativ (1. Vergleichsform)	comparative /kəmˈpærətɪv/	faster, better, more beautiful, more loudly	10
Modalverb	modal verb /ˈməʊdl vɜːb/	can, must	13R, 14R
Nomen (Substantiv, Hauptwort)	noun /naʊn/	apple, friend, milk, water	1, 2, 4R

Deutscher Begriff	Englischer Begriff mit Aussprache	Beispiele	LiF
Objekt direktes Objekt indirektes Objekt	object /ˈɒbdʒɪkt/ direct object /dɪˌrekt‿ˈɒbdʒɪkt/ indirect object /ɪndɪˌrekt‿ˈɒbdʒɪkt/	Bill is writing an email. He gave her a book. He gave her a book.	1, 8R, 9R
Partizip Perfekt	past participle /ˌpɑːst ˈpɑːtɪsɪpl/	played, been, taken	7R, 17
Passiv	passive /ˈpæsɪv/	A tower is built.	7R
Perfekt	present perfect /ˌpreznt ˈpɜːfɪkt/	have gone, has been, has visited	16
Personalpronomen	personal pronoun /ˌpɜːsnl ˈprəʊnaʊn/	I, you, we, they	1
Plural (Mehrzahl)	plural /ˈplʊərəl/	apples	2, 5
Reflexivpronomen	reflexive pronoun /rɪˌfleksɪv ˈprəʊnaʊn/	myself, yourself, ourselves	1
Singular (Einzahl)	singular /ˈsɪŋgjʊlə/	apple	2
Steigerung (Vergleichsformen) von Adverbien	comparison of adverbs /kɒmˌpærɪsn‿əv‿ˈædvɜːbz/	more quickly than …, as beautifully as …, the most quickly	10
Stützwort	prop word /ˈprɒp wɜːd/	the blue one, the red ones	2
Subjekt (Satzgegenstand)	subject /ˈsʌbdʒekt/	Bill is writing an email.	1, 8R
Superlativ (2. Vergleichsform)	superlative /suːˈpɜːlətɪv/	biggest, nicest, most interesting, best	10
Verb (Tätigkeitswort) regelmäßig unregelmäßig	verb /vɜːb/ regular /ˈregjʊlə/ irregular /ɪˈregjʊlə/	 play, like, watch, walk go, do, have	8R 17 17
Vergangenheitsform	past form /ˈpɑːst fɔːm/	played, liked, went, did	14R
Verlaufsform der Gegenwart	present progressive /ˌpreznt prəʊˈgresɪv/	We are having a party.	16
Verlaufsform der Vergangenheit	past progressive /ˌpɑːst prəʊˈgresɪv/	was reading, were running	16
Verlaufsform des Perfekts	present perfect progressive /ˌpreznt ˌpɜːfɪkt prəʊˈgresɪv/	She has been running for half an hour.	6
Vorvergangenheit (Plusquamperfekt)	past perfect /ˌpɑːst ˈpɜːfɪkt/	had left, had gone, had been	17

Theme 1

LiF 1 Reflexivpronomen – *reflexive pronouns*

Du verwendest Reflexivpronomen, wenn das Subjekt und das Objekt in einem Satz dieselbe Person bezeichnen.

*I enjoyed **myself** at the party.*

***The players** are preparing **themselves** for the next match.*

Personalpronomen	Reflexivpronomen
I	**myself**
you	**yourself**
he	**himself**
she	**herself**
it	**itself**
we	**ourselves**
you	**yourselves**
they	**themselves**

*The girls are looking at **themselves** in the mirror.*

! Nicht immer sind Verben, die im Deutschen reflexiv sind, auch im Englischen reflexiv:

I can't concentrate. – Ich kann mich nicht konzentrieren. (*concentrate* = sich konzentrieren)
The friends met at school. – Die Freunde trafen sich in der Schule. (*meet* = sich treffen)

LiF 2 Stützwörter *one/ones – prop words one/ones (optional)*

One oder *ones* kann für ein Nomen stehen, das schon erwähnt wurde oder aus dem Zusammenhang klar ist und deshalb nicht wiederholt werden muss.

Du benutzt *one*, um ein Nomen im Singular zu ersetzen:

*Which is your T-shirt? The yellow **one** or the blue **one**?*
(statt: *The yellow **T-shirt** or the blue **T-shirt**?*)
Welches ist dein T-Shirt? Das gelbe oder das blaue?

Wenn ein Nomen im Plural ersetzt wird, dann benutzt du *ones*:

*Alex likes hot dogs, especially the **ones** in New York.*
(statt: ... *the **hot dogs** in New York.*)
Alex mag Hotdogs, besonders die in New York.

LiF 3 Zusammensetzungen mit *some/any* – *compounds with some/any (optional)*

Mit *some* und *any* bezeichnet man unbestimmte Mengen. In bejahten Aussagesätzen verwendet man *some*, in verneinten Aussagesätzen und in Fragen in der Regel *any*.

Nach denselben Regeln wie *some* und *any* benutzt du auch ihre Zusammensetzungen wie *something/anything*, *somewhere/anywhere*, *somebody/anybody* und *someone/anyone*.

Bejahte Aussagesätze mit *some* und Zusammensetzungen mit *some*

I spent some time in New York. I met somebody from Brooklyn.	*Ich habe etwas Zeit in New York verbracht.* *Ich habe jemanden aus Brooklyn getroffen.*

Verneinte Aussagesätze mit *any* und Zusammensetzungen mit *any*

We haven't got any plans for tomorrow yet. I don't know anyone in New York.	*Wir haben noch keine Pläne für morgen.* *Ich kenne niemanden in New York.*

Fragen mit *any* und Zusammensetzungen mit *any*

Have you taken any photos? Have you been anywhere in the USA?	*Hast du (irgendwelche) Fotos gemacht?* *Warst du schon irgendwo in den USA?*

! Wenn man höflich um etwas bittet oder etwas anbietet, benutzt man *some* auch in Fragen:

Fragen mit *some* und Zusammensetzungen mit *some*

Can I have some milk, please? Would you like something to drink?	*Kann ich bitte (etwas) Milch haben?* *Möchtest du etwas zu trinken?*

Have you seen my keys?
I can't find them anywhere.

Theme 2

LiF 4R Das Gerundium – *the gerund (revision)*

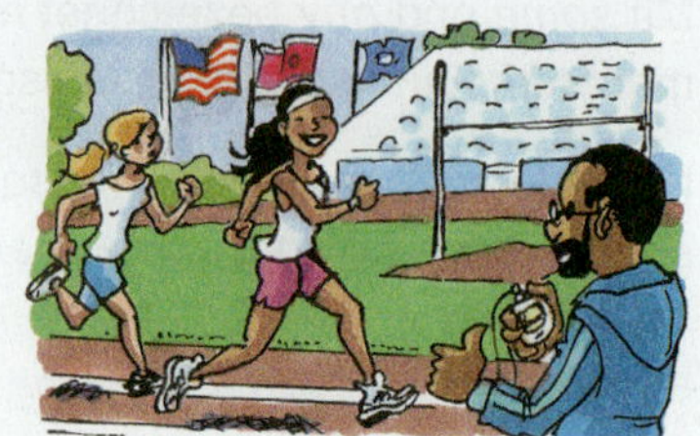

Wird ein Verb durch Anhängen von *-ing* zu einem Nomen, nennt man es Gerundium *(gerund)*.

Das Gerundium kann Subjekt eines Satzes sein:
***Running** keeps you fit.*

Das Gerundium folgt oft nach bestimmten Verben wie *like, love, enjoy, hate, start* und *stop*:
*She enjoys **helping** people.*
*I stopped **smoking** a year ago.*

Du benutzt das Gerundium auch nach bestimmten Ausdrücken wie zum Beispiel *proud of*:
*You can be proud of **winning** a race.*

Achte auf die Schreibweise:
dance – dancing, make – making, run – running, hit – hitting, stop – stopping usw.

LiF 5 Indirekte Befehlssätze – *reported commands*

Der Imperativ (die Befehlsform) hat im Englischen dieselbe Form wie der Infinitiv und lautet im Singular und Plural gleich.
***Help** me, please.* – Bitte **hilf** mir./Bitte **helft** mir.

Wenn jemand etwas nicht tun soll, steht *do not* oder *don't* vor dem Verb.
***Don't forget** your keys.*

Wenn du einen Befehlssatz in der indirekten Rede wiedergeben willst, benutzt du den Infinitiv mit *to*:

Close the door, please. — *The teacher tells the pupils **to close** the door.*

Wenn der Originalsatz negativ ist, steht *not* vor dem Infinitiv mit *to*:

Don't open the window. — *She tells them **not to open** the window.*

Denke auch daran, Bezugswörter anzupassen, wenn nötig.

Do your homework. — *She tells them to do **their** homework.*

LiF 6 Die Verlaufsform des Perfekts – *present perfect progressive (optional)*

Das *present perfect progressive* verwendest du, wenn du über etwas sprechen möchtest, das in der Vergangenheit begonnen hat und immer noch andauert.

Tim has been running for thirty minutes (and he is still running).
Miriam has been helping in the fields for a few years (and she is still helping every year).

a Aussagesätze im *present perfect progressive*

So bildest du das *present perfect progressive*:

have/has + been + ***-ing*-Form**:

*I **have been cleaning** shoes since I was nine.*
*Jacob **has been looking** for a job for three months.*

*She **has been doing** her homework for two hours.*

Bei Verneinungen fügst du *not* hinter *have* oder *has* ein:

have/has + not + been + ***-ing*-Form**:

*I **haven't been working** for long.*
*He **hasn't been going** to school for a long time.*

b Fragen und Kurzantworten im *present perfect progressive*

Entscheidungsfragen im *present perfect progressive* bildest du, indem du *have* oder *has* an den Satzanfang stellst. *Have* bzw. *has* wird in den Kurzantworten aufgegriffen.

Have you been working for long? – *Yes, I have./No, I haven't.*
Has he been going to school for six years? – *Yes, he has./No, he hasn't.*

Bei Fragen mit Fragewörtern steht das Fragewort vor *have* oder *has*.

What have you been doing all day?
How long has Raoul been working as a shoe shine boy?

c *since* und *for*

Geht es bei einer Zeitangabe um einen genauen Zeitpunkt, an dem etwas begonnen hat, dann benutzt du *since*, z. B. *since 2011, since ten o'clock, since I was six years old.*

Miriam has been going to school since she was eight years old.

Bei einem Zeitraum benutzt du *for*, z. B. *for six months, for ten years, for a long time.*

Raoul has been attending the local school for two years.

LiF7R Das Passiv – *the passive (revision)*

Aktivsätze sagen uns, wer oder was handelt. Wenn es aber nicht wichtig oder nicht bekannt ist, wer etwas tut, kannst du in vielen Fällen das Passiv verwenden.

Aktiv	Passiv
The men build a **tower**.	**A tower** is built.

Passivsätze kannst du in allen Zeiten bilden. Die Verbformen haben dieses Muster:

Form von *be* + **Partizip Perfekt *(past participle)***

simple present:

The vines are selected by a village elder.
Land diving isn't done in the wet season.

simple past:

The vines were selected by my grandfather last year.
Land diving wasn't done last month.

present perfect:

The vines have already been selected.
The trees haven't been cut yet.

will-future:

The vines will be selected soon.
The trees won't be cut soon.

Mit *by* („von", „durch") kannst du die handelnde Person oder die Ursache hinzufügen:
A tower is built ***by*** *the men.*
The tower was destroyed ***by*** *fire.*

Theme 3

LiF8R Die Stellung der Satzglieder – *word order (revision)*

a Satzstellung Subjekt – Verb – Objekt (S – V – O)

Im englischen Aussagesatz ist die Satzstellung meist:

Subjekt *(subject)* S	Verb *(verb)* V	Objekt *(object)* O
I	have lost	my phone number.
We	would make	a great pair.

b Verben mit zwei Objekten

Wie im Deutschen gibt es auch im Englischen einige Verben, die zwei Objekte haben können, zum Beispiel *give, offer, show, ask, send*.

Man unterscheidet direkte und indirekte Objekte.

Das indirekte Objekt steht oft für eine oder mehrere Personen, während das direkte Objekt oft für eine Sache steht.

Das indirekte Objekt steht entweder vor dem direkten Objekt oder unmittelbar danach.
Wenn es nachgestellt wird, muss das indirekte Objekt durch *to* oder *for* eingeleitet werden.

Subjekt
Verb
indirektes Objekt
direktes Objekt
I
She
would buy
sent
my friend
her friend
a present.
a text message.
Subjekt
Verb
direktes Objekt
indirektes Objekt
I
She
would buy
sent
a present
a text message
for my friend.
to her friend.

c Ortsangaben und Zeitangaben

Orts- und Zeitangaben stehen in der Regel am Ende eines Satzes. Wenn sie zusammen in einem Satz vorkommen, steht die Ortsangabe vor der Zeitangabe („Ort“ vor „Zeit“).

Ortsangabe
Zeitangabe
I was born
My parents came
in New York
to the USA
in 2004.
twenty years ago.

Um eine Zeitangabe stärker zu betonen, kannst du sie auch an den Satzanfang stellen.

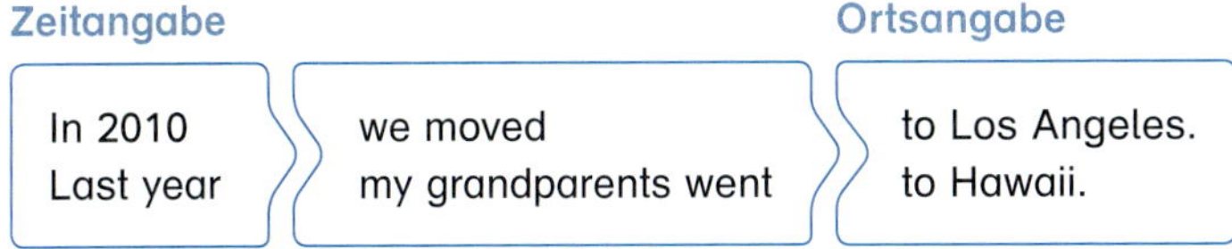

Zeitangabe
Ortsangabe
In 2010
Last year
we moved
my grandparents went
to Los Angeles.
to Hawaii.

LiF 9R Adverbien der Art und Weise – *adverbs of manner (revision)*

Wenn du eine Person, ein Tier oder eine Sache beschreibst, benutzt du ein Adjektiv.

The music is loud. *She is happy.*

Wenn du beschreiben möchtest, wie jemand etwas tut oder wie etwas geschieht, benutzt du ein Adverb der Art und Weise.

The girl sings loudly. *She smiled happily.*

Adverbien der Art und Weise bildest du, indem du an das Adjektiv die Endung *-ly* anhängst:

Adjektiv	Adverb	
loud	loudly	The boys speak very loudly.
bad	badly	Susan sings badly.
slow	slowly	Tom walks slowly.

He sings badly.

Manchmal ändert sich die Schreibweise, wenn *-ly* angehängt wird:

Adjektiv	Adverb	
easy	easily	We'll solve the problem easily.
happy	happily	The woman laughed happily.
terrible	terribly	Simon dances terribly.
beautiful	beautifully	Mona sings beautifully.

! Einige Adverbien haben Sonderformen, die du wie Vokabeln lernen musst.

Adjektiv	Adverb	
good	well	Rob is a good guitar player. He plays the guitar well.
fast	fast	Jack is a fast runner. He runs fast.
hard	hard	Emma is a hard worker. She works hard.

Adverbien der Art und Weise stehen nach dem Verb.
In Sätzen mit Objekt stehen sie nach dem Objekt.

Subjekt	Verb	Objekt	Adverb
Emma	walks		quickly.
Rob	plays	the guitar	well.

Rajiv dances very well.

LiF 10 Die Steigerung von Adverbien – *comparison of adverbs*

Für die Steigerung von Adverbien gelten die gleichen Regeln wie für die Steigerung von Adjektiven.

Einsilbige Adverbien werden durch das Anhängen von *-er* und *-est* gesteigert.

Tom runs faster than the other boys.

Adverb	Komparativ	Superlativ
fast	faster	(the) fastest
hard	harder	(the) hardest

Tim runs the fastest.

Zwei- und mehrsilbige Adverbien, die auf *-ly* enden, steigerst du mit *more* und *most*.

Janet talks more quickly than Liz.

Adverb	Komparativ	Superlativ
slowly	more slowly	(the) most slowly
quickly	more quickly	(the) most quickly
loudly	more loudly	(the) most loudly
happily	more happily	(the) most happily
beautifully	more beautifully	(the) most beautifully

Es gibt auch unregelmäßige Steigerungsformen, die du wie Vokabeln lernen musst.

Tony skates better than all the others.
He skates the best.

Adverb	Komparativ	Superlativ
well	better	(the) best
badly	worse	(the) worst
much	more	(the) most

Vergleichsätze bildest du wie bei den Adjektiven mit *than* oder mit *as … as*:

Ann sings more beautifully than Janet.
Jason sings as beautifully as Ann.

LiF11R Indirekte Rede 1 – *reported speech 1 (revision)*

Wenn du berichten willst, was jemand gesagt hat, benutzt du indirekte Rede.

Indirekte Rede besteht aus einem Begleitsatz und der wiedergegebenen Aussage.

	Begleitsatz	wiedergegebene Aussage
"I hope nobody recognises me."	Romeo says (that)	he hopes nobody recognises him.

Beide Satzteile können durch *that* verbunden werden. Wenn der Begleitsatz in der Gegenwart steht, verändern sich die Zeiten in der wiedergegebenen Aussage nicht.

You look beautiful tonight, Juliet.

Wenn die Originalaussage Wörter enthält, die nur aus dem Zusammenhang richtig zu verstehen sind, musst du sie in der wiedergegebenen Aussage anpassen:

*"**You** look beautiful."*
*Romeo tells Juliet (that) **she** looks beautiful.*

LiF12 Indirekte Fragesätze – *reported questions*

Wenn du eine Frage wiedergeben willst, die jemand anderes gestellt hat, benutzt du *if* oder *whether*:

Did Juliet talk about Romeo?

*The Prince wants to know **whether** Juliet talked about Romeo.*

Did they fall in love at first sight?

*The Prince asks **if** they fell in love at first sight.*

Wenn die Frage mit einem Fragewort eingeleitet wird, übernimmst du das Fragewort:

When did they get married?

*The Prince wants to know **when** they got married.*

Theme 4

LiF13R Bedingungssätze 1 – *conditional 1 (revision)*

Wenn du sagen willst, was unter bestimmten Bedingungen passiert, verwendest du einen Bedingungssatz. Dieser besteht aus einem *if*-Satz *(if-clause)* und einem Hauptsatz *(main clause)*.

Der *if*-Satz nennt eine Bedingung und steht im *simple present*. Der Hauptsatz drückt aus, was passiert, wenn die Bedingung erfüllt ist. Im Hauptsatz steht häufig das *will-future*.

if-Satz (*simple present*)	Hauptsatz (*will-future*)
If you become a flight attendant,	you will travel a lot.
If you become a baker,	you will have to get up early.
If you get a job in your town,	you won't have to move to another place.

Im Hauptsatz kannst du auch Modalverben (z. B. *must, should, can*) oder den Imperativ verwenden:

if-Satz (*simple present*)	Hauptsatz (Modalverb oder Imperativ)
If you want to earn a lot of money,	you must work hard.
If you feel sick,	you should stay at home.
If you need help,	ask your boss.

Wenn der *if*-Satz vor dem Hauptsatz steht, muss er mit einem Komma getrennt werden. Steht er allerdings nach dem Hauptsatz, so verwendest du kein Komma:

If I find a good job, I'll be happy.
I'll be happy if I find a good job.

If oder *when*?

Beide Wörter kannst du mit „wenn" übersetzen. Sie werden aber unterschiedlich verwendet:

- *If I see Ben on Monday, I'll give him the book.*
  Der Sprecher verwendet *if*, weil er nicht sicher ist, ob er Ben am Montag sieht. Du kannst *if* hier mit „wenn" oder „falls" übersetzen.

- *When I see Ben on Monday, I'll give him the book.*
  Der Sprecher weiß, dass er Ben am Montag sehen wird. Dann wird er ihm auch das Buch geben. Du kannst *when* hier mit „wenn" übersetzen, aber nicht mit „falls".

LiF 14R Modalverben – *modal verbs (revision, optional)*

Mithilfe von Modalverben kannst du z. B. ausdrücken, was jemand tun kann, darf, muss oder sollte.

a Fähigkeit: *can/can't/be able to*

Mit *can* kannst du sagen, was jemand tun kann.

Keith **can** paint. I **can't** paint very well.	*Keith kann malen. Ich kann nicht gut malen.*

Can steht mit dem Infinitiv und bleibt in allen Personen gleich.

! Die Ersatzform von *can* ist ***be able to***. Im *simple past* kannst du auch ***could*** benutzen.

Keith **was able to** draw very well. The artist **could** sell all his paintings. I **will be able to** go to art school next year.	*Keith konnte sehr gut malen. Der Künstler konnte alle seine Bilder verkaufen. Ich werde nächstes Jahr auf die Kunstschule gehen können.*

b Erlaubnis: *can/can't – be allowed to/not be allowed to – may/may not – must not*

Mit *can/can't, (not) be allowed to, may/may not* und *must not* kannst du sagen, was jemand tun oder nicht tun darf. Du benutzt es auch, wenn du

- um Erlaubnis fragst oder jemandem etwas erlaubst
- um etwas bittest
- etwas verbietest.

Can I paint on this wall? – No, sorry, you **are not allowed to**. The children **were allowed to** work with Keith Haring. **May** I use your pencil? You **mustn't** touch the painting.	*Darf ich auf dieser Wand malen? – Nein, tut mir leid, das darfst du nicht. Die Kinder durften mit Keith Haring arbeiten. Darf ich deinen Bleistift benutzen? Du darfst das Gemälde nicht anfassen.*

! ***Must not*** oder die Kurzform ***mustn't*** klingt wie im Deutschen „muss nicht“, heißt aber „nicht dürfen“.

You *mustn't* talk now.

Ihr dürft jetzt nicht sprechen.

c Notwendigkeit: *must/have to – don't have to/needn't*

Must bedeutet „müssen". In der Regel kannst du ***must*** auch durch ***have to/has to*** ersetzen.

You **must** practise a lot to get better at drawing. *oder* You **have to** practise a lot to get better at drawing.	*Du musst viel üben um im Zeichnen besser zu werden.*

Must hat keine eigene Vergangenheitsform. Daher wird die *simple past*-Form von ***have to*** benutzt.

Keith Haring **had to** move to New York.	*Keith Haring musste nach New York ziehen.*

Wenn du sagen willst, was jemand *nicht* tun muss oder musste, benutzt du ***don't/doesn't have to*** bzw. ***didn't have to***.

People **didn't have to** pay much for Keith Haring's posters.	*Die Leute mussten nicht viel für Keith Harings Poster bezahlen.*

Auch mit ***needn't*** (Kurzform von ***need not***) kannst du ausdrücken, dass jemand etwas nicht tun muss.

You **needn't** do your homework now, you can do it later.	*Du musst deine Hausaufgaben nicht jetzt machen, du kannst sie später machen.*

d Empfehlung: *should/shouldn't*

Mit *should/shouldn't* drückst du aus, dass etwas deiner Ansicht nach passieren oder nicht passieren sollte:

*You **should** study art, you're really good at it.*

*I probably **shouldn't** choose art as an elective.*

Mit *should* kannst du auch die Meinung einer anderen Person erfragen:

*What do you think I **should** do?*

LiF15 Bedingungssätze 2 – *conditional 2*

Bedingungssätze können realistische oder unrealistische Bedingungen nennen.
Ist eine Bedingung erfüllbar, verwendet man den Bedingungssatz 1 (siehe auch LiF13R auf Seite 187):

***If you study hard**, you will get a good mark.*

Ist eine Bedingung jedoch unwahrscheinlich oder unmöglich, verwendet man den Bedingungssatz 2.

***If my mom had the money**, she would send me to art school.*

Da die Mutter das Geld im Moment nicht hat, ist die Bedingung nicht erfüllbar.

Bei dieser zweiten Art von Bedingungssätzen steht der *if*-Satz im *simple past*. Im Hauptsatz steht *would* (oder auch *could*) mit einem Hauptverb im Infinitiv.

***if*-Satz** *(simple past)*	**Hauptsatz** *(would/could + Infinitiv)*
If Emma's brother **didn't help** her,	Emma **would fail** completely in math.
If she **was** fitter,	she **would choose** basketball.
If Emma **chose** graphic design,	she **would be** happier.
If Emma's mother **had** more money,	Emma **could go** to art school.

*Mr Batson **would be** very happy if he **found** a new job.*

If I were …

Bei *if*-Sätzen heiβt es manchmal *If I were …*, aber du kannst auch *If I was …* sagen.
Beide Formen sind hier möglich.

*If I **were** Emma, I would choose graphic design.*
oder:
*If I **was** Emma, I would choose graphic design.*

LiF16 Zeitverschiebung in indirekter Rede – *tense shift in reported speech*

Wenn du berichten willst, was jemand sagt oder gesagt hat, verwendest du die indirekte Rede *(reported speech)* (siehe auch LiF 11R auf Seite 186).

Wenn im Begleitsatz die Zeitform der Gegenwart verwendet wird, ändert sich die Zeitform in der wiedergegebenen Aussage nicht.

Oft steht jedoch das Verb im Begleitsatz in der Vergangenheit. Dann musst du die Zeitform in der indirekten Rede anpassen. Sie rückt sozusagen eine Stufe weiter in die Vergangenheit:

Mr. Cameron: You **have to** be on time.

→ *Mr. Cameron* ***told*** *Nick that he* ***had to*** *be on time.*

Mr. Cameron: You **will** have to work later this evening.

→ *Mr. Cameron* ***told*** *Nick that he* ***would*** *have to work later that evening.*

Nick: I'm **cleaning** the floor.

→ *Nick* ***said*** *that he* ***was cleaning*** *the floor.*

Nick: I **will** be on time tomorrow.

→ *Nick* ***said*** *that he* ***would*** *be on time the next day.*

Denke daran, Bezugswörter, die nur aus dem Zusammenhang richtig zu verstehen sind, in der wiedergegebenen Aussage anzupassen. Dies sind zum Beispiel Personalpronomen und Adverbien wie *tomorrow* und *here*.

*Mr. Cameron: "**I**'m not happy."* → *Mr. Cameron said that **he** wasn't happy.*
*Nick: "**I**'ll work harder **tomorrow**."* → *Nick said that **he** would work harder **the next day**.*
*Caroline: "**I** like working **here**."* → *Caroline said that **she** liked working **there**.*

Aus dieser Tabelle kannst du ablesen, wie sich die Zeiten verändern.

Direkte Rede		Indirekte Rede
simple present	→	*simple past*
present progressive	→	*past progressive*
will	→	*would*
can	→	*could*
should	→	*should*
(simple past	→	*past perfect, s. LiF 17)*
(present perfect	→	*past perfect, s. LiF 17)*

Theme 5

LiF17 Die Vorvergangenheit – *past perfect*

Das *past perfect* verwendest du, wenn du über eine Handlung sprechen möchtest, die vor einer anderen Handlung in der Vergangenheit stattgefunden hat. Die zweite Handlung steht im *simple past*. Beide Handlungen sind abgeschlossen.

*After Annie's parents **had gone** to America, they found jobs in New York.*
Nachdem Annies Eltern nach Amerika gegangen waren, fanden sie Arbeit in New York.

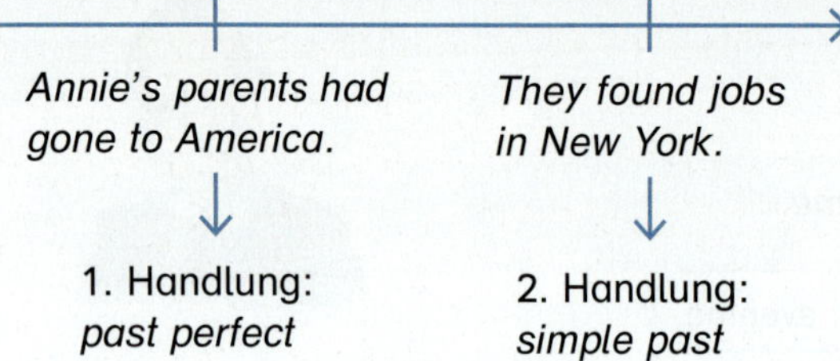
Annie's parents had gone to America.
They found jobs in New York.
1. Handlung: past perfect
2. Handlung: simple past

Das *past perfect* bildest du so: ***had*** + **Partizip Perfekt *(past participle)***

1. Handlung ***past perfect***	**2. Handlung** ***simple past***
After Annie **had boarded** the ship, *Nachdem Annie an Bord gegangen war,*	her journey began. *begann ihre Reise.*
Annie's family **had lived** in Ireland *Annies Familie hatte in Irland gelebt,*	before they came to the USA. *bevor sie in die USA kamen.*

Die Verneinung bildest du mit ***hadn't*** + **Partizip Perfekt *(past participle)***.

1. Handlung ***past perfect***	**2. Handlung** ***simple past***
Annie's parents **hadn't had** any money *Annies Eltern hatten kein Geld gehabt,*	before they moved to New York. *bevor sie nach New York zogen.*

Wenn du das *past perfect* bildest, musst du auf das Partizip Perfekt achten.
Bei regelmäßigen Verben endet es auf *-ed*.
Bei unregelmäßigen Verben musst du die Formen wie neue Vokabeln lernen.

Auf den Seiten 306 bis 308 findest du eine Liste mit unregelmäßigen Verben.

Erläuterung der Wortlisten

Alphabetische Wortlisten *(Dictionary)*

Du kannst in der alphabetischen Liste *(Dictionary English-German)* ab Seite 253 die Bedeutung von Wörtern, die im Buch vorgekommen sind, oder von Lernwörtern aus Band I, II oder III (5., 6. oder 7. Klasse) nachschlagen. Unbekanntes Vokabular aus den Arbeitsanweisungen findest du ebenfalls dort. Die wichtigsten Arbeitsanweisungen findest du in der Liste auf den Seiten 196–199 und in Kästen innerhalb der Wortlisten nach Kapiteln. Einige Wörter, die im Englischen wie im Deutschen gleich sind, findest du mit ihrer Lautschrift auf Seite 195. Im *Dictionary German-English* ab Seite 292 kannst du nachschlagen, wenn dir eins der englischen Lernwörter nicht einfällt.

Wortlisten nach Kapiteln *(Words)*

Hier werden die neuen Vokabeln an der Stelle aufgelistet, an der sie zum ersten Mal vorkommen oder zum Lernwort werden. Die Lernwörter sind fett gedruckt. Du solltest sie dir auf jeden Fall merken. Hier siehst du, wie du die Wortlisten nach Kapiteln (ab Seite 201) benutzen kannst:

Links stehen die englischen Wörter mit ihrer Lautschrift.

Die Lautschrift zeigt an, wie man ein Wort ausspricht.

Hier findest du die Übersetzungen.

Fett gedruckte Wörter solltest du dir merken.

Zu dieser Aufgabe gehören die folgenden Wörter.

(AE) bedeutet: Dies ist ein Wort aus dem amerikanischen Englisch.

(BE) bedeutet: Dies ist das englische Wort oder die englische Schreibweise eines Wortes, das im Text im amerikanischen Englisch vorkommt.

(pl) weist auf eine unregelmäßige Mehrzahlform hin oder darauf, dass ein Wort in seiner Mehrzahlform vorkommt.

(no pl) bedeutet: Dieses Wort hat keine Mehrzahl.

W

Words

I	hurricane /ˈhʌrɪkeɪn/	Orkan	To find out what happens next in a book, you must *read on*.
	read on /ˌriːd‿ˈɒn/	weiterlesen	
	famine /ˈfæmɪn/	Hungersnot	
	settler /ˈsetlə/	Siedler/in	
	immigration /ˌɪmɪˈgreɪʃn/	Einwanderung, Immigration	*Immigration* describes the process in which people enter a different country in order to live there.
	journey /ˈdʒɜːni/	reisen	
	glory /ˈglɔːri/	Ruhm	
	motive /ˈməʊtɪv/	Motiv	
	response /rɪˈspɒns/	Antwort; Reaktion	
A1	arithmetic /əˈrɪθmətɪk/	Arithmetik	
	public school *(AE)* /ˌpʌblɪk ˈskuːl/	staatliche Schule	
	what makes somebody tick /wɒt ˌmeɪks‿ˌsʌmbədi ˈtɪk/	was jemanden bewegt	
	in front /ɪn ˈfrʌnt/	vorn	
	behind /bɪˈhaɪnd/	hinten	
	aisle /aɪl/	Gang	*I am craving* chocolate! = I really, really want some chocolate!
	crave (for) /kreɪv/	sich sehnen nach	
	Italian /ɪˈtæljən/	Italienisch	
	Polish /ˈpəʊlɪʃ/	Polnisch	
	colored *(AE)* = coloured *(BE)* /ˈkʌləd/	farbig	
	Russian /ˈrʌʃn/	Russe, Russin; russisch	
	Grecian /ˈgriːʃn/	griechisch	
	Chinese /ˌtʃaɪˈniːz/	Chinese, Chinesin; chinesisch	
	regular /ˈregjʊlə/	normal	
	ark /ɑːk/	Arche	
	graduation /ˌgrædʒuˈeɪʃn/	(Studien)abschluss	
	across /əˈkrɒs/	gegenüber	
	African American /ˌæfrɪkən‿əˈmerɪkən/	afroamerikanisch	
	traditional /trəˈdɪʃnəl/	traditionell	
	racist /ˈreɪsɪst/	Rassist/in; rassistisch	
	kitchen utensils *(pl)* /ˈkɪtʃən‿juːˌtenslz/	Küchengeräte	
	get *(irr)* /get/	werden	
	meat loaf /ˌmiːt ˈləʊf/	Hackbraten	
	pasta /ˈpæstə/	Nudeln	
	wife (*pl* wives) /waɪf, waɪvz/	Ehefrau	
	artwork *(no pl)* /ˈɑːtˌwɜːk/	Kunstwerk(e)	
	background /ˈbækˌgraʊnd/	Hintergrund	
	you guys *(informal)* /ˈjuː gaɪz/	ihr, euch	

Früher war die britische Schreibweise von Wörtern mit *'-ise'* bzw. *'-isation'* eindeutig die mit 's', die amerikanische die mit 'z'. Mittlerweile werden kaum noch Unterschiede gemacht. Viele Briten schreiben ganz selbstverständlich *'realize'*, *'organize'* oder *'organization'*. In vielen Wörterbüchern wird sogar die Schreibweise mit 'z' als die häufiger vorkommende gelistet.

Kleine Bilder und Beispielsätze helfen dabei, dir Wörter besser einzuprägen.

Hier findest du wichtige Vokabel-Lerntipps.

(irr) bedeutet: Dieses Verb hat unregelmäßige Formen. Du findest sie in der Liste ab S. 306.

(informal) bedeutet: Dieses Wort ist umgangssprachlich.

The English alphabet

/eɪ/	/biː/	/siː/	/diː/	/iː/	/ef/	/dʒiː/	/eɪtʃ/	/aɪ/
a	b	c	d	e	f	g	h	i
/dʒeɪ/	/keɪ/	/el/	/em/	/en/	/əʊ/	/piː/	/kjuː/	/ɑː/
j	k	l	m	n	o	p	q	r
/es/	/tiː/	/juː/	/viː/	/ˈdʌbljuː/	/eks/	/waɪ/	/zed/	
s	t	u	v	w	x	y	z	

English sounds

Im Englischen spricht man Wörter oft anders aus, als man sie schreibt. Die Aussprache der Wörter wird mit Hilfe der Lautschrift in jedem Wörterbuch angegeben. Man kann so auch neue Wörter richtig aussprechen, ohne sie vorher gehört zu haben.
Die Lautschrift ist eine Schrift, deren Symbole jeden Laut genau bezeichnen.
Hier ist eine Liste mit den Symbolen dieser Lautschrift zusammen mit Beispielwörtern, in denen der entsprechende Laut vorkommt.

Vokale

/ɑː/ arm
/ʌ/ but
/e/ desk
/ə/ a, an
/ɜː/ girl, bird
/æ/ apple
/ɪ/ in, it
/i/ happy
/iː/ easy, eat
/ɒ/ orange, sorry
/ɔː/ all, call
/ʊ/ look
/u/ January
/uː/ boot

Doppellaute

/aɪ/ eye, by, buy
/aʊ/ our
/eə/ air, there
/eɪ/ take, they
/ɪə/ here
/ɔɪ/ boy
/əʊ/ go, old
/ʊə/ tourist

Konsonanten

/b/ bag, club
/d/ duck, card
/f/ fish, laugh
/g/ get, dog
/h/ hot
/j/ you
/k/ can, duck
/l/ lot, small
/m/ more, mum
/n/ now, sun
/ŋ/ song, long
/p/ present, top
/r/ red, around
/s/ sister, class (stimmlos)
/z/ nose, dogs (stimmhaft)
/t/ time, cat
/ʒ/ television
/dʒ/ sausage
/ʃ/ fresh
/tʃ/ child, cheese
/ð/ these, mother (stimmhaft)
/θ/ bathroom, think (stimmlos)
/v/ very, have
/w/ what, word

/ˈ/ Betonungszeichen für die folgende Silbe (Hauptbetonung)
/ˌ/ Betonungszeichen für die folgende Silbe (Nebenbetonung)

Words

Viele Wörter, die im Englischen wie im Deutschen so gut wie gleich sind und in deinem Buch vorkommen, findest du hier. Sie sind nicht in den Wortlisten der einzelnen Kapitel, weil sie dir ja nicht neu sind. Bei denen, die anders ausgesprochen werden als im Deutschen, haben wir die Lautschrift farbig hervorgehoben.

ABC /ˌeɪbiːˈsiː/
adverb /ˈædvɜːb/
alternative /ɔːlˈtɜːnətɪv/
anorak /ˈænəræk/
anti- /ˈænti/
arm /ɑːm/
baby /ˈbeɪbi/
badminton /ˈbædmɪntən/
ball /bɔːl/
baseball /ˈbeɪsˌbɔːl/
basketball /ˈbɑːskɪtˌbɔːl/
biodiesel /ˌbaɪəʊˈdiːzl/
bitter /ˈbɪtə/
blog /blɒg/
blues /bluːz/
boss /bɒs/
bungee jump /ˈbʌndʒiː ˌdʒʌmp/
burger, hamburger /ˈbɜːgə, ˈhæmˌbɜːgə/
burrito /bəˈriːtəʊ/
bus /bʌs/
butter /ˈbʌtə/
button /ˈbʌtən/
café, cafeteria /ˈkæfeɪ, ˌkæfəˈtɪəriə/
carsharing /ˈkɑː ˌʃeərɪŋ/
cartoon /kɑːˈtuːn/
CD, DVD /ˌsiːˈdiː, ˌdiːviːˈdiː/
chance /tʃɑːns/
cheerleader /ˈtʃɪəˌliːdə/
chicken nugget /ˌtʃɪkɪn ˈnʌgɪt/
chili con carne /ˌtʃɪli kɒn ˈkɑːni/
clip /klɪp/
coach /kəʊtʃ/
collage /ˈkɒlɑːʒ/
comic /ˈkɒmɪk/
cool /kuːl/
cranberry /ˈkrænbri/
darts /dɑːts/
definition /ˌdefəˈnɪʃn/
designer boutique /dɪˌzaɪnə buːˈtiːk/
detail /ˈdiːteɪl/
digital /ˈdɪdʒɪtl/
dollar /ˈdɒlə/
drama /ˈdrɑːmə/
email /ˈiːmeɪl/
episode /ˈepɪsəʊd/
essay /ˈeseɪ/
expedition /ˌekspəˈdɪʃn/
explosion /ɪkˈspləʊʒn/
fan /fæn/
fast food /ˌfɑːst ˈfuːd/
film /fɪlm/
finger /ˈfɪŋgə/
fit /fɪt/
flyer /ˈflaɪə/
form /fɔːm/
gang /gæŋ/
generation /ˌdʒenəˈreɪʃn/
gin tonic /ˌdʒɪn ˈtɒnɪk/
global /ˈgləʊbl/
gold /gəʊld/
graffiti /grəˈfiːti/
hand /hænd/
hobby /hɒbi/
hockey /ˈhɒki/
hot dog /ˌhɒt ˈdɒg/
hotel /həʊˈtel/
hunger /ˈhʌŋgə/
illegal /ɪˈliːgl/
illustration /ˌɪləˈstreɪʃn/
info /ˈɪnfəʊ/
installation /ˌɪnstəˈleɪʃn/
international, national /ˌɪntəˈnæʃnəl, ˈnæʃnəl/
Internet /ˈɪntəˌnet/
interview /ˈɪntəˌvjuː/
intro /ˈɪntrəʊ/
isolation /ˌaɪsəˈleɪʃn/
journalist /ˈdʒɜːnəlɪst/
lacrosse /ləˈkrɒs/
land /lænd/
link /lɪŋk/
live /laɪv/
make-up /ˈmeɪkʌp/
marathon /ˈmærəθn/
marketing /ˈmɑːkɪtɪŋ/
material /məˈtɪəriəl/
migration /maɪˈgreɪʃn/
million /ˈmɪljən/
mineral /ˈmɪnrəl/
mini golf /ˈmɪni gɒlf/
minute /ˈmɪnɪt/
modern /ˈmɒdən/
moment /ˈməʊmənt/
monster /ˈmɒnstə/
motor /ˈməʊtə/
motto /ˈmɒtəʊ/
museum /mjuːˈziːəm/
musical /ˈmjuːzɪkl/
name /neɪm/
New Yorker /ˌnjuː ˈjɔːkə/
newsletter /ˈnjuːzˌletə/
normal /ˈnɔːml/
online /ˈɒnlaɪn/
organisation /ˌɔːgənaɪˈzeɪʃn/
original /əˈrɪdʒnəl/
park /pɑːk/
partner /ˈpɑːtnə/
patient /ˈpeɪʃnt/
person /ˈpɜːsn/
peso /ˈpeɪsəʊ/
pilot /ˈpaɪlət/
pizza /ˈpiːtsə/
plan /plæn/
planet /ˈplænɪt/
plural /ˈplʊərəl/
podcast /ˈpɒdˌkɑːst/
polyester /ˌpɒliˈestə/
pony /ˈpəʊni/
poster /ˈpəʊstə/
problem /ˈprɒbləm/
professor /prəˈfesə/
quiz /kwɪz/
radio /ˈreɪdiəʊ/
recycling /riːˈsaɪklɪŋ/
religion /rɪˈlɪdʒn/
reporter /rɪˈpɔːtə/
rest /rest/
restaurant /ˈrestrɒnt/
rose /rəʊz/
sandwich /ˈsænwɪdʒ/
sauerkraut /ˈsaʊəˌkraʊt/
second-hand /ˌsekənd ˈhænd/
selfie /ˈselfi/
shampoo /ʃæmˈpuː/
sherry /ˈʃeri/
shorts /ʃɔːts/
show /ʃəʊ/
signal /ˈsɪgnl/
situation /ˌsɪtʃuˈeɪʃn/
slogan /ˈsləʊgən/
so /səʊ/
softball /ˈsɒftˌbɔːl/
sound check /ˈsaʊnd‿tʃek/
sponsor /ˈspɒnsə/
stand /stænd/
statue /ˈstætʃuː/
status /ˈsteɪtəs/
street art /ˈstriːt‿ɑːt/
stress /stres/
studio /ˈstjuːdiəʊ/
stunt /stʌnt/
surf board /ˈsɜːfbɔːd/
symbol /ˈsɪmbl/
talent /ˈtælənt/
taxi /ˈtæksi/
team, teamwork /tiːm, ˈtiːmˌwɜːk/
terrorist /ˈterərɪst/
text /tekst/
ticket /ˈtɪkɪt/
toast /təʊst/
tour, tourist /tʊə, ˈtʊərɪst/
training /ˈtreɪnɪŋ/
trendsetter /ˈtrendˌsetə/
trifle /ˈtraɪfl/
tube /tjuːb/
unfair /ʌnˈfeə/
uniform /ˈjuːnɪfɔːm/
utensil /juːˈtensl/
verb /vɜːb/
video (clip) /ˈvɪdiəʊ (klɪp)/
vitamin /ˈvɪtəmɪn/
watt /wɒt/
webcode, website /ˈwebˌkəʊd, ˈwebˌsaɪt/
whiteboard /ˈwaɪtˌbɔːd/
zone /zəʊn/

Übersicht über in diesem Buch verwendete Arbeitsanweisungen

Act out the dialogue.	Spielt den Dialog nach.
Add one sentence/some more information.	Füg einen Satz/einige weitere Informationen hinzu.
Add the others' ideas to your section of the placemat.	Füg die Ideen der anderen deinem Bereich des Platzdeckchens hinzu.
Add to it during the project.	Erweitert es während des Projekts.
Agree on one problem that you want to investigate and work on for your project.	Einigt euch auf ein Problem, das ihr untersuchen und an dem ihr für euer Projekt arbeiten wollt.
Answer each other's questions.	Beantwortet einander die Fragen.
Answer the questions using the information in brackets.	Beantworte die Fragen, indem du die in Klammern stehenden Informationen benutzt.
Ask a partner to check your pronunciation.	Bitte einen Partner/eine Partnerin, deine Aussprache zu überprüfen.
Be a language detective.	Sei ein Sprachendetektiv/eine Sprachendetektivin.
Be creative!	Seid kreativ!
Carry out your research.	Führt eure Untersuchungen durch.
Change the tense of the verb in the first action.	Verändere die Zeitform des Verbs in der ersten Handlung.
Check with the LiF.	Überprüf es mit dem LiF.
Check your answers/definitions/lists/phrases/questions/results/sentences/word pairs.	Überprüf deine Antworten/Definitionen/Listen/Ausdrücke/Fragen/Ergebnisse/Sätze/Wortpaare.
Choose a scene/title for each of the six paragraphs/version/one phrase from the song.	Wähl eine Szene/Überschrift für jeden der sechs Absätze/Version/einen Ausdruck aus dem Lied aus.
Choose one of the poems/quotes/situations.	Wählt eines der Gedichte/Zitate/eine der Situationen.
Choose the right question word/statement that you think is the most important.	Such das richtige Fragewort/die Aussage, die deiner Meinung nach am wichtigsten ist, aus.
Close your books.	Schließt eure Bücher.
Collect facts/ideas/information in the table in your workbook/pictures.	Sammle Fakten/Ideen/Informationen in der Tabelle in deinem Arbeitsheft/Bilder.
Comment on the other photos.	Äußere dich zu den anderen Fotos.
Compare in class/with a partner.	Vergleicht in der Klasse/mit einem Partner/einer Partnerin.
Compare your ideas with the definition at the bottom of the page.	Vergleicht eure Ideen mit der Definition am Seitenende.
Complete it using the modal verbs.	Vervollständige es, indem du die Modalverben benutzt.
Complete … with …	Vervollständige … mit …
Concentrate on the most important information.	Konzentriert euch auf die wichtigsten Informationen.
Copy the lists/sentences/table/three pieces of advice.	Schreib die Listen/Sätze/Tabelle/drei Ratschläge ab.
Create a quiz/an action plan/your part of the display.	Erstellt ein Quiz/einen Aktionsplan/euren Teil der Ausstellung.
Decide as a class what you want to include in your display/who does what.	Entscheidet euch als Klasse, was ihr in eure Ausstellung einbeziehen wollt/wer was macht.
Decide on a topic and a product.	Entscheidet euch für ein Thema und ein Produkt.
Decide on the aspects you want to focus on/the best solution.	Entscheidet euch, auf welche Aspekte ihr euch konzentrieren wollt/für die beste Lösung.
Decide whether …/which topic you want to work on.	Entscheide, ob …/an welchem Thema du arbeiten möchtest.
Describe the characters/your everyday life.	Beschreib die Figuren/euren Alltag.
Design a teen magazine.	Entwirf eine Jugendzeitschrift.
Discuss issues from your topic that affect your school, home or community/possible solutions to your problem/the following points.	Besprecht Fragen von eurem Thema, die eure Schule, euer Zuhause oder eure Gemeinde betreffen/mögliche Lösungen für euer Problem/die folgenden Punkte.
Display the map.	Hängt die Karte aus.
Do a class survey in your class.	Mach eine Umfrage in deiner Klasse.
Do some research/your own research online.	Recherchiert/selbst online.
Do the activities/quiz/step …	Macht die Aktivitäten/das Quiz/Schritt …
Don't forget to think about a cover and a table of contents.	Vergesst nicht, an einen Umschlag und ein Inhaltsverzeichnis zu denken.
Draw a picture or symbol to go with it.	Zeichne ein Bild oder Symbol, das dazu passt.

Edit your work.	Bearbeitet eure Arbeit.
Explain the terms in German.	Erklär auf Deutsch die Begriffe.
Fill in the missing words.	Trag die fehlenden Wörter ein.
Find a definition/map/more adverts/more examples/pictures.	Finde eine Definition/Karte/weitere Werbung/weitere Beispiele/Bilder.
Find out about …	Finde etwas über … heraus.
Find out if the statements are right or wrong/if you were right.	Finde heraus, ob die Aussagen richtig oder falsch sind/ob du recht hattest.
Find out who he calls.	Finde heraus, wen er anruft.
Find phrases or chunks/sentences/words.	Finde Ausdrücke oder Wendungen/Sätze/Wörter.
Find the American words for these British English words/matching pairs/the word that rhymes with …/words and expressions in the lyrics that describe…	Finde die amerikanischen Wörter für diese britischen Wörter/die passenden Paare/das Wort, das sich auf … reimt/Wörter und Ausdrücke in dem Liedtext, die … beschreiben.
Get into a group with classmates who want to do the same topic as you.	Kommt in einer Gruppe mit Klassenkameraden/Klassenkameradinnen zusammen, die dasselbe Thema machen wollen wie ihr.
Get into groups of three or four.	Kommt in Dreier- oder Vierergruppen zusammen.
Get together in small groups.	Kommt in Kleingruppen zusammen.
Give a short summary.	Schreib eine kurze Zusammenfassung.
Give each other feedback.	Gebt einander Rückmeldung.
Give reasons.	Gib Gründe an.
Give your presentation.	Haltet eure Präsentation.
Go straight to step …	Geht direkt zu Schritt …
Go to www.diesterweg.de/webcodes.	Geht auf www.diesterweg.de/webcodes.
Have a look at this sentence.	Sieh dir diesen Satz an.
Imagine …	Stell dir vor, …
Inform other group members about what you found out.	Informiert andere Gruppenmitglieder darüber, was ihr herausgefunden habt.
Interview someone from a different generation or someone from a different cultural background.	Befrage jemanden aus einer anderen Generation oder jemanden mit einem anderen kulturellen Hintergrund.
Label …	Beschrifte …
Listen again.	Hört noch einmal zu.
Listen to …	Hör … zu./Hör dir … an.
Listen to the description/end of the story/full film reviews/news reports/other presentations/podcast/report/rest of the conversation/statements/scene.	Hört euch die Beschreibung/das Ende der Geschichte/die vollständigen Filmkritiken/Nachrichtenmeldungen/anderen Präsentationen/den Podcast/Bericht/Rest der Unterhaltung/die Äußerungen/Szene an.
Look at … for help.	Sieh dir zur Hilfe … an.
Look at both versions of the text/page …	Sieh dir beide Versionen des Texts/Seite … an.
Look at the bar chart/picture.	Sieh dir das Balkendiagramm/Bild an.
Look at the map/photos and the boxes below/questions in the speech bubbles/situations in the box/title/works of art.	Sieh dir die Karte/Fotos und die Kästen unten/Fragen in den Sprechblasen/Situationen im Kasten/Überschrift/Kunstwerke an.
Look at the CV/chorus/title and headings of the report on the next page.	Sieh dir den Lebenslauf/Refrain/Titel und die Überschriften des Berichts auf der nächsten Seite an.
Look through the three topics in this Theme.	Sieh durch die drei Themen in diesem Kapitel.
Look up the words in brackets in your German-English dictionary.	Schlag die Wörter in Klammern in deinem Deutsch-Englisch-Wörterbuch nach.
Look up words you don't know.	Schlag Wörter nach, die du nicht kennst.
Make a class display/collage/fact file/freeze-frame/plan/poster.	Macht eine Klassenausstellung/Collage/einen Steckbrief/ein Standbild/einen Plan/ein Poster.
Make a list/word web with … in the middle.	Erstell eine Liste/ein Wortnetz mit … in der Mitte.
Make notes about …/for …	Mach dir Notizen über …/für …
Make sentences.	Bilde Sätze.
Make sure that …	Stellt sicher, dass …
Make two lists.	Mach zwei Listen.
Mark the comparisons.	Markiere die Vergleiche.

Match the photos and the descriptions/questions and answers/responsibilites with the rights.	Ordne die Fotos und die Beschreibungen/Fragen und Antworten/Pflichten und die Rechte einander zu.
Match the sentence parts/words and phrases in the box to the definitions below.	Ordne die Satzteile einander/Wörter und Ausdrücke im Kasten den Definitionen unten zu.
Mill around.	Lauft umher.
Mime it.	Stell es pantomimisch dar.
Plan what you need to do.	Plant, was ihr tun müsst.
Plan your magazine in more detail.	Plant eure Zeitschrift ausführlicher.
Play it to a small group.	Spiel es einer kleinen Gruppe vor.
Practise acting out the scenes/reading it out loud.	Übt, die Szenen nachzuspielen/es laut vorzulesen.
Practise the dialogue/interview several times.	Übt den Dialog/das Vorstellungsgespräch mehrere Male.
Prepare a placemat/presentation.	Bereite ein Platzdeckchen/eine Präsentation vor.
Present your findings/part of the display.	Präsentiert eure Ergebnisse/euren Teil der Ausstellung.
Publish a print or digital edition.	Veröffentlicht eine Druckversion oder eine digitale Version.
Put … in the right place.	Setz … an die richtige Stelle.
Put the magazine together/your pages together to make a brochure.	Stellt die Zeitschrift zusammen/eure Seiten zusammen, um eine Broschüre zu machen.
Put your plan into action.	Setzt euren Plan in die Tat um.
Put your product on the wall.	Hängt euer Produkt an die Wand.
Quote from the text.	Zitiert aus dem Text.
Read about …	Lies über …
Read along.	Lies mit.
Read the blog entries/comments/definition/health warnings/film review/first line of each text/names/nouns/poems/reply.	Lies die Blogeinträge/Kommentare/Definition/Warnhinweise/Filmkritik/erste Zeile jedes Texts/Namen/Hauptwörter/Gedichte/Antwort.
Read the first paragraph/lyrics/report/rest of the story from line … onwards.	Lies den ersten Absatz/Liedtext/Bericht/Rest der Geschichte ab Zeile …
Read the words out loud.	Lies die Wörter laut vor.
Read this flyer/summary/version of …	Lies diesen Flyer/diese Zusammenfassung/Version von …
Record the interview.	Nimm das Vorstellungsgespräch auf.
Remember the rules for reported speech.	Denk an die Regeln für die indirekte Rede.
Repeat the plural nouns/words in the box.	Wiederhol die Hauptwörter im Plural/Wörter im Kasten.
Replace the marked word in each sentence with …	Ersetze die markierten Wörter in jedem Satz mit …
Reply to …	Antworte auf …
Report the advice to a friend.	Berichte den Ratschlag einem Freund/einer Freundin.
Report the questions.	Gib die Fragen wieder.
Research the problem/your topic.	Recherchiert das Problem/euer Thema.
Say what advice the person gives him/which of the two people is American and which is British.	Sag, welchen Rat ihm die Person gibt/welcher der beiden Menschen amerikanisch und welcher britisch ist.
Scan the text for reasons for migration.	Such den Text nach Gründen für Migration ab.
Share your answers/ideas/notes.	Teilt eure Antworten/Ideen/Notizen.
Show your brochure or guide to	Zeigt … eure Broschüre oder euren Reiseführer.
Skim the information/text.	Überflieg die Informationen/den Text.
Sort the reasons for migration into two lists.	Sortiert die Gründe für Migration in zwei Listen.
Split the class into four groups.	Teilt die Klasse in vier Gruppen ein.
Split up your group so that different people explore different texts.	Teilt eure Gruppe auf, sodass verschiedene Leute verschiedene Texte untersuchen.
Start a wordbank for your topic.	Fangt ein Wortfeld für euer Thema an.
Swap with a partner.	Tauscht mit einem Partner/einer Partnerin.
Take a look at …	Sieh dir … an.
Take a map of the world.	Nimm eine Weltkarte.
Take a selfie or photo.	Mach ein Selfie oder Foto.
Take notes on at least four of the following questions/the following points/the questions.	Mach dir zu mindestens vier der folgenden Fragen/den folgenden Punkten/den Fragen Notizen.
Take turns.	Wechselt euch ab.
Talk about a film you have seen/the characters.	Redet über einen Film, den ihr gesehen habt/die Figuren.
Talk about the problem/project/your findings.	Sprecht über das Problem/Projekt/eure Ergebnisse.
Talk to …	Sprich mit …

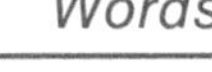

Tell a partner the most important facts in English/German/which comments you like best.	Erzähl einem Partner/einer Partnerin die wichtigsten Tatsachen auf Englisch/Deutsch/welche Kommentare dir am besten gefallen.
Tell him or her in your own words what the article says.	Sag ihm oder ihr in deinen eigenen Worten, was in dem Artikel steht.
Think about a cover and a title.	Denkt über einen Einband und eine Überschrift nach.
Think about her feelings, hopes, fears, ...	Denk an ihre Gefühle, Hoffnungen, Ängste, ...
Think about how you would say the sentences in German.	Denk darüber nach, wie du die Sätze auf Deutsch sagen würdest.
Think about research, writing texts, finding or drawing pictures, ...	Denkt über Recherche, das Schreiben von Texten, das Finden oder Zeichnen von Bildern, ... nach.
Think about the number of immigrants, their homelands, journeys, languages, ...	Denkt über die Zahl der Einwanderer, ihre Heimatländer, Reisen, Sprachen, ... nach.
Think of a question you can ask the class at the end of your presentation.	Denkt euch eine Frage aus, die ihr der Klasse am Ende eurer Präsentation stellen könnt.
Think of a title for the poem you read.	Denk dir eine Überschrift für das Gedicht aus, das du gelesen hast.
Think of reasons why ...	Denkt an Gründe, warum ...
Think up a different title for the story.	Denk dir eine andere Überschrift für die Geschichte aus.
Turn the placemat.	Dreh das Platzdeckchen.
Type in the webcode of your topic.	Tippt den Webcode eures Themas ein.
Underline the part of each sentence that tells you what happened first/syllables that are stressed/past perfect form.	Unterstreich den Teil von jedem Satz, der dir sagt, was zuerst passiert ist/die Silben, die betont sind/die Form des Plusquamperfekt.
Unscramble the chat-up lines/facts/following sentences/words.	Ordne die Anmachsprüche/Tatsachen/folgenden Sätze/Wörter.
Use a dictionary/the phrases and chunks from .../ the verbs in the box/ these phrases/your answers/your imagination/notes.	Benutz ein Wörterbuch/die Ausdrücke und Wendungen aus .../die Verben im Kasten/ diese Ausdrücke/deine Antworten/Vorstellungskraft/Notizen.
Use a dictionary for help.	Benutz ein Wörterbuch, wenn du Hilfe brauchst.
Use adjectives/adverbs/the phrases/webcode.	Benutz Adjektive/Adverbien/die Ausdrücke/den Webcode.
Use the words in brackets to join the two actions.	Verwende die Wörter in Klammern, um die zwei Handlungen zu verbinden.
Watch the interview/video clip.	Sieh dir das Interview/den Videoclip an.
Work alone, in pairs or in groups.	Arbeitet alleine, paarweise oder in Gruppen.
Work on your part of the magazine/presentation.	Arbeitet an eurem Teil der Zeitschrift/eurer Präsentation.
Work out how many points you scored.	Errechne, wie viele Punkte du erzielt hast.
Write a dialogue/diary entry/letter/short blog comment/text/a few different examples.	Schreib einen Dialog/Tagebucheintrag/Brief/kurzen Blogkommentar/Text/ein paar verschiedene Beispiele.
Write a list of the contents on the board/short film review/summary/text message.	Schreibt eine Liste der Inhalte an die Tafel/kurze Filmkritik/Zusammenfassung/SMS.
Write about the bar chart/characters/situation.	Schreib über das Balkendiagramm/die Figuren/Situation.
Write down at least four questions/everything it makes you think of.	Schreib mindestens vier Fragen/alles, an das es dich denken lässt, auf.
Write down his activities in order.	Schreib seine Aktivitäten in einer Reihenfolge auf.
Write down how you feel and why.	Schreib auf, wie du dich fühlst und warum.
Write down key phrases for each paragraph.	Schreibt euch wesentliche Ausdrücke für jeden Absatz auf.
Write down questions you would like to ask your character.	Schreib Fragen auf, die du deiner Figur gern stellen würdest.
Write down similar sentences/what .../your conversation/opinion.	Schreib ähnliche Sätze/was .../dein Gespräch/deine Meinung auf.
Write down the letters that you choose for each question/them down next to the question.	Schreib die Buchstaben auf, die du für jede Frage wählst/sie neben der Frage auf.
Write down the two lines in the poem that reflect his opinion/tips for pupils starting work experience.	Schreib die zwei Zeilen im Gedicht auf, die seine Meinung zum Ausdruck bringen/Tipps auf für Schüler/Schülerinnen, die ihr Praktikum beginnen.
Write sentences/statements/thought or speech bubbles.	Schreib Sätze/Aussagen/Gedanken- oder Sprechblasen.
Write the words in the correct list.	Schreib die Wörter in die richtige Liste.

Numbers

0 oh, zero, nil /əʊ, ˈzɪərəʊ, nɪl/
1 one /wʌn/
2 two /tuː/
3 three /θriː/
4 four /fɔː/
5 five /faɪv/
6 six /sɪks/
7 seven /sevn/
8 eight /eɪt/
9 nine /naɪn/
10 ten /ten/
11 eleven /ɪˈlevn/
12 twelve /twelv/
13 thirteen /ˌθɜːˈtiːn/
14 fourteen /ˌfɔːˈtiːn/
15 fifteen /ˌfɪfˈtiːn/
16 sixteen /ˌsɪksˈtiːn/
17 seventeen /ˌsevnˈtiːn/
18 eighteen /ˌeɪˈtiːn/
19 nineteen /ˌnaɪnˈtiːn/
20 twenty /ˈtwenti/
21 twenty-one /ˌtwentiˈwʌn/
22 twenty-two /ˌtwentiˈtuː/
30 thirty /ˈθɜːti/
33 thirty-three /ˌθɜːtiˈθriː/
34 thirty-four /ˌθɜːtiˈfɔː/
40 forty /ˈfɔːti/
45 forty-five /ˌfɔːtiˈfaɪv/
50 fifty /ˈfɪfti/
56 fifty-six /ˌfɪftiˈsɪks/
60 sixty /ˈsɪksti/
67 sixty-seven /ˌsɪkstiˈsevn/
70 seventy /ˈsevnti/
78 seventy-eight /ˌsevntiˈeɪt/
80 eighty /ˈeɪti/
89 eighty-nine /ˌeɪtiˈnaɪn/
90 ninety /ˈnaɪnti/
100 a/one hundred /ə/wʌn ˈhʌndrəd/
101 one hundred and one /wʌn ˌhʌndrəd‿ən ˈwʌn/
102 one hundred and two /wʌn ˌhʌndrəd‿ən ˈtuː/
110 one hundred and ten /wʌn ˌhʌndrəd‿ən ˈten/
200 two hundred /tuː ˈhʌndrəd/

1,000 a/one thousand /ə/wʌn ˈθauznd/
1,001 one thousand and one /wʌn ˌθauznd‿ən ˈwʌn/
1,111 one thousand one hundred and eleven /wʌn ˌθauznd wʌn ˌhʌndrəd‿ən‿ɪˈlevn/
2,000 two thousand /tuː ˈθauznd/
10,000 ten thousand /ten ˈθauznd/
100,000 a/one hundred thousand /ə/wʌn ˌhʌndrəd ˈθauznd/
1,000,000 a/one million /ə/wʌn ˈmiljən/
1,000,000,000 a/one billion /ə/wʌn ˈbiljən/

1st first /fɜːst/
2nd second /ˈsekənd/
3rd third /θɜːd/
4th fourth /fɔːθ/
5th fifth /fɪfθ/
6th sixth /sɪksθ/
7th seventh /ˈsevnθ/
8th eighth /eɪtθ/
9th ninth /naɪnθ/
10th tenth /tenθ/
11th eleventh /ɪˈlevnθ/
12th twelfth /twelfθ/
13th thirteenth /ˌθɜːˈtiːnθ/
14th fourteenth /ˌfɔːˈtiːnθ/
15th fifteenth /ˌfɪfˈtiːnθ/
16th sixteenth /ˌsɪksˈtiːnθ/
17th seventeenth /ˌsevnˈtiːnθ/
18th eighteenth /ˌeɪˈtiːnθ/
19th nineteenth /ˌnaɪnˈtiːnθ/
20th twentieth /ˈtwentiəθ/
21st twenty-first /ˌtwentiˈfɜːst/
22nd twenty-second /ˌtwentiˈsekənd/
23rd twenty-third /ˌtwentiˈθɜːd/

30th thirtieth /ˈθɜːtiəθ/
40th fortieth /ˈfɔːtiəθ/
50th fiftieth /ˈfɪftiəθ/
60th sixtieth /ˈsɪkstiəθ/
70th seventieth /ˈsevntiəθ/
80th eightieth /ˈeɪtiəθ/
90th ninetieth /ˈnaɪntiəθ/
100th hundredth /ˈhʌndrədθ/

$\frac{1}{2}$ a/one half /ə/wʌn ˈhaːf/
$\frac{1}{3}$ a/one third /ə/wʌn ˈθɜːd/
$\frac{1}{4}$ a/one quarter /ə/wʌn ˈkwɔːtə/
$\frac{1}{8}$ a/one eighth /ə/wʌn‿ˈeɪtθ/
$\frac{3}{4}$ three quarters /θriː ˈkwɔːtəz/

Months

January /ˈdʒænjuəri/	Januar	July /dʒʊˈlaɪ/	Juli
February /ˈfebruəri/	Februar	August /ˈɔːgəst/	August
March /maːtʃ/	März	September /sepˈtembə/	September
April /ˈeɪprəl/	April	October /ɒkˈtəʊbə/	Oktober
May /meɪ/	Mai	November /nəʊˈvembə/	November
June /dʒuːn/	Juni	December /dɪˈsembə/	Dezember

Quiz

lots /lɒts/	viel, jede Menge	
correct /kəˈrekt/	richtig, korrekt	*correct* = right
make *(irr)* /meɪk/	*hier:* ergeben	
state /steɪt/	(Bundes)staat	The *capital* is the city where a country has its government.
capital /ˈkæpɪtl/	Hauptstadt	
president /ˈprezɪdənt/	Präsident/in; Vorsitzende/r	
ranger /ˈreɪndʒə/	(Park)aufseher/in	
most important /ˌməʊst‿ɪmˈpɔːtnt/	wichtigste(r, s)	important → more important → *most important*
American /əˈmerɪkən/	Amerikaner/in; amerikanisch	
award /əˈwɔːd/	Preis, Auszeichnung	
holiday /ˈhɒlɪdeɪ/	*hier:* Feiertag	
Thanksgiving /ˈθæŋksˌɡɪvɪŋ/	Thanksgiving *(amerikanisches Erntedankfest)*	*Thanksgiving* is an *American holiday.*
Independence Day /ˌɪndɪˈpendəns deɪ/	Unabhängigkeitstag	
Pancake Day /ˈpænkeɪk deɪ/	Pfannkuchentag	
the Statue of Liberty /ðə ˌstætʃu‿əv ˈlɪbəti/	Freiheitsstatue	
the very first /ðə ˌveri ˈfɜːst/	der/die/das allererste	
Africa /ˈæfrɪkə/	Afrika	
Asia /ˈeɪʒə/	Asien	
Australia /ɒˈstreɪliə/	Australien	
(the) US (= United States) /ðə ˌju‿ˈes, juːˌnaɪtɪd ˈsteɪts/	US, Vereinigte Staaten (von Amerika); US-	
the Nobel Peace Prize /ðə nəʊˌbel ˈpiːs praɪz/	Friedensnobelpreis	
peace /piːs/	Frieden	
African American /ˌæfrɪkən‿əˈmerɪkən/	Afroamerikaner/in; afroamerikanisch	
flag /flæɡ/	Fahne, Flagge	
moccasin /ˈmɒkəsɪn/	Mokassin	
kayak /ˈkaɪæk/	Kajak	
Native American /ˌneɪtɪv‿əˈmerɪkən/	amerikanische/r Ureinwohner/in	
language /ˈlæŋɡwɪdʒ/	Sprache	
European /ˌjʊərəˈpiːən/	Europäer/in; europäisch	
stand for /ˈstænd fɔː/	für etwas stehen	
bake /beɪk/	backen	They *have* just *baked* a cake.
dealer /ˈdiːlə/	Händler/in; *hier:* Verhandlungsführer/in	
police department /pəˈliːs dɪˌpɑːtmənt/	Polizeidienststelle	
popular /ˈpɒpjələ/	beliebt	Ice cream is a *popular* dessert. Lots of people like it.
disco /ˈdɪskəʊ/	Disko	

Nur zehn Minuten
Übe die Vokabeln immer nur fünf bis zehn Minuten, dafür aber oft und regelmäßig! Das ist viel wirkungsvoller, als selten eine ganze Stunde zu üben.

This is the *flag* of the *United States*.

They *have* just *baked* a cake.

Super Bowl /'suːpə bəʊl/	*Finale der US-amerikan. American Football-Profiliga*	
cooking /'kʊkɪŋ/	Kochen; Koch-	

Theme 1

I	travel blog /'trævl blɒg/	Reiseblog	Especially on the first day of a new job you want to make a good *impression*.
	tip /tɪp/	Tipp	
	impression /ɪm'preʃn/	Eindruck	

A1

What comes to mind when you think of the USA?	Was fällt dir ein, wenn du an die USA denkst?
Look at the map at the front of the book.	Sieh dir die Karte vorne im Buch an.

	south /saʊθ/	Süden	
	centre /'sentə/	Zentrum, Mitte	I live in the town *centre*.
A2	secondary school /'sekəndri skuːl/	weiterführende Schule	
	subject /'sʌbdʒɪkt/	*hier:* Betreff	
	luckily /'lʌkɪli/	zum Glück, glücklicherweise	
	grade *(AE)* /greɪd/	Klasse	
	form /fɔːm/	Klasse	
	instead of /ɪn'sted‿əv/	anstatt	
	be like *(informal)* /ˌbiː 'laɪk/	*hier etwa:* sagen	
	enjoy oneself /ɪn'dʒɔɪ wʌnˌself/	sich amüsieren	They really *enjoyed themselves* at the zoo.
	email /'iːmeɪl/	mailen	
	you guys *(informal)* /'juː gaɪz/	ihr, euch	

Collect information about his high school.	Sammle Informationen über seine Highschool.
Take notes about Bill's new schedule.	Mach dir über Bills neuen Stundenplan Notizen.

schedule *(AE)* /'skeˌdʒul, 'ʃedjuːl/	*hier:* Stundenplan	*schedule (AE)* = timetable *(BE)*
period *(AE)* /'pɪəriəd/	Stunde	
computer science /kəmˌpjuːtə 'saɪəns/	Informatik	
math *(AE, informal)* /mæθ/	Mathe *(Schulfach)*	
social studies /'səʊʃl ˌstʌdiz/	*Schulfach, das unter anderem Erdkunde, Geschichte, Soziologie umfasst*	He is learning *Spanish* because he is going on holiday to Spain.
Spanish /'spænɪʃ/	Spanisch	

Words

study hall /ˈstʌdi hɔːl/	*Freistunde zur Stillbeschäftigung*	to *study* = to learn about a subject by going to school or university
study /ˈstʌdi/	studieren; lernen	
student *(AE)* /ˈstjuːdnt/	Schüler/in; Student/in	
laugh oneself silly *(informal)* /ˌlɑːf ˌwʌnself ˈsɪli/	sich kaputtlachen	
soccer /ˈsɒkə/	Fußball	
score /skɔː/	Punktestand	
gee *(AE, informal)* /dʒiː/	Wahnsinn, Mannomann	
shock /ʃɒk/	Schock	
make something *(informal)* /ˈmeɪk ˌsʌmθɪŋ/	etwas schaffen; *hier:* sich qualifizieren	
football /ˈfʊtˌbɔːl/	*hier:* American Football	 He dreams of a *career* as a football player.
career /kəˈrɪə/	Karriere, Laufbahn	
while /waɪl/	Weile	
team spirit /ˌtiːm ˈspɪrɪt/	Teamgeist	

> Write down at least four questions. — Schreib mindestens vier Fragen auf.

A3

detective /dɪˈtektɪv/	Detektiv/in	

> What do you notice? — Was fällt dir auf?
> Can you find a pattern? — Kannst du ein Muster finden?
> Complete the sentences with the words from the box. — Vervollständige die Sätze mit den Wörtern aus dem Kasten.

himself /hɪmˈself/	sich; sich selbst	
herself /həˈself/	sich; sich selbst	
ourselves /aʊəˈselvz/	uns; wir selbst	
themselves /ðəmˈselvz/	sich; sie selbst	
make somebody do something /ˌmeɪk ˌsʌmbədi ˈduː ˌsʌmθɪŋ/	jemanden dazu bringen, etwas zu tun	
guys *(pl, informal)* /gaɪz/	Leute	 They are preparing a *farewell party* for a friend.
farewell party /feəˈwel ˌpɑːti/	Abschiedsfeier	

A4

> Copy the table and fill it in. — Schreib die Tabelle ab und füll sie aus.

athlete /ˈæθliːt/	Athlet/in	
represent /ˌreprɪˈzent/	präsentieren, vertreten	
community /kəˈmjuːnəti/	Gemeinde, Gemeinschaft	
take place /ˌteɪk ˈpleɪs/	stattfinden	
diamond /ˈdaɪəmənd/	*Spielfeld im Baseball*	
contact somebody /ˈkɒntækt ˌsʌmbədi/	sich mit jemandem in Verbindung setzen	 *Chess* can be a very long game.
chess /tʃes/	Schach	

bring together /ˌbrɪŋ təˈgeðə/	zusammenbringen	
skill /skɪl/	Fähigkeit, Geschick	
discipline /ˈdɪsəplɪn/	Disziplin	
sportsmanship /ˈspɔːtsmənʃɪp/	Fairness	A *variety* is a number of people or things that are all different from one another.
variety /vəˈraɪəti/	Vielfalt	
food science /ˈfuːd ˌsaɪəns/	*hier:* Ernährungswissenschaft	
development /dɪˈveləpmənt/	Entwicklung	
creation /kriˈeɪʃn/	(Er)schaffung	

Do you have the same or similar clubs at your school?	Hast du in deiner Schule dieselben oder ähnliche AGs?
A5 Find out if the statements are right or wrong.	Finde heraus, ob die Aussagen richtig oder falsch sind.

similar /ˈsɪmɪlə/	ähnlich	
yard /jaːd/	*hier:* Yard *(Maßeinheit)*	
touchdown /ˈtʌtʃˌdaʊn/	Versuch, Touchdown	You often hear *chants* at football games.
point /pɔɪnt/	Punkt	
A6 **support** /səˈpɔːt/	(unter)stützen	
chant /tʃaːnt/	Sprechgesang	
field /fiːld/	Feld	
stick /stɪk/	Schläger	
soft /sɒft/	weich	*soft* ≠ hard
wrestling /ˈreslɪŋ/	Ringkampf	
pin /pɪn/	*hier:* drücken	
ground /graʊnd/	Boden	
net /net/	Netz	

Match the photos and the descriptions.	Ordne die Fotos und die Beschreibungen einander zu.

A7 turkey /ˈtɜːki/	Truthahn, Pute	
pumpkin /ˈpʌmpkɪn/	Kürbis	
pie /paɪ/	Pastete, Kuchen	
French fries *(AE, pl)* /ˌfrentʃ ˈfraɪz/	Pommes frites	
totally /ˈtəʊtli/	völlig, total	
organic /ɔːˈgænɪk/	*hier:* aus biologischem Anbau	
farmers' market /ˈfaːməz ˌmaːkɪt/	Bauernmarkt	Vegetables are really fresh at the *farmers' market*.
traditional /trəˈdɪʃnəl/	traditionell	
meat loaf /ˌmiːt ˈləʊf/	Hackbraten	
settler /ˈsetlə/	Siedler/in	
that way /ˈðæt weɪ/	so, auf diese Weise	

like that /ˌlaɪk ˈðæt/	so	
background /ˈbækˌgraʊnd/	Hintergrund	
Italy /ˈɪtəli/	Italien	*Italy* is famous for its *pasta*.
pasta /ˈpæstə/	Nudeln	
in my opinion /ɪn ˈmaɪ‿əˌpɪnjən/	meiner Meinung nach	

A8 Make a word web. — Erstell ein Wortnetz.

A9 anyone /ˈeniˌwʌn/	jede(r, s), (irgend)jemand
date /deɪt/	datieren
beginning /bɪˈgɪnɪŋ/	Anfang; Beginn
the Declaration of Independence /ðə ˌdekləˌreɪʃn‿əv ‿ˌɪndɪˈpendəns/	*die Unabhängigkeitserklärung der USA*
man (*pl* men) /mæn, men/	Mensch
create /kriˈeɪt/	erschaffen, erzeugen
equal /ˈiːkwəl/	gleich
right /raɪt/	Recht
liberty /ˈlɪbəti/	Freiheit
pursuit of /pəˈsjuːt‿əv/	Streben nach
happiness /ˈhæpinəs/	Glück; Zufriedenheit
judge /dʒʌdʒ/	(be)urteilen, (ein)schätzen
distance /ˈdɪstəns/	Distanz, Entfernung
reality /riˈæləti/	Realität, Wirklichkeit
nightmare /ˈnaɪtˌmeə/	Albtraum
realize (= realise) /ˈrɪəlʌɪz/	*hier:* verwirklichen
human /ˈhjuːmən/	menschlich
maximize /ˈmæksɪmaɪz/	maximieren
minimum wage /ˌmɪnɪməm ˈweɪdʒ/	Mindestlohn
A10 **culture** /ˈkʌltʃə/	Kultur

Vokabelspiel
Teilt euch in zwei Gruppen auf. Für die jeweils andere Gruppe schreibt ihr zehn Wörter mit dem gleichen Anfangsbuchstaben auf. Eure Gegenspieler/Gegenspielerinnen sollen diese Wörter nun möglichst schnell alphabetisch ordnen. Welche Gruppe ist die schnellste?
Sammelt um die Wette Wörter nach bestimmten Kriterien, z. B. zusammengesetzte Wörter, Wörter mit Doppelvokalen oder Doppelkonsonanten, oder Wörter mit einer bestimmten Buchstabenzahl.
Gebt euren Gegenspielern/Gegenspielerinnen einige Wörter vor und lasst sie herausfinden, auf welcher Seite im Words-Teil sie stehen. Zu welchen Wörtern können sie den Gegensatz nennen? Gibt es bei Substantiven passende Verben oder Adjektive dazu?

You are going to give a presentation about life in the USA.	Ihr werdet eine Präsentation über das Leben in den USA halten.
Get into small groups and decide on a topic and a product.	Kommt in kleinen Gruppen zusammen und entscheidet euch für ein Thema und ein Produkt.

fact file /ˈfækt faɪl/	Steckbrief	
license plate *(AE)* /ˈlaɪsns pleɪt/	Nummernschild	
starting point /ˈstɑːtɪŋ pɔɪnt/	Ausgangspunkt	
inhabitant /ɪnˈhæbɪtənt/	Einwohner/in, Bewohner/in	They are *inhabitants* of the same city.
presentation /ˌpreznˈteɪʃn/	Präsentation, Vortrag	

Words

Research your topics and collect information and pictures.	Recherchiert eure Themen und sammelt Informationen und Bilder.
Give your presentation in class.	Haltet eure Präsentation in der Klasse.
Give each other feedback.	Gebt einander Rückmeldung.

P1	explain /ɪk'spleɪn/	erklären	The teacher *explained* to the class how to do a presentation.
P2	reflexive /rɪ'fleksɪv/	reflexiv, rückbezüglich	

	Decide whether you need a word from the green box or the yellow box to complete the sentences.	Entscheide, ob du ein Wort aus dem grünen oder dem gelben Kasten brauchst, um die Sätze zu vervollständigen.
	Complete the sentences with words from the box.	Vervollständige die Sätze mit Wörtern aus dem Kasten.
P3	Look up the words in brackets in your German-English dictionary.	Schlag die Wörter in Klammern in deinem Deutsch-Englisch-Wörterbuch nach.
	Then complete the sentences.	Vervollständige dann die Sätze.
P4	Unscramble the words and write them down.	Ordne die Wörter und schreib sie auf.
	Check your words and repeat them.	Überprüf deine Wörter und wiederhole sie.
P5	Unscramble the sentences.	Ordne die Sätze.

	California /ˌkælə'fɔːniə/	Kalifornien	
	known /nəʊn/	bekannt	
	surfing /'sɜːfɪŋ/	Surfen	*surfing*
P6	stand up paddleboarding /ˌstænd‿ʌp 'pædlbɔːdɪŋ/	Stehpaddeln	
	exchange student /ɪks'tʃeɪndʒ ˌstjuːdnt/	Austauschschüler/in	

P7	Listen to the words and repeat them.	Hör dir die Wörter an und wiederhol sie.

B1	glimpse /ɡlɪmps/	flüchtiger Blick

What is your first impression of New York?	Was ist dein erster Eindruck von New York?

B2	post /pəʊst/	posten, bekannt geben	
	take somebody on a tour /ˌteɪk ˌsʌmbədi‿ɒn‿ə 'tʊə/	mit jemandem einen Ausflug machen	
	up close /ʌp 'kləʊs/	aus der Nähe	*highlight* = the most exciting part of an event
	highlight /'haɪˌlaɪt/	Höhepunkt	
	immigrant /'ɪmɪɡrənt/	Einwanderer/in, Immigrant/in	
	severe /sɪ'vɪə/	schlimm, stark	*severe* = very bad
	physical /'fɪzɪkl/	körperlich	
	yellow cab *(AE)* /'jeləʊ kæb/	Taxi	

avenue /ˈævəˌnjuː/	Boulevard, Allee, Straße	She made a *comment* about the weather. = She said something about the weather.
joke /dʒəʊk/	scherzen, Spaß machen	
comment /ˈkɒment/	Kommentar, Bemerkung	
French /frentʃ/	Franzose/Französin; französisch	
care /keə/	sich kümmern um, achten auf; Zuneigung fühlen	There are lots of *skyscrapers* in New York. 
skyscraper /ˈskaɪˌskreɪpə/	Wolkenkratzer	
elevator *(AE)* /ˈeləveɪtə/	Aufzug	
to the top /tʊ ðə ˈtɒp/	nach oben	
view /vjuː/	(Aus)sicht	
up there /ˌʌp ˈðeə/	dort oben	to *complain* = to say that you are not happy with something
complain /kəmˈpleɪn/	sich beklagen	
floor /flɔː/	*hier:* Stockwerk	
step /step/	Stufe; Schritt	
imagine /ɪˈmædʒɪn/	sich etwas vorstellen	
downtown *(AE)* /ˌdaʊnˈtaʊn/	in der Innenstadt, im Zentrum	If you are *jealous*, you are unhappy because someone has something that you would like to have.
film /fɪlm/	drehen, filmen	
movie *(AE)* /ˈmuːvi/	Film	
jealous /ˈdʒeləs/	eifersüchtig, neidisch	

B3

Look at the maps at the back of the book.	Sieh dir die Karten hinten im Buch an.
Read the blog and the comments again.	Lies den Blog und die Kommentare noch einmal.
Write down his activities in order.	Schreib seine Aktivitäten in einer Reihenfolge auf.

B4

What do the words 'one' and 'ones' stand for in these sentences?	Wofür stehen die Wörter *‚one'* und *‚ones'* in diesen Sätzen?
Find more examples.	Finde weitere Beispiele.

cab *(AE)* /kæb/	Taxi

Copy the sentences and complete them with 'one' or 'ones'.	Schreib die Sätze ab und vervollständige sie mit *‚one'* oder *‚ones'*.

case /keɪs/	*hier:* Hülle	
normally /ˈnɔːmli/	normalerweise	
Chinatown /ˈtʃaɪnəˌtaʊn/	Chinesenviertel	*'Big Apple'* is a nickname for New York.
Big Apple /ˌbɪg‿ˈæpl/	*Spitzname für New York*	
B5 borough /ˈbʌrə/	Verwaltungsbezirk; *hier:* Stadtteil	

Find the boroughs on the map at the back of the book.	Finde die Stadtbezirke auf der Karte hinten im Buch.

apartment *(AE)* /ə'pɑ:tmənt/	Wohnung	
north /nɔ:θ/	Norden	
truck /trʌk/	Lastwagen	
hardly /'hɑ:dli/	kaum	
stadium /'steɪdiəm/	Stadion	*stadium*
park /pɑ:k/	parken	
parking lot *(AE)* /'pɑ:kɪŋ lɒt/	Parkplatz	
somebody /'sʌmbədi/	jemand, irgendwer	*somebody* = someone
the best /ðə 'best/	der/die/das beste	
grow up /ˌgrəʊ‿'ʌp/	*hier:* aufwachsen	
high school *(AE)* /'haɪ sku:l/	Highschool, weiterführende Schule	
latest /'leɪtɪst/	neueste(r, s)	
sneaker *(AE)* /'sni:kə/	Turnschuh	This is a *sneaker*.
special /'speʃl/	*hier:* besonders, speziell	
neighborhood *(AE)* /'neɪbəˌhʊd/	Viertel, Nachbarschaft	
washroom *(AE)* /'wɒʃˌru:m/	Toilette	It is very *busy* in town today. There are a lot of people and cars.
tiny /'taɪni/	winzig	
busy /'bɪzi/	belebt; verkehrsreich	
mostly /'məʊstli/	meistens	
South America /ˌsaʊθ‿ə'merɪkə/	Südamerika	A lot of people speak Spanish in *South America*.
the Caribbean /ðə ˌkærɪ'biən/	Karibik, karibische Inseln	
reputation /ˌrepjʊ'teɪʃn/	Ruf	
high /haɪ/	hoch	
crime rate /'kraɪm reɪt/	Kriminalitätsrate	
favorite *(AE)* /'feɪvrət/	Liebling; Lieblings-	
ringtone /'rɪŋˌtəʊn/	Klingelton	*cellphone (AE)* = mobile phone *(BE)* 
cellphone *(AE)* /'sel fəʊn/	Handy	
mom *(AE)* /mɒm/	Mama	
shop /ʃɒp/	einkaufen	
quiet /'kwaɪət/	leise; ruhig	
club /klʌb/	*hier:* Club, Diskothek	A *flat* is a number of rooms for living in.
flat /flæt/	Wohnung	
lorry /'lɒri/	Lastwagen	
car park /'kɑ: pɑ:k/	Parkplatz	
city centre /ˌsɪti 'sentə/	Innenstadt	
lift /lɪft/	Aufzug	

Find phrases or chunks that show how the people feel about their borough.	Finde Ausdrücke oder Wendungen, die zeigen, was die Leute von ihrem Stadtbezirk halten.
B6 Complete the following sentences.	Vervollständige die folgenden Sätze.
B7 Swap and do the quizzes.	Tauscht und macht euer Quiz.
Find out about a TV show set in New York.	Finde etwas über eine Fernsehshow heraus, die in New York spielt.

Words

B8	voice /vɔɪs/	Stimme	
	siren /ˈsaɪrən/	Sirene	
	all around /ˌɔːl‿əˈraʊnd/	überall	*all around* = everywhere
	mean *(AE)* /miːn/	aggressiv, gefährlich	
	marquee *(AE)* /mɑːˈkiː/	Markise, Vordach	Achtung! Manche Wörter haben im amerikanischen und britischen Englisch unterschiedliche Bedeutungen: *‚mean‘* beispielsweise bedeutet ‚aggressiv, gefährlich‘ im amerikanischen Englisch und ‚gemein‘ oder ‚geizig‘ im britischen Englisch.
	ain't (= am/are/is not) *(informal)* /eɪnt/	nicht sein	
	chorus (*pl* choruses) /ˈkɔːrəs, ˈkɔːrəsɪz/	Refrain	
	concrete jungle /ˌkɒŋkriːt ˈdʒʌŋgl/	Betonwüste	
	brand-new /ˌbrænd ˈnjuː/	brandneu	
	inspire /ɪnˈspaɪə/	inspirieren	
	curfew /ˈkɜːfjuː/	Ausgangssperre	
	melting pot /ˈmeltɪŋ pɒt/	Schmelztiegel	
	rock *(informal)* /rɒk/	*hier:* Crack *(Rauschgift)*	
	preacher /ˈpriːtʃə/	Geistliche/r, Prediger/in	When you *pray* to *God*, you speak to *God*, usually to ask for help or give thanks.
	pray /preɪ/	beten	
	God (= god) /gɒd/	Gott	
	hail /heɪl/	*hier:* rufen	
	gypsy cab *(informal)* /ˈdʒɪpsi kæb/	*illegales Taxi*	
	gonna (= going to) *(informal)* /ˈgʌnə, ˈgəʊɪŋ tʊ/	werden	
	by any means /ˌbaɪ‿ˌeni ˈmiːnz/	auf jeden Fall	*by any means* = for sure
	lighter /ˈlaɪtə/	Feuerzeug	The *lyrics* are the words of a song.
	lyrics *(pl)* /ˈlɪrɪks/	Liedtext	

	Find words and expressions in the lyrics that describe the city and the people.	Finde Wörter und Ausdrücke in dem Liedtext, die die Stadt und die Menschen beschreiben.
B9	Take notes.	Mach dir Notizen.
	What is her first impression?	Was ist ihr erster Eindruck?

B10	rain /reɪn/	regnen
	review /rɪˈvjuː/	Kritik, Rezension

	Think about a cover and a title, too.	Denkt auch über einen Einband und eine Überschrift nach.
	Think about research, writing texts, finding or drawing pictures, …	Denkt über Recherche, das Schreiben von Texten, das Finden oder Zeichnen von Bildern, … nach.
 P9	Copy these sentences and replace the marked word in each sentence with 'one' or 'ones'.	Schreib diese Sätze ab und ersetze die markierten Wörter in jedem Satz mit *‚one‘* oder *‚ones‘*.
 P10	Complete the sentences with 'one' or 'ones'.	Vervollständige die Sätze mit *‚one‘* oder *‚ones‘*.

	especially /ɪˈspeʃli/	besonders, vor allem	
P12	Look at the maps at the back of the book and complete the sentences.	Sieh dir die Karten hinten im Buch an und vervollständige die Sätze.	
	Write down similar sentences for a partner.	Schreib ähnliche Sätze für einen Partner/eine Partnerin auf.	
	Take turns.	Wechselt euch ab.	
P14	accent /ˈæksnt/	Akzent	
	Listen to these statements.	Hör dir diese Aussagen an.	
	For each scene, say which of the two people is American and which is British.	Sag für jede Szene, welcher der beiden Menschen amerikanisch und welcher britisch ist.	

Theme 2

I	**challenge** /ˈtʃæləndʒ/	Herausforderung	
	all over the world /ˌɔːl‿ˌəʊvə ðə ˈwɜːld/	auf der ganzen Welt	
	schoolwork /ˈskuːlˌwɜːk/	Schularbeiten	
	take a look at /ˌteɪk‿ə ˈlʊk‿ət/	sich ansehen	
	youth /juːθ/	Jugend; Jugendliche/r	
	helpline /ˈhelpˌlaɪn/	*telefonischer Beratungsdienst*	
	land diving /ˈlænd‿ˌdaɪvɪŋ/	*Lianenspringen*	
A1	go out with somebody /ˌɡəʊ‿ˈaʊt wɪð ˌsʌmbədi/	mit jemandem ausgehen	
	smoking /ˈsməʊkɪŋ/	Rauchen	
	elderly /ˈeldəli/	ältere(r, s)	

This boy is helping the *elderly* lady to cross the road.

	Write them down.	Schreib sie auf.	
A2	**attractive** /əˈtræktɪv/	attraktiv; reizvoll	*attractive* = nice to look at
	spray /spreɪ/	sprühen	
	stand up to somebody /ˌstænd‿ˈʌp tə ˌsʌmbədi/	sich jemandem widersetzen	
	bully /ˈbʊli/	*Person, die mobbt*	
	own /əʊn/	besitzen	
	climb /klaɪm/	auf etwas (hinauf)steigen, klettern	to *climb* = to go up something towards the top
	graduate *(AE)* /ˈɡrædʒueɪt/	die Abschlussprüfung bestehen	

Take a selfie or photo that has something to do with pride and write a caption.	Mach ein Selfie oder Foto, das etwas mit Stolz zu tun hat, und schreib eine Bildunterschrift.
Show your photos in the classroom and comment on the other photos.	Zeig deine Fotos im Klassenzimmer und äußere dich zu den anderen Fotos.
Interview someone from a different generation or someone from a different cultural background.	Befrage jemanden aus einer anderen Generation oder jemanden mit einem anderen kulturellen Hintergrund.
Report to the class.	Berichte der Klasse.
Choose one of the people in the pictures in … and write a diary entry for them.	Wähl einen der Menschen aus den Bildern in … aus und schreib einen Tagebucheintrag für ihn oder sie.

mind /maɪnd/	Geist, Verstand	
reflection /rɪˈflekʃn/	Reflexion	
fear /fɪə/	Angst	
leave behind /ˌliːv bɪˈhaɪnd/	zurücklassen	
step out of /ˌstep‿ˈaʊt‿əv/	heraustreten aus	
the ordinary /ði‿ˈɔːdnri/	das Übliche, das Normale	to *ascend* = to climb a mountain or stairs etc.
ascend /əˈsend/	aufsteigen	
stop /stɒp/	stoppen; aufhalten	
make a break /ˌmeɪk‿ə ˈbreɪk/	ausbrechen	
for /fɔː/	*hier:* in die	
freedom /ˈfriːdəm/	Freiheit	
realize (= realise) /ˈrɪəlaɪz/	sich bewusst sein, erkennen	
change /tʃeɪndʒ/	Veränderung	
spirit /ˈspɪrɪt/	Geist; Stimmung	
'cause (= because) /kɔːz, bɪˈkɒz/	weil, da	The *horizon* is the line where the sky seems to meet the earth.
horizon /həˈraɪzn/	Horizont	

Copy your three favourite phrases from the song.	Schreib deine drei Lieblingsphrasen aus dem Lied ab.
Write a few different examples.	Schreib ein paar verschiedene Beispiele.

couch potato /ˌkaʊtʃ pəˈteɪtəʊ/	Couchpotato, Fernsehglotzer/in	to *train* = to practise a sport regularly
train /treɪn/	trainieren	

biggest /ˈbɪgɪst/	größte(r, s)

Is it possible to tell who faced which challenge?	Ist es möglich, zu sagen, wer welcher Herausforderung gegenüber gestanden hat?

quit *(irr)* /kwɪt/	aufhören mit

break up /ˌbreɪk‿ˈʌp/	Schluss machen	to *deal with* something = to take action to do something
deal with /ˈdiːl wɪð/	sich befassen mit	
adapt /əˈdæpt/	sich anpassen	

Make notes and talk to a partner.	Mach dir Notizen und sprich mit einem Partner/einer Partnerin.
How did you cope with it?	Wie bist du damit zurechtgekommen?

A6

come out /ˈkʌm‿aʊt/	herauskommen; *hier:* sich outen	If you *accept* somebody as they are you make them feel welcome and part of your group.
gay /geɪ/	homosexuell	
accept /əkˈsept/	anerkennen, akzeptieren	
lesbian /ˈlezbiən/	lesbisch	
bisexual /baɪˈsekʃʊəl/	bisexuell	
transgender /trænsˈdʒendə/	transsexuell	
queer /kwɪə/	*hier:* homosexuell	
questioning /ˈkwestʃnɪŋ/	*hier:* zweifelnd	
adopt /əˈdɒpt/	adoptieren	A *rumour* is a piece of information that may or may not be true.
spread *(irr)* /spred/	verbreiten	
rumour /ˈruːmə/	Gerücht	
mean /miːn/	gemein	
rude /ruːd/	unhöflich; primitiv	
isolated /ˈaɪsəˌleɪtɪd/	isoliert, einsam	
worthless /ˈwɜːθləs/	wertlos	

Watch the video clip again and take notes on the questions in the box.	Sieh dir den Videoclip noch einmal an und mach dir zu den Fragen im Kasten Notizen.

A7

be about /ˌbi‿əˈbaʊt/	gehen um, handeln von	
butt *(informal)* /bʌt/	Kippe	
smoke /sməʊk/	rauchen	
fit in /ˌfɪt‿ˈɪn/	*hier:* dazugehören	to *fit in* = to belong
seem /siːm/	scheinen	
peer pressure /ˈpɪə ˌpreʃə/	Gruppenzwang	
somehow /ˈsʌmhaʊ/	irgendwie	
energy /ˈenədʒi/	Energie, Kraft	*energy* = power
smell of /ˈsmel‿əv/	nach etwas riechen	When there is a fire, there is always *smoke*.
smoke /sməʊk/	Rauch	
nicotine /ˈnɪkətiːn/	Nikotin	
gum /gʌm/	Kaugummi	
cigarette /ˌsɪgəˈret, ˈsɪgəˌret/	Zigarette	
at first /ət ˈfɜːst/	zuerst	to *gain weight* = to put on weight
gain weight /ˌgeɪn ˈweɪt/	zunehmen	
skin /skɪn/	Haut	To '*advise*' means to tell somebody what you think they should do.
advise /ədˈvaɪz/	raten, beraten; informieren	
ruin /ˈruːɪn/	zerstören, verderben	

A8 health warning /ˈhelθ ˌwɔːnɪŋ/ Warnhinweis

Read the health warnings from some American cigarette packets.	Lies die Warnhinweise von einigen amerikanischen Zigarettenschachteln.

Surgeon General *(AE)* /ˌsɜːdʒn ˈdʒenrəl/	Gesundheitsminister/in	
warning /ˈwɔːnɪŋ/	Warnung	to *contain* = to include something or have it as a part
contain /kənˈteɪn/	enthalten	
carbon monoxide /ˌkɑːbən məˈnɒksaɪd/	Kohlenmonoxid	
cause /kɔːz/	verursachen	
lung cancer /ˈlʌŋ ˌkænsə/	Lungenkrebs	
disease /dɪˈziːz/	Krankheit	
emphysema /ˌemfɪˈsiːmə/	Emphysem	
complicate /ˈkɒmplɪkeɪt/	verkomplizieren	
pregnancy /ˈpregnənsi/	Schwangerschaft	
pregnant /ˈpregnənt/	schwanger	
result in /rɪˈzʌlt‿ɪn/	zur Folge haben, führen zu	
fetal *(AE)* = foetal *(BE)* /ˈfiːtl/	fötal, fetal	
injury /ˈɪndʒəri/	Verletzung	
premature /ˈpremətʃə/	verfrüht, vorzeitig	
birth /bɜːθ/	Geburt	

He had to see a doctor because of his leg *injury*.

Do they have an effect on you?	Haben sie eine Wirkung auf dich?

A9 smoke-free /ˌsməʊk ˈfriː/ rauchfrei

Which piece of advice do you find most useful?	Welchen Ratschlag findest du am nützlichsten?

break the habit /ˌbreɪk ðə ˈhæbɪt/	sich etwas abgewöhnen	
non-smoking /ˌnɒn ˈsməʊkɪŋ/	Nichtraucher-	
normally /ˈnɔːmli/	normalerweise	
exercise /ˈeksəsaɪz/	trainieren	It is healthy to *exercise* often.
keep oneself busy /ˌkiːp wʌnˌself ˈbɪzi/	sich mit etwas beschäftigen	
carrot /ˈkærət/	Möhre, Karotte	
celery /ˈseləri/	Sellerie	
munch /mʌntʃ/	mampfen	

carrots

Make notes with a partner and discuss in class.	Macht euch mit einem Partner/einer Partnerin Notizen und diskutiert in der Klasse darüber.
A10 Read the reply that Steven gets. Copy three pieces of advice.	Lies die Antwort, die Steven bekommt. Schreib drei Ratschläge ab.

panic /ˈpænɪk/	in Panik geraten	

Work with a partner.	Arbeitet mit einem Partner/einer Partnerin zusammen.

firstly /ˈfɜːsli/	erstens	Ruby *is hiding* in the box.
hide *(irr)* /haɪd/	(sich) verstecken	
leave *(irr)* /liːv/	zurücklassen; (übrig) lassen	
deadline /ˈdedˌlaɪn/	letzter Termin, Stichtag	

A11 Discuss the following points and make notes.	Besprecht die folgenden Punkte und macht euch Notizen.

teen /tiːn/	jugendlich, Teenager-	
personal /ˈpɜːsnəl/	persönlich	Young people *face* a lot of problems today.
face /feɪs/	gegenüberstehen	

Write a list of the contents on the board.	Schreibt eine Liste der Inhalte an die Tafel.
Don't forget to think about a cover and a table of contents.	Vergesst nicht, an einen Umschlag und ein Inhaltsverzeichnis zu denken.
You could even publish a print or digital edition.	Ihr könntet sogar eine Druckversion oder eine digitale Version veröffentlichen.
P1 Explain what you have to do.	Erklär, was du tun sollst.
P3 What are typical challenges that teenagers face?	Was sind typische Herausforderungen, denen Jugendliche gegenüberstehen?
Write down your ideas.	Schreib deine Ideen auf.
P4 Choose at least four words or phrases and explain what they mean.	Wähl mindestens vier Wörter und Ausdrücke aus und erklär, was sie bedeuten.
P5 Report what the teacher told her class to do and what not to do.	Berichte, was die Lehrerin ihrer Klasse gesagt hat, was sie tun und nicht tun soll.
P6 Listen to the teacher talking to a group of pupils about how to quit smoking.	Hör zu, was der Lehrer einer Schülergruppe darüber erzählt, wie man mit dem Rauchen aufhört.
Report the advice to a friend.	Berichte den Ratschlag einem Freund/einer Freundin.

tell somebody to do something /ˌtel ˌsʌmbədi tə ˈduː ˌsʌmθɪŋ/	jemandem sagen, dass er/sie etwas tun soll

P7 Listen to the CD and repeat the words in the box.	Hör dir die CD an und wiederhol die Wörter im Kasten.
Is the stress on the first, the second or the third syllable?	Liegt die Betonung auf der ersten, der zweiten oder der dritten Silbe?
B1 Describe your everyday life.	Beschreibt euren Alltag.

of one's own /əv wʌnz‿ˈəʊn/	eigene(r, s)

B2 Read at least the first two profiles. — Lies dir mindestens die ersten zwei Porträts durch.

another /əˈnʌðə/	*hier:* weitere	
peanut /ˈpiːˌnʌt/	Erdnuss	
harvest /ˈhɑːvɪst/	ernten	
all day /ˌɔːl ˈdeɪ/	den ganzen Tag lang	
collect /kəˈlekt/	*hier:* holen	A *shoe shine boy* earns money by cleaning shoes.
shoe shine boy /ˈʃuːʃaɪn bɔɪ/	Schuhputzer	
accident /ˈæksɪdnt/	Unfall	
get on /ˌget‿ˈɒn/	*hier:* mitfahren	
hang on to /ˌhæŋ‿ˈɒn tʊ/	sich festhalten an	
back /bæk/	*hier:* Rückseite	
jump off /ˌdʒʌmp‿ˈɒf/	herunterspringen	
all morning /ˌɔːl ˈmɔːnɪŋ/	den ganzen Morgen lang	
in the evening /ˌɪn ði‿ˈiːvnɪŋ/	am Abend	
get *(irr)* /get/	werden	
trailer park /ˈtreɪlə pɑːk/	Wohnwagenabstellplatz	
aluminum *(AE)* = aluminium *(BE)* /əˈluːmɪnəm, ˌæləˈmɪniəm/	Aluminium	
cash /kæʃ/	Geld; Bargeld	The boy isn't paying by card, he is paying with *cash* instead.
store *(AE)* /stɔː/	Laden	
trailer /ˈtreɪlə/	Wohnwagen	
AC (= air conditioning) /ˌeɪ ˈsiː/	Klimaanlage	
run *(irr)* /rʌn/	*hier:* in Betrieb sein	
that /ðæt/	so	The *residents* of a house or flat are the people who live in it.
resident /ˈrezɪdnt/	Bewohner/in	
leave around /ˌliːv‿əˈraʊnd/	herumliegen lassen	
trash *(AE)* /træʃ/	Müll, Abfall	

Each person chooses a text and reads it in more detail.	Jede Person sucht sich einen Text aus und liest ihn ausführlicher.
Collect information in the table in your workbook.	Sammle Informationen in der Tabelle in deinem Arbeitsheft.
In your group, compare the children's lives to your lives.	Vergleicht in eurer Gruppe die Leben der Kinder mit euren.

B3

responsibility /rɪˌspɒnsəˈbɪləti/	Verantwortung; Pflicht
explain /ɪkˈspleɪn/	erklären

B4

Look at these two sentences from Miriam's profile.	Sieh dir diese zwei Sätze aus Miriams Porträt an.
What do you notice about the verb after 'have been'?	Was fällt dir an dem Verb hinter *‚have been'* auf?

B5

Find more examples in the profiles.	Finde weitere Beispiele in den Porträts.
The children in … live on different continents.	Die Kinder in … leben auf verschiedenen Kontinenten.
Who comes from which continent?	Wer kommt von welchem Kontinent?
What do you know about these continents?	Was weißt du über diese Kontinente?
Choose a continent and make a poster.	Wähl einen Kontinent aus und mach ein Poster.
Choose one of the countries: Ghana, Mexico or the USA.	Wählt eines der Länder aus: Ghana, Mexiko oder die USA.

Mexico /ˈmeksɪkəʊ/	Mexiko	

Make a fact file.	Mach einen Steckbrief.
Write a diary entry for one of the children.	Schreib einen Tagebucheintrag für eins der Kinder.

sheet /ʃiːt/	Blatt, Bogen	About 50 per cent of the world's *population* is female.
population /ˌpɒpjʊˈleɪʃn/	Bevölkerung	

B6

Listen again and complete the sentences.	Hört noch einmal zu und vervollständigt die Sätze.

report /rɪˈpɔːt/	Bericht	*Windmills* are often used to produce power.
windmill /ˈwɪnˌmɪl/	Windmühle	
manage /ˈmænɪdʒ/	schaffen	
bring *(irr)* /brɪŋ/	*hier:* bringen	

B7

Read what he says about land diving.	Lies, was er über das *Lianenspringen* sagt.

test /test/	prüfen, testen	
courage /ˈkʌrɪdʒ/	Mut	
dive /daɪv/	tauchen	
no longer /ˌnəʊ ˈlɒŋɡə/	nicht mehr	*no longer* = not anymore
wooden /ˈwʊdn/	Holz-, hölzern	
practise /ˈpræktɪs/	*hier:* machen, praktizieren	
century /ˈsentʃəri/	Jahrhundert	a *century* = 100 years
cut *(irr)* /kʌt/	*hier:* fällen	
body /ˈbɒdi/	*hier:* Hauptteil	
site /saɪt/	Stelle, Platz, Ort	
clear /klɪə/	*hier:* frei räumen	to *remove* = to take something away from a place
remove /rɪˈmuːv/	entfernen	
soil /sɔɪl/	Boden, Erde	
scaffolding /ˈskæfəʊldɪŋ/	Gerüst	
pole /pəʊl/	Stange, Pfahl	
stabilise (= stabilize) /ˈsteɪbəlaɪz/	stabilisieren	

front /frʌnt/	Vorderseite	
high /haɪ/	hoch	*high* ≠ low
top /tɒp/	oberes Ende, Spitze	
bend /bend/	sich biegen	
downwards /ˈdaʊnwədz/	abwärts, nach unten	
absorb /əbˈzɔːb/	*hier:* abfangen	
force /fɔːs/	Kraft; Wucht	
vine /vaɪn/	Rankengewächs	
tie /taɪ/	binden	
ankle /ˈæŋkl/	(Fuß)knöchel	
village elder /ˌvɪlɪdʒ‿ˈeldə/	Dorfälteste/r	
diver /ˈdaɪvə/	*hier:* Springer/in	
elastic /ɪˈlæstɪk/	elastisch, flexibel	
break *(irr)* /breɪk/	*hier:* reißen	
that's why /ˈðæts ˌwaɪ/	deshalb	
wet season /ˌwet ˈsiːzn/	Regenzeit	
safety /ˈseɪfti/	Sicherheit; Sicherheits-	
below /bɪˈləʊ/	unten, unter	
turn over the soil /ˌtɜːn‿ˌəʊvə ðə ˈsɔɪl/	den Boden umgraben	
soften /ˈsɒfn/	weicher machen	
dive /daɪv/	Sprung	
beneath /bɪˈniːθ/	unter	Ruby is *beneath* the box.
keep away /ˌkiːp‿əˈweɪ/	fernhalten	
evil /ˈiːvl/	böse	
respect /rɪˈspekt/	respektieren	
B8 the United Nations /ðə juːˌnaɪtɪd ˈneɪʃnz/	die Vereinten Nationen	
convention /kənˈvenʃn/	*hier:* Abkommen	
adequately /ˈædɪkwətli/	ausreichend	
feed *(irr)* /fiːd/	*hier:* ernähren	
educate /ˈedjʊkeɪt/	ausbilden, unterrichten	
relax /rɪˈlæks/	entspannen	to *waste* = to use more of something than is necessary
waste /weɪst/	verschwenden	
as best somebody can /əz ˌbest ˌsʌmbədi ˈkæn/	so gut (wie) jemand kann	

Vielseitige Verben
Im Englischen kann ein Verb verschiedene Bedeutungen haben – je nachdem, mit welchen Wörtern es kombiniert wird. Zum Beispiel kann ‚*take*' nicht nur mit ‚nehmen', sondern auch mit ‚machen' oder ‚bringen' übersetzt werden:
- *take a photo* – ein Foto machen
- *take notes* – sich Notizen machen
- *take somebody to the hospital* – jemanden ins Krankenhaus bringen

Kannst du ähnliche Beispiele für ‚*get*' finden?

B9

Choose the statement that you think is the most important.	Wähl die Aussage, die deiner Meinung nach am wichtigsten ist.
Choose a country where you think children live completely differently from you.	Wähl ein Land aus, von dem du denkst, dass Kinder dort völlig anders als du leben.
Do some research.	Recherchiert.
The presentation should contain five slides and last three minutes.	Die Präsentation sollte fünf Folien enthalten und drei Minuten dauern.
Take notes and answer the other groups' questions.	Macht euch Notizen und beantwortet die Fragen der anderen Gruppen.

poverty /ˈpɒvəti/	Armut	*poverty* = the state of being poor
war /wɔː/	Krieg	
right /raɪt/	Recht	

P11 Complete the sentences with chunks from the box. — Vervollständige die Sätze mit Wendungen aus dem Kasten.

P12 Answer the questions using the information in brackets. — Beantworte die Fragen, indem du die in Klammern stehenden Informationen benutzt.

Write down your answers. — Schreib deine Antworten auf.

P14 Listen to the report about William Kamkwamba and his invention again. — Hör dir noch einmal den Bericht über William Kamkwamba und seine Erfindung an.

Take notes on the following points. — Mach dir zu folgenden Punkten Notizen.

Use your notes to give a short summary of the report to a partner in German. — Verwende deine Notizen, um einem Partner/einer Partnerin auf Deutsch eine kurze Zusammenfassung des Berichts zu geben.

Theme 3

I

love /lʌv/	Liebe	*'Friendship'* is a relationship between people who are friends.
friendship /ˈfrenʃɪp/	Freundschaft	
chat-up line /ˈtʃætʌp ˌlaɪn/	Anmache, Anmachspruch	
romantic /rəʊˈmæntɪk/	romantisch	
check out *(informal)* /ˌtʃek‿ˈaʊt/	sich ansehen	

A1 Tell a partner which comments you like best. — Sag einem Partner/einer Partnerin, welche Kommentare du am liebsten magst.

A3 One of you takes notes on what Carrie says, the other on what Seb says. — Eine/r von euch macht sich Notizen dazu, was Carrie sagt, der/die andere dazu, was Seb sagt.

A4

coward /ˈkaʊəd/	Feigling	
place /pleɪs/	*hier:* Wohnung	
whatever /wɒtˈevə/	was (auch immer)	
mirror /ˈmɪrə/	Spiegel	
practice *(AE)* /ˈpræktɪs/	üben	
nasty /ˈnɑːsti/	gemein	
none /nʌn/	keine(r, s); nichts	
admit /ədˈmɪt/	zugeben	
stare at /ˈsteər‿æt/	anstarren	They all *stared at* the baby gorilla.
ask somebody out on a date /ˌɑːsk ˌsʌmbədi‿ˌaʊt‿ɒn‿ə ˈdeɪt/	jemanden fragen, ob er/sie mit einem ausgehen will	

date /deɪt/	Datum, Termin, Verabredung	
guy *(informal)* /gaɪ/	Kerl, Typ	*'Guy'* is an *informal* word for 'man'.
pass /pɑːs/	vorbeigehen an	
snack bar /ˈsnæk bɑː/	Imbissbude	to *chat* = to have a conversation with someone
chat /tʃæt/	schwätzen, plaudern	
pretend /prɪˈtend/	vorgeben, vortäuschen	

Think up a different title for the story.	Denk dir eine andere Überschrift für die Geschichte aus.
Split the class into four groups.	Teilt die Klasse in vier Gruppen ein.
Each group chooses a different character.	Jede Gruppe wählt eine andere Figur aus.
One person in your group takes the role of the character.	Eine Person in eurer Gruppe nimmt die Rolle der Figur an.
A5 With a partner, write down your conversation.	Schreib dein Gespräch mit einem Partner/einer Partnerin auf.

shocked /ˈʃɒkt/	schockiert, entsetzt

A6 Look at the chorus.	Sieh dir den Refrain an.
Write down your ideas and compare with a partner.	Schreib deine Ideen auf und vergleiche mit einem Partner/einer Partnerin.

broke *(informal)* /brəʊk/	pleite	When you have no money, you are *broke*.
love life /ˈlʌv laɪf/	Liebesleben	
D.O.A. (= Dead On Arrival) /ˌdiː‿əʊ‿ˈeɪ, ˌded‿ɒn‿əˈraɪvl/	*etwa:* tot, bevor es Rettung gibt	
be stuck /ˌbiː ˈstʌk/	*hier:* festhängen	
gear /gɪə/	Gang	When it *pours* with rain, rain is falling heavily.
pour /pɔː/	*hier:* schütten	
so far /ˈsəʊ fɑː/	bisher	
et al. /et‿ˈæl/	u.a. (= und andere)	

Listen to the song again and read along.	Hör dir das Lied noch einmal an und lies mit.
What problems are mentioned in the song?	Welche Probleme weden im Lied erwähnt?
Quote from the text and explain.	Zitier aus dem Text und erklär.

A7 were /wɜː/	wäre(st, n, t)	
pick /pɪk/	aussuchen; pflücken, sammeln	
I'd (= I would) /aɪd, ˈaɪ wʊd/	ich würde	
grow *(irr)* /grəʊ/	wachsen; werden; anbauen	
cultivate /ˈkʌltɪveɪt/	anbauen; *hier:* pflegen	

It can be fun to *grow* and *cultivate* vegetables.

Theme 3

care /keə/	Betreuung, Pflege; Sorgfalt	*Well done! I can see that a lot of care has gone into your work!*
forever /fər'evə/	ewig	
anonymous /ə'nɒnɪməs/	anonym	
inclusive /ɪn'klu:sɪv/	allumfassend	
whether /'weðə/	ob	
straight /streɪt/	*hier:* heterosexuell	
race /reɪs/	Rasse	
outer space /ˌaʊtə 'speɪs/	Weltraum	
whoever /hu:'evə/	wer auch immer	
movie star /'mu:vi ˌstɑ:/	Filmstar	
sibling /'sɪblɪŋ/	Geschwister	
speaker /'spi:kə/	Sprecher/in	

A *speaker* is someone who speaks in front of a group of people.

A8

Practise reading the poem out loud and present it in class.	Übt, das Gedicht laut zu lesen, und stellt es in der Klasse vor.
Draw a picture or make a collage of the three boys standing in front of the mirror.	Zeichne ein Bild oder mach eine Collage von den drei Jungen, die vor dem Spiegel stehen.
Write thought or speech bubbles.	Schreib Gedanken- oder Sprechblasen.
A friend lets you down.	Ein Freund/eine Freundin lässt dich im Stich.

let somebody down /ˌlet ˌsʌmbədi 'daʊn/	jemanden im Stich lassen

A9

Read the definition of a chat-up line.	Lies die Definition eines Anmachspruchs.

conversation /ˌkɒnvə'seɪʃn/	Gespräch, Unterhaltung	
lose *(irr)* /lu:z/	verlieren	Her favourite pen had *disappeared*. She couldn't find it anywhere.
magician /mə'dʒɪʃn/	Zauberkünstler/in	
disappear /ˌdɪsə'pɪə/	verschwinden	
pair /peə/	Paar	

Unscramble these chat-up lines and write them down.	Ordne diese Anmachsprüche und schreib sie auf.

anytime /'eniˌtaɪm/	jederzeit	The boys *took pictures* of all the sights.
take a picture /ˌteɪk‿ə 'pɪktʃə/	ein Bild machen	
angel /'eɪndʒl/	Engel	
exist /ɪg'zɪst/	existieren	
stupid /'stju:pɪd/	dumm, blöd	*stupid* ≠ clever
chocolate /'tʃɒklət/	Praline	
A10 truly /'tru:li/	wirklich, wahrhaftig	
madly /'mædli/	wie verrückt	
deeply /'di:pli/	sehr, äußerst	

The *director* tells the actors what to do.

release date /rɪˈliːs deɪt/	Erscheinungsdatum	
the UK (= United Kingdom) /ðə ˌjuː ˈkeɪ, juːˌnaɪtɪd ˈkɪŋdəm/	Vereinigtes Königreich	
running time /ˈrʌnɪŋ taɪm/	Laufzeit	
cast /kɑːst/	Besetzung	
director /dəˈrektə/	Regisseur/in	
pianist /ˈpiːənɪst/	Pianist/in	
cellist /ˈtʃelɪst/	Cellist/in	
go on /ˌɡəʊ‿ˈɒn/	fortsetzen, fortfahren	*go on* = carry on
properly /ˈprɒpəli/	richtig	
lead *(irr)* /liːd/	führen	to *lead* a life = to live a life
notice /ˈnəʊtɪs/	bemerken; wahrnehmen	
cheerfully /ˈtʃɪəfli/	fröhlich, vergnügt	
bored /bɔːd/	gelangweilt	
passionately /ˈpæʃnətli/	leidenschaftlich	

Work with a partner and write a short summary of the film.	Arbeite mit einem Partner/einer Partnerin und schreibt eine kurze Zusammenfassung des Films.
Be a language detective.	Sei ein Sprachendetektiv/eine Sprachendetektivin.
Find sentences with adverbs and write them down.	Finde Sätze mit Adverbien und schreib sie auf.
Some of the sentences contain comparisons with 'than'.	Manche der Sätze enthalten Vergleiche mit ‚*than*'.
Write them down and mark the comparisons.	Schreib sie auf und markiere die Vergleiche.
What do you notice about the adverbs?	Was fällt dir an den Adverbien auf?

A11 **branch** /brɑːntʃ/ — Zweig, Ast; Zweigstelle

Agree on what you would like to hang on the tree.	Einigt euch auf das, was ihr gern an den Baum hängen würdet.

quote /kwəʊt/ — Zitat

	Work on your part of the tree alone, in pairs or in groups.	Arbeitet alleine, paarweise oder in Gruppen an eurem Teil des Baums.
P3	Find the word that rhymes with 'these'.	Finde das Wort, das sich auf ‚*these*' reimt.
	Listen to the words and repeat.	Hör dir die Wörter an und wiederhole.
	Copy the table and write the words into two lists.	Schreib die Tabelle ab und schreib die Wörter in zwei Listen.
 P4	Look at the sentences and complete them with words from the box.	Sieh dir die Sätze an und vervollständige sie mit Wörtern aus dem Kasten.
 P5	Unscramble the following sentences and write them down.	Ordne die folgenden Sätze und schreib sie ab.

P6	comparison /kəmˈpærɪsn/	Vergleich

> Use the adverbs in the box to complete the sentences. — Benutz die Adverbien im Kasten, um die Sätze zu vervollständigen.
> Compare with a partner. — Vergleich mit einem Partner/einer Partnerin.

B1

> What do you need for a good love story? — Was braucht man für eine gute Liebesgeschichte?
> Read this version of 'Romeo and Juliet'. — Lies diese Version von ‚Romeo und Julia'.

enemy /ˈenəmi/	Feind/in	*enemy* ≠ friend
fish finger /ˌfɪʃ ˈfɪŋgə/	Fischstäbchen	
out of /ˈaʊt‿əv/	aus	*out of* ≠ into
miserable /ˈmɪzrəbl/	miserabel	
palace /ˈpæləs/	Palast	If you are *in disguise*, nobody will recognize you.
in disguise /ɪn dɪsˈgaɪz/	verkleidet	
at first sight /ət ˌfɜːst ˈsaɪt/	auf den ersten Blick	
get to know somebody /ˌget tə‿ˈnəʊ ˌsʌmbədi/	jemanden kennenlernen	
come down /ˌkʌm ˈdaʊn/	herunterkommen	
might /maɪt/	könnte(st, n, t)	Birds have *wings* so that they can fly.
wing /wɪŋ/	Flügel	
leave *(irr)* /liːv/	weggehen	
dangerous /ˈdeɪndʒərəs/	gefährlich	
lover /ˈlʌvə/	Liebende/r	
get married /ˌget ˈmærid/	heiraten	
in secret /ɪn ˈsiːkrət/	heimlich	
because of /bɪˈkɒz‿əv/	wegen	
fight /faɪt/	Kampf; Streit	
say goodbye /ˌseɪ gʊdˈbaɪ/	Abschied nehmen, Wiedersehen sagen	
no matter what /nəʊ ˌmætə ˈwɒt/	was auch (immer) passiert	
promise /ˈprɒmɪs/	versprechen	
count /kaʊnt/	Graf	
friar /ˈfraɪə/	Mönch	
be asleep /ˌbi‿əˈsliːp/	schlafen	 This girl *is asleep*.
dead /ded/	tot	
wake somebody up /ˌweɪk ˌsʌmbədi‿ˈʌp/	jemanden aufwecken	
Here goes! /ˌhɪə ˈgəʊz/	Los geht's!	
poison /ˈpɔɪzn/	Gift	You can kill people with *poison*.
get somebody to do something /ˌget ˌsʌmbədi tə ˈduː ˌsʌmθɪŋ/	jemanden dazu bringen, etwas zu tun	

B2

> Make a list of the characters. — Erstell eine Liste der Figuren.
> Unscramble the sentences and write them down. — Ordne die Sätze und schreib sie auf.

Words

B3 play /pleɪ/ — Spiel, (Theater)stück

> Read this summary of the play from a theatre guide. — Lies diese Zusammenfassung des Stücks aus einem Theaterführer.

disguise /dɪsˈgaɪz/	sich verkleiden
take up /ˌteɪk‿ˈʌp/	*hier:* annehmen
prince /prɪns/	Prinz; Fürst
ban /bæn/	*hier:* verbannen
wife (*pl* wives) /waɪf, waɪvz/	Ehefrau
meanwhile /ˈmiːnˌwaɪl/	inzwischen, unterdessen, mittlerweile
marriage /ˈmærɪdʒ/	Ehe, Heirat
drug /drʌg/	Medikament; Droge
rescue /ˈreskjuː/	retten, befreien
rush /rʌʃ/	eilen

Schiffe versenken
Du kennst bestimmt das Spiel ‚Schiffe versenken'. Das kannst du auch mit englischen Vokabeln spielen: Statt Schiffe in dein Raster einzutragen, trägst du einfach englische Vokabeln ein. Wer von euch hat als Erste/r alle Wörter gefunden?

> Romeo and Juliet both die tragically. — Romeo und Julia sterben beide tragisch.
> Explain how it came to that. — Erklär, wie es dazu kam.

B4 dramatic /drəˈmætɪk/	dramatisch
character /ˈkærəktə/	*hier:* Figur
B5 nurse /nɜːs/	*hier:* Kindermädchen

> Report the questions. — Gib die Fragen wieder.

death /deθ/ — Tod

B6
> Skim the information about the three films. — Überflieg die Informationen über die drei Filme.
> What do they have in common? — Was haben sie gemeinsam?

PG (= parental guidance) /ˌpiː ˈdʒiː, pəˌrentl ˈgaɪdəns/	nicht jugendfrei	
genre /ˈʒɒnrə/	Genre, Gattung	A *genre* is a particular type of literature or film.
romance /rəʊˈmæns/	Romanze	
originally /əˈrɪdʒnəli/	ursprünglich	*originally* = at first
be a shame /ˌbi‿ə ˈʃeɪm/	schade sein	A *crime* is an illegal activity. For example, stealing is a *crime*.
crime /kraɪm/	Verbrechen, Kriminalität	
version /ˈvɜːʃn/	Version, Fassung	
be in love /ˌbi‿ɪn ˈlʌv/	verliebt sein	
comedy /ˈkɒmədi/	Komödie	*Comedies* are very funny.
be set in /ˌbiː ˈset‿ɪn/	spielen in	
at the beginning /ˌæt‿ðə bɪˈgɪnɪŋ/	am Anfang	*at the beginning* ≠ at the end

Listen to the full film reviews.	Hört euch die vollständigen Filmkritiken an.
Which film does the reviewer like most?	Welchen Film mag die Kritikerin am liebsten?
Which film does she like least?	Welchen Film mag sie am wenigsten?
Listen to the review again and take notes on at least three of the following topics.	Hör dir die Kritik noch einmal an und mach dir zu mindestens drei der folgenden Themen Notizen.

reviewer /rɪˈvjuːə/	Kritiker/in

	Get into groups with other people who chose the same review.	Kommt in Gruppen mit anderen Leuten zusammen, die die gleiche Kritik wie ihr gewählt haben.
	Use your notes to talk about it.	Verwendet eure Notizen, um darüber zu sprechen.
B7	Choose a scene from the comic version of 'Romeo and Juliet'.	Wählt eine Szene aus der Comic-Version von ‚Romeo und Julia' aus.
	Make a freeze-frame of your scene.	Macht ein Standbild von eurer Szene.
	Find out more about the Globe theatre.	Finde mehr über das Globe Theater heraus.
B8	Listen to this scene at the Capulets' party in Shakespearean and modern English and read along.	Hör dir diese Szene auf der Party bei den Capulets auf Shakespeare-Englisch und modernem Englisch an und lies mit.

madam /ˈmædəm/	gnädige Frau	I *am craving* chocolate! = I really, really want some chocolate!
crave (for) /kreɪv/	sich sehnen nach	
marry *(veraltet)* /ˈmæri/	*hier etwa:* Ei nun!	
bachelor /ˈbætʃələ/	Junggeselle	
wise /waɪz/	weise	
virtuous /ˈvɜːtʃʊəs/	tugendhaft, rechtschaffen	
nurse /nɜːs/	pflegen, stillen	
withal *(veraltet, nachgestellt)* /wɪðˈɔːl/	mit	
lay hold of somebody /ˌleɪ ˈhəʊld‿əv ˌsʌmbədi/	jemanden bekommen	Nowadays, you would say 'purse' instead of '*chink*'.
chink *(veraltet)* /tʃɪŋk/	Geldbeutel	
aside /əˈsaɪd/	auf die Seite	
dear /dɪə/	*hier:* teuer	
account /əˈkaʊnt/	*hier:* Preis	
foe /fəʊ/	Feind	I borrowed a lot of money and now I have a big *debt*.
debt /det/	Schuld	
indeed /ɪnˈdiːd/	wirklich, in der Tat	*indeed* = really
whom /huːm/	wem; wen; der/die/das	
wealthy /ˈwelθi/	reich, wohlhabend	*wealthy* = rich

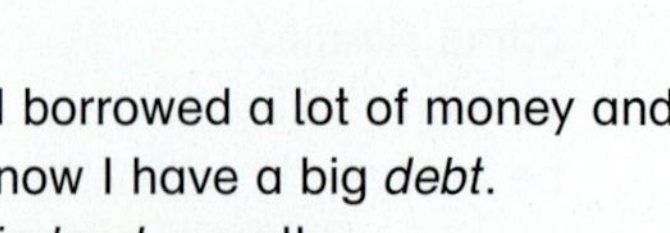

Words

Look at both versions of the text and find the answers to these questions. Make notes.	Sieh dir beide Textfassungen an und finde die Antworten auf die Fragen. Mach dir Notizen.

express /ɪk'spres/ — ausdrücken

Choose the modern or the Shakespearean version and practise reading it out loud.	Wählt die moderne oder die Shakespeare-Version aus und übt, sie laut vorzulesen.

B9 love story /'lʌv ˌstɔ:ri/ — Liebesgeschichte

Create your own modern love story.	Erfindet eure eigene moderne Liebesgeschichte.

short story /ʃɔ:t 'stɔ:ri/	Kurzgeschichte	They wanted to *shoot* the film in Hollywood.
shoot *(irr)* /ʃu:t/	*hier:* filmen, drehen	
main /meɪn/	Haupt-	The film had a good *ending*. Everyone was happy.
ending /'endɪŋ/	Ende, Schluss	
P9 adjective /'ædʒɪktɪv/	Adjektiv	

P10

Listen to the words in the box and repeat them.	Hör dir die Wörter im Kasten an und wiederhol sie.
Copy the words.	Schreib die Wörter ab.
Underline the syllables that are stressed.	Unterstreich die Silben, die betont sind.
Now read the words out loud.	Lies die Wörter nun laut vor.
Ask a partner to check your pronunciation.	Bitte einen Partner/eine Partnerin, deine Aussprache zu überprüfen.

P11 nosy /'nəʊzi/ — neugierig

P12

A local English theatre group is performing a play at your school and you want to see it.	Eine ortsansässige Theatergruppe spielt an deiner Schule ein Stück vor und du möchtest es dir ansehen.

rival /'raɪvl/	rivalisierend	The *admission fee* is the amount of money that you pay to go into a building or to an event.
leader /'li:də/	Leiter/in, Führer/in	
risk /rɪsk/	riskieren	
admission fee /əd'mɪʃn fi:/	Eintritt	

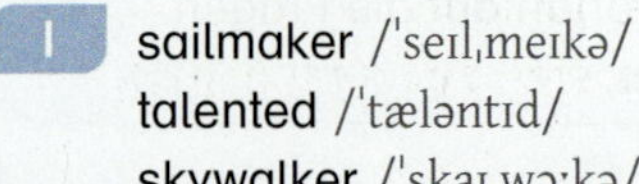

Theme 4

I

sailmaker /ˈseɪlˌmeɪkə/	Segelmacher/in	The sails on this boat were made by a *sailmaker*.
talented /ˈtæləntɪd/	talentiert	
skywalker /ˈskaɪˌwɔːkə/	*Bauarbeiter/in, der/die Wolkenkratzer baut bzw. auf diesen arbeitet*	
smoke-jumper /ˈsməʊkˌdʒʌmpə/	*Feuerspringer/in*	
snake-milker /ˈsneɪkˌmɪlkə/	Schlangenmelker/in	
vocational /vəʊˈkeɪʃnəl/	beruflich	In *training* you will gain a lot of experience.
training /ˈtreɪnɪŋ/	Ausbildung, Schulung	

A1 Match them with the jobs in the box. — Ordne sie den Berufen im Kasten zu.

secretary /ˈsekrətri/	Sekretär/in	
flight attendant /ˈflaɪt‿əˌtendənt/	Flugbegleiter/in	
software developer /ˈsɒfˌweə dɪˌveləpə/	Softwareentwickler/in	A *software developer* must be able to program a computer.
physiotherapist /ˌfɪziəʊˈθerəpɪst/	Physiotherapeut/in	
social worker /ˈsəʊʃl ˌwɜːkə/	Sozialarbeiter/in	
plumber /ˈplʌmə/	Klempner/in	
lifeguard /ˈlaɪfˌgɑːd/	Bademeister/in, Rettungsschwimmer/in	A *lifeguard* must be able to swim very well.
doctor's assistant /ˈdɒktəz‿əˌsɪstnt/	Arzthelfer/in	
develop /dɪˈveləp/	erarbeiten, entwickeln	
passenger /ˈpæsɪndʒə/	Fahrgast, Passagier/in	There are a lot of *passengers* on this tour bus.
install /ɪnˈstɔːl/	installieren	
heating system /ˈhiːtɪŋ ˌsɪstəm/	Heizungsanlage	
water system /ˈwɔːtə ˌsɪstəm/	Wasseranlage	
medical /ˈmedɪkl/	medizinisch	
create /kriˈeɪt/	erschaffen, erzeugen	
computer program /kəmˈpjuːtə ˌprəʊgræm/	Computerprogramm	
doctor's office /ˈdɒktəz‿ˌɒfɪs/	Praxis	Doctor's assistants work at a *doctor's office*.

Listen and take notes. — Hör zu und mach dir Notizen.
Compare your notes with a partner. — Vergleich deine Notizen mit einem Partner/einer Partnerin.
What do you think about the jobs? — Was hältst du von den Berufen?

stressful /ˈstresfl/	stressig, anstrengend	If a job is *well-paid*, it means you earn lots of money.
well-paid /ˌwel ˈpeɪd/	gut bezahlt	
badly-paid /ˌbædli ˈpeɪd/	schlecht bezahlt	

A2	Close your books and write down all the jobs you know.	Schließt eure Bücher und schreibt alle Berufe auf, die ihr kennt.
	Compare your lists with the other groups.	Vergleicht eure Listen mit den anderen Gruppen.
	You get one point for each job that the other groups do not have and an extra point if you can give information about the jobs.	Ihr kriegt einen Punkt für jeden Beruf, den die anderen Gruppen nicht haben, und einen zusätzlichen Punkt, wenn ihr Informationen über die Berufe geben könnt.
A3	What is necessary to do these jobs?	Was braucht man, um diese Berufe auszuüben?

apprenticeship /əˈprentɪsʃɪp/ Ausbildung, Lehre

Compare your sentences with a partner.	Vergleich deine Sätze mit einem Partner/einer Partnerin.

A4	sail /seɪl/	Segel
	sum up /ˌsʌm‿ˈʌp/	zusammenfassen

Give reasons.	Gib Gründe an.

A6	**unusual** /ʌnˈjuːʒuəl/	ungewöhnlich	
	violinist /ˌvaɪəˈlɪnɪst/	Violinist/in, Geiger/in	
	specialise in /ˈspeʃəlaɪz‿ɪn/	sich spezialisieren auf	A *violinist* plays the
	violin /ˌvaɪəˈlɪn/	Violine, Geige	*violin*.
	bow /baʊ/	Bogen	

	Listen to what Amanda says about how she turned her talent into a profession.	Hör dir an, was Amanda darüber erzählt, wie sie ihr Talent zu einem Beruf gemacht hat.
	Take notes in your workbook.	Mach dir in deinem Arbeitsheft Notizen.
	Amanda says: "My hands have been my most important tool for as long as I can remember."	Amanda sagt: „Meine Hände sind, solange ich mich erinnern kann, mein wichtigstes Werkzeug gewesen."
A7	Look at the works of art.	Sieh dir die Kunstwerke an.
	Listen and read along.	Hör zu und lies mit.

extremely /ɪkˈstriːmli/	äußerst, höchst, außerordentlich
at the age of /æt ði‿ˈeɪdʒ‿əv/	im Alter von
academy /əˈkædəmi/	Akademie, Schule
sculptor /ˈskʌlptə/	Bildhauer/in
performance artist /pəˈfɔːməns‿ɑːtɪst/	Performancekünstler/in
style /staɪl/	Stil
subway *(AE)* /ˈsʌbˌweɪ/	U-Bahn

The statue was made by a *sculptor*.

panel /ˈpænl/	Tafel	
look out for /ˌlʊk‿ˈaʊt fɔː/	Ausschau halten nach	
space /speɪs/	*hier:* Reklamefläche	
whenever /wenˈevə/	wann auch immer	
realize (= realise) /ˈrɪəlaɪz/	sich bewusst sein, erkennen	
rub out /ˌrʌb‿ˈaʊt/	ausradieren	
communicate /kəˈmjuːnɪkeɪt/	kommunizieren, sprechen	
image /ˈɪmɪdʒ/	Bild	
product /ˈprɒdʌkt/	Produkt	
wall painting /ˈwɔːl ˌpeɪntɪŋ/	Wandgemälde	
documentary /ˌdɒkjʊˈmentri/	Dokumentarfilm	
release /rɪˈliːs/	veröffentlichen, herausbringen	
A8	profession /prəˈfeʃn/	Beruf

Früher war die britische Schreibweise von Wörtern mit ‚*-ise*' bzw. ‚*-isation*' eindeutig die mit ‚s', die amerikanische die mit ‚z'. Mittlerweile werden kaum noch Unterschiede gemacht. Viele Briten schreiben ganz selbstverständlich ‚*realize*', ‚*organize*' oder ‚*organization*'. In vielen Wörterbüchern wird sogar die Schreibweise mit ‚z' als die häufiger vorkommende gelistet.

A9

Complete the sentences.	Vervollständige die Sätze.
Read the text again and take notes on important moments in Keith Haring's life.	Lies die Texte nochmal und mach dir Notizen zu wichtigen Momenten in Keith Harings Leben.

A10

obvious, obviously /ˈɒbviəs, ˈɒbviəsli/	offensichtlich

Listen to Emma talking to her guidance counselor at school.	Hör dir an, was Emma ihrem Beratungslehrer von der Schule erzählt.

guidance counselor *(AE)* /ˈgaɪdns ˌkaʊnslə/	Beratungslehrer/in

Listen again and read along.	Hör noch einmal zu und lies mit.

at the end /ˌæt ðiˈend/	schließlich
take a seat /ˌteɪk‿ə ˈsiːt/	sich setzen
elective /ɪˈlektɪv/	Wahlfach
yet /jet/	schon; noch
honestly /ˈɒnɪsli/	ehrlich, wirklich
right now /ˌraɪt ˈnaʊ/	im Moment
fail /feɪl/	durchfallen
credit /ˈkredɪt/	*hier:* Leistungsnachweis
offer /ˈɒfə/	anbieten
graphic design /ˌgræfɪk dɪˈzaɪn/	Grafikdesign
right /raɪt/	genau, direkt
perfect /ˈpɜːfɪkt/	perfekt

If my brother didn't help me, I would fail. Wenn mein Bruder mir nicht helfen würde, würde ich durchfallen.

If I was fitter, I would take that course. Wenn ich fitter wäre, würde ich den Kurs nehmen.

If she had the money, she would send me to art school. Wenn sie das Geld hätte, würde sie mich zur Kunstschule schicken.

Words

A11	Find the sentences with 'if' in the dialogue and write them down. Compare your sentences with the sentences in …	Finde die Sätze mit ‚if' im Dialog und schreib sie auf. Vergleich deine Sätze mit den Sätzen in …

result /rɪˈzʌlt/ — Ergebnis

A12	Make a jobs and talents word web. Make a job quiz for a partner. Do a class survey of talents in your class. Explain it to your classmates.	Erstell ein Wortnetz über Jobs und Talente. Mach ein Jobquiz für einen Partner/eine Partnerin. Mach eine Umfrage über Talente in deiner Klasse. Erklär es deinen Klassenkameraden/Klassenkameradinnen.
A13	Prepare a placemat. Write the things you are good at in your section of the placemat.	Bereite ein Platzdeckchen vor. Schreib die Dinge, in denen du gut bist, in deinen Teil des Platzdeckchens.

patient /ˈpeɪʃnt/ — geduldig — You have to be *patient* and wait in a queue.
well-organised /ˌwel‿ˈɔːgənaɪzd/ — gut organisiert

	Turn the placemat and read what the others have written. Add the others' ideas to your section of the placemat.	Dreh das Platzdeckchen und lies, was die anderen geschrieben haben. Füg die Ideen der anderen deinem Bereich des Platzdeckchens hinzu.
A14	Make a class display about jobs you and your class think are interesting.	Macht eine Klassenausstellung über Berufe, die du und deine Klasse interessant finden.

display /dɪˈspleɪ/ — *hier:* Ausstellung

You can also present someone who turned his or her talent into a profession. Create your part of the display.	Du kannst auch jemanden vorstellen, der/die sein oder ihr Talent in einen Beruf umgewandelt hat. Erstellt euren Teil der Ausstellung.

effective /ɪˈfektɪv/ — wirksam, effektiv
precise /prɪˈsaɪs/ — genau, präzise
paragraph /ˈpærəˌgrɑːf/ — Absatz, Abschnitt
underline /ˌʌndəˈlaɪn/ — unterstreichen
heading /ˈhedɪŋ/ — Überschrift, Titel

A *paragraph* is a section of a text that begins on a new line and contains one or more sentences.

P3	Listen to the CD and repeat the words. Copy the lists and fill in the words. The third list is for words with a silent 'g'.	Hör dir die CD an und wiederhol die Wörter. Schreib die Listen ab und trag die Wörter ein. Die dritte Liste ist für Wörter mit einem stummen ‚g'.

P4	Use the simple present in the if-clause and the will-future in the main clause.	Benutz die Formen der einfachen Gegenwart im *if*-Satz und das *will*-Futur im Hauptsatz.
	Listen to the CD and check your sentences.	Hör dir die CD an und überprüf deine Sätze.
P6	Complete it using the modal verbs from the box.	Vervollständige sie, indem du die Modalverben aus dem Kasten benutzt.
	There is more than one solution.	Es gibt mehr als eine Lösung.

	Columbia /kə'lʌmbiə/	Kolumbien	A *future* event is an event that hasn't happened yet.
B1	future /'fju:tʃə/	zukünftig	

Think of a job and mime it.	Denk dir einen Beruf aus und stell ihn pantomimisch dar.
Look at the pictures and the questions in the speech bubbles.	Sieh dir die Bilder und die Fragen in den Sprechblasen an.
Talk to a partner and make notes.	Sprich mit einem Partner/einer Partnerin und mach dir Notizen.

indoors /ˌɪn'dɔ:z/	drinnen, im Haus	
outdoors /ˌaʊt'dɔ:z/	draußen, im Freien	*outdoors ≠ indoors*
social /'səʊʃl/	gesellschaftlich; sozial	

Using your answers from ..., collect and write down ideas for jobs that each of you could do.	Sammelt und schreibt Ideen für Berufe auf, die jede/r von euch machen könnte, indem ihr eure Antworten aus ... verwendet.
Mill around and share your ideas with your classmates.	Lauft umher und teilt eure Ideen mit euren Klassenkameraden/Klassenkameradinnen.

B2	programme /'prəʊgræm/	Programm

Listen to what Angie says about her job.	Hör zu, was Angie über ihren Beruf sagt.
Imagine your younger sister wants to be a hotel receptionist.	Stell dir vor, dass deine jüngere Schwester Empfangsdame in einem Hotel werden will.

B3	**work experience** /'wɜ:k‿ɪkˌspɪəriəns/	Praktikum, Berufserfahrung

Where do you think Nick is doing his work experience?	Wo macht Nick deiner Meinung nach sein Praktikum?
What does he complain about?	Über was beklagt er sich?

sports shop /'spɔ:ts‿ʃɒp/	Sportgeschäft	The boy *is skateboarding*.
skateboard /'skeɪtbɔ:d/	Skateboard fahren	
demonstrate /'demənˌstreɪt/	zeigen, vorführen	

Words

disaster /dɪˈzɑːstə/	Katastrophe	
task /tɑːsk/	Aufgabe	If you are never late you are always *on time*.
on time /ˌɒn ˈtaɪm/	pünktlich	
send off /ˌsend‿ˈɒf/	wegschicken	
cardboard box /ˈkɑːdbɔːd bɒks/	Karton	You can recycle *cardboard boxes*.
basement /ˈbeɪsmənt/	Keller	
shoelace /ˈʃuːˌleɪs/	Schnürsenkel	*shoelace* →
sweep *(irr)* /swiːp/	fegen, kehren	
fall asleep /ˌfɔːl‿əˈsliːp/	einschlafen	
make up /ˌmeɪk‿ˈʌp/	*hier:* ausgleichen	
cash register /ˈkæʃ ˌredʒɪstə/	Registrierkasse	
pull out /ˈpʊl‿ˌaʊt/	herausziehen	
text /tekst/	eine SMS schreiben	
appear /əˈpɪə/	erscheinen, auftauchen	
from nowhere /frəm ˈnəʊweə/	aus dem Nichts	
sit around /ˌsɪt‿əˈraʊnd/	herumsitzen	
storeroom /ˈstɔːˌruːm/	Lagerraum, Abstellkammer	Between them they ate a *whole* pizza. It was huge.
whole /həʊl/	ganz, gesamt	
B4 telephone call /ˈtelɪfəʊn kɔːl/	Telefonanruf	

Then listen to what Nick told his sister Melanie on the phone and read along.	Dann hör dir an, was Nick seiner Schwester Melanie am Telefon erzählt hat und lies mit.

awful /ˈɔːfl/	schrecklich	*awful* = terrible
to-do list /təˈduː ˌlɪst/	To-do-Liste	

	Listen to the rest of the conversation and check your sentences.	Hör dir den Rest der Unterhaltung an und überprüf deine Sätze.
B5	Make a list of work places in your area where you or your classmates could try to get work experience.	Erstell eine Liste von Arbeitsplätzen in deiner Region, wo du oder deine Klassenkameraden/Klassenkameradinnen versuchen könnten, einen Praktikumsplatz zu bekommen.
B6	Read this American magazine article.	Lies diesen amerikanischen Zeitschriftenartikel.

take *(irr)* /teɪk/	erfordern, benötigen	If you want a job, you have to *apply for* it.
apply for /əˈplaɪ fɔː/	sich bewerben um	
work placement /ˈwɜːk ˌpleɪsmənt/	Praktikum, Praktikumsstelle	*Employers hire* people to work for them.
employer /ɪmˈplɔɪə/	Arbeitgeber/in	
hire *(AE)* /ˈhaɪə/	einstellen	
soft skill /ˌsɒft ˈskɪl/	*persönliche, soziale und methodische Kompetenzen*	
hard skill /ˌhɑːd ˈskɪl/	*berufstypische Qualifikationen*	

example /ɪgˈzɑːmpl/	Beispiel	
typing /ˈtaɪpɪŋ/	Maschineschreiben	She uses a special *program* to help her write her CV.
programming /ˈprəʊˌgræmɪŋ/	Programmieren	
program /ˈprəʊgræm/	Computerprogramm	
politeness /pəˈlaɪtnəs/	Höflichkeit	
reliability /rɪˌlaɪəˈbɪlɪti/	Zuverlässigkeit	Good *communication* means that you are good at talking and listening to people.
communication /kəˌmjuːnɪˈkeɪʃn/	Verständigung, Kommunikation	
ability /əˈbɪləti/	Fähigkeit	
interview /ˈɪntəˌvjuː/	Vorstellungsgespräch	
likely /ˈlaɪkli/	wahrscheinlich	*likely* = probably
babysit /ˈbeɪbiˌsɪt/	babysitten	
neighbor *(AE)* /ˈneɪbə/	Nachbar/in	
reliable /rɪˈlaɪəbl/	verlässlich, zuverlässig	
responsible /rɪˈspɒnsəbl/	verantwortungsbewusst, verantwortlich	
improve /ɪmˈpruːv/	verbessern; besser werden	to *improve* = to get better or to make something better
feedback /ˈfiːdbæk/	Feedback, Rückmeldung	
take a course /ˌteɪk‿ə ˈkɔːs/	einen Kurs machen	
list /lɪst/	auflisten	to *list* = to make a list
résumé *(AE)* /ˈrezjuːmeɪ/	Lebenslauf	

Collect hard and soft skills in the article and make two lists.	Sammle berufstypische Qualifikationen sowie persönliche, soziale und methodische Kompetenzen im Artikel und mach zwei Listen.
Read the text again and write down the answers to the questions.	Lies den Text noch einmal und schreib die Antworten auf die Fragen auf.

B7

check /tʃek/	Überprüfung, Kontrolle
sit down /ˌsɪt‿ˈdaʊn/	sich hinsetzen
apologize (= apologise) /əˈpɒlədʒaɪz/	sich entschuldigen
individual /ˌɪndɪˈvɪdʒuəl/	individuell; einzeln
playground /ˈpleɪˌgraʊnd/	*hier:* Schulhof
carefully /ˈkeəfli/	*hier:* genau
specific /spəˈsɪfɪk/	genau, bestimmte(r, s); spezifisch
out of /ˈaʊt‿əv/	aus
due /djuː/	fällig
in order to /ˌɪn‿ˈɔːdə tʊ/	um zu
on one's own /ˌɒn ˌwʌnz‿ˈəʊn/	allein

Relativsatz-Rallye

Mit Relativsätzen kannst du Dinge oder Personen näher beschreiben – dass diese Beschreibung nicht nach einem Satz enden muss, beweist dieses Spiel!

Spielt in Gruppen gegeneinander. Eine Gruppe beginnt einen Satz, danach hängt jemand aus der anderen Gruppe einen Relativsatz an usw. Welche Gruppe kann den längsten Satz bilden?

Beispiel: *This is Mr Miller – who teaches English – which is my favourite subject – …*

Work out how many points you scored.	Errechne, wie viele Punkte du erzielt hast.
Look at page … and check your result.	Sieh dir Seite … an und überprüf dein Ergebnis.

	organisational /ˌɔ:gənaɪ'zeɪʃnəl/	organisatorisch	
	take initiative /ˌteɪk‿ɪ'nɪʃətɪv/	die Initiative ergreifen	
B8	staff manager /'stɑ:f ˌmænɪdʒə/	Personalchef/in	
	placement /'pleɪsmənt/	Stelle; *hier:* Praktikumsstelle	The *staff manager* is greeting the boy on the first day of his *placement*.
	gain experience /ˌgeɪn‿ɪk'spɪəriəns/	Erfahrungen sammeln	
	help out /ˌhelp‿'aʊt/	aushelfen	
	other than that … /ˌʌðə ðən 'ðæt/	abgesehen davon …	*other than that* = apart from that
	be done with *(informal)* /ˌbi: 'dʌn wɪð/	fertig sein mit	

	Remember the rules for reported speech.	Denk an die Regeln für die indirekte Rede.
	What would you answer the staff manager?	Was würdest du dem Personalchef/der Personalchefin antworten?
B9	Think of the hard skills and the soft skills you need for the job.	Denk an die berufstypischen Qualifikationen und die persönlichen, sozialen und methodischen Kompetenzen, die du für den Job brauchst.
	You will hear interview questions for a two week placement.	Du wirst Bewerbungsfragen für ein zweiwöchiges Praktikum hören.
	Record the interview.	Nimm das Vorstellungsgespräch auf.
	Do your classmates think you will get the work placement?	Glauben deine Klassenkameraden/Klassenkameradinnen, dass du die Praktikumsstelle bekommen wirst?
P8	Report what these people said.	Berichte, was diese Leute gesagt haben.

P9	positive /'pɒzətɪv/	positiv

	What hard and soft skills does Mrs Michael mention?	Welche berufstypischen Qualifikationen und persönlichen, sozialen und methodischen Kompetenzen erwähnt Frau Michael?
P10	Look at Aidan's CV.	Sieh dir Aidans Lebenslauf an.
	He wants to do a work placement as a car mechanic.	Er möchte ein Praktikum als Automechaniker machen.
	Work with a partner and make notes for a telephone interview: one of you is the employer, the other is Aidan.	Arbeite mit einem Partner/einer Partnerin zusammen und macht euch Notizen für ein Vorstellungsgespräch am Telefon: eine/r von euch ist der/die Arbeitgeber/in, der/die andere ist Aidan.

date of birth /ˌdeɪt‿əv ˈbɜːθ/	Geburtsdatum	
place of birth /ˌpleɪs‿əv ˈbɜːθ/	Geburtsort	She is working
garage /ˈgærɑːʒ/	Werkstatt	at a *garage*.
service /ˈsɜːvɪs/	Service, Dienst	
education /ˌedjʊˈkeɪʃn/	Bildung, Ausbildung	
primary school /ˈpraɪməri skuːl/	Grundschule	

Theme 5

immigration /ˌɪmɪˈgreɪʃn/	Einwanderung, Immigration	
read on /ˌriːd‿ˈɒn/	weiterlesen	To find out what happens next in a book, you must *read on*.
hurricane /ˈhʌrɪkeɪn/	Orkan	
Irish /ˈaɪrɪʃ/	irisch	
famine /ˈfæmɪn/	Hungersnot	

A1 Listen to the poem and read along. — Hör dir das Gedicht an und lies mit.

arithmetic /əˈrɪθmətɪk/	Arithmetik	*Arithmetic* is a part of mathematics.
public school *(AE)* /ˌpʌblɪk ˈskuːl/	staatliche Schule	
what makes somebody tick /wɒt ˌmeɪks‿ˌsʌmbədi ˈtɪk/	was jemanden bewegt	
in front /ɪn ˈfrʌnt/	vorn	
behind /bɪˈhaɪnd/	hinten	*in front ≠ behind*
aisle /aɪl/	Gang	
Italian /ɪˈtæljən/	Italiener/in; italienisch	
Polish /ˈpəʊlɪʃ/	Polnisch; polnisch	
colored *(AE)* = coloured *(BE)* /ˈkʌləd/	farbig	These are *coloured* pencils.
Russian /ˈrʌʃn/	Russe, Russin; russisch	
Jewish /ˈdʒuːɪʃ/	jüdisch	
Grecian /ˈgriːʃn/	griechisch	
Chinese /ˌtʃaɪˈniːz/	Chinese, Chinesin; chinesisch	
regular /ˈregjʊlə/	regelmäßig; üblich, normal	*'Ark'* is the name of the boat in the Bible that Noah built.
ark /ɑːk/	Arche	
race /reɪs/	Rasse	
graduation /ˌgrædʒuˈeɪʃn/	(Studien)abschluss	
across /əˈkrɒs/	gegenüber	A *writer* is a person whose job it is to write books, articles, stories, etc.
bubble /ˈbʌbl/	Blase	
writer /ˈraɪtə/	Autor/in	
identity /aɪˈdentɪti/	Identität	

consider /kən'sɪdə/	halten für; nachdenken; betrachten	
racist /'reɪsɪst/	Rassist/in; rassistisch	

Choose one of the quotes.	Wähl eines der Zitate.
How diverse is your class?	Wie vielfältig ist eure Klasse?
In his poem Hughes criticises the idea of categorising people according to nationality or appearance.	In seinem Gedicht kritisiert Hughes den Gedanken, Menschen nach ihrer Nationalität oder ihrem Aussehen zu kategorisieren.
Write down the two lines in the poem that reflect his opinion.	Schreib die zwei Zeilen im Gedicht auf, die seine Meinung zum Ausdruck bringen.
A2 Read about Ireland in the 19th century.	Lies über Irland im 19. Jahrhundert.

once /wʌns/	früher	
isle /aɪl/	(kleine) Insel	You feel *pain* when something hurts you.
pain /peɪn/	Schmerz	
disease /dɪ'zi:z/	Krankheit	*disease* = illness
destroy /dɪ'strɔɪ/	zerstören	
starve /stɑ:v/	verhungern	
sick /sɪk/	krank	A lot of people decide to *emigrate* if they are unhappy where they live.
as a result /əz‿ə rɪ'zʌlt/	als Folge	
emigrate /'emɪgreɪt/	auswandern	
Canada /'kænədə/	Kanada	
at that time /æt 'ðæt‿taɪm/	zu jener Zeit	
journey /'dʒɜ:ni/	Reise	There is *little* space in the car park. 
Atlantic Ocean /ətˌlæntɪk‿'əʊʃn/	Atlantik	
overcrowded /ˌəʊvə'kraʊdɪd/	überfüllt	
little /'lɪtl/	wenig	

A3 What is the song about?	Worum geht es in dem Lied?

shadow /'ʃædəʊ/	Schatten	A *hill* is smaller than a mountain.
hill /hɪl/	Hügel	
deadly /'dedli/	tödlich	
drive from /'draɪv‿frəm/	vertreiben	
journey /'dʒɜ:ni/	reisen	
glory /'glɔ:ri/	Ruhm	A *motive* is a reason why you do something.
motive /'məʊtɪv/	Motiv	
greed /'gri:d/	Gier	In the 19th century, the *voyage* to America could take over a month.
voyage /'vɔɪɪdʒ/	Reise, Seereise	
survival /sə'vaɪvl/	Überleben	
stormy /'stɔ:mi/	stürmisch	If your car costs a *fortune*, you must be very rich.
fortune /'fɔ:tʃən/	Vermögen; Schicksal; Glück	
fame /feɪm/	Ruhm	
hardship /'hɑ:dʃɪp/	Not, Elend	
upon /ə'pɒn/	auf, an	

plain /pleɪn/	Ebene	
spread *(irr)* /spred/	sich ausbreiten	
throughout /θruːˈaʊt/	im ganzen/in der ganzen	A *nation* is a country that has its own government and land.
nation /ˈneɪʃn/	Land, Nation	
railroad car *(AE)* /ˈreɪlˌrəʊd kɑː/	Eisenbahnwaggon	
ease /iːz/	beruhigen	

A4

What do you learn about her and her family?	Was erfährst du über sie und ihre Familie?

board a ship /ˌbɔːd‿ə ˈʃɪp/	ein Schiff besteigen
hold /həʊld/	Frachtraum
space /speɪs/	Raum, Platz
crowded /ˈkraʊdɪd/	überfüllt
reach /riːtʃ/	erreichen
almost /ˈɔːlməʊst/	fast, beinahe
captain /ˈkæptɪn/	Kapitän/in; Mannschaftsführer/in
announce /əˈnaʊns/	bekannt geben
dock /dɒk/	anlegen
gift /gɪft/	Geschenk

had gone	war(en) gefahren
had arrived	war(en) angekommen
had been	war(en) gewesen
had boarded	hatte(n) (ein Schiff) bestiegen
had seen	hatte(n) gesehen

Choose a title for each of the six paragraphs.	Wähl eine Überschrift für jeden der sechs Absätze.

arrival /əˈraɪvl/	Ankunft
mixed /mɪkst/	gemischt

Answer questions 1 to 6 above.	Beantworte die Fragen 1 bis 6 von oben.
Swap with a partner and answer the questions.	Tauscht mit einem Partner/einer Partnerin und beantwortet die Fragen.
A5 Have a look at this sentence.	Sieh dir diesen Satz an.

after /ˈɑːftə/	nachdem

Find more examples in …	Finde weitere Beispiele in …
Copy the sentences and underline the past perfect form.	Schreib die Sätze ab und unterstreich die Form des Plusquamperfekt.
Match the sentence parts and write them down.	Ordne die Satzteile einander zu und schreib sie auf.
A6 Write thought bubbles for Annie when she leaves Ireland or when she arrives in New York.	Schreib Gedankenblasen für Annie, als sie Irland verlässt oder als sie in New York ankommt.
Think about her feelings, hopes, fears, …	Denk an ihre Gefühle, Hoffnungen, Ängste, …

Words

	Imagine how Annie felt when she left Ireland and when she arrived in New York.	Stell dir vor, wie sich Annie gefühlt hat, als sie Irland verlassen hat und als sie in New York angekommen ist.
	Use adjectives from the box to write about her.	Benutz Adjektive aus dem Kasten, um über sie zu schreiben.
	Imagine what it was like when Annie said goodbye to her best friend or when she met her parents in New York.	Stell dir vor, wie es war, als Annie von ihrer besten Freundin Abschied genommen hat oder als sie ihre Eltern in New York getroffen hat.
A7	Look at the bar chart and listen to the description of the situation in 1850 and 2000.	Sieh dir das Balkendiagramm an und hör dir die Beschreibung der Situation in den Jahren 1850 und 2000 an.

	Philippines /ˈfɪləpiːnz/	Philippinen	
	total /ˈtəʊtl/	gesamt, völlig	*total* = complete
	compare /kəmˈpeə/	vergleichen	
	top /tɒp/	oberste(r, s)	When you leave one country and enter another, you cross a *border*.
	half (*pl* halves) /hɑːf, hɑːvz/	Hälfte	
A8	border /ˈbɔːdə/	Grenze	
	travel caution /ˈtrævl ˌkɔːʃn/	*etwa:* Reisewarnung	
	smuggle /ˈsmʌgl/	schmuggeln	
	encounter /ɪnˈkaʊntə/	treffen, begegnen	A sign that says '*No trespassing!*' means you are not allowed to enter that place or area.
	No trespassing! /ˌnəʊ ˈtrespəsɪŋ/	Kein Durchgang!	
	restricted area /rɪˌstrɪktɪd‿ˈeəriə/	Sperrgebiet	

A9	Then skim the text.	Überflieg dann den Text.

run *(irr)* /rʌn/	*hier:* verlaufen	
around /əˈraʊnd/	ungefähr	
illegally /ɪˈliːgli/	ungesetzlich, illegal	*illegally* ≠ legally
violence /ˈvaɪələns/	Gewalt	You should *avoid* unhealthy food. = You shouldn't eat unhealthy food.
Mexican /ˈmeksɪkən/	Mexikaner/in; mexikanisch	
avoid /əˈvɔɪd/	meiden, vermeiden	
border patrol /ˈbɔːdə pəˌtrəʊl/	Grenzstreife	
desert /ˈdezət/	Wüste	
die /daɪ/	sterben	
thirst /θɜːst/	Durst	
heat exhaustion /ˈhiːt‿ɪgˌzɔːstʃn/	Hitzschlag	
deportee /ˌdiːpɔːˈtiː/	Abzuschiebende/r, Abgeschobene/r	
make *(irr)* /meɪk/	*hier:* schaffen	
immediately /ɪˈmiːdiətli/	sofort	
impossible /ɪmˈpɒsəbl/	unmöglich	*impossible* ≠ possible

side /saɪd/	Seite	

Write down key phrases for each paragraph. — Schreibt euch wesentliche Ausdrücke für jeden Absatz auf.
Read the questions below. — Lest die Fragen unten.
Use your answers to write a summary. — Verwendet eure Antworten, um eine Zusammenfassung zu schreiben.
A10 Read the first paragraph. — Lies den ersten Absatz.

coyote *(AE)* /kaɪˈəʊti/	Schlepper/in	
perfectly /ˈpɜːfɪkli/	ganz genau	
cross into a country /ˌkrɒs‿ˌɪntu‿ə ˈkʌntri/	die Grenze in ein Land passieren	
pang /pæŋ/	(plötzliches) Schmerzgefühl	She feels a *pang* of pain in her *stomach*.
stomach /ˈstʌmək/	Magen, Bauch	
weak /wiːk/	schwach	*weak* ≠ strong
thief (*pl* thieves) /θiːf, θiːvz/	Dieb	
once more /ˌwʌns ˈmɔː/	noch einmal	
across /əˈkrɒs/	*hier:* durch	
valley /ˈvæli/	Tal	
bush /bʊʃ/	Busch	
on /ɒn/	weiter; vorwärts	
lie down /ˌlaɪ ˈdaʊn/	sich hinlegen	
breathe /briːð/	(ein)atmen	
darkness /ˈdɑːknəs/	Dunkelheit	
whisper /ˈwɪspə/	flüstern, wispern	They *are* not *whispering*, they are talking loudly.

Does Rosa make it across the border? — Schafft Rosa es über die Grenze?
A11 Make a class display about immigration in the USA. — Macht eine Klassenausstellung über Einwanderung in den Vereinigten Staaten.
Decide as a class what you want to include in your display. — Entscheidet euch als Klasse, was ihr in eure Ausstellung einbeziehen wollt.

chart /tʃɑːt/	Diagramm	I always write *captions* under my photos.
caption /ˈkæpʃn/	Bildunterschrift	
timeline /ˈtaɪmlaɪn/	Zeitachse	

Think about the number of immigrants, their homelands, journeys, languages … — Denkt über die Zahl der Einwanderer, ihre Heimatländer, Reisen, Sprachen … nach.
Research your topic and work on your product with a partner or in a small group. — Recherchiert euer Thema und arbeitet mit einem Partner/einer Partnerin oder in einer Kleingruppe an eurem Produkt.
P2 What are the nationalities? — Welches sind die Nationalitäten?

Poland /ˈpəʊlənd/	Polen	
Spain /speɪn/	Spanien	

Russia /ˈrʌʃə/ — Russland

Write at least five more pairs.	Schreib wenigstens fünf weitere Paare.

P3 scrambled /ˈskræmbld/ — durcheinander gebracht

Unscramble the facts about the Irish potato famine and write them down.	Ordne die Tatsachen über die irische Hungersnot und schreib sie auf.
P4 Copy the table.	Schreib die Tabelle ab.
P5 Copy the sentences and fill in the missing words.	Schreib die Sätze ab und trag die fehlenden Wörter ein.

P6 move /muːv/ — umziehen

Use the words in brackets to join the two actions.	Verwende die Wörter in Klammern, um die zwei Handlungen zu verbinden.
Change the tense of the verb in the first action.	Verändere die Zeitform des Verbs in der ersten Handlung.
P7 Make sentences and copy them.	Bilde Sätze und schreib sie ab.
Compare your ideas with a partner.	Vergleiche deine Ideen mit einem Partner/einer Partnerin.
Did you write down the same sentences?	Habt ihr die gleichen Sätze aufgeschrieben?

B1 on the move /ˌɒn ðə ˈmuːv/ — unterwegs

Make notes.	Macht euch Notizen.

school exchange /ˈskuːl‿ɪksˌtʃeɪndʒ/	Schüleraustausch	
B2 **war** /wɔː/	Krieg	Every *war* is horrible.
flood /flʌd/	Überschwemmung, Hochwasser	
earthquake /ˈɜːθˌkweɪk/	Erdbeben	
political /pəˈlɪtɪkl/	politisch	
natural disaster /ˌnætʃrəl dɪˈzɑːstə/	Naturkatastrophe	*Floods* and *earthquakes* are both *natural disasters*.
flee *(irr)* /fliː/	fliehen	

Listen to the news reports.	Hör dir die Nachrichtenmeldungen an.
Match them to the photos.	Ordne sie den Fotos zu.
Choose one of the situations.	Wähl eine der Situationen.
Listen again and take notes.	Hör noch einmal zu und mach dir Notizen.
B3 Now skim the text and find out if you were right.	Überflieg nun den Text und finde heraus, ob du recht hattest.

be born /biː ˈbɔːn/	geboren werden	We *are moving* house next week.
move /muːv/	umziehen	

standard of living /ˌstændəd‿əv ˈlɪvɪŋ/	Lebensstandard	
pull factor /ˈpʊl ˌfæktə/	Pull-Faktor	
unsafe /ʌnˈseɪf/	unsicher, gefährlich	
impossible /ɪmˈpɒsəbl/	unmöglich	
persecute /ˈpɜːsɪˌkjuːt/	verfolgen	They couldn't go for a walk *due to* the rain.
due to /ˈdjuː tʊ/	wegen	
nationality /ˌnæʃəˈnæləti/	Nationalität	
opinion /əˈpɪnjən/	Meinung, Ansicht	your *opinion* = what you think
escape /ɪˈskeɪp/	fliehen, entkommen	to *escape* = to get away from a place where you have been in danger
extreme /ɪkˈstriːm/	äußerste(r, s), extrem	
push factor /ˈpʊʃ ˌfæktə/	Push-Faktor	
push /pʊʃ/	schieben, stoßen	

Scan the text for reasons for migration.	Such den Text nach Gründen für Migration ab.
With your partner, sort the reasons for migration into two lists: 'push factors' and 'pull factors'.	Sortiert mit eurem Partner/eurer Partnerin die Gründe für Migration in zwei Listen: ‚Push-Faktoren' und ‚Pull-Faktoren'.
Read the definitions and look up the words 'migrant', 'refugee', 'asylum seeker' and 'internally displaced person'.	Lies die Definitionen und schlag die Wörter *‚migrant'*, *‚refugee'*, *‚asylum seeker'* und *‚internally displaced person'* nach.
Explain the terms to a partner in German.	Erklär einem Partner/einer Partnerin auf Deutsch die Begriffe.

migrant /ˈmaɪgrənt/	Zuwanderer/in	
move around /ˌmuːv‿əˈraʊnd/	umherreisen	
within /wɪðˈɪn/	innerhalb	
economic /ˌiːkəˈnɒmɪk/	wirtschaftlich	
sort /sɔːt/	Sorte, Art	The *government* is the group of people who are responsible for controlling a state or country.
refugee /ˌrefjʊˈdʒiː/	Flüchtling	
government /ˈgʌvənmənt/	Regierung	
law /lɔː/	Gesetz, Recht	
asylum seeker /əˈsaɪləm ˌsiːkə/	Asylsuchende/r	You can see *fear* on the man's face.
fear /fɪə/	Angst	
internally displaced /ɪnˌtɜːnli dɪsˈpleɪst/	*intern vertrieben*	
force /fɔːs/	zwingen	
B4 displace /dɪsˈpleɪs/	vertreiben	

Listen to …	Hör/Hört … zu.
What is your first reaction to his story?	Was ist deine erste Reaktion auf seine Geschichte?
Collect your thoughts on the board.	Sammelt eure Gedanken an der Tafel.
Write down your opinion.	Schreib deine Meinung auf.

evacuation /ɪˌvækjuˈeɪʃn/	Evakuierung, Räumung

Words

airlift /ˈeəˌlɪft/	per Flugzeug evakuieren	
helicopter /ˈhelɪˌkɒptə/	Hubschrauber, Helikopter	
flood /flʌd/	überschwemmen, unter Wasser setzen	If water *floods* a place, it covers it.

B5

What can you find out about his or her hopes for the future?	Was kannst du über seine oder ihre Hoffnungen für die Zukunft herausfinden?
Write it down.	Schreib es auf.
Compare Hassan and Muzoon's lives.	Vergleicht das Leben von Hassan und Muzoon.

Syria /ˈsɪriə/	Syrien
Syrian /ˈsɪriən/	syrisch
Turkey /ˈtɜːki/	Türkei
sewing machine /ˈsəʊɪŋ məˌʃiːn/	Nähmaschine
pair /peə/	Paar
housekeeper /ˈhaʊsˌkiːpə/	Haushälter/in
rent /rent/	Miete
feed *(irr)* /fiːd/	*hier:* ernähren
campaign /kæmˈpeɪn/	kämpfen, sich engagieren
education /ˌedjʊˈkeɪʃn/	Bildung, Ausbildung
refugee camp /ˈrefjʊˌdʒiː kæmp/	Flüchtlingslager
Jordan /ˈdʒɔːdn/	Jordanien
camp /kæmp/	*hier:* Flüchtlingslager
senior school /ˈsiːniə skuːl/	Oberstufenschule
university /ˌjuːnɪˈvɜːsəti/	Universität
return /rɪˈtɜːn/	zurückkehren, zurückkommen
rebuild /ˌriːˈbɪld/	wieder aufbauen

False friends
Im Englischen gibt es viele Wörter, die deutschen Wörtern sehr ähnlich sehen, aber eine ganz andere Bedeutung haben. Man nennt sie *false friends* = falsche Freunde. ‚*gymnasium*' ist z. B. keine Schulform, sondern eine Turnhalle, ‚*prize*' meint nicht den Preis, sondern den Gewinn, ‚*gift*' ist kein Gift, sondern ein Geschenk. Für diese Wörter kannst du dir eine Extra-Abteilung in deinem Karteikasten anlegen, um sie zu lernen.

B6

Label countries that are currently in the news because of refugees or migrants.	Beschrifte Länder, die zurzeit wegen Flüchtlingen oder Zuwanderern in den Nachrichten sind.
Display and explain the map in class.	Hängt die Karte aus und erklärt sie in der Klasse.

B7

goal /gəʊl/	Ziel

Listen to the poems and read along.	Hör dir die Gedichte an und lies mit.
Which one do you like better?	Welches gefällt dir besser?

blister /ˈblɪstə/	Blase	If a baby bird *hatches*, it comes out of its egg and is born.
hatch /hætʃ/	schlüpfen	
shell /ʃel/	Schale	
warrior /ˈwɒriə/	Krieger/in	

explode /ɪk'spləʊd/	explodieren	*blazing hot* = very hot because the sun is shining strongly
blazing hot /ˌbleɪzɪŋ 'hɒt/	glühend heiß	
sunray /'sʌnreɪ/	Sonnenstrahl	
feast /fiːst/	schlemmen	
strive for /'straɪv‿fɔː/	streben nach	
gray *(AE)* = grey *(BE)* /greɪ/	grau	*crammed* = completely filled with people or things
crammed /kræmd/	vollgestopft	
just like me /ˌdʒʌst laɪk 'miː/	genau wie ich	
sweaty /'sweti/	verschwitzt	
disembark /ˌdɪsɪm'bɑːk/	von Bord gehen	
eatery /'iːtəri/	Restaurant, Esslokal	
sense /sens/	Sinn; Gefühl	
topping /'tɒpɪŋ/	*hier:* Belag	
combine /kəm'baɪn/	verbinden	
wish /wɪʃ/	wünschen	He *wishes* he had a full English breakfast instead of cornflakes.
B8 **hope** /həʊp/	Hoffnung	

What hopes might they have?	Welche Hoffnungen könnten sie haben?

Turkish /'tɜːkɪʃ/	Türkisch	
Greece /griːs/	Griechenland	
B9 **response** /rɪ'spɒns/	Antwort; Reaktion	*response* = answer, reaction

There are lots of ways to express yourself.	Es gibt viele Wege, wie du dich ausdrücken kannst.

fiction /'fɪkʃn/	Erfindung, Fiktion, Erzählliteratur
non-fiction /ˌnɒn 'fɪkʃn/	Sachliteratur

You can share your products in class if you want to – maybe in a gallery walk.	Wenn ihr möchtet, könnt ihr eure Produkte in der Klasse teilen, vielleicht in einer Gruppendiskussion in Stationsarbeit.
P9 Listen to the CD and repeat the plural nouns.	Hör dir die CD an und wiederhol die Hauptwörter im Plural.

P10 noun /naʊn/	Hauptwort, Substantiv, Nomen	*'Reaction'* is a *noun*, 'react' is a verb.

Write down the word pairs.	Schreib die Wortpaare auf.
P11 Make notes about your ideas.	Mach dir über deine Ideen Notizen.
Share your ideas with a partner.	Teilt eure Ideen mit einem Partner/einer Partnerin.
Are they similar?	Sind sie ähnlich?
P12 Work with a partner and check your definitions.	Arbeitet mit einem Partner/einer Partnerin und überprüft eure Definitionen.
P13 Compare in class.	Vergleicht in der Klasse.

Theme 6

I

go green /ˌgəʊ ˈgriːn/	umweltbewusst werden	
green /griːn/	*hier:* umweltbewusst	
take *(irr)* /teɪk/	*hier:* machen	
toxic /ˈtɒksɪk/	giftig	
fashion /ˈfæʃn/	Mode	These girls love *fashion* and always buy lots of cool clothes.
handy /ˈhændi/	praktisch	
navigation bar /ˌnævɪˈgeɪʃn bɑː/ 	Navigationsleiste	
introduction /ˌɪntrəˈdʌkʃn/	Einleitung	

P p. 116

How green are you?	Wie umweltbewusst bist du?

switch off /ˌswɪtʃ ˈɒf/	ausschalten	*Cycling* to work is more *eco-friendly* than driving.
cycle /ˈsaɪkl/	Rad fahren, radeln	
reuse /riːˈjuːz/	wiederverwenden	
plastic bag /ˌplæstɪk ˈbæg/	Plastiktüte	
household waste /ˈhaʊsˌhəʊld weɪst/	Haushaltsmüll	
recycle /riːˈsaɪkl/	recyceln, wiederaufbereiten	You could decide to *go green* and *recycle* all your rubbish.

Share your answers in class.	Teilt eure Antworten in der Klasse.
What can you say about the results?	Was könnt ihr über die Ergebnisse sagen?

eco- /ˈiːkəʊ/	Öko-

P p. 117

What comes to mind?	Was fällt dir ein?
Talk in class.	Redet in der Klasse darüber.
Compare your ideas with the definition at the bottom of the page.	Vergleicht eure Ideen mit der Definition am Seitenende.

clean /kliːn/	sauber	
chemical /ˈkemɪkl/	Chemikalie	
clothing /ˈkləʊðɪŋ/	Kleidung	He loves his *electric* guitar.
electric /ɪˈlektrɪk/	elektrisch, Elektro-	
traffic /ˈtræfɪk/	Verkehr	
pollute /pəˈluːt/	verschmutzen	
be aware of something /ˌbi‿əˈweər‿əv ˌsʌmθɪŋ/	sich einer Sache bewusst sein	If you *are aware of* something, you know about it.
ecological footprint /ˌiːkəˌlɒdʒɪkl ˈfʊtprɪnt/	ökologischer Fußabdruck	
environment /ɪnˈvaɪrənmənt/	Umgebung, Umfeld; Umwelt	The *environment* is the world around us.

p. 118

Look through the three topics in this Theme.	Sieh durch die drei Themen in diesem Kapitel.

explore /ɪkˈsplɔː/ — erforschen, untersuchen

On the second and third pages there are pictures, facts and figures, newspaper articles, podcasts, and much more, for example …	Auf den zweiten und dritten Seiten gibt es Bilder, Fakten und Zahlen, Zeitungsartikel, Podcasts und vieles mehr, zum Beispiel …

urban /ˈɜːrbən/ — städtisch
gardening /ˈɡɑːdnɪŋ/ — Gartenarbeit, Gärtnern
NYC (= New York City) /ˌen waɪ ˈsiː, ˌnjuː jɔːk ˈsɪti/ — *die Stadt New York*
edible /ˈedɪbəl/ — essbar, genießbar
rooftop /ˈruːfˌtɒp/ — Dach
farm /fɑːm/ — Bauernhof
vertical /ˈvɜːtɪkl/ — vertikal, senkrecht

My grandma loves *gardening* and has lots of plants in her garden.

Split up your group so that different people explore different texts.	Teilt eure Gruppe auf, sodass verschiedene Leute verschiedene Texte untersuchen.
If you want to find out even more, go to www.diesterweg.de/webcodes and type in the webcode of your topic.	Wenn ihr sogar noch mehr herausfinden wollt, geht auf www.diesterweg.de/webcodes und tippt den Webcode eures Themas ein.
As a group, start a wordbank now for your topic.	Fangt jetzt als Gruppe ein Wortfeld für euer Thema an.
Add to it during the project.	Erweitert es während des Projekts.
Inform other group members about what you found out.	Informiert andere Gruppenmitglieder darüber, was ihr herausgefunden habt.

p. 119

spotlight /ˈspɒtˌlaɪt/ — Scheinwerfer, Aufmerksamkeit

On the fourth page you will find a text called 'Spotlight on …'.	Auf der vierten Seite findest du einen Text, der *‚Spotlight on …'* heißt.
This text goes into a bit more detail than the others.	Dieser Text geht etwas mehr ins Detail als die anderen.
Read the text as a group, take notes and talk about it.	Lest den Text als Gruppe, macht euch Notizen und redet darüber.

get ready /ˌɡet ˈredi/ — sich fertig machen, sich vorbereiten — In the mornings I wake up and *get ready* for school.

It is time to share your knowledge with your class.	Es ist Zeit, dass ihr euer Wissen mit eurer Klasse teilt.
Prepare a presentation.	Bereitet eine Präsentation vor.
You could make a poster, a computer presentation, a fact file, …	Ihr könntet ein Poster, eine Computerpräsentation, einen Steckbrief, … machen.
Decide on the aspects you want to focus on.	Entscheidet euch, auf welche Aspekte ihr euch konzentrieren wollt.

Be prepared for questions and feedback from the other groups.	Seid vorbereitet auf Fragen und Feedback von den anderen Gruppen.
If as a class you want to go further and carry out your own projects, do step 6.	Wenn ihr als Klasse weitermachen und eure eigenen Projekte durchführen wollt, macht Schritt 6.
If not, go straight to step 7.	Falls nicht, geht direkt zu Schritt 7.
Each group can now plan their own project based on their topic.	Jetzt kann jede Gruppe basierend auf ihrem Thema ihr eigenes Projekt planen.
Each group would need to …	Jede Gruppe müsste …

identify /aɪˈdentɪfaɪ/	identifizieren	
research /rɪˈsɜːtʃ/	recherchieren	I am sure we can find a *solution* to your problem.
solution /səˈluːʃn/	Lösung	
put into action /ˌpʊt‿ɪntʊ ˈækʃn/	in die Tat umsetzen	
detail /ˈdiːteɪl/	Detail, Einzelheit	

After the project is over, you have a chance to think about how it went and reflect on the work you have done.	Nachdem das Projekt vorbei ist, habt ihr die Gelegenheit, darüber nachzudenken, wie es gelaufen ist, und über die Arbeit zu reflektieren, die ihr gemacht habt.
You can find a questionnaire to help you with this in your workbook.	Ihr könnt in eurem Arbeitsheft einen Fragebogen finden, der euch dabei helfen kann.
 PA p. 120 What makes a green city?	Was macht eine umweltbewusste Stadt aus?

public transport /ˌpʌblɪk ˈtrænspɔːt/	öffentliche Verkehrsmittel	Buses are a kind of *public transport*.
garden /ˈɡɑːdn/	Garten	
bike lane /ˈbaɪk leɪn/	Fahrradweg	
PA p. 121 Iceland /ˈaɪslənd/	Island	Electricity is often made with *fossil fuels*.
fossil fuel /ˌfɒsl ˈfjuːəl/	fossiler Brennstoff	
ban /bæn/	verbieten	
Sweden /ˈswiːdn/	Schweden	
energy-efficient /ˈenədʒi‿ɪˌfɪʃnt/	energiesparend	*Renewable* energy cannot be completely used up, it replaces itself by natural processes.
renewable /rɪˈnjuːəbl/	erneuerbar	
carpet /ˈkɑːpɪt/	Teppich	
citizen /ˈsɪtɪzn/	Bürger/in	
consume /kənˈsjuːm/	konsumieren; verbrauchen	
gasoline /ˈɡæsəliːn/	Benzin	A car needs *gasoline* to run.
compact /kəmˈpækt/	kompakt	If something is *compact*, it is normally quite small.
get around /ˌɡet‿əˈraʊnd/	herumkommen	
apartment building /əˈpɑːtmənt ˌbɪldɪŋ/	Wohnblock	
carbon footprint /ˌkɑːbən ˈfʊtprɪnt/	CO_2-Fußabdruck, CO_2-Bilanz	The more you fly, the bigger your *carbon footprint*.

PA p. 122	resource /rɪˈzɔːs/	Quelle, Ressource	You should *reduce* the amount of plastic that you use.
	reduce /rɪˈdjuːs/	reduzieren	
	waste /weɪst/	Abfall	*waste* = litter
	access /ˈækses/	Zugang	
	affordable /əˈfɔːdəbl/	erschwinglich	
	set a good example /ˌset‿ə gʊd‿ɪgˈzɑːmpl/	mit gutem Beispiel vorangehen	Adults should *set a good example* for children.

Here are some ideas for search terms. — Hier sind ein paar Ideen für Suchbegriffe.

PA p. 123	unused /ʌnˈjuːzd/	unbenutzt	*unused* = not used
	plot of land /ˌplɒt‿əv ˈlænd/	ein Stück Land	
	organization *(AE)* = organisation *(BE)* /ˌɔːgənaɪˈzeɪʃn/	Organisation	
	plot /plɒt/	*hier:* Parzelle	A *plot* is a piece of land.
	single /ˈsɪŋgl/	einzige(r, s)	
	acre /ˈeɪkə/	Morgen *(Maßeinheit zur Flächenbestimmung)*	
	full-time /ˌfʊl ˈtaɪm/	Vollzeit-	
	compost /ˈkɒmpɒst/	Kompost	
	put up /ˌpʊt‿ˈʌp/	errichten, bauen	
	fencing /ˈfensɪŋ/	Einzäunung	
	lay the soil /ˌleɪ ðə ˈsɔɪl/	*hier:* den Boden vorbereiten	
	plant /plɑːnt/	pflanzen	
	volunteer /ˌvɒlənˈtɪə/	sich freiwillig melden; ehrenamtlich arbeiten	
	by (+ *-ing*) *(oder nur Verbform mit -ing)* /baɪ/	indem	The man is getting to the other side *by* climb*ing* over the *fencing*.
	sustainability /səˌsteɪnəˈbɪləti/	Nachhaltigkeit	
PB p. 124	wildlife /ˈwaɪldˌlaɪf/	Tier- und Pflanzenwelt, Flora und Fauna	
	drop /drɒp/	fallen lassen	to *drop* = to let something fall
	irresponsible /ˌɪrɪˈspɒnsəbl/	unverantwortlich, verantwortungslos	
	pollution /pəˈluːʃn/	Verschmutzung	The pollution on this beach is horrible. 
	packaging /ˈpækɪdʒɪŋ/	Verpackung	

Do you think they show solutions to the problems? — Zeigen sie deiner Meinung nach Lösungen für die Probleme?

	reusable /riːˈjuːzəbl/	wiederverwendbar	It is better to use a *reusable* bag than a plastic bag.
	recycling bin /riːˈsaɪklɪŋ bɪn/	Wertstoffsammelbehälter	

Talk in your group and make notes. — Sprecht in eurer Gruppe darüber und macht euch Notizen.

Words

PB p. 125	toy /tɔɪ/	Spielzeug	Children love to play with *toys*.
	effect /ɪˈfekt/	Effekt, Wirkung	
	package /ˈpækɪdʒ/	verpacken	to *transport* = to move people or things from one place to another
	transport /trænsˈpɔːt/	transportieren	
	good /gʊd/	Ware	
	threat /θret/	Bedrohung, Gefahr	
	biodegrade /ˌbaɪəʊdɪˈgreɪd/	sich zersetzen	*Plastics* do not *biodegrade*.
	break down /ˌbreɪk ˈdaʊn/	sich aufspalten	
	Zanzibar /ˈzænzɪbɑː/	Sansibar	
	ocean /ˈəʊʃn/	Ozean, Meer	
	tens of thousands /ˌtenz‿əv ˈθaʊzndz/	zehntausende	
	whale /weɪl/	Wal	*whale* 
	seal /siːl/	Seehund, Robbe	
	turtle /ˈtɜːtl/	Schildkröte	
	mistake for /mɪˈsteɪk fɔː/	verwechseln mit	
	Dr (= Doctor) /ˈdɒktə/	Dr. (= Doktor)	
	marine biologist /məˌriːn baɪˈɒlədʒɪst/	Meeresbiologe/in	
	Australian /ɒˈstreɪliən/	Australier/in; australisch	This is the *Australian* flag.
	institute /ˈɪnstɪˌtjuːt/	Institut	
	marine /məˈriːn/	Meeres-, See-	
	save /seɪv/	sparen; aufheben	To *save* money, spend less!
	recycled /riːˈsaɪkld/	wiederverwertet, Recycling-	
	power /ˈpaʊə/	antreiben	
	light bulb /ˈlaɪt bʌlb/	Glühbirne	*light bulb* 
	raw material /ˌrɔː məˈtɪəriəl/	Rohstoff	
PB p. 126	figure /ˈfɪgə/	Zahl, Wert	
	take action /ˌteɪk‿ˈækʃn/	handeln	
	billion /ˈbɪljən/	Milliarde	a *billion* = one thousand million
	ton /tʌn/	Tonne	
	wrap /ræp/	einwickeln	
	microbead /ˈmaɪkrəʊˌbiːd/	*winzige Plastikpartikel*	
	end up /ˌend‿ˈʌp/	schließlich landen	
	on average /ˌɒn‿ˈævərɪdʒ/	durchschnittlich	
	preferably /ˈprefrəbli/	vorzugsweise	
	natural /ˈnætʃrəl/	natürlich	
	returnable /rɪˈtɜːnəbl/	Mehrweg-	I'm going to *replace* the old poster in my room with a new one.
	coffee shop /ˈkɒfi ʃɒp/	Kaffeebar, Café	
	replace /rɪˈpleɪs/	ersetzen	
	lunchbox /ˈlʌntʃbɒks/	Frühstücksdose	
	use /juːs/	Verwendung; Einsatz	
	rather than /ˈrɑːðə ðæn/	anstatt	
	throw away /ˌθrəʊ‿əˈweɪ/	wegwerfen	
	necessary /ˈnesəsri/	notwendig, erforderlich	A polluted beach needs a *clean-up*.
	clean-up /ˈkliːn‿ʌp/	*Aufräumaktion*	

	English	German	Example / Explanation
	environmental organization *(AE)* = environmental organisation *(BE)* /ɪnvaɪrən,mentl‿ɔːgənaɪˈzeɪʃn/	Umweltschutzorganisation	

Use the webcode or do your own research online.	Benutz den Webcode oder recherchier selbst online.

	English	German	Example / Explanation
	majestic /məˈdʒestɪk/	majestätisch, erhaben	There is a *ban* on all mobile phones in my school.
	ban /bæn/	Verbot	
PB	preserve /prɪˈzɜːv/	erhalten	
p. 127	bottle cap /ˈbɒtl kæp/	Flaschenverschluss	
	frequently /ˈfriːkwəntli/	häufig	*frequently* = often
	recyclable /riːˈsaɪkləbl/	recycelbar, wiederverwertbar	
	literally /ˈlɪtrəli/	(wort)wörtlich	
	fall through the cracks /ˌfɔːl θruː ðə ˈkræks/	durch die Maschen schlüpfen	
	unique /juːˈniːk/	einzigartig	
	cap /kæp/	*hier:* Verschluss, Deckel	They *organised* an event to raise money for new computers for the school.
	organize *(AE)* = organise *(BE)* /ˈɔːgənaɪz/	organisieren	
	collection bin /kəˈlekʃn bɪn/	Sammelbehälter	
	carrier /ˈkæriə/	Träger	
	razor /ˈreɪzə/	Rasierer	
PC	trace /treɪs/	Spur	
p. 128	hidden /ˈhɪdn/	versteckt	*hidden* = not to be found easily
	hazardous /ˈhæzədəs/	gefährlich	A *sweatshop* is a factory where people work very hard in bad conditions and earn very little money.
	outdoor gear /aʊtˌdɔː ˈgɪə/	Outdoor-Ausrüstung	
	sweatshop /ˈswetˌʃɒp/	Ausbeuterbetrieb	
	swap shop /ˈswɒp ʃɒp/	Tauschbörse	
	child labour /ˈtʃaɪld ˌleɪbə/	Kinderarbeit	
	trading company /ˈtreɪdɪŋ ˌkʌmpni/	Handelsgesellschaft	
	certified /ˈsɜːtɪfaɪd/	geprüft, garantiert	A *label* gives information about something.
	label /ˈleɪbl/	Etikett, Schildchen	
	production /prəˈdʌkʃn/	Produktion	
PC	speak out /ˌspiːk‿ˈaʊt/	seine Meinung deutlich vertreten	
p. 129			Let's *swap* mobile numbers. You give me yours and I'll give you mine.
	eco-friendly /ˌiːkəʊ ˈfrendli/	umweltfreundlich	
	swap /swɒp/	tauschen	
	closet /ˈklɒzɪt/	Schrank	
	restyle /riːˈstaɪl/	neu entwerfen	
	button /ˈbʌtən/	Knopf	
	dye /daɪ/	färben	
	color *(AE)* /ˈkʌlə/	Farbe	A *dye* is used for changing the colour of something.
	dye /daɪ/	Färbemittel	

	English	German	Notes
	purse /pɜːs/	Portmonee	I've lost my *purse*. It had all my money in it!
	bamboo /ˌbæmˈbuː/	Bambus	
	hemp /hemp/	Hanf	
	detox /ˈdiːtɒks/	Entgiftung	
	loser /ˈluːzə/	Verlierer/in	*loser* ≠ winner
	put pressure on /ˌpʊt ˈpreʃər‿ɒn/	Druck ausüben auf	
	brand /brænd/	Marke	
	textile /ˈtekstaɪl/	Textil	*conventional* = not new or different
	conventional /kənˈvenʃnəl/	konventionell, herkömmlich	
	growing /ˈɡrəʊɪŋ/	Anbau	
	fertilizer *(AE)* = fertiliser *(BE)* /ˈfɜːtəlaɪzə/	Dünger	
	make a living /ˌmeɪk‿ə ˈlɪvɪŋ/	seinen Lebensunterhalt verdienen	You need a job to *make a living*.
	decent /ˈdiːsnt/	angemessen, annehmbar	
	method /ˈmeθəd/	Methode	
	bug /bʌɡ/	Wanze, Ungeziefer	
	in addition to /ˌɪn‿əˈdɪʃn tʊ/	zusätzlich zu	
PC	chance /tʃɑːns/	Möglichkeit, Gelegenheit	
p. 130	Asian /ˈeɪʒn/	Asiat/in; asiatisch	
	Indonesia /ˌɪndəʊˈniːʒə/	Indonesien	
	Bangladesh /ˌbæŋɡləˈdeʃ/	Bangladesch	
	India /ˈɪndiə/	Indien	
	worker /ˈwɜːkə/	Arbeiter/in	
	wage /weɪdʒ/	Lohn	
	profit /ˈprɒfɪt/	Gewinn	
	drinking water /ˈdrɪŋkɪŋ ˌwɔːtə/	Trinkwasser	
	not exactly /ˌnɒt‿ɪɡˈzækli/	eigentlich nicht; nicht gerade	
	labor *(AE)* = labour *(BE)* /ˈleɪbə/	Arbeit	
	join /dʒɔɪn/	sich zu jemandem gesellen	
	worldwide /ˌwɜːldˈwaɪd/	weltweit	
	definitely /ˈdefnətli/	eindeutig, definitiv	
	synthetic /sɪnˈθetɪk/	synthetisch	
	formaldehyde /fɔːˈmældɪˌhaɪd/	Formaldehyd	If you are *allergic* to some foods, you can't eat them without getting a reaction.
	allergic /əˈlɜːdʒɪk/	allergisch	
	reaction /riˈækʃn/	Reaktion	
	illness /ˈɪlnəs/	Krankheit	to *found* = to start an organisation, company etc.
PC	found /faʊnd/	gründen	
p. 131	company /ˈkʌmpni/	Firma, Unternehmen	
	accessory /əkˈsesəri/	Accessoire	
	artwork *(no pl)* /ˈɑːtˌwɜːk/	Kunstwerk(e)	*artwork* = work of art
	use up /ˌjuːz‿ˈʌp/	verbrauchen	

Vorsilben

Oft kann man durch Hinzufügen einer Vorsilbe die Bedeutung eines Wortes verändern bzw. ins Gegenteil verkehren. Ganz einfach ist es mit *‚un-'*. Es weist auf das Gegenteil hin, z. B.

tidy ≠ untidy
happy ≠ unhappy
important ≠ unimportant
friendly ≠ unfriendly
fair ≠ unfair

Kannst du noch weitere Beispiele finden?

leather /ˈleðə/	Leder	
silk /sɪlk/	Seide	You can make clothes from *silk* or *wool*.
wool /wʊl/	Wolle	
fabric /ˈfæbrɪk/	Stoff	I *donate* money to charity once a month.
donate /dəʊˈneɪt/	spenden	
separate /ˈseprət/	separat, gesondert	
non-profit /ˌnɒnˈprɒfɪt/	gemeinnützig, nicht gewinnorientiert	
environmentalist /ɪnˌvaɪrənˈmentlɪst/	Umweltschützer/in	*Environmentalists* want to protect the world.

P p. 132

In your group, discuss issues from your topic that affect your school, home or community.	Besprecht in eurer Gruppe Fragen von eurem Thema, die eure Schule, euer Zuhause oder eure Gemeinde betreffen.
Agree on one problem that you want to investigate and work on for your project.	Einigt euch auf ein Problem, das ihr untersuchen und an dem ihr für euer Projekt arbeiten wollt.
Research the problem.	Recherchiert das Problem.

survey /ˈsɜːveɪ/	Umfrage

Make a plan and carry out your research.	Macht einen Plan und führt eure Untersuchungen durch.
Talk about your findings and discuss possible solutions to your problem.	Sprecht über eure Ergebnisse und diskutiert über mögliche Lösungen für euer Problem.
Which ones would be most practical and effective?	Welche wären am praktischsten und effektivsten?
Create an action plan for your solution.	Erstellt einen Aktionsplan für eure Lösung.
Here's an example.	Hier ist ein Beispiel.

school playground /ˌskuːl ˈpleɪˌgraʊnd/	Schulhof	
seed /siːd/	Samen	
tool /tuːl/	Werkzeug	
advertise /ˈædvətaɪz/	für etwas Werbung machen	
total /ˈtəʊtl/	Gesamtsumme	Everybody was *involved* in the group project.
involved /ɪnˈvɒlvd/	beteiligt	

p. 133

Now put your plan into action.	Setzt nun euren Plan in die Tat um.

carry out /ˌkæri‿ˈaʊt/	durchführen, betreiben	
action plan /ˈækʃn plæn/	Handlungsplan, Maßnahmenplan	
leaflet /ˈliːflət/	Prospekt, Broschüre	*leaflet* 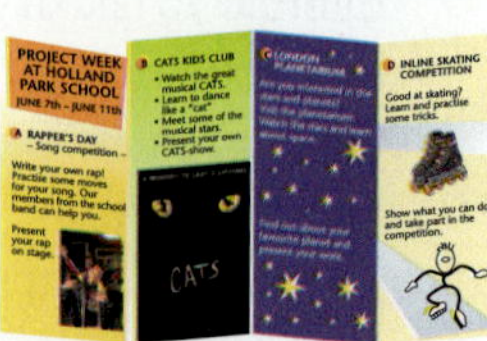
fundraising *(no pl)* /ˈfʌndreɪzɪŋ/	*Geldbeschaffung zu Wohltätigkeitszwecken*	*Progress* is the process of developing or improving.
progress /ˈprəʊgres/	Fortschritt	

Words

Be creative and use your imagination!	Seid kreativ und benutzt eure Vorstellungskraft!
Your presentation could include …	Eure Präsentation könnte … beinhalten.

slide show /ˈslaɪd ʃəʊ/	Diavortrag	
projector /prəˈdʒektə/	Projektor, Vorführgerät	
role play /ˈrəʊl pleɪ/	Rollenspiel	A *debate* is a kind of discussion.
debate /dɪˈbeɪt/	Debatte, Diskussion	

PA p. 134

Listen to the other presentations and take notes.	Hört euch die anderen Präsentationen an und macht euch Notizen.
Match the words and phrases in the box to the definitions below.	Ordne die Wörter und Ausdrücke im Kasten den Definitionen unten zu.

situated /ˈsɪtʃueɪtɪd/	gelegen	
measure /ˈmeʒə/	Maß, Maßeinheit	
oil /ɔɪl/	Öl	
coal /kəʊl/	Kohle	*Oil* and *coal* are fossil fuels.
run out of /ˌrʌn‿ˈaʊt‿əv/	nicht mehr haben	

Match the words to make phrases that have something to do with green cities.	Ordne die Wörter einander zu, um Ausdrücke zu bilden, die etwas mit umweltbewussten Städten zu tun haben.

sustainable /səˈsteɪnəbl/	nachhaltig	
metropolis /məˈtrɒpəlɪs/	Metropole	A *metropolis* is a big city.
housing *(no pl)* /ˈhaʊzɪŋ/	Wohnungen, Unterkünfte	*public transport* = buses, trains
transport /ˈtrænspɔːt/	Transport, Verkehrsmittel	etc. that everyone can use

Write statements about green cities using the phrases.	Schreib Aussagen über umweltbewusste Städte, in denen du die Ausdrücke benutzt.
Talk about making your community a greener place and reducing your carbon footprint.	Sprich darüber, wie du aus deiner Gemeinde einen umweltbewussteren Ort machen und deinen CO_2-Fußabdruck reduzieren kannst.

PB p. 135

define /dɪˈfaɪn/	definieren
principle /ˈprɪnsəpl/	Prinzip

Match the words in the box to the definitions below.	Ordne die Wörter im Kasten den Definitionen unten zu.

rot /rɒt/	verrotten, verfaulen	
harm /hɑːm/	schaden	to *harm* = to damage
substance /ˈsʌbstəns/	Substanz, *hier:* Chemikalie	

Match the words to make phrases that have something to do with 'A plastic planet'.	Ordne die Wörter einander zu, um Ausdrücke zu bilden, die etwas mit *'A plastic planet'* zu tun haben.

kitchen utensils *(pl)* /ˈkɪtʃən‿juːˌtenslz/	Küchengeräte

Write statements about 'A plastic planet' using the phrases.	Schreib Aussagen über *'A plastic planet'*, in denen du die Ausdrücke benutzt.

discussion /dɪˈskʌʃn/	Diskussion

Talk about the problem of plastic and what you can do about it.	Sprecht über das Problem von Plastik und was ihr dagegen machen könnt.

PC p. 136

environmental /ɪnˌvaɪrənˈmentl/	Umwelt-	
pesticide /ˈpestɪsaɪd/	Pestizid, Schädlingsbekämpfungsmittel	*Pesticides* and *herbicides* are chemicals that are very bad for the environment and your health.
herbicide /ˈhɜːbɪsaɪd/	Herbizid, Unkrautvernichtungsmittel	
harmful /ˈhɑːmfl/	schädlich	
damage /ˈdæmɪdʒ/	Schaden	A storm can cause a lot of *damage* to a ship.
e.g. (= exempli gratia) /ˌiː ˈdʒiː/	z.B. (= zum Beispiel)	
chemical /ˈkemɪkl/	chemisch	
insect /ˈɪnsekt/	Insekt	
weed /wiːd/	Unkraut	
non-natural /ˌnɒn‿ˈnætʃrəl/	nicht natürlich	
condition /kənˈdɪʃn/	Zustand; Bedingung	

Match the words to make phrases that have something to do with toxic fashion.	Ordne die Wörter einander zu, um Ausdrücke zu bilden, die etwas mit giftiger Mode zu tun haben.

rely on /rɪˈlaɪ‿ɒn/	sich verlassen auf
detox /diːˈtɒks/	entgiften

Write statements about toxic fashion using the phrases.	Schreib Aussagen über giftige Mode, in denen du die Ausdrücke benutzt.
Talk about the problem of toxic fashion and what you can do about it.	Sprecht über das Problem von giftiger Mode und was ihr dagegen machen könnt.

Dictionary

Hier findest du alphabetisch sortiert alle Wörter aus dem vorliegenden Buch sowie die Lernwörter aus den vorigen Bänden.
I bedeutet: Dieses Wort kommt in Band I (5. Klasse) vor, entsprechend steht II für Band 2, III für Band 3 und IV für Band 4.
5/A3 bedeutet: Dieses Wort kommt in *Theme* 5, Aufgabe A3 das erste Mal vor oder wird erst an dieser Stelle zum Lernwort gemacht.
6/Project steht hinter Wörtern aus dem Projektkapitel.
BS markiert ein Wort aus einem *Book stop*-Text. O markiert ein Wort aus einem *Optional*. Diese Wörter sind zusätzlich mit einem ° versehen.

Folgende Abkürzungen werden verwendet:
sth = something, sb = somebody, etw = etwas, jd = jemand, jdm = jemandem, jdn = jemanden

A

a/an /ə, eɪ / ən/ ein(e) I:Welcome
a /ə/ pro III:3/A4
ability /ə'bɪləti/ Fähigkeit IV:4/B6
be able to do sth /ˌbi‿ˌeɪbl tə 'du: ˌsʌmθɪŋ/ etw tun können II:3/A1
about /ə'baʊt/ über; an I:1/I; ungefähr I:5/A4
above /ə'bʌv/ obige(r, s); oben genannte(n) IV:5/A4
abroad /ə'brɔ:d/ im Ausland, ins Ausland II:6/B1
go abroad /ˌgəʊ‿ə'brɔ:d/ ins Ausland fahren II:1/A3
absorb /əb'zɔ:b/ *hier:* abfangen IV:2/B7
AC (= air conditioning) /ˌeɪ 'si:/ Klimaanlage IV:2/B2
academy /ə'kædəmi/ Akademie; Schule IV:4/A7
accent /'æksnt/ Akzent IV:1/P14
accept /ək'sept/ anerkennen; akzeptieren IV:2/A6
access /'ækses/ Zugang IV:6/Project A p.122
accessory /ək'sesəri/ Accessoire IV:6/Project C p.131
accident /'æksɪdnt/ Unfall IV:2/B2
according to /ə'kɔ:dɪŋ ˌtu:/ nach; gemäß II:2/A8
account /ə'kaʊnt/ *hier:* Preis IV:3/B8
°achieve /ə'tʃi:v/ erreichen IV:5/O
°achievement /ə'tʃi:vmənt/ Leistung IV:BS/9
acre /'eɪkə/ Morgen *(Maßeinheit zur Flächenbestimmung)* IV:6/Project A p.123
across /ə'krɒs/ über II:2/A2
across /ə'krɒs/ gegenüber IV:5/A1; *hier:* durch IV:5/A10
act /ækt/ handeln; *hier:* spielen II:3/A8
act out /ˌækt‿'aʊt/ nachspielen; vorspielen II:6/B11
action /'ækʃn/ Handlung I:3/A13
put into action /ˌpʊt‿ɪntʊ 'ækʃn/ in die Tat umsetzen IV:6/Project p.119
action plan /'ækʃn plæn/ Handlungsplan, Maßnahmenplan IV:6/Project p.132
activity /æk'tɪvəti/ Aktivität II:1/A10
actor/actress /'æktə, 'æktrəs/ Schauspieler/in II:3/A8
actually /'æktʃuəli/ eigentlich; übrigens II:4/A3
°actually /'æktʃuəli/ *hier:* wirklich IV:BS/3
°ad (= advertisement) /æd, əd'vɜ:tɪsmənt/ Anzeige IV:BS/8
adapt /ə'dæpt/ sich anpassen IV:2/A5
add /æd/ hinzufügen III:1/B5
add to /'æd‿tʊ/ beitragen; *hier:* erweitern IV:6/Project p.118
adequately /'ædɪkwətli/ ausreichend IV:2/B8
adjective /'ædʒɪktɪv/ Adjektiv IV:3/P9
admission fee /əd'mɪʃn fi:/ Eintritt IV:3/P12
admit /əd'mɪt/ zugeben IV:3/A4
adopt /ə'dɒpt/ adoptieren IV:2/A6
adult /'ædʌlt/ Erwachsene/r II:2/A8
°advancement /əd'vɑ:nsmənt/ Vorankommen, Weiterkommen IV:BS/9
adventure /əd'ventʃə/ Abenteuer III:2/A9
°adventurous /əd'ventʃrəs/ abenteuerlich IV:5/O
advertise /'ædvətaɪz/ für etw Werbung machen IV:6/Project p.132
advertisement (= advert) /əd'vɜ:tɪsmənt, 'ædvɜ:t/ Werbung; Anzeige III:2/B13
advice *(no pl)* /əd'vaɪs/ Rat(schlag) III:4/B2
advise /əd'vaɪz/ raten, beraten; informieren IV:2/A7
affect /ə'fekt/ betreffen; beeinflussen IV:6/Project p.132
afford /ə'fɔ:d/ sich leisten III:2/A7
affordable /ə'fɔ:dəbl/ erschwinglich IV:6/Project A p.122
Africa /'æfrɪkə/ Afrika IV:Quiz
African American /ˌæfrɪkən‿ə'merɪkən/ Afroamerikaner/in; afroamerikanisch IV:Quiz
after /'ɑ:ftə/ nachdem IV:5/A5; nach I:3/A1
after that /ˌɑ:ftə 'ðæt/ danach II:1/A7

afternoon /ˌɑːftəˈnuːn/ Nachmittag I:4/A11
all afternoon /ˌɔːl‿ˌɑːftəˈnuːn/ den ganzen Nachmittag lang II:6/A6
in the afternoon /ˌɪn ði‿ɑːftəˈnuːn/ am Nachmittag II:4/B8
afterwards /ˈɑːftəwədz/ anschließend; später III:4/B4
again /əˈgen/ wieder; noch einmal I:1/A2
against /əˈgenst/ gegen II:5/A8
age /eɪdʒ/ Alter I:1/A9
at the age of /æt ði‿ˈeɪdʒ‿əv/ im Alter von IV:4/A7
°aged /eɪdʒd/ alt IV:5/O
°take ages *(informal)* /ˌteɪk‿ˈeɪdʒɪz/ ewig dauern IV:3/O
ago /əˈgəʊ/ vor III:3/A4
agree /əˈgriː/ zustimmen II:5/B3
agree on /əˈgriː‿ɒn/ sich einigen auf IV:3/A11
ain't (= am/are/is not) *(informal)* /eɪnt/ nicht sein IV:1/B8
air /eə/ Luft III:5/A2
airlift /ˈeəˌlɪft/ per Flugzeug evakuieren IV:5/B4
airport /ˈeəpɔːt/ Flughafen II:2/A2
aisle /aɪl/ Gang IV:5/A1
alarm clock /əˈlɑːm klɒk/ Wecker II:5/B2
°alive /əˈlaɪv/ lebendig IV:BS/4
all /ɔːl/ alle; alles I:Welcome; ganz; völlig III:2/B4
all afternoon /ˌɔːl‿ˌɑːftəˈnuːn/ den ganzen Nachmittag lang II:6/A6
all around /ˌɔːl‿əˈraʊnd/ überall IV:1/B8
°all around the world /ˌɔːl‿əˌraʊnd ðə ˈwɜːld/ überall auf der Welt IV:1/O
all day /ˌɔːl ˈdeɪ/ den ganzen Tag lang IV:2/B2
all kinds of /ˌɔːl ˈkaɪndz‿əv/ alle möglichen II:6/B11
all morning /ˌɔːl ˈmɔːnɪŋ/ den ganzen Morgen lang IV:2/B2
all over the world /ˌɔːl‿ˌəʊvə ðə ˈwɜːld/ auf der ganzen Welt IV:2/I
all right /ˌɔːl ˈraɪt/ in Ordnung III:2/A7
all the time /ˌɔːl ðə ˈtaɪm/ die ganze Zeit II:4/B5
all week /ˌɔːl ˈwiːk/ die ganze Woche lang II:6/A2
allergic /əˈlɜːdʒɪk/ allergisch IV:6/Project C p.130
allow /əˈlaʊ/ erlauben II:5/A8
°allow /əˈlaʊ/ *hier:* einplanen IV:2/O
almost /ˈɔːlməʊst/ fast; beinahe IV:5/A4
alone /əˈləʊn/ allein III:4/A1
°along with /əˈlɒŋ wɪð/ zusammen mit IV:1/O
alphabet /ˈælfəˌbet/ Alphabet I:2/B9
already /ɔːlˈredi/ schon; bereits II:3/A1
also /ˈɔːlsəʊ/ auch I:3/B6
°although /ɔːlˈðəʊ/ obwohl IV:1/O
altogether /ˌɔːltəˈgeðə/ insgesamt I:4/B6
aluminum *(AE)* = aluminium *(BE)* /əˈluːmɪnəm, ˌæləˈmɪniəm/ Aluminium IV:2/B2
always /ˈɔːlweɪz/ immer I:1/A5
am (= ante meridiem) /ˌeɪˈem, ˌænti məˈrɪdiəm/ morgens, vormittags *(nur hinter Uhrzeit zwischen Mitternacht und 12 Uhr mittags)* I:3/A4
amazing *(informal)* /əˈmeɪzɪŋ/ toll III:5/A1
°ambition /æmˈbɪʃn/ Ehrgeiz IV:5/O
America /əˈmerɪkə/ Amerika II:4/A1
American /əˈmerɪkən/ Amerikaner/in; amerikanisch IV:Quiz
among /əˈmʌŋ/ unter; zwischen II:2/A2
amount /əˈmaʊnt/ Menge; Betrag II:6/B11
and /ænd/ und I:Welcome ...
angel /ˈeɪndʒl/ Engel IV:3/A9
angry, angrily /ˈæŋgri, ˈæŋgrili/ verärgert II:3/B1
animal /ˈænɪml/ Tier I:Welcome ...
ankle /ˈæŋkl/ (Fuß)knöchel IV:2/B7
announce /əˈnaʊns/ bekannt geben IV:5/A4
annoyed /əˈnɔɪd/ verärgert II:5/A1
anonymous /əˈnɒnɪməs/ anonym IV:3/A7
another /əˈnʌðə/ noch ein/e I:3/A13; ein anderer/ein anderes/eine andere II:5/B10
another /əˈnʌðə/ *hier:* weitere IV:2/B2
answer /ˈɑːnsə/ *(be)*antworten I:2/B7; Antwort I:3/B6
answer the phone /ˌɑːnsə ðə ˈfəʊn/ ans Telefon gehen I:5/B3
°ant /ænt/ Ameise IV:BS/4
°the Antarctic /ði‿æntˈɑːktɪk/ Antarktis IV:BS/3
°Antarctica /ænˈtɑːktɪkə/ Antarktis IV:BS/3
any /ˈeni/ (irgend)ein(e) I:3/B4
anybody /ˈenibɒdi/ irgendjemand; jede(r, s) I:3/A1
anyone /ˈeniˌwʌn/ jede(r, s); (irgend)jemand IV:1/A9
anything /ˈeniˌθɪŋ/ irgendetwas III:2/A7
not anything /ˌnɒt‿ˈeniˌθɪŋ/ nichts II:1/A7
anything else /eniˌθɪŋ‿ˈels/ noch etwas I:4/B6
Anything else? /eniˌθɪŋ‿ˈels/ Sonst noch etwas?, Darf es noch etwas sein? I:4/B6
anytime /ˈeniˌtaɪm/ jederzeit IV:3/A9
anyway /ˈeniweɪ/ jedenfalls I:4/B9; sowieso; überhaupt II:4/A7
anywhere /ˈeniˌweə/ irgendwo II:1/A6
apartment *(AE)* /əˈpɑːtmənt/ Wohnung IV:1/B5
apartment building /əˈpɑːtmənt ˌbɪldɪŋ/ Wohnblock IV:6/Project A p.121

apologize (= apologise) /əˈpɒlədʒaɪz/ sich entschuldigen IV:4/B7
appear /əˈpɪə/ erscheinen, auftauchen IV:4/B3
appearance /əˈpɪərəns/ Erscheinen, Aussehen IV:5/A1
°appetite /ˈæpətaɪt/ Appetit IV:BS/6
apple /ˈæpl/ Apfel I:Welcome
apply for /əˈplaɪ fɔː/ sich bewerben um IV:4/B6
apprenticeship /əˈprentɪsʃɪp/ Ausbildung, Lehre IV:4/A3
April /ˈeɪprəl/ April I:5/B7
°architect /ˈɑːkɪˌtekt/ Architekt/in IV:5/O
Are there …? /ˈɑː ðeə/ Gibt es …? I:1/B3
Are you ready to order? /ɑː juː ˌredi tʊ‿ˈɔːdə/ Möchten Sie bestellen? III:1/A4
How are you? /ˌhaʊ‿ˈɑː jʊ/ Wie geht es dir? / Wie geht es Ihnen? I:4/B9
Where are you from? /ˌweər‿ə jʊ ˈfrɒm/ Woher kommst du? I:1/A3
area /ˈeəriə/ Gebiet, Region III:1/A9
arithmetic /əˈrɪθmətɪk/ Arithmetik IV:5/A1
ark /ˈɑːk/ Arche IV:5/A1
around /əˈraʊnd/ um; herum, umher II:2/I
around /əˈraʊnd/ ungefähr IV:5/A9
°see you around *(informal)* /ˌsiː jʊ‿əˈraʊnd/ bis demnächst IV:3/O
arrival /əˈraɪvl/ Ankunft IV:5/A4
arrive /əˈraɪv/ ankommen II:1/A2
art /ɑːt/ Kunst I:5/A2
article /ˈɑːtɪkl/ Artikel I:4/A11
artist /ˈɑːtɪst/ Künstler/in III:6/B1
artwork *(no pl)* /ˈɑːtˌwɜːk/ Kunstwerk(e) IV:6/Project C p. 131
as /əz/ als; wie; während II:1/B11
as … as /æz æz/ so … wie II:4/B3
°as a matter of fact /əz‿ə ˌmætər‿əv‿ˈfækt/ übrigens IV:BS/8
as a result /əz‿ə rɪˈzʌlt/ als Folge IV:5/A2
as best sb can /əz ˌbest ˌsʌmbədi ˈkæn/ so gut (wie) jd kann IV:2/B8
°as long as /əz ˈlɒŋ‿əz/ solange IV:BS/7
as well /ˌəz‿ˈwel/ auch II:6/B11
°as well as /əz ˈwel‿əz/ ebenso wie IV:BS/3
ascend /əˈsend/ aufsteigen IV:2/A4
Asia /ˈeɪʒə/ Asien IV:Quiz
Asian /ˈeɪʒn/ Asiat/in; asiatisch IV:6/Project C p. 130
aside /əˈsaɪd/ auf die Seite IV:3/B8
ask /ɑːsk/ fragen; bitten I:3/A5
ask questions /ˌɑːsk ˈkwestʃnz/ Fragen stellen III:4/B2
ask sb out on a date /ˌɑːsk ˌsʌmbədi‿ˌaʊt‿ɒn‿ə ˈdeɪt/ jdn fragen, ob er / sie mit einem ausgehen will IV:3/A4
be asleep /ˌbi‿əˈsliːp/ schlafen IV:3/B1
aspect /ˈæspekt/ Aspekt; Gesichtspunkt IV:6/Project p. 119
assembly /əˈsembli/ (Schüler)versammlung I:5/A3
°assembly line /əˈsembli laɪn/ Fließband IV:BS/8
°association /əˌsəʊsiˈeɪʃn/ Vereinigung IV:BS/9
asylum seeker /əˈsaɪləm ˌsiːkə/ Asylsuchende/r IV:5/B3
at /æt/ an; in; bei; um I:Welcome
at all /ət‿ˈɔːl/ überhaupt II:1/B1
at first /ət ˈfɜːst/ zuerst IV:2/A7
at first sight /ət ˌfɜːst ˈsaɪt/ auf den ersten Blick IV:3/B1
at home /ˌæt ˈhəʊm/ zu Hause I:3/A9
at last /ət ˈlɑːst/ endlich; schließlich II:6/A2
at least /ət ˈliːst/ mindestens; wenigstens III:3/B1
at midnight /æt ˈmɪdˌnaɪt/ um Mitternacht II:4/B8
at night /æt ˈnaɪt/ nachts II:1/B11
at that time /æt ˈðæt‿taɪm/ zu jener Zeit IV:5/A2
at the age of /æt ði‿ˈeɪdʒ‿əv/ im Alter von IV:4/A7
at the back /ˌæt ðə ˈbæk/ hinten IV:1/B3
at the beginning /ˌæt‿ðə bɪˈgɪnɪŋ/ am Anfang IV:3/B6
at the bottom /ˌæt‿ðə ˈbɒtəm/ unten IV:6/Project p. 117
at the end /ˌæt ði‿ˈend/ schließlich IV:4/A10
at the front /ˌæt ðə ˈfrʌnt/ vorn(e) IV:1/A1
at the moment /ˌæt‿ðə ˈməʊmənt/ im Moment I:3/B6
°at the time /ˌæt‿ðə ˈtaɪm/ damals; zu dem Zeitpunkt IV:BS/9
at the weekend /ˌæt‿ðə ˈwiːkend/ am Wochenende I:2/A12
athlete /ˈæθliːt/ Athlet/in IV:1/A4
Atlantic Ocean /ətˌlæntɪk‿ˈəʊʃn/ Atlantik IV:5/A2
attack /əˈtæk/ angreifen II:5/B10
°attempt /əˈtempt/ Versuch IV:BS/3
attractive /əˈtræktɪv/ attraktiv; reizvoll IV:2/A2
audience /ˈɔːdiəns/ Publikum II:6/B6
August /ˈɔːgəst/ August I:5/B7
aunt /ɑːnt/ Tante I:5/B3
Australia /ɒˈstreɪliə/ Australien IV:Quiz
Australian /ɒˈstreɪliən/ Australier/in; australisch IV:6/Project B p. 125
autumn /ˈɔːtəm/ Herbst I:Welcome
available /əˈveɪləbl/ verfügbar III:1/A9
avenue /ˈævəˌnjuː/ Boulevard, Allee, Straße IV:1/B2
average /ˈævərɪdʒ/ durchschnittlich III:1/A9
on average /ˌɒn‿ˈævərɪdʒ/ durchschnittlich IV:6/Project B p. 126
avoid /əˈvɔɪd/ meiden; vermeiden IV:5/A9
award /əˈwɔːd/ Preis; Auszeichnung IV:Quiz; verleihen; auszeichnen; zusprechen IV:BS/9

be aware of sth /ˌbi‿əˈweər‿əv ˌsʌmθɪŋ/ sich einer Sache bewusst sein IV:6/Project p. 117
away /əˈweɪ/ weg II:2/B2
awesome /ˈɔːsm/ spitze; super; beeindruckend II:2/B6
awful /ˈɔːfl/ schrecklich IV:4/B4

B

babysit /ˈbeɪbiˌsɪt/ babysitten IV:4/B6
bachelor /ˈbætʃələ/ Junggeselle IV:3/B8
back /bæk/ Rücken I:2/A1; zurück I:4/A11
back /bæk/ *hier:* Rückseite IV:2/B2
at the back /ˌæt ðə ˈbæk/ hinten IV:1/B5
°back then /ˌbæk ˈðen/ damals IV:4/O
backache *(no pl)* /ˈbækeɪk/ Rückenschmerzen III:3/B2
background /ˈbækˌɡraʊnd/ Hintergrund IV:1/A7
bacon /ˈbeɪkən/ Schinkenspeck I:2/A8
bad /bæd/ schlecht; schlimm II:1/B10
bad luck /ˌbæd ˈlʌk/ Pech II:1/B6
badly-paid /ˌbædli ˈpeɪd/ schlecht bezahlt IV:4/A1
bag /bæɡ/ Tasche II:3/A1
bake /beɪk/ backen IV:Quiz
baked beans *(pl)* /ˌbeɪkt ˈbiːnz/ Bohnen in Tomatensauce I:2/A7
baker /ˈbeɪkə/ Bäcker/in II:3/A6
balloon /bəˈluːn/ Luftballon I:5/B3
bamboo /ˌbæmˈbuː/ Bambus IV:6/Project C p. 129
ban /bæn/ *hier:* verbannen IV:3/B3; verbieten IV:6/Project A p. 121; Verbot IV:6/Project B p. 126
banana /bəˈnɑːnə/ Banane I:Welcome
bandage /ˈbændɪdʒ/ Verband III:3/B1
Bangladesh /ˌbæŋɡləˈdeʃ/ Bangladesch IV:6/Project C p. 130
bar chart /ˈbɑː tʃɑːt/ Balkendiagramm; Säulendiagramm IV:5/A7
°barbecue /ˈbɑːbɪˌkjuː/ Grill; *hier:* Grillparty IV:BS/4
°barely /ˈbeəli/ kaum IV:BS/6
°base camp /ˈbeɪs kæmp/ Basislager IV:BS/3
based on /ˈbeɪst‿ɒn/ basierend auf IV:6/Project p. 119
basement /ˈbeɪsmənt/ Keller IV:4/B3
bat /bæt/ Fledermaus I:WB/1
bathroom /ˈbɑːθˌruːm/ Badezimmer I:2/A2
°battle /ˈbætl/ Kampf IV:BS/3
be *(irr)* /biː/ sein I:1/A2
be a shame /ˌbi‿ə ˈʃeɪm/ schade sein IV:3/B6
be able to do sth /ˌbi‿eɪbl tə ˈduː ˌsʌmθɪŋ/ etw tun können II:3/A1
be about /ˌbi‿əˈbaʊt/ gehen um; handeln von IV:2/A7
be afraid of /ˌbi‿əˈfreɪd‿əv/ Angst haben vor III:4/B9
be allowed to /ˌbi‿əˈlaʊd‿tə/ dürfen II:5/A4
be asleep /ˌbi‿əˈsliːp/ schlafen IV:3/B1
be aware of sth /ˌbi‿əˈweər‿əv ˌsʌmθɪŋ/ sich einer Sache bewusst sein IV:6/Project p. 117
be born /biː ˈbɔːn/ geboren werden IV:5/B3
be done with *(informal)* /ˌbiː ˈdʌn wɪð/ fertig sein mit IV:4/B8
be good at sth /ˌbiː ˈɡʊd‿æt ˌsʌmθɪŋ/ gut in etw sein II:4/A7
°be in a rush /ˌbi‿ɪn‿ə ˈrʌʃ/ in Eile sein IV:BS/6
be in love /ˌbi‿ɪn ˈlʌv/ verliebt sein IV:3/B6
be like *(informal)* /ˌbiː ˈlaɪk/ *hier etwa:* sagen IV:1/A2
be one's turn /ˌbiː wʌnz ˈtɜːn/ an der Reihe sein I:4/B1
be out of breath /ˌbi‿aʊt‿əv ˈbreθ/ außer Atem sein; atemlos sein III:3/A1
°be out of sight /ˌbi‿ˌaʊt‿əv ˈsaɪt/ außer Sichtweite sein IV:3/O
be prepared /ˌbiː prɪˈpeəd/ vorbereitet sein auf IV:6/Project p. 119
be right /ˌbiː ˈraɪt/ recht haben II:1/B7
be scared (of) /ˌbiː ˈskeəd‿əv/ Angst haben (vor) II:1/B3
be set in /ˌbiː ˈset‿ɪn/ spielen in IV:1/B7
°be sick of *(informal)* /ˌbiː ˈsɪk‿əv/ satthaben IV:BS/6
be stressed /ˌbiː ˈstrest/ betont werden IV:3/P10
be stuck /ˌbiː ˈstʌk/ *hier:* festhängen IV:3/A6
beach /biːtʃ/ Strand II:1/A11
baked beans *(pl)* /ˌbeɪkt ˈbiːnz/ Bohnen in Tomatensauce I:2/A7
beat *(irr)* /biːt/ schlagen I:3/A6
beautiful /ˈbjuːtəfl/ schön II:4/A1
because /bɪˈkɒz/ weil; da I:4/B3
because of /bɪˈkɒz‿əv/ wegen IV:3/B1
become *(irr)* /bɪˈkʌm/ werden II:1/A6
bed /bed/ Bett I:4/A1
before /bɪˈfɔː/ vor I:2/A12; bevor II:1/B11; vorher; zuvor II:6/A2
begin *(irr)* /bɪˈɡɪn/ anfangen; beginnen II:1/B3
beginning /bɪˈɡɪnɪŋ/ Anfang; Beginn IV:1/A9
at the beginning /ˌæt‿ðə bɪˈɡɪnɪŋ/ am Anfang IV:3/B6
behind /bɪˈhaɪnd/ hinten IV:5/A1; hinter I:4/A3
believe (in) /bɪˈliːv‿ɪn/ glauben (an) III:2/B9
belong (to) /bɪˈlɒŋ/ gehören (zu) II:5/A6
below /bɪˈləʊ/ unten, unter IV:2/B7
bend /bend/ sich biegen IV:2/B7
beneath /bɪˈniːθ/ unter IV:2/B7
best /best/ beste(r, s) I:1/A4; am liebsten II:4/A1
like best /ˌlaɪk ˈbest/ am liebsten mögen I:5/B12

the best /ðə ˈbest/ der/die/das beste IV:1/B5
best wishes /ˌbest ˈwɪʃɪz/ viele Grüße II:6/A8
better /ˈbetə/ besser I:5/A2
between /bɪˈtwiːn/ zwischen I:4/B5
bicycle /ˈbaɪsɪkl/ Fahrrad III:5/B1
big /bɪg/ groß I:1/A4
Big Apple /ˌbɪg‿ˈæpl/ *Spitzname für New York* IV:1/B4
biggest /ˈbɪgɪst/ größte(r, s) IV:2/A5
bike /baɪk/ Fahrrad I:1/A4
by bike /ˌbaɪ ˈbaɪk/ mit dem Fahrrad I:5/A7
ride a bike /ˌraɪd‿ə ˈbaɪk/ Fahrrad fahren I:1/A4
bike lane /ˈbaɪk leɪn/ Fahrradweg IV:6/Project A p. 120
bill /bɪl/ Rechnung III:1/A4
billion /ˈbɪljən/ Milliarde IV:6/Project B p. 126
bin /bɪn/ Abfalleimer I:2/B1
biodegrade /ˌbaɪəʊdɪˈgreɪd/ sich zersetzen IV:6/Project B p. 125
°biography /baɪˈɒgrəfi/ Biographie IV:BS/9
bird /bɜːd/ Vogel I:WB/1
birth /bɜːθ/ Geburt IV:2/A8
date of birth /ˌdeɪt‿əv ˈbɜːθ/ Geburtsdatum IV:4/P10
place of birth /ˌpleɪs‿əv ˈbɜːθ/ Geburtsort IV:4/P10
birthday /ˈbɜːθdeɪ/ Geburtstag I:5/B2
Happy birthday (to you)! /ˌhæpi ˈbɜːθdeɪ tʊ juː/ Herzlichen Glückwunsch zum Geburtstag! I:5/B1
biscuit /ˈbɪskɪt/ Keks I:4/B5
bisexual /baɪˈsekʃʊəl/ bisexuell IV:2/A6
a (little) bit /ə ˌlɪtl ˈbɪt/ ein (kleines) bisschen II:1/B1
black /blæk/ schwarz I:Welcome
blackboard /ˈblækˌbɔːd/ Tafel I:2/B1
blazing hot /ˌbleɪzɪŋ ˈhɒt/ glühend heiß IV:5/B7
blister /ˈblɪstə/ Blase IV:5/B7
blue /bluː/ blau I:Welcome
board /bɔːd/ Tafel; Brett IV:2/A11
board a ship /ˌbɔːd‿ə ˈʃɪp/ ein Schiff besteigen IV:5/A4
boat /bəʊt/ Boot II:1/A7
body /ˈbɒdi/ Körper I:2/A3
body /ˈbɒdi/ *hier:* Hauptteil IV:2/B7; *hier:* Leiche IV:BS/3
boil /bɔɪl/ kochen *(Flüssigkeit)* III:5/B7
°boiled /bɔɪld/ gekocht IV:BS/4
bone /bəʊn/ Knochen III:4/A1
book /bʊk/ Buch I:2/A3
exercise book /ˈeksəsaɪz ˌbʊk/ Heft I:2/B4
boot /buːt/ Stiefel I:WB/1
border /ˈbɔːdə/ Grenze IV:5/A8
border patrol /ˈbɔːdə pəˌtrəʊl/ Grenzstreife IV:5/A9
bored /bɔːd/ gelangweilt IV:3/A10
boring /ˈbɔːrɪŋ/ langweilig I:4/A11
borough /ˈbʌrə/ Verwaltungsbezirk; *hier:* Stadtteil IV:1/B5
borrow /ˈbɒrəʊ/ (aus)leihen II:5/A6
both /bəʊθ/ beide III:3/A4
bottle /ˈbɒtl/ Flasche III:1/A3
bottle cap /ˈbɒtl kæp/ Flaschenverschluss IV:6/Project B p. 127
bow /baʊ/ Bogen IV:4/A6
bowl /bəʊl/ Schüssel, Schale III:1/B11
box /bɒks/ Kasten; Kiste II:4/A1
Boxing Day /ˈbɒksɪŋ deɪ/ zweiter Weihnachtsfeiertag II:4/A1
boy /bɔɪ/ Junge I:3/A1
boyfriend /ˈbɔɪˌfrend/ Freund *(Partner)*; Partner III:4/B4
bracket /ˈbrækɪt/ Klammer IV:1/P3
branch /brɑːntʃ/ Zweig, Ast; Zweigstelle IV:3/A11
°branch manager /ˈbrɑːntʃ ˌmænɪdʒə/ Filialleiter/in IV:BS/8
brand /brænd/ Marke IV:6/Project C p. 129
brand-new /ˌbrænd ˈnjuː/ brandneu IV:1/B8
°brave /breɪv/ mutig IV:BS/3
°bravery /ˈbreɪvəri/ Tapferkeit, Mut IV:BS/3
bread /bred/ Brot III:1/A3
break /breɪk/ Pause I:Welcome
break *(irr)* /breɪk/ brechen; zerbrechen; kaputt machen II:6/A6
break *(irr)* /breɪk/ *hier:* reißen IV:2/B7
break down /ˌbreɪk ˈdaʊn/ sich aufspalten IV:6/Project B p. 125
break the habit /ˌbreɪk ðə ˈhæbɪt/ sich etw abgewöhnen IV:2/A9
break up /ˌbreɪk‿ˈʌp/ Schluss machen IV:2/A5
breakfast /ˈbrekfəst/ Frühstück I:2/A7
for breakfast /fə ˈbrekfəst/ zum Frühstück I:2/A12
have breakfast /ˌhæv ˈbrekfəst/ frühstücken I:2/A12
be out of breath /ˌbi‿ˌaʊt‿əv ˈbreθ/ außer Atem sein; atemlos sein III:3/A1
breathe /briːð/ (ein)atmen IV:5/A10
bricklayer /ˈbrɪkˌleɪə/ Maurer/in II:3/A8
bridge /brɪdʒ/ Brücke II:2/A2
bright /braɪt/ intelligent; strahlend, hell III:5/B8
brilliant /ˈbrɪljənt/ genial, klasse III:2/B5
bring *(irr)* /brɪŋ/ mitbringen I:3/A4
bring *(irr)* /brɪŋ/ *hier:* bringen IV:2/B6
bring together /ˌbrɪŋ təˈgeðə/ zusammenbringen IV:1/A4
Britain /ˈbrɪtn/ Großbritannien III:1/B9
British /ˈbrɪtɪʃ/ britisch III:1/I
broke *(informal)* /brəʊk/ pleite IV:3/A6
broken /ˈbrəʊkən/ zerbrochen; gebrochen; kaputt III:2/B5
brother /ˈbrʌðə/ Bruder I:Welcome
brothers and sisters /ˈbrʌðəz‿ænd ˌsɪstəz/ Geschwister II:Last year
brown /braʊn/ braun I:Welcome
bruised /bruːzd/ geprellt III:3/B1

brush /brʌʃ/ putzen; bürsten I:2/A1
brush one's teeth /ˌbrʌʃ wʌnz ˈtiːθ/ sich die Zähne putzen I:2/A1
bubble /ˈbʌbl/ Blase IV:5/A1
°bubble up /ˌbʌbl‿ˈʌp/ aufsteigen IV:3/O
budgie /ˈbʌdʒi/ Wellensittich I:WB/1
bug /bʌg/ Wanze; Ungeziefer IV:6/Project C p. 129
build *(irr)* /bɪld/ bauen II:3/A8
building /ˈbɪldɪŋ/ Gebäude III:5/A6
bully /ˈbʊli/ mobben II:5/B9
bully /ˈbʊli/ *Person, die mobbt* IV:2/A2
bullying /ˈbʊliɪŋ/ Mobben II:5/I
burn *(irr)* /bɜːn/ (ver)brennen II:3/B8
by bus /ˌbaɪ ˈbʌs/ mit dem Bus I:5/A7
go by bus /ˌgəʊ baɪ ˈbʌs/ mit dem Bus fahren I:5/A4
°bus pass /ˈbʌs pɑːs/ Buskarte, Monatskarte IV:3/O
bus stop /ˈbʌs‿stɒp/ Bushaltestelle II:5/B9
bush /bʊʃ/ Busch IV:5/A10
business /ˈbɪznəs/ Geschäft; Handel III:2/B9
busy /ˈbɪzi/ belebt; verkehrsreich IV:1/B5; arbeitsreich; beschäftigt I:4/A6
keep oneself busy /ˌkiːp wʌnˌself ˈbɪzi/ sich mit etw beschäftigen IV:2/A9
but /bʌt/ aber I:1/A4
butt *(informal)* /bʌt/ Kippe IV:2/A7
butterfly /ˈbʌtəˌflaɪ/ Schmetterling II:3/A1
button /ˈbʌtən/ Knopf IV:6/Project C p. 129
buy *(irr)* /baɪ/ kaufen I:3/B6
by /baɪ/ von; mit II:1/A10; *hier:* (spätestens) bis II:5/A3
by (+ *-ing*) *(oder nur Verbform mit -ing)* /baɪ/ indem IV:6/Project A p. 123
by any means /ˌbaɪ‿eni ˈmiːnz/ auf jeden Fall IV:1/B8
by bike /ˌbaɪ ˈbaɪk/ mit dem Fahrrad I:5/A7
by bus /ˌbaɪ ˈbʌs/ mit dem Bus I:5/A7
by the way /ˌbaɪ ðə ˈweɪ/ übrigens II:1/B1
bye /baɪ/ tschüs(s) I:3/A5

C

cab *(AE)* /kæb/ Taxi IV:1/B4
cage /keɪdʒ/ Käfig II:2/B2
cake /keɪk/ Kuchen I:4/B5
calendar /ˈkælɪndə/ Kalender I:2/B1
California /ˌkæləˈfɔːniə/ Kalifornien IV:1/P5
call /kɔːl/ anrufen I:3/B6; rufen II:1/B11; Anruf; Gespräch II:6/A9
telephone call /ˈtelɪfəʊn kɔːl/ Telefonanruf IV:4/B4
call sb names /ˌkɔːl ˌsʌmbədi ˈneɪmz/ jdn beschimpfen II:5/B10
called /kɔːld/ genannt; namens II:Last year
(be) **called** /ˌbiː ˈkɔːld/ heißen, genannt werden II:1/A7
camera /ˈkæmrə/ Kamera; Fotoapparat III:2/B9
camp /kæmp/ *hier:* Flüchtlingslager IV:5/B5
campaign /kæmˈpeɪn/ kämpfen; sich engagieren IV:5/B5
can /kæn/ Dose; Büchse III:1/A3
can / can't /kæn / kɑːnt/ können / nicht können I:Welcome
Can I help you? /ˌkæn‿aɪ ˈhelp juː/ Kann ich dir / Ihnen helfen? I:3/B4
Canada /ˈkænədə/ Kanada IV:5/A2
candle /ˈkændl/ Kerze I:5/B11
cap /kæp/ Mütze I:1/A5
cap /kæp/ *hier:* Verschluss; Deckel IV:6/Project B p. 127
capital /ˈkæpɪtl/ Hauptstadt IV:Quiz
captain /ˈkæptɪn/ Kapitän/in; Mannschaftsführer/in IV:5/A4
caption /ˈkæpʃn/ Bildunterschrift IV:5/A11
car /kɑː/ Auto I:1/B4
toy car /ˌtɔɪ ˈkɑː/ Spielzeugauto I:3/B5
°car factory /ˈkɑː ˌfæktri/ Autofabrik IV:BS/8
car park /ˈkɑː pɑːk/ Parkplatz IV:1/B5
carbon footprint /ˌkɑːbən ˈfʊtprɪnt/ CO_2-Fußabdruck; CO_2-Bilanz IV:6/Project A p. 121
carbon monoxide /ˌkɑːbən məˈnɒksaɪd/ Kohlenmonoxid IV:2/A8
card /kɑːd/ Karte I:3/B5
cardboard box /ˈkɑːdbɔːd bɒks/ Karton IV:4/B3
care /keə/ sich kümmern um; achten auf; Zuneigung fühlen IV:1/B2; Betreuung; Pflege; Sorgfalt IV:3/A7
career /kəˈrɪə/ Karriere, Laufbahn IV:1/A2
carefully /ˈkeəfli/ vorsichtig II:3/B7
carefully /ˈkeəfli/ *hier:* genau IV:4/B7
the Caribbean /ðə ˌkærɪˈbiən/ Karibik; karibische Inseln IV:1/B5
carnival /ˈkɑːnɪvl/ Karneval III:2/I
carpet /ˈkɑːpɪt/ Teppich IV:6/Project A p. 121
carrier /ˈkæriə/ Träger IV:6/Project B p. 127
carrot /ˈkærət/ Möhre, Karotte IV:2/A9
carry /ˈkæri/ tragen II:4/A1
carry on /ˌkæri‿ˈɒn/ weitermachen III:3/A4
carry out /ˌkæri‿ˈaʊt/ durchführen, betreiben IV:6/Project p. 119
pencil case /ˈpensl ˌkeɪs/ Federmäppchen I:2/B4
case /keɪs/ *hier:* Hülle IV:1/B4
cash /kæʃ/ Geld; Bargeld IV:2/B2
cash register /ˈkæʃ ˌredʒɪstə/ Registrierkasse IV:4/B3
cast /kɑːst/ Besetzung IV:3/A10
cat /kæt/ Katze I:1/A5
catch *(irr)* /kætʃ/ fangen II:2/B2
catch a train /ˌkætʃ‿ə ˈtreɪn/ einen Zug nehmen II:2/A2

categorise /ˈkætɪgəraɪz/ kategorisieren, in Gruppen unterteilen IV:5/A1

°caterpillar /ˈkætəˌpɪlə/ Raupe IV:BS/4

°cauliflower /ˈkɒliˌflaʊə/ Blumenkohl IV:BS/5

cause /kɔːz/ verursachen IV:2/A8

'cause (= because) /kɔːz, bɪˈkɒz/ weil, da IV:2/A4

celebrate /ˈseləˌbreɪt/ feiern II:4/A1

celebration /ˌseləˈbreɪʃn/ Feier II:4/I

celery /ˈseləri/ Sellerie IV:2/A9

cellist /ˈtʃelɪst/ Cellist/in IV:3/A10

cellphone *(AE)* /ˈsel fəʊn/ Handy IV:1/B5

centre /ˈsentə/ Zentrum; Mitte IV:1/A1

century /ˈsentʃəri/ Jahrhundert IV:2/B7

certainly /ˈsɜːtnli/ sicher; gerne III:1/A7

certified /ˈsɜːtɪfaɪd/ geprüft; garantiert IV:6/Project C p. 128

chair /tʃeə/ Stuhl I:2/B1

chalk /tʃɔːk/ Kreide I:2/B1

challenge /ˈtʃæləndʒ/ Herausforderung IV:2/I

chance /tʃɑːns/ Möglichkeit; Gelegenheit IV:6/Project p. 119

change /tʃeɪndʒ/ wechseln; umsteigen I:4/B3; Wechselgeld I:4/B6; ändern; verändern II:5/A8

change /tʃeɪndʒ/ Veränderung IV:2/A4

chant /tʃɑːnt/ Sprechgesang IV:1/A6

character /ˈkærəktə/ *hier:* Figur IV:3/A4

charge /tʃɑːdʒ/ aufladen III:5/B7

charity /ˈtʃærəti/ Wohltätigkeitsorganisation III:3/I

chart /tʃɑːt/ Diagramm IV:5/A11

chat /tʃæt/ schwätzen; plaudern IV:3/A4

chat-up line /ˈtʃætʌp ˌlaɪn/ Anmache, Anmachspruch IV:3/I

cheap /tʃiːp/ billig II:2/B6

check /tʃek/ überprüfen; kontrollieren II:4/A7

check /tʃek/ Überprüfung, Kontrolle IV:4/B7

check out *(informal)* /ˌtʃek‿ˈaʊt/ sich ansehen IV:3/I

°cheek /tʃiːk/ Wange IV:BS/6

cheerfully /ˈtʃɪəfli/ fröhlich, vergnügt IV:3/A10

cheese /tʃiːz/ Käse I:Welcome

chemical /ˈkemɪkl/ Chemikalie IV:6/Project p. 117; chemisch IV:6/Project C p. 136

chess /tʃes/ Schach IV:1/A4

chicken /ˈtʃɪkɪn/ Huhn I:WB/1

°chief /tʃiːf/ Häuptling IV:BS/2

child (*pl* **children**) /tʃaɪld, ˈtʃɪldrən/ Kind I:Welcome

child labour /ˈtʃaɪld ˌleɪbə/ Kinderarbeit IV:6/Project C p. 128

Chinatown /ˈtʃaɪnəˌtaʊn/ Chinesenviertel IV:1/B4

Chinese /ˌtʃaɪˈniːz/ Chinese, Chinesin; chinesisch IV:5/A1

chink *(veraltet)* /tʃɪŋk/ Geldbeutel IV:3/B8

chips *(pl)* /tʃɪps/ Pommes frites II:1/B11

chocolate /ˈtʃɒklət/ Schokolade I:4/B1

chocolate /ˈtʃɒklət/ Praline IV:3/A9

hot chocolate /ˌhɒt ˈtʃɒklət/ (heißer) Kakao I:4/B9

°chocolate-covered /ˈtʃɒklət ˌkʌvəd/ mit Schokolade umhüllt IV:BS/4

choice /tʃɔɪs/ Wahl III:1/A7

choose *(irr)* /tʃuːz/ wählen; sich entscheiden I:1/B5

chorus (*pl* choruses) /ˈkɔːrəs, ˈkɔːrəsɪz/ Refrain IV:1/B8

Christmas Day /ˌkrɪsməs ˈdeɪ/ erster Weihnachtsfeiertag II:2/A8

Christmas Eve /ˌkrɪsməs‿ˈiːv/ Heiligabend II:4/A1

chunk /tʃʌŋk/ *hier:* Wendung IV:1/B5

church /tʃɜːtʃ/ Kirche II:4/A1

cigarette /ˌsɪgəˈret, ˈsɪgəˌret/ Zigarette IV:2/A7

cinema /ˈsɪnəmə/ Kino I:1/B3

circle /ˈsɜːkl/ Kreis III:2/A9

citizen /ˈsɪtɪzn/ Bürger/in IV:6/Project A p. 121

city /ˈsɪti/ Stadt; Innenstadt I:Welcome

city centre /ˌsɪti ˈsentə/ Innenstadt IV:1/B5

class /klɑːs/ Klasse I:2/A13

°class /klɑːs/ *hier:* (Unterrichts)stunde IV:BS/6

classmate /ˈklɑːsˌmeɪt/ Klassenkamerad/in II:4/A3

classroom /ˈklɑːsˌruːm/ Klassenzimmer I:2/B1

clause /klɔːz/ Satzglied, Satzteil IV:4/P4

clean /kliːn/ sauber IV:6/Project p. 117; sauber machen I:4/A6

clean up /ˌkliːn‿ˈʌp/ sauber machen II:5/A6

clean-up /ˈkliːn‿ʌp/ *Aufräumaktion* IV:6/Project B p. 126

clear /klɪə/ *hier:* frei räumen IV:2/B7

°clearly /ˈklɪəli/ klar; deutlich IV:4/O

clever /ˈklevə/ klug; schlau II:3/B7

climb /klaɪm/ auf etw (hinauf)steigen; klettern IV:2/A2

clock /klɒk/ Uhr I:2/B1

close /kləʊz/ zumachen; schließen IV:4/A2

up close /ʌp ˈkləʊs/ aus der Nähe IV:1/B2

closet /ˈklɒzɪt/ Schrank IV:6/Project C p. 129

clothes *(pl)* /kləʊðz/ Kleider, Kleidung I:Welcome

clothing /ˈkləʊðɪŋ/ Kleidung IV:6/Project p. 117

cloud /klaʊd/ Wolke I:WB/1

cloudy /ˈklaʊdi/ bewölkt; bedeckt I:WB/1

club /klʌb/ Klub; AG I:3/I

club /klʌb/ *hier:* Club, Diskothek IV:1/B5

coal /kəʊl/ Kohle IV:6/Project A p.134
°coat /kəʊt/ Mantel IV:BS/8
coffee /ˈkɒfi/ Kaffee III:1/A3
coffee shop /ˈkɒfi ʃɒp/ Kaffeebar; Café IV:6/Project B p.126
coin /kɔɪn/ Münze II:6/B11
cold /kəʊld/ kalt I:2/A2; Erkältung I:3/A5
°cold /kəʊld/ Kälte IV:BS/2
collect /kəˈlekt/ sammeln I:3/A13
collect /kəˈlekt/ *hier:* holen IV:2/B2
collection /kəˈlekʃn/ Sammlung I:3/B5
collection bin /kəˈlekʃn bɪn/ Sammelbehälter IV:6/Project B p.127
color *(AE)* /ˈkʌlə/ Farbe IV:6/Project C p.129
colored *(AE)* = coloured *(BE)* /ˈkʌləd/ farbig IV:5/A1
colour /ˈkʌlə/ Farbe I:Welcome ...
colourful /ˈkʌləfl/ farbenfroh; bunt II:4/A1
Columbia /kəˈlʌmbiə/ Kolumbien IV:4/P6
column /ˈkɒləm/ Kolumne IV:6/Project C p.129
combine /kəmˈbaɪn/ verbinden IV:5/B7
come *(irr)* /kʌm/ kommen I:Welcome
come down /ˌkʌm ˈdaʊn/ herunterkommen IV:3/B1
Come in. /ˌkʌm‿ˈɪn/ Komm(t) herein! I:5/B3
come to mind /ˌkʌm tə ˈmaɪnd/ einfallen IV:1/A1
come out /ˈkʌm‿aʊt/ herauskommen; *hier:* sich outen IV:2/A6
comedy /ˈkɒmədi/ Komödie IV:3/B6
comfortable /ˈkʌmftəbl/ bequem I:4/A4
comment /ˈkɒment/ Kommentar, Bemerkung IV:1/B2; kommentieren IV:2/A3
°committee /kəˈmɪti/ Ausschuss; Komitee IV:5/O

communicate /kəˈmju:nɪkeɪt/ kommunizieren, sprechen IV:4/A7
communication /kəˌmju:nɪˈkeɪʃn/ Verständigung; Kommunikation IV:4/B6
community /kəˈmju:nəti/ Gemeinde, Gemeinschaft IV:1/A4
compact /kəmˈpækt/ kompakt IV:6/Project A p.121
company /ˈkʌmpni/ Firma, Unternehmen IV:6/Project C p.131
compare /kəmˈpeə/ vergleichen IV:2/B2
comparison /kəmˈpærɪsn/ Vergleich IV:3/P6
competition /ˌkɒmpəˈtɪʃn/ Wettbewerb II:1/B6
complain /kəmˈpleɪn/ sich beklagen IV:1/B2
complete /kəmˈpli:t/ vervollständigen; zu Ende bringen IV:1/A3
completely /kəmˈpli:tli/ völlig, absolut IV:2/B9
complicate /ˈkɒmplɪkeɪt/ verkomplizieren IV:2/A8
compost /ˈkɒmpɒst/ Kompost IV:6/Project A p.123
computer game designer /kəmˈpju:tə geɪm dɪˌzaɪnə/ Computerspielentwickler/in II:3/A8
computer program /kəmˈpju:tə ˌprəʊgræm/ Computerprogramm IV:4/A1
computer science /kəmˌpju:tə ˈsaɪəns/ Informatik IV:1/A2
concentrate /ˈkɒnsnˌtreɪt/ sich konzentrieren II:3/A1
concert /ˈkɒnsət/ Konzert III:6/I
concrete jungle /ˌkɒŋkri:t ˈdʒʌŋgl/ Betonwüste IV:1/B8
condition /kənˈdɪʃn/ Zustand; Bedingung IV:6/Project C p.136
Congratulations! /kənˌgrætʃʊˈleɪʃnz/ Glückwunsch!; Gratuliere! II:1/B3
consider /kənˈsɪdə/ halten für; nachdenken; betrachten IV:5/A1

°constantly /ˈkɒnstəntli/ ständig; dauernd IV:5/O
consume /kənˈsju:m/ konsumieren; verbrauchen IV:6/Project A p.121
contact sb /ˈkɒntækt ˌsʌmbədi/ sich mit jdm in Verbindung setzen IV:1/A4
contain /kənˈteɪn/ enthalten IV:2/A8
content /ˈkɒntent/ Inhalt IV:2/A11
continent /ˈkɒntɪnənt/ Kontinent IV:2/B5
°contribute /kənˈtrɪbju:t/ *hier:* spenden IV:BS/10
control /kənˈtrəʊl/ Kontrolle III:2/B4; kontrollieren III:6/A3
convention /kənˈvenʃn/ *hier:* Abkommen IV:2/B8
conventional /kənˈvenʃnəl/ konventionell; herkömmlich IV:6/Project C p.129
conversation /ˌkɒnvəˈseɪʃn/ Gespräch; Unterhaltung IV:3/A9
cook /kʊk/ Koch/Köchin III:Last year; kochen; braten; backen III:1/I
°cookbook /ˈkʊkˌbʊk/ Kochbuch IV:BS/4
do the cooking /ˌdu: ðə ˈkʊkɪŋ/ kochen I:4/A6
cooking /ˈkʊkɪŋ/ Kochen; Koch- IV:Quiz
copy /ˈkɒpi/ abschreiben IV:1/A4
corner /ˈkɔ:nə/ Ecke II:1/A11
correct /kəˈrekt/ richtig, korrekt IV:Quiz
°corridor /ˈkɒrɪdɔ:/ Flur, Gang IV:BS/6
cost *(irr)* /kɒst/ kosten II:4/A7
costume /ˈkɒstju:m/ Kostüm III:2/B1
cotton /ˈkɒtn/ Baumwolle; Baumwoll- II:4/B3
couch potato /ˌkaʊtʃ pəˈteɪtəʊ/ Couchpotato; Fernsehglotzer/in IV:2/A4
could /kʊd/ könnte(st, n, t) I:4/B6
couldn't (= could not) /ˈkʊdnt, ˈkʊd nɒt/ *Vergangenheitsform von can't* II:1/A7

count /kaʊnt/ zählen; wichtig sein; ankommen auf II:4/B3
count /kaʊnt/ Graf IV:3/B1
country /ˈkʌntri/ Land II:1/A11
courage /ˈkʌrɪdʒ/ Mut IV:2/B7
°courageous /kəˈreɪdʒəs/ mutig IV:BS/10
course /kɔːs/ Kurs I:5/A7
°course /kɔːs/ Gang IV:BS/5
take a course /ˌteɪk‿ə ˈkɔːs/ einen Kurs machen IV:4/B6
cousin /ˈkʌzn/ Cousin/e I:1/A2
cover /ˈkʌvə/ bedecken III:1/B5
cover /ˈkʌvə/ Einband IV:1/B10
cow /kaʊ/ Kuh I:WB/1
coward /ˈkaʊəd/ Feigling IV:3/A4
coyote *(AE)* /kɔɪˈəʊti/ Schlepper/in IV:5/A10
crammed /kræmd/ vollgestopft IV:5/B7
crave (for) /kreɪv/ sich sehnen nach IV:3/B8
°crawl /krɔːl/ krabbeln; kriechen IV:BS/4
crazy /ˈkreɪzi/ verrückt; wahnsinnig II:1/B1
cream /kriːm/ Sahne II:4/B5; Creme; Salbe III:3/B1
°creamy /ˈkriːmi/ cremig IV:BS/4
create /kriˈeɪt/ erschaffen; erzeugen IV:4/A1
create /kriˈeɪt/ *hier:* erstellen IV:6/Project p. 132
creation /kriˈeɪʃn/ (Er)schaffung IV:1/A4
creative /kriˈeɪtɪv/ kreativ IV:6/Project p. 133
credit /ˈkredɪt/ *hier:* Leistungsnachweis IV:4/A10
°cricket /ˈkrɪkɪt/ Grille IV:BS/4
crime /kraɪm/ Verbrechen; Kriminalität IV:3/B6
crime rate /ˈkraɪm reɪt/ Kriminalitätsrate IV:1/B5
crisps *(pl)* /krɪsps/ Chips I:4/B5
criticise /ˈkrɪtɪsaɪz/ kritisieren IV:5/A1
crocodile /ˈkrɒkədaɪl/ Krokodil I:WB/1
°crop /krɒp/ Ernte IV:BS/10
cross /krɒs/ überqueren II:1/B3
°cross /ˌkrɒs/ Kreuz IV:BS/10
cross into a country /ˌkrɒs‿ˌɪntu‿ə ˈkʌntri/ die Grenze in ein Land passieren IV:5/A10
crowd /kraʊd/ Menschenmenge III:2/B9
crowded /ˈkraʊdɪd/ überfüllt IV:5/A4
cry /kraɪ/ weinen; schreien III:4/B9
cuddly toy /ˌkʌdli ˈtɔɪ/ Kuscheltier I:3/B5
cultivate /ˈkʌltɪveɪt/ anbauen; *hier:* pflegen IV:3/A7
°cultural /ˈkʌltʃrəl/ kulturell IV:BS/9
culture /ˈkʌltʃə/ Kultur IV:1/A10
cup /kʌp/ Tasse I:2/A9
cup final /ˈkʌp ˌfaɪnl/ Pokalendspiel, Cupfinale I:3/A4
cupboard /ˈkʌbəd/ Schrank I:2/B1
curfew /ˈkɜːfjuː/ Ausgangssperre IV:1/B8
°curly /ˈkɜːli/ lockig IV:3/O
°curry /ˈkʌri/ Curry(gericht) IV:BS/4
customer /ˈkʌstəmə/ Kunde/Kundin I:3/B4
cut *(irr)* /kʌt/ schneiden II:3/A8
cut *(irr)* /kʌt/ *hier:* fällen IV:2/B7
cute /kjuːt/ süß; niedlich II:1/B10
CV (= curriculum vitae) /ˌsiː ˈviː/ Lebenslauf IV:4/P10
cycle /ˈsaɪkl/ Rad fahren, radeln IV:6/Project p. 116

D

dad /dæd/ Papa; Vati I:2/A7
damage /ˈdæmɪdʒ/ beschädigen, schaden III:6/A3
damage /ˈdæmɪdʒ/ Schaden IV:6/Project C p. 136
dance /dɑːns/ tanzen I:4/A11; Tanz II:4/A1
dancing /ˈdɑːnsɪŋ/ Tanzen II:Last year
dangerous /ˈdeɪndʒərəs/ gefährlich IV:3/B1
dark /dɑːk/ dunkel I:2/A3
darkness /ˈdɑːknəs/ Dunkelheit IV:5/A10
date /deɪt/ Datum; Termin; Verabredung IV:3/A4
date /deɪt/ datieren IV:1/A9
ask sb out on a date /ˌɑːsk ˌsʌmbədi‿ˌaʊt‿ɒn‿ə ˈdeɪt/ jdn fragen, ob er/sie mit einem ausgehen will IV:3/A4
release date /rɪˈliːs deɪt/ Erscheinungsdatum IV:3/A10
date of birth /ˌdeɪt‿əv ˈbɜːθ/ Geburtsdatum IV:4/P10
daughter /ˈdɔːtə/ Tochter I:5/B7
day /deɪ/ Tag I:Welcome
one day /ˌwʌn ˈdeɪ/ eines Tages II:1/B7
dead /ded/ tot IV:3/B1
deadline /ˈdedˌlaɪn/ letzter Termin, Stichtag IV:2/A10
deadly /ˈdedli/ tödlich IV:5/A3
deal with /ˈdiːl wɪð/ sich befassen mit IV:2/A5
dealer /ˈdiːlə/ Händler/in; *hier:* Verhandlungsführer/in IV:Quiz
dear /dɪə/ liebe/r *(Anrede)* II:5/A4
dear /dɪə/ *hier:* teuer IV:3/B8
death /deθ/ Tod IV:3/B5
debate /dɪˈbeɪt/ Debatte; Diskussion IV:6/Project p. 133
debt /det/ Schuld IV:3/B8
December /dɪˈsembə/ Dezember I:5/B7
decent /ˈdiːsnt/ angemessen; annehmbar IV:6/Project C p. 129
decide /dɪˈsaɪd/ entscheiden; sich entscheiden II:1/B7
the Declaration of Independence /ðə ˌdekləˌreɪʃn‿əv‿ˌɪndɪˈpendəns/ *die Unabhängigkeitserklärung der USA* IV:1/A9
°deep down /diːp ˈdaʊn/ im Innersten; tief in mir IV:5/O
deeply /ˈdiːpli/ sehr, äußerst IV:3/A10
define /dɪˈfaɪn/ definieren IV:6/Project B p. 135
definitely /ˈdefnətli/ eindeutig, definitiv IV:6/Project C p. 130; *hier:* bestimmt IV:BS/10
definition /ˌdefəˈnɪʃn/ IV:6/Project B p. 135

delicious /dɪˈlɪʃəs/ köstlich, lecker III:1/A1
°deliver /dɪˈlɪvə/ liefern, zustellen IV:4/O
demonstrate /ˈdemənˌstreɪt/ zeigen, vorführen IV:4/B3
police department /pəˈliːs dɪˌpɑːtmənt/ Polizeidienststelle IV:Quiz
department store /dɪˈpɑːtmənt stɔː/ Kaufhaus II:4/B3
deportee /ˌdiːpɔːˈtiː/ Abzuschiebende/r; Abgeschobene/r IV:5/A9
describe /dɪˈskraɪb/ beschreiben I:3/B6
description /dɪˈskrɪpʃn/ Beschreibung IV:1/A6
desert /ˈdezət/ Wüste IV:5/A9
°deserve /dɪˈzɜːv/ verdienen IV:BS/8
design /dɪˈzaɪn/ entwerfen II:3/A8
computer game designer /kəmˈpjuːtə geɪm dɪˌzaɪnə/ Computerspielentwickler/in II:3/A8
desk /desk/ Schreibtisch I:2/B1
°despite /dɪˈspaɪt/ trotz IV:5/O
dessert /dɪˈzɜːt/ Nachtisch III:1/A3
destroy /dɪˈstrɔɪ/ zerstören IV:5/A2
detail /ˈdiːteɪl/ Detail, Einzelheit IV:6/Project p. 119
go into detail /ˌɡəʊ‿ɪntə ˈdiːteɪl/ ins Detail gehen IV:6/Project p. 119
detective /dɪˈtektɪv/ Detektiv/in IV:1/A3
detox /ˈdiːtɒks/ Entgiftung IV:6/Project C p. 129
detox /diːˈtɒks/ entgiften IV:6/Project C p. 136
develop /dɪˈveləp/ erarbeiten; entwickeln IV:4/A1
development /dɪˈveləpmənt/ Entwicklung IV:1/A4
dialogue /ˈdaɪəˌlɒɡ/ Gespräch, Dialog II:5/A1
diamond /ˈdaɪəmənd/ *Spielfeld im Baseball* IV:1/A4
diary /ˈdaɪəri/ Tagebuch II:1/A7
dictionary /ˈdɪkʃənri/ Lexikon; Wörterbuch I:2/B10
die /daɪ/ sterben II:1/B7
different /ˈdɪfrənt/ anders; andere(r, s); verschiedene(r, s) II:2/A7
difficult /ˈdɪfɪklt/ schwierig; schwer II:1/B7
dinner /ˈdɪnə/ Abendessen I:4/B1
°dipped /dɪpt/ eingetaucht IV:BS/4
°direct /dɪˈrekt/ Regie führen IV:5/O
direct speech /daɪˌrekt ˈspiːtʃ/ direkte Rede, wörtliche Rede II:3/B9
°directly /dɪˈrekli/ direkt IV:1/O
director /dəˈrektə/ Regisseur/in IV:3/A10
dirty /ˈdɜːti/ dreckig; schmutzig II:2/B3
disappear /ˌdɪsəˈpɪə/ verschwinden IV:3/A9
°disappointed /ˌdɪsəˈpɔɪntɪd/ enttäuscht IV:BS/3
disaster /dɪˈzɑːstə/ Katastrophe IV:4/B3
discipline /ˈdɪsəplɪn/ Disziplin IV:1/A4
disco /ˈdɪskəʊ/ Disko IV:Quiz
discover /dɪˈskʌvə/ entdecken III:4/I
discuss /dɪˈskʌs/ besprechen; diskutieren III:3/A10
discussion /dɪˈskʌʃn/ Diskussion IV:6/Project A p. 134
disease /dɪˈziːz/ Krankheit IV:5/A2
disembark /ˌdɪsɪmˈbɑːk/ von Bord gehen IV:5/B7
disguise /dɪsˈɡaɪz/ sich verkleiden IV:3/B3
in disguise /ɪn dɪsˈɡaɪz/ verkleidet IV:3/B1
disgusting /dɪsˈɡʌstɪŋ/ widerlich III:1/A1
dish (*pl* **dishes**) /dɪʃ, ˈdɪʃɪz/ Gericht III:1/I
displace /dɪsˈpleɪs/ vertreiben IV:5/B4
display /dɪˈspleɪ/ *hier:* Ausstellung IV:4/A14; aushängen IV:5/B6
distance /ˈdɪstəns/ Distanz, Entfernung IV:1/A9
°distinguished /dɪˈstɪŋɡwɪʃt/ hervorragend, ausgezeichnet IV:BS/9
dive /daɪv/ tauchen; Sprung IV:2/B7
diver /ˈdaɪvə/ *hier:* Springer/in IV:2/B7
diverse /daɪˈvɜːs/ vielfältig, unterschiedlich IV:5/A1
land diving /ˈlænd‿ˌdaɪvɪŋ/ *Lianenspringen* IV:2/I
do *(irr)* /duː/ tun; machen I:3/A8
do gymnastics /ˌduː dʒɪmˈnæstɪks/ Turnen I:3/A8
do research /ˌduː rɪˈsɜːtʃ/ *hier:* recherchieren IV:2/B9
do the cooking /ˌduː ðə ˈkʊkɪŋ/ kochen I:4/A6
do the shopping /ˌduː ðə ˈʃɒpɪŋ/ einkaufen I:4/A6
do the washing up /ˌduː ðə ˌwɒʃɪŋ‿ˈʌp/ abspülen I:4/A6
D.O.A. (= Dead On Arrival) /ˌdi‿əʊ‿ˈeɪ, ˌded‿ɒn‿əˈraɪvl/ *etwa:* tot, bevor es Rettung gibt IV:3/A6
dock /dɒk/ anlegen IV:5/A4
doctor /ˈdɒktə/ Arzt/Ärztin; *hier:* Doktor II:2/A8
doctor's assistant /ˈdɒktəz‿əˌsɪstnt/ Arzthelfer/in IV:4/A1
doctor's office /ˈdɒktəz‿ˌɒfɪs/ Praxis IV:4/A1
documentary /ˌdɒkjʊˈmentri/ Dokumentarfilm IV:4/A7
dog /dɒɡ/ Hund I:1/A5
walk the dog /ˌwɔːk ðə ˈdɒɡ/ den Hund ausführen I:5/A4
°dog food /ˈdɒɡ fuːd/ Hundefutter IV:BS/7
°dog surfing /ˈdɒɡ ˌsɜːfɪŋ/ Hundesurfen IV:BS/7
Don't worry. /ˌdəʊnt ˈwʌri/ Mach dir keine Sorgen. II:3/B1
donate /dəʊˈneɪt/ spenden IV:6/Project C p. 131
well done /ˌwel ˈdʌn/ gut gemacht II:1/B3

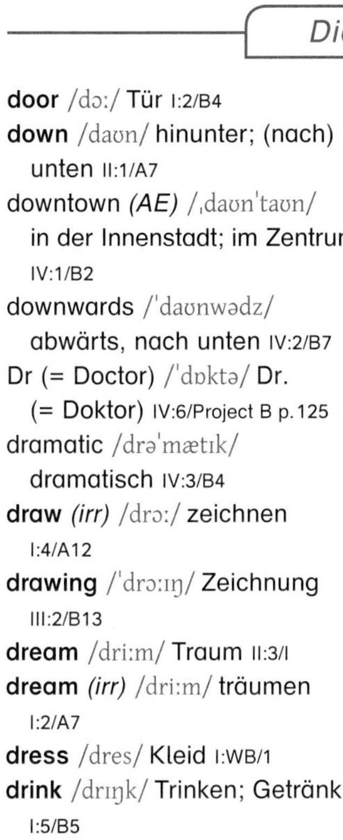

door /dɔ:/ Tür I:2/B4
down /daʊn/ hinunter; (nach) unten II:1/A7
downtown *(AE)* /ˌdaʊn'taʊn/ in der Innenstadt; im Zentrum IV:1/B2
downwards /'daʊnwədz/ abwärts, nach unten IV:2/B7
Dr (= Doctor) /'dɒktə/ Dr. (= Doktor) IV:6/Project B p. 125
dramatic /drə'mætɪk/ dramatisch IV:3/B4
draw *(irr)* /drɔ:/ zeichnen I:4/A12
drawing /'drɔ:ɪŋ/ Zeichnung III:2/B13
dream /dri:m/ Traum II:3/I
dream *(irr)* /dri:m/ träumen I:2/A7
dress /dres/ Kleid I:WB/1
drink /drɪŋk/ Trinken; Getränk I:5/B5
drink *(irr)* /drɪŋk/ trinken I:2/A8
drinking water /'drɪŋkɪŋ ˌwɔ:tə/ Trinkwasser IV:6/Project C p. 130
drive *(irr)* /draɪv/ fahren II:1/B11
drive from /'draɪv‿frəm/ vertreiben IV:5/A3
drop /drɒp/ fallen lassen IV:6/Project B p. 124
drug /drʌg/ Medikament; Droge IV:3/B3
due /dju:/ fällig IV:4/B7
due to /'dju: tʊ/ wegen IV:5/B3
during /'djʊərɪŋ/ während II:5/B1
°Dutch /dʌtʃ/ holländisch; niederländisch IV:BS/1
duvet /'du:veɪ/ Steppdecke; Daunendecke I:4/A1
dye /daɪ/ Färbemittel; färben IV:6/Project C p. 129

E

each /i:tʃ/ jede(r, s) II:1/A6
each other /ˌi:tʃ‿'ʌðə/ einander II:1/B10
ear /ɪə/ Ohr I:2/A2
early /'ɜ:li/ früh II:4/A1
earn /ɜ:n/ verdienen III:2/A7
earth /ɜ:θ/ Erde II:1/B11
°earthkeeper /'ɜ:θˌki:pə/ *etwa:* Erdbewahrer/in IV:BS/10
earthquake /'ɜ:θˌkweɪk/ Erdbeben IV:5/B2
ease /i:z/ beruhigen IV:5/A3
easiest /'i:ziɪst/ leichteste(r, s) IV:2/A5
easily /'i:zɪli/ leicht; mühelos II:3/B1
east /i:st/ Osten III:4/A9
Easter /'i:stə/ Ostern II:4/A1
easy /'i:zi/ leicht; einfach I:3/B6
eat *(irr)* /i:t/ essen I:2/A12
eat out /ˌi:t‿'aʊt/ auswärts essen; im Restaurant essen III:1/I
eatery /'i:təri/ Restaurant, Esslokal IV:5/B7
eating habit /'i:tɪŋ ˌhæbɪt/ Essgewohnheit III:1/I
eco- /'i:kəʊ/ Öko- IV:6/Project p. 116
eco-friendly /ˌi:kəʊ 'frendli/ umweltfreundlich IV:6/Project C p. 129
ecological footprint /ˌi:kəˌlɒdʒɪkl 'fʊtprɪnt/ ökologischer Fußabdruck IV:6/Project p. 117
economic /ˌi:kə'nɒmɪk/ wirtschaftlich IV:5/B3
edible /'edɪbəl/ essbar; genießbar IV:6/Project p. 118
edit /'edɪt/ bearbeiten II:3/B9
edition /ɪ'dɪʃn/ Ausgabe, Edition IV:2/A11
educate /'edjʊkeɪt/ ausbilden; unterrichten IV:2/B8
education /ˌedjʊ'keɪʃn/ Bildung; Ausbildung IV:5/B5
effect /ɪ'fekt/ Effekt, Wirkung IV:2/A8
effective /ɪ'fektɪv/ wirksam, effektiv IV:4/A14
e.g. (= exempli gratia) /ˌi: 'dʒi:/ z.B. (= zum Beispiel) IV:6/Project C p. 136
egg /eg/ Ei I:2/A8
fried egg /ˌfraɪd‿'eg/ Spiegelei I:2/A7
either ... or ... /ˌaɪðə 'ɔ:/ entweder ... oder ... III:1/B7
elastic /ɪ'læstɪk/ elastisch; flexibel IV:2/B7
village elder /ˌvɪlɪdʒ‿'eldə/ Dorfälteste/r IV:2/B7
elderly /'eldəli/ ältere(r, s) IV:2/A1
°elect /ɪ'lekt/ wählen IV:BS/9
elective /ɪ'lektɪv/ Wahlfach IV:4/A10
electric /ɪ'lektrɪk/ elektrisch; Elektro- IV:6/Project p. 117
electricity /ɪˌlek'trɪsəti/ Elektrizität, Strom III:5/B7
elephant /'elɪfənt/ Elefant I:WB/1
elevator *(AE)* /'eləveɪtə/ Aufzug IV:1/B2
else /els/ anders; sonst III:4/B9
anything else /eniˌθɪŋ‿'els/ noch etwas I:4/B6
Anything else? /eniˌθɪŋ‿'els/ Sonst noch etwas?, Darf es noch etwas sein? I:4/B6
what else /ˌwɒt‿'els/ was sonst I:2/A8
email /'i:meɪl/ mailen IV:1/A2
embarrassing /ɪm'bærəsɪŋ/ unangenehm; peinlich II:6/B6
°emerging /ɪ'mɜ:dʒɪŋ/ aufstrebend IV:BS/9
emigrate /'emɪgreɪt/ auswandern IV:5/A2
emphysema /ˌemfɪ'si:mə/ Emphysem IV:2/A8
°employee /ɪm'plɔɪi:/ Mitarbeiter/in; Angestellter/in IV:BS/8
employer /ɪm'plɔɪə/ Arbeitgeber/in IV:4/B6
empty /'empti/ ausleeren; ausräumen I:4/A9; leer (stehend); unbewohnt II:3/B7
encounter /ɪn'kaʊntə/ treffen; begegnen IV:5/A8
°encourage /ɪn'kʌrɪdʒ/ ermutigen IV:5/O
end /end/ enden; beenden I:5/A3; Ende; Schluss II:1/B3
at the end /ˌæt ði‿'end/ schließlich IV:4/A10
end up /ˌend‿'ʌp/ schließlich landen IV:6/Project B p. 126
ending /'endɪŋ/ Ende; Schluss IV:3/B9
enemy /'enəmi/ Feind/in IV:3/B1
energy /'enədʒi/ Energie; Kraft IV:2/A7

energy-efficient /ˈenədʒi‿ɪˌfɪʃnt/ energiesparend IV:6/Project A p. 121
engineer /ˌendʒɪˈnɪə/ Ingenieur/in III:4/B4
English /ˈɪŋɡlɪʃ/ Englisch; englisch I:Welcome ...
in English /ˌɪn‿ˈɪŋɡlɪʃ/ auf Englisch II:3/A8
°the English *(pl)* /ði‿ˈɪŋɡlɪʃ/ die Engländer IV:BS/1
enjoy /ɪnˈdʒɔɪ/ genießen II:1/B3
enjoy oneself /ɪnˈdʒɔɪ wʌnˌself/ sich amüsieren IV:1/A2
enough /ɪˈnʌf/ genug II:4/B5
enter /ˈentə/ betreten III:5/A1
°enthusiastic /ɪnˌθjuːziˈæstɪk/ enthusiastisch; begeistert IV:BS/6
°entire /ɪnˈtaɪə/ ganz; gesamt IV:BS/2
entry /ˈentri/ Eintrag IV:1/B2
envelope /ˈenvələʊp/ Briefumschlag II:4/A3
environment /ɪnˈvaɪrənmənt/ Umgebung, Umfeld; Umwelt IV:6/Project p. 117
environmental /ɪnˌvaɪrənˈmentl/ Umwelt- IV:6/Project B p. 135
environmental organization *(AE)* = environmental organisation *(BE)* /ɪnvaɪrənˌmentl‿ɔːɡənaɪˈzeɪʃn/ Umweltschutzorganisation IV:6/Project B p. 126
environmentalist /ɪnˌvaɪrənˈmentlɪst/ Umweltschützer/in IV:6/Project C p. 131
equal /ˈiːkwəl/ gleich IV:1/A9
equipment /ɪˈkwɪpmənt/ Ausrüstung; Ausstattung II:6/B11
escape /ɪˈskeɪp/ fliehen; entkommen IV:5/B3
especially /ɪˈspeʃli/ besonders; vor allem IV:1/P10
et al. /et‿ˈæl/ u. a. (= und andere) IV:3/A6
Europe /ˈjʊərəp/ Europa II:2/A2
European /ˌjʊərəˈpiːən/ Europäer/in; europäisch IV:Quiz

evacuation /ɪˌvækjuˈeɪʃn/ Evakuierung, Räumung IV:5/B4
even /ˈiːvn/ selbst; sogar II:2/A2
even though /ˌiːvn ˈðəʊ/ obwohl IV:3/O
evening /ˈiːvnɪŋ/ Abend I:4/A11
event /ɪˈvent/ Ereignis, Veranstaltung III:2/A11
ever /ˈevə/ jemals II:6/A6
every /ˈevri/ jede(r, s) I:2/A7
everybody /ˈevriˌbɒdi/ alle; jeder I:Welcome
everyday life /ˌevrideɪ ˈlaɪf/ Alltag IV:2/B1
everyone /ˈevriwʌn/ alle; jeder I:3/B8
everything /ˈevriθɪŋ/ alles I:4/B6
evil /ˈiːvl/ böse IV:2/B7
exactly /ɪɡˈzækli/ genau III:3/B1
exam /ɪɡˈzæm/ Prüfung III:4/B1
example /ɪɡˈzɑːmpl/ Beispiel IV:4/B6
for example /fər‿ɪɡˈzɑːmpl/ zum Beispiel II:4/A12
set a good example /ˌset‿ə ɡʊd‿ɪɡˈzɑːmpl/ mit gutem Beispiel vorangehen IV:6/Project A p. 122
except /ɪkˈsept/ außer II:2/A8
exchange student /ɪksˈtʃeɪndʒ ˌstjuːdnt/ Austauschschüler/in IV:1/P6
excited, excitedly /ɪkˈsaɪtɪd, ɪkˈsaɪtɪdli/ aufgeregt II:3/B2
°excitement /ɪkˈsaɪtmənt/ Aufregung IV:3/O
exciting /ɪkˈsaɪtɪŋ/ aufregend II:1/B6
Excuse me! /ɪkˈskjuːz ˌmi/ Entschuldigen Sie bitte!, Entschuldigung! III:1/A4
exercise /ˈeksəsaɪz/ Bewegung; Übung III:3/A4
exercise /ˈeksəsaɪz/ trainieren IV:2/A9
exercise book /ˈeksəsaɪz ˌbʊk/ Heft I:2/B4
exhibition /ˌeksɪˈbɪʃn/ Ausstellung II:2/A2
exist /ɪɡˈzɪst/ existieren IV:3/A9
°expect /ɪkˈspekt/ erwarten IV:5/O

expensive /ɪkˈspensɪv/ teuer II:2/B6
experience /ɪkˈspɪəriəns/ Erfahrung III:2/B5
gain experience /ˌɡeɪn‿ɪkˈspɪəriəns/ Erfahrungen sammeln IV:4/B8
°experience /ɪkˈspɪəriəns/ erleben; erfahren IV:5/O
experiment /ɪkˈsperɪmənt/ Experiment, Versuch III:5/A1
explain /ɪkˈspleɪn/ erklären IV:2/B3
explode /ɪkˈspləʊd/ explodieren IV:5/B7
explore /ɪkˈsplɔː/ erforschen; untersuchen IV:6/Project p. 118
°explorer /ɪkˈsplɔːrə/ Forscher/in IV:BS/1
express /ɪkˈspres/ ausdrücken IV:3/B8
expression /ɪkˈspreʃn/ Ausdruck IV:1/B8
extra /ˈekstrə/ zusätzlich IV:4/A2
extreme /ɪkˈstriːm/ äußerste(r, s); extrem IV:5/B3
extremely /ɪkˈstriːmli/ äußerst, höchst; außerordentlich IV:4/A7
eye /aɪ/ Auge I:2/A2
°meet one's eye /ˌmiːt wʌnz‿ˈaɪ/ jdm in die Augen gucken IV:3/O
°take one's eyes off sth /ˌteɪk wʌnz‿ˈaɪz‿ɒf ˌsʌmθɪŋ/ sich von einem Anblick trennen IV:3/O

fabric /ˈfæbrɪk/ Stoff IV:6/Project C p. 131
face /feɪs/ gegenüberstehen IV:2/A11; Gesicht I:2/A1
fact /fækt/ Tatsache; Fakt III:Last year
°as a matter of fact /əz‿ə ˌmætər‿əv‿ˈfækt/ übrigens IV:BS/8
fact file /ˈfækt faɪl/ Steckbrief IV:1/A10
factory /ˈfæktri/ Fabrik III:5/B3
fail /feɪl/ durchfallen IV:4/A10
fall *(irr)* /fɔːl/ fallen II:3/A1

fall asleep /ˌfɔːl‿əˈsliːp/ einschlafen IV:4/B3
fall in love /ˌfɔːl‿ɪn ˈlʌv/ sich verlieben III:2/A9
fall off /ˌfɔːl‿ˈɒf/ (herunter)fallen III:3/B11
fall through the cracks /ˌfɔːl θruː ðə ˈkræks/ durch die Maschen schlüpfen IV:6/Project B p. 127
fame /feɪm/ Ruhm IV:5/A3
family /ˈfæmli/ Familie I:3/A4
famine /ˈfæmɪn/ Hungersnot IV:5/I
famous /ˈfeɪməs/ berühmt II:1/A2
fantastic /fænˈtæstɪk/ fantastisch; super I:3/A6
far /fɑː/ weit II:1/B6; *hier:* fern II:6/B2
far away /ˌfɑːr‿əˈweɪ/ weit weg II:1/B10
farewell party /feəˈwel ˌpɑːti/ Abschiedsfeier IV:1/A3
farm /fɑːm/ Bauernhof I:WB/1
°farm /fɑːm/ Land bebauen IV:BS/10
farmer /ˈfɑːmə/ Bauer/Bäuerin II:3/B1
farmers' market /ˈfɑːməz ˌmɑːkɪt/ Bauernmarkt IV:1/A7
fashion /ˈfæʃn/ Mode IV:6/I
fast /fɑːst/ schnell I:Welcome
father /ˈfɑːðə/ Vater I:5/B7
fault /fɔːlt/ Schuld III:2/A9
favorite *(AE)* /ˈfeɪvrət/ Liebling; Lieblings- IV:1/B5
favourite /ˈfeɪvrət/ Liebling; Lieblings- I:Welcome ...
fear /fɪə/ Angst IV:5/B3
feast /fiːst/ schlemmen IV:5/B7
February /ˈfebruəri/ Februar I:5/B7
admission fee /ədˈmɪʃn fiː/ Eintritt IV:3/P12
feed *(irr)* /fiːd/ *hier:* ernähren IV:5/B5; füttern I:4/A8
feedback /ˈfiːdbæk/ Feedback, Rückmeldung IV:4/B6
feel *(irr)* /fiːl/ (sich) fühlen II:1/A7
feel sorry for /ˌfiːl ˈsɒri fə/ leid tun III:4/B2

feeling /ˈfiːlɪŋ/ Gefühl III:4/A2
°female /ˈfiːmeɪl/ weiblich IV:4/O
°feminine /ˈfemənɪn/ feminin; weiblich IV:5/O
fencing /ˈfensɪŋ/ Einzäunung IV:6/Project A p. 123
ferry /ˈferi/ Fähre II:6/B2
fertilizer *(AE)* = fertiliser *(BE)* /ˈfɜːtəlaɪzə/ Dünger IV:6/Project C p. 129
festival /ˈfestɪvl/ Fest; Festival II:4/A1
fetal *(AE)* = foetal *(BE)* /ˈfiːtl/ fötal, fetal IV:2/A8
a few /ə ˈfjuː/ einige; wenige III:1/A9
fiction /ˈfɪkʃn/ Erfindung; Fiktion; Erzählliteratur IV:5/B9
field /fiːld/ Feld IV:1/A6
fifth /fɪfθ/ fünfte(r, s) I:5/A3
fight /faɪt/ Kampf; Streit IV:3/B1
fight *(irr)* /faɪt/ kämpfen II:3/A8; bekämpfen; ankämpfen gegen III:4/A11
figure /ˈfɪgə/ Zahl; Wert IV:6/Project p. 118
fill in /ˌfɪl‿ˈɪn/ eintragen, ausfüllen IV:1/A4
film /fɪlm/ drehen, filmen IV:1/B2
cup final /ˈkʌp ˌfaɪnl/ Pokalendspiel, Cupfinale I:3/A4
finally /ˈfaɪnli/ schließlich; endlich II:2/B6
find *(irr)* /faɪnd/ finden I:3/B6
find out /ˌfaɪnd‿ˈaʊt/ herausfinden II:2/A2
finding /ˈfaɪndɪŋ/ Ergebnis IV:1/O
fine /faɪn/ in Ordnung, gut II:1/B11
I'm fine, thanks. /aɪm ˈfaɪn ˌθæŋks/ Es geht mir gut, danke. I:4/B9
finish /ˈfɪnɪʃ/ beenden; enden I:5/A7
fire /ˈfaɪə/ Feuer II:3/A8
°firefighter /ˈfaɪəˌfaɪtə/ Feuerwehrmann/-frau IV:4/O
°fireman (*pl* firemen) /ˈfaɪəmən, ˈfaɪəmən/ Feuerwehrmann IV:4/O
fireworks *(pl)* /ˈfaɪəˌwɜːks/ Feuerwerk II:4/A1

first /fɜːst/ zuerst I:4/B1; erste(r, s) I:5/A3
the very first /ðə ˌveri ˈfɜːst/ der/die/das allererste IV:Quiz
first aid kit /ˌfɜːst‿ˈeɪd kɪt/ Verbandskasten III:4/A11
firstly /ˈfɜːsli/ erstens IV:2/A10
fish finger /ˌfɪʃ ˈfɪŋgə/ Fischstäbchen IV:3/B1
fish (*pl* fish *or* fishes) /fɪʃ, fɪʃ, fɪʃɪz/ Fisch I:WB/1
fit /fɪt/ passen; zusammenpassen IV:5/A10
fit in /ˌfɪt‿ˈɪn/ *hier:* dazugehören IV:2/A7
flag /flæg/ Fahne, Flagge IV:Quiz
flat /flæt/ Wohnung IV:1/B5
°flavour /ˈfleɪvə/ Geschmack; Aroma IV:BS/4
flee *(irr)* /fliː/ fliehen IV:5/B2
flight /flaɪt/ Flug II:1/B1
flight attendant /ˈflaɪt‿əˌtendənt/ Flugbegleiter/in IV:4/A1
°flight school /ˈflaɪt skuːl/ Flugschule IV:5/O
flood /flʌd/ Überschwemmung; Hochwasser IV:5/B2; überschwemmen; unter Wasser setzen IV:5/B4
floor /flɔː/ *hier:* Stockwerk IV:1/B2; Fußboden I:4/A3
flour /ˈflaʊə/ Mehl II:4/B5
flower /ˈflaʊə/ Blume II:1/A11
fly /flaɪ/ Fliege I:WB/1
fly *(irr)* /flaɪ/ fliegen I:5/A8
focus on /ˈfəʊkəs‿ɒn/ sich konzentrieren auf IV:6/Project p. 119
foe /fəʊ/ Feind IV:3/B8
follow /ˈfɒləʊ/ folgen; verfolgen II:1/B7
following /ˈfɒləʊɪŋ/ folgende(r, s) III:3/A10
food /fuːd/ Essen I:2/A7
°food depot /ˈfuːd ˌdepəʊ/ Nahrungsmitteldepot IV:BS/3
food science /ˈfuːd ˌsaɪəns/ *hier:* Ernährungswissenschaft IV:1/A4
foot (*pl* feet) /fʊt, fiːt/ Fuß I:2/A1
on foot /ˌɒn ˈfʊt/ zu Fuß II:6/B2

football /ˈfʊtˌbɔːl/ Fußball I:Welcome
football /ˈfʊtˌbɔːl/ *hier:* American Football IV:1/A2
football player /ˈfʊtbɔːl ˌpleɪə/ Fußballspieler/in II:3/A6
for /fɔː/ für I:2/A8
for *(+ Zeitraum)* /fɔː/ … lang II:1/B7
for /fɔː/ *hier:* in die IV:2/A4
for breakfast /fə ˈbrekfəst/ zum Frühstück I:2/A12
for example /fər‿ɪgˈzɑːmpl/ zum Beispiel II:4/A12
for free /fə ˈfriː/ gratis II:2/A2
for help /fə ˈhelp/ nach Hilfe, als Hilfe II:5/B11
force /fɔːs/ Kraft; Wucht IV:2/B7
force /fɔːs/ zwingen IV:5/B3
forest /ˈfɒrɪst/ Wald II:3/A12
forever /fərˈevə/ ewig IV:3/A7
forget *(irr)* /fəˈget/ vergessen I:2/A2
fork /fɔːk/ Gabel I:2/A8
form /fɔːm/ Klasse IV:1/A2
formaldehyde /fɔːˈmældɪˌhaɪd/ Formaldehyd IV:6/Project C p. 130
fortune /ˈfɔːtʃən/ Vermögen; Schicksal; Glück IV:5/A3
fossil fuel /ˌfɒsl ˈfjuːəl/ fossiler Brennstoff IV:6/Project A p. 121
found /faʊnd/ gründen IV:6/Project C p. 131
°foundation /faʊnˈdeɪʃn/ Stiftung IV:BS/10
fourth /fɔːθ/ vierte(r, s) I:5/A3
fox /fɒks/ Fuchs I:WB/1
°frame /freɪm/ einrahmen IV:3/O
free /friː/ frei; kostenlos III:1/A9
for free /fə ˈfriː/ gratis II:2/A2
free time /friː ˈtaɪm/ Freizeit I:3/I
freedom /ˈfriːdəm/ Freiheit IV:2/A4
freeze-frame /ˈfriːzˌfreɪm/ Standbild IV:3/B7
French /frentʃ/ Franzose/Französin; französisch IV:1/B2
French fries *(AE, pl)* /ˌfrentʃ ˈfraɪz/ Pommes frites IV:1/A7
°the French *(pl)* /ðə ˈfrentʃ/ die Franzosen IV:BS/1

frequently /ˈfriːkwəntli/ häufig IV:6/Project B p. 127
fresh /freʃ/ neu; frisch III:1/A7
friar /ˈfraɪə/ Mönch IV:3/B1
Friday /ˈfraɪdeɪ/ Freitag I:1/B2
fridge /frɪdʒ/ Kühlschrank II:1/A11
°fried /fraɪd/ gebraten IV:BS/4
fried egg /ˌfraɪd‿ˈeg/ Spiegelei I:2/A7
friend /frend/ Freund/in I:Welcome
friendly /ˈfrendli/ freundlich I:1/B2
friendship /ˈfrenʃɪp/ Freundschaft IV:3/I
frightened /ˈfraɪtnd/ verängstigt II:5/A1
frog /frɒg/ Frosch I:WB/1
from /frɒm/ von; aus I:Welcome …
°from all over the world /frəm‿ɔːl‿ˌəʊvə ðə ˈwɜːld/ aus der ganzen Welt IV:BS/1
from nowhere /frəm ˈnəʊweə/ aus dem Nichts IV:4/B3
front /frʌnt/ Vorderseite IV:2/B7
at the front /ˌæt ðə ˈfrʌnt/ vorn(e) IV:1/A1
°frostbite /ˈfrɒsˌbaɪt/ Erfrierung IV:BS/3
°frozen /ˈfrəʊzn/ gefroren IV:BS/3
fruit *(no pl)* /fruːt/ Frucht; Obst I:4/B5
frustrated /frʌˈstreɪtɪd/ frustriert II:5/A1
full /fʊl/ voll; satt III:1/A7
full /fʊl/ *hier:* vollständig IV:3/B6
full-time /ˌfʊl ˈtaɪm/ Vollzeit- IV:6/Project A p. 123
fun /fʌn/ Spaß I:4/B1; lustig; witzig I:4/B12
be (good/great) fun /ˌbiː ˌgʊd/ ˌgreɪt ˈfʌn/ (viel) Spaß machen II:1/B1
have (a lot of) fun /ˌhæv‿ə ˌlɒt‿əv‿ˈfʌn/ (viel) Spaß haben II:1/B3
°fund /fʌnd/ finanzieren IV:BS/10
fundraising *(no pl)* /ˈfʌndreɪzɪŋ/ *Geldbeschaffung zu Wohltätigkeitszwecken* IV:6/Project p. 133
funny /ˈfʌni/ lustig; komisch I:3/A4

further /ˈfɜːðə/ weiter II:6/B11
future /ˈfjuːtʃə/ Zukunft II:3/A1
future /ˈfjuːtʃə/ zukünftig IV:4/B1

G

gain experience /ˌgeɪn‿ɪkˈspɪəriəns/ Erfahrungen sammeln IV:4/B8
gain weight /ˌgeɪn ˈweɪt/ zunehmen IV:2/A7
game /geɪm/ Spiel I:3/B4
garage /ˈgærɑːʒ/ Werkstatt IV:4/P10
garden /ˈgɑːdn/ Garten I:1/B2
gardener /ˈgɑːdnə/ Gärtner/in II:3/A8
gardening /ˈgɑːdnɪŋ/ Gartenarbeit; Gärtnern IV:6/Project p. 118
gasoline /ˈgæsəliːn/ Benzin IV:6/Project A p. 121
gay /geɪ/ homosexuell IV:2/A6
gear /gɪə/ Ausrüstung III:6/A3
gear /gɪə/ Gang IV:3/A6
gee *(AE, informal)* /dʒiː/ Wahnsinn, Mannomann IV:1/A2
genre /ˈʒɒnrə/ Genre; Gattung IV:3/B6
geography /dʒiːˈɒgrəfi/ Erdkunde I:5/A3
German /ˈdʒɜːmən/ Deutsch; deutsch I:Welcome …
in German /ˌɪn ˈdʒɜːmən/ auf Deutsch I:2/B1
Germany /ˈdʒɜːməni/ Deutschland I:1/A9
get *(irr)* /get/ werden IV:2/B2; bekommen I:4/A11; kommen; gelangen II:1/A10; *hier:* kaufen II:4/B3
get around /ˌget‿əˈraʊnd/ herumkommen IV:6/Project A p. 121
get into groups /ˌget‿ɪntʊ ˈgruːps/ in Gruppen zusammenkommen IV:3/B6
get into trouble /ˌget‿ɪntʊ ˈtrʌbl/ in Schwierigkeiten geraten II:5/B11
get to know sb /ˌget tə‿ˈnəʊ ˌsʌmbədi/ jdn kennenlernen IV:3/B1
get lost /ˌget ˈlɒst/ sich verirren II:1/B10

get married /ˌget ˈmærid/ heiraten IV:3/B1
°get off /ˌget‿ˈɒf/ *hier:* aussteigen IV:3/O
get on /ˌget‿ˈɒn/ *hier:* mitfahren IV:2/B2; *hier:* einsteigen IV:3/O
get out /ˌget‿ˈaʊt/ aussteigen I:4/B3
get ready /ˌget ˈredi/ sich fertig machen; sich vorbereiten IV:6/Project p.119
get sb to do sth /ˌget ˌsʌmbədi tə ˈduː ˌsʌmθɪŋ/ jdn dazu bringen, etw zu tun IV:3/B1
get up /ˌget‿ˈʌp/ aufstehen I:2/B7
Get well soon! /ˌget ˌwel ˈsuːn/ Gute Besserung! II:6/A12
ghost /gəʊst/ Geist; Gespenst I:4/B1
gift /gɪft/ Geschenk IV:5/A4
giraffe /dʒəˈrɑːf/ Giraffe I:WB/1
girl /gɜːl/ Mädchen I:3/A1
girlfriend /ˈgɜːlˌfrend/ Freundin; Partnerin II:2/B2
give *(irr)* /gɪv/ geben I:Welcome
give a presentation /ˌgɪv‿ə ˌpreznˈteɪʃn/ eine Präsentation halten IV:1/A10
give a reason /ˌgɪv‿ə ˈriːzn/ einen Grund nennen IV:4/A4
°give thanks /ˌgɪv ˈθæŋks/ Dank sagen IV:BS/2
give up /ˌgɪv‿ˈʌp/ aufgeben III:4/B4
glad /glæd/ glücklich, froh III:1/A7
glass /glɑːs/ Glas III:1/A7
glasses *(pl)* /ˈglɑːsɪz/ Brille I:2/A6
glimpse /glɪmps/ flüchtiger Blick IV:1/B1
glory /ˈglɔːri/ Ruhm IV:5/A3
glove /glʌv/ Handschuh I:WB/1
go *(irr)* /gəʊ/ gehen; fahren I:Welcome
Here you go. /ˌhɪə ju ˈgəʊ/ Hier, bitte! I:4/B6
go abroad /ˌgəʊ‿əˈbrɔːd/ ins Ausland fahren II:1/A3
go by bus /ˌgəʊ baɪ ˈbʌs/ mit dem Bus fahren I:5/A4
go green /ˌgəʊ ˈgriːn/ umweltbewusst werden IV:6/I
go into detail /ˌgəʊ‿ɪntə ˈdiːteɪl/ ins Detail gehen IV:6/Project p.119
go on /ˌgəʊ‿ˈɒn/ passieren; weitergehen, weiterfahren; weiterreden III:1/I
go on /ˌgəʊ‿ˈɒn/ fortsetzen; fortfahren IV:3/A10
go on holiday /ˌgəʊ‿ɒn ˈhɒlɪdeɪ/ in Urlaub fahren II:1/A1
go out /ˌgəʊ‿ˈaʊt/ (hinaus)gehen; ausgehen III:3/B4
go out with sb /ˌgəʊ‿ˈaʊt wɪð ˌsʌmbədi/ mit jdm ausgehen IV:2/A1
°go red /ˌgəʊ ˈred/ erröten, rot werden IV:BS/6
go shopping /ˌgəʊ ˈʃɒpɪŋ/ Einkaufen gehen II:1/A2
go swimming /ˌgəʊ ˈswɪmɪŋ/ Schwimmen gehen I:3/A9
go with /ˌgəʊ ˈwɪθ/ gehören zu; passen zu II:5/A1
Let's go! /ˌlets ˈgəʊ/ Lass(t) uns gehen! I:1/A2
goal /gəʊl/ Ziel IV:5/B7
score a goal /ˌskɔːr‿ə ˈgəʊl/ ein Tor schießen I:3/A6
God (= god) /gɒd/ Gott IV:1/B8
be going to do sth /biː ˌgəʊɪŋ tə ˈduː ˌsʌmθɪŋ/ etw tun werden II:4/A7
goldfish (*pl* goldfish) /ˈgəʊldˌfɪʃ/ Goldfisch I:1/A4
gonna (= going to) *(informal)* /ˈgʌnə, ˈgəʊɪŋ tʊ/ werden IV:1/B8
good /gʊd/ gut I:Welcome
good /gʊd/ Ware IV:6/Project B p.125
be good at sth /ˌbiː ˈgʊd‿æt ˌsʌmθɪŋ/ gut in etw sein II:4/A7
be good fun /biː ˌgʊd ˈfʌn/ viel Spaß machen I:4/A11
Good luck! /ˌgʊd ˈlʌk/ Viel Glück! I:3/B6
Good morning! /ˌgʊd ˈmɔːnɪŋ/ Guten Morgen! I:2/I
good-looking /ˌgʊdˈlʊkɪŋ/ gut aussehend I:2/A3
Goodbye. /ˌgʊdˈbaɪ/ Auf Wiedersehen. I:Welcome
say goodbye /ˌseɪ gʊdˈbaɪ/ Abschied nehmen; Wiedersehen sagen IV:5/A5
government /ˈgʌvənmənt/ Regierung IV:5/B3
grade *(AE)* /greɪd/ Klasse IV:1/A2
graduate *(AE)* /ˈgrædʒueɪt/ die Abschlussprüfung bestehen IV:2/A2
graduation /ˌgrædʒuˈeɪʃn/ (Studien)abschluss IV:5/A1
granddaughter /ˈgrænˌdɔːtə/ Enkelin I:5/B7
grandfather /ˈgrænˌfɑːðə/ Großvater I:5/B7
grandmother /ˈgrænˌmʌðə/ Großmutter I:5/B7
grandparent /ˈgrænˌpeərənt/ Großelternteil I:5/B7
grandparents *(pl)* /ˈgrænˌpeərənts/ Großeltern II:1/A2
grandson /ˈgrænˌsʌn/ Enkel I:5/B7
graphic design /ˌgræfɪk dɪˈzaɪn/ Grafikdesign IV:4/A10
grass /grɑːs/ Gras; Wiese II:2/A2
°grasshopper /ˈgrɑːsˌhɒpə/ Grashüpfer IV:BS/4
grateful /ˈgreɪtfl/ dankbar III:4/A2
gray *(AE)* = grey *(BE)* /greɪ/ grau IV:5/B7
great /greɪt/ groß; großartig I:Welcome
Great Britain /ˌgreɪt ˈbrɪtn/ Großbritannien II:4/A1
°great-grandfather /ˌgreɪt ˈgrænˌfɑːðə/ Urgroßvater IV:BS/8
°Greater New York /ˌgreɪtə ˌnjuː ˈjɔːk/ Großraum New York IV:BS/1
Grecian /ˈgriːʃn/ griechisch IV:5/A1
Greece /griːs/ Griechenland IV:5/B8
greed /ˈgriːd/ Gier IV:5/A3
green /griːn/ *hier:* umweltbewusst IV:6/I; grün I:Welcome
greetings *(pl)* /ˈgriːtɪŋz/ Grüße II:1/A2
grey /greɪ/ grau I:2/A6
°grilled /grɪld/ gegrillt IV:BS/4

ground /graʊnd/ Boden IV:1/A6

°ground /graʊnd/ gemahlen IV:BS/4

group /gruːp/ Gruppe II:2/A10

grow *(irr)* /grəʊ/ wachsen; werden; anbauen IV:3/A7

grow up /ˌgrəʊ‿ˈʌp/ erwachsen sein, erwachsen werden II:3/A8

grow up /ˌgrəʊ‿ˈʌp/ *hier:* aufwachsen IV:1/B5

growing /ˈgrəʊɪŋ/ Anbau IV:6/Project C p. 129

guess /ges/ (er)raten II:1/B10; annehmen; vermuten II:4/A3

guest /gest/ Gast II:4/B8

guidance counselor *(AE)* /ˈgaɪdns ˌkaʊnslə/ Beratungslehrer/in IV:4/A10

guide /gaɪd/ Führer/in III:6/B2

travel guide /ˈtrævl ˌgaɪd/ Reiseführer IV:1/B10

guinea pig /ˈgɪni ˌpɪg/ Meerschweinchen I:WB/1

guitar /gɪˈtɑː/ Gitarre I:1/A5

play the guitar /ˌpleɪ ðə gɪˈtɑː/ Gitarre spielen II:Last year

gum /gʌm/ Kaugummi IV:2/A7

guy *(informal)* /gaɪ/ Kerl, Typ IV:3/A4

you guys *(informal)* /ˈjuː gaɪz/ ihr; euch IV:1/A2

guys *(pl, informal)* /gaɪz/ Leute IV:1/A3

gym (= gymnasium) /dʒɪm, dʒɪmneɪziəm/ Turnhalle I:3/A9

do gymnastics /ˌduː dʒɪmˈnæstɪks/ Turnen I:3/A8

gypsy cab *(informal)* /ˈdʒɪpsi kæb/ *illegales Taxi* IV:1/B8

H

hail /heɪl/ *hier:* rufen IV:1/B8

hair /heə/ Haar I:2/A1

hairdresser, hair stylist /ˈheəˌdresə, heə ˈstaɪlɪst/ Friseur/in II:3/A8

half /hɑːf/ halb I:2/A7

half *(pl* halves*)* /hɑːf, hɑːvz/ Hälfte IV:5/A7

°ham /hæm/ Schinken IV:BS/5

hamster /ˈhæmstə/ Hamster I:WB/1

handkerchief *(pl* **handkerchiefs / handkerchieves)** /ˈhæŋkəˌtʃɪf, ˈhæŋkəˌtʃɪfs, ˈhæŋkəˌtʃiːvz/ Taschentuch II:4/B3

handsome /ˈhænsm/ gut aussehend II:3/A1

handy /ˈhændi/ praktisch IV:6/I

°hang around *(informal)* /ˌhæŋ‿əˈraʊnd/ rumhängen IV:BS/8

hang on to /ˌhæŋ‿ˈɒn tʊ/ sich festhalten an IV:2/B2

happen /ˈhæpən/ geschehen; passieren II:3/B3

happiness /ˈhæpinəs/ Glück; Zufriedenheit IV:1/A9

happy /ˈhæpi/ glücklich I:1/B2

Happy birthday (to you)! /ˌhæpi ˈbɜːθdeɪ tʊ juː/ Herzlichen Glückwunsch zum Geburtstag! I:5/B1

Happy New Year! /ˌhæpi njuː ˈjɪə/ Frohes Neues Jahr! II:4/A1

hard /hɑːd/ hart; anstrengend II:2/B2

hard skill /ˌhɑːd ˈskɪl/ *berufstypische Qualifikationen* IV:4/B6

hardly /ˈhɑːdli/ kaum IV:1/B5

hardship /ˈhɑːdʃɪp/ Not; Elend IV:5/A3

harm /hɑːm/ schaden IV:6/Project B p. 135

harmful /ˈhɑːmfl/ schädlich IV:6/Project C p. 136

harvest /ˈhɑːvɪst/ ernten IV:2/B2; Ernte IV:BS/2

hat /hæt/ Hut I:WB/1

hatch /hætʃ/ schlüpfen IV:5/B7

hate /heɪt/ hassen; nicht ausstehen können I:Welcome

have *(irr)* /hæv/ haben; essen, trinken I:1/B2

°have a dinner party /ˌhæv‿ə ˈdɪnə ˌpɑːti/ ein Abendessen geben IV:BS/4

have a look at /ˌhæv‿ə ˈlʊk‿ət/ sich ansehen IV:5/A5

have (a lot of) fun /ˌhæv‿ə ˌlɒt‿əv‿ˈfʌn/ (viel) Spaß haben II:1/B3

have a picnic /ˌhæv‿ə ˈpɪknɪk/ ein Picknick machen I:5/B11

have a temperature /ˌhæv‿ə ˈtemprɪtʃə/ Fieber haben III:3/B4

have breakfast /ˌhæv ˈbrekfəst/ frühstücken I:2/A12

have got /ˌhæv ˈgɒt/ haben I:1/A5

have in common /ˌhæv‿ɪn ˈkɒmən/ gemeinsam haben IV:3/B6

have to /ˈhæv tə/ müssen I:4/B1

hazardous /ˈhæzədəs/ gefährlich IV:6/Project C p. 128

he /hiː/ er I:Welcome

head /hed/ Kopf III:5/B3

°shake one's head /ˌʃeɪk wʌnz ˈhed/ den Kopf schütteln IV:BS/6

headache /ˈhedeɪk/ Kopfschmerzen III:3/B4

heading /ˈhedɪŋ/ Überschrift, Titel IV:4/A14

health /helθ/ Gesundheit III:3/B4

health warning /ˈhelθ ˌwɔːnɪŋ/ Warnhinweis IV:2/A8

healthy /ˈhelθi/ gesund III:3/A4

hear *(irr)* /hɪə/ hören II:2/A7

heart /hɑːt/ Herz III:2/B4

heat exhaustion /ˈhiːt‿ɪgˌzɔːstʃn/ Hitzschlag IV:5/A9

heating system /ˈhiːtɪŋ ˌsɪstəm/ Heizungsanlage IV:4/A1

heavy /ˈhevi/ schwer II:4/A1

hedgehog /ˈhedʒˌhɒg/ Igel I:WB/1

helicopter /ˈhelɪˌkɒptə/ Hubschrauber; Helikopter IV:5/A4

hello /həˈləʊ/ hallo I:Welcome

help /help/ helfen I:3/B4; Hilfe II:1/B7

Can I help you? /ˌkæn‿aɪ ˈhelp juː/ Kann ich dir/Ihnen helfen? I:3/B4

for help /fə ˈhelp/ nach Hilfe, als Hilfe II:5/B11

help out /ˌhelp‿ˈaʊt/ aushelfen IV:4/B8

helpful /ˈhelpfl/ hilfreich; nützlich III:4/B3

°helpless /ˈhelpləs/ hilflos IV:BS/6
helpline /ˈhelpˌlaɪn/ *telefonischer Beratungsdienst* IV:2/I
hemp /hemp/ Hanf IV:6/Project C p. 129
her /hɜː/ ihr/ihre; sie I:Welcome
herbicide /ˈhɜːbɪsaɪd/ Herbizid; Unkrautvernichtungsmittel IV:6/Project C p. 136
here /hɪə/ hier; hierher I:1/B2
Here goes! /ˌhɪə ˈgəʊz/ Los geht's! IV:3/B1
Here you are. /ˌhɪə ju‿ˈɑː/ Hier, bitte! I:2/B10
Here you go. /ˌhɪə ju ˈgəʊ/ Hier, bitte! I:4/B6
hero (*pl* heroes) /ˈhɪərəʊ, ˈhɪərəʊz/ Held II:3/A12
hers /hɜːz/ ihre(r, s) III:4/B2
herself /həˈself/ sich; sich selbst IV:1/A3
hidden /ˈhɪdn/ versteckt IV:6/Project C p. 128
hide *(irr)* /haɪd/ (sich) verstecken IV:2/A10
high /haɪ/ hoch IV:2/B7
high school *(AE)* /ˈhaɪ skuːl/ Highschool, weiterführende Schule IV:1/A2
highlight /ˈhaɪˌlaɪt/ Höhepunkt IV:1/B2
hill /hɪl/ Hügel IV:5/A3
him /hɪm/ ihm, ihn I:4/A6
himself /hɪmˈself/ sich; sich selbst IV:1/A3
hire *(AE)* /ˈhaɪə/ einstellen IV:4/B6
his /hɪz/ sein; seine(r, s) I:Welcome
history /ˈhɪstri/ Geschichte I:5/A2
hit *(irr)* /hɪt/ treffen, stoßen gegen; schlagen III:4/A1
hold /həʊld/ Frachtraum IV:5/A4
hold *(irr)* /həʊld/ (fest)halten II:6/B4
lay hold of sb /ˌleɪ ˈhəʊld‿əv ˌsʌmbədi/ jdn bekommen IV:3/B8
hole /həʊl/ Loch II:5/A3
holiday(s) /ˈhɒlɪdeɪ(z)/ Ferien; Urlaub II:1/I
holiday /ˈhɒlɪdeɪ/ *hier: Feiertag* IV:Quiz
go on holiday /ˌgəʊ‿ɒn ˈhɒlɪdeɪ/ in Urlaub fahren II:1/A1
home /həʊm/ Zuhause; Haus I:1/B2; nach Hause II:3/B1
at home /ˌæt ˈhəʊm/ zu Hause I:3/A9
homeland /ˈhəʊmˌlænd/ Heimat(land) IV:5/A11
homework /ˈhəʊmwɜːk/ Hausaufgaben I:2/B1
honestly /ˈɒnɪsli/ ehrlich; wirklich IV:4/A10
hope /həʊp/ Hoffnung IV:5/B8; hoffen I:1/B2
horizon /həˈraɪzn/ Horizont IV:2/A4
°horrible /ˈhɒrəbl/ schrecklich; gemein IV:BS/4
horse /hɔːs/ Pferd I:3/A8
ride a horse /ˌraɪd‿ə ˈhɔːs/ reiten I:3/A8
hot /hɒt/ heiß I:Welcome; scharf III:1/A1
hot chocolate /ˌhɒt ˈtʃɒklət/ (heißer) Kakao I:4/B9
hour /ˈaʊə/ Stunde II:1/B1
house /haʊs/ Haus I:1/B2
household waste /ˈhaʊsˌhəʊld weɪst/ Haushaltsmüll IV:6/Project p. 116
housekeeper /ˈhaʊsˌkiːpə/ Haushälter/in IV:5/B5
°housewife (*pl* housewives) /ˈhaʊsˌwaɪf, ˈhaʊsˌwaɪvz/ Hausfrau IV:4/O
housing *(no pl)* /ˈhaʊzɪŋ/ Wohnungen, Unterkünfte IV:6/Project A p. 134
how /haʊ/ wie I:1/A3
How about ...? /ˈhaʊ‿əˌbaʊt/ Wie wäre es mit ...? III:3/A9
How are you? /ˌhaʊ‿ˈɑː jʊ/ Wie geht es dir?/Wie geht es Ihnen? I:4/B9
how many /haʊ ˈmeni/ wie viele I:3/B5
how much /haʊ ˈmʌtʃ/ wie viel I:4/B6
How much is it? /ˌhaʊ mʌtʃ‿ˈɪz‿ɪt/ Wie viel kostet es? I:3/B4
How old are you? /haʊ‿ˈəʊld‿ɑː ˌjʊ/ Wie alt bist du? I:Welcome ...
how to /ˈhaʊ tʊ/ wie man I:3/A1
huge /hjuːdʒ/ riesig II:2/B6
human /ˈhjuːmən/ menschlich IV:1/A9
hungry /ˈhʌŋgri/ hungrig I:4/B9
°hunt /hʌnt/ jagen IV:BS/2
hurricane /ˈhʌrɪkeɪn/ Orkan IV:5/I
hurry (up) /ˌhʌri‿ˈʌp/ sich beeilen I:2/A2
Hurry up! /ˌhʌri‿ˈʌp/ Beeil dich! I:2/A7
hurt *(irr)* /hɜːt/ wehtun, schmerzen III:3/B1

I /aɪ/ ich I:Welcome ...
I don't know. /ˌaɪ ˌdəʊnt ˈnəʊ/ Ich weiß es nicht. I:3/B6
I don't like ... /ˌaɪ ˈdəʊnt laɪk/ Ich mag ... nicht. I:2/A7
I don't understand. /ˌaɪ ˌdəʊnt‿ˌʌndəˈstænd/ Ich verstehe es nicht. I:3/A4
I'd (= I would) /aɪd, ˈaɪ wʊd/ ich würde IV:3/A7
I'd rather ... /ˌaɪd ˈrɑːðə/ Ich würde lieber ... I:5/A2
I'll take it. /ˌaɪl ˈteɪk‿ɪt/ Ich nehme es. I:3/B4
I'm (= I am) /aɪm, ˈaɪ‿æm/ ich bin, ich heiße I:Welcome ...
I'm fine, thanks. /aɪm ˈfaɪn ˌθæŋks/ Es geht mir gut, danke. I:4/B9
I'm sorry. /ˌaɪm ˈsɒri/ Es tut mir leid., Entschuldigung. III:1/A7
I've got (= I have got) /ˌaɪv ˈgɒt, ˌaɪ hæv ˈgɒt/ ich habe I:Welcome
ice cream /ˈaɪs ˌkriːm/ Eis II:1/A1
Iceland /ˈaɪslənd/ Island IV:6/Project A p. 121
ICT (= Information and Communication Technology) /ˌaɪˌsiːˈtiː, ɪnfəˈmeɪʃn‿ən kəˌmjuːnɪˈkeɪʃn tekˌnɒlədʒi/ Informationstechnologie, IT I:5/A3
idea /aɪˈdɪə/ Idee II:1/B7; *hier:* Vorstellung II:3/A1

identify /aɪˈdentɪfaɪ/ identifizieren IV:6/Project p. 119
identity /aɪˈdentɪti/ Identität IV:5/A1
if /ɪf/ wenn; falls II:1/B7; ob II:5/A4
ignore /ɪɡˈnɔː/ ignorieren II:5/B10
ill /ɪl/ krank II:3/A8
illegally /ɪˈliːɡli/ ungesetzlich, illegal IV:5/A9
illness /ˈɪlnəs/ Krankheit IV:6/Project C p. 130
image /ˈɪmɪdʒ/ Bild IV:4/A7
imagination /ɪˌmædʒɪˈneɪʃn/ Fantasie, Vorstellungskraft IV:6/Project p. 133
imagine /ɪˈmædʒɪn/ sich etw vorstellen IV:1/B2
immediately /ɪˈmiːdiətli/ sofort IV:5/A9
immigrant /ˈɪmɪɡrənt/ Einwanderer/in; Immigrant/in IV:1/B2
immigration /ˌɪmɪˈɡreɪʃn/ Einwanderung; Immigration IV:5/I
important /ɪmˈpɔːtnt/ wichtig II:5/B3
impossible /ɪmˈpɒsəbl/ unmöglich IV:5/B3
impression /ɪmˈpreʃn/ Eindruck IV:1/I
impressive /ɪmˈpresɪv/ beeindruckend III:6/A3
improve /ɪmˈpruːv/ verbessern; besser werden IV:4/B6
in /ɪn/ in; auf I:Welcome
in addition to /ˌɪn‿əˈdɪʃn tʊ/ zusätzlich zu IV:6/Project C p. 129
in detail /ɪn ˈdiːteɪl/ ausführlich IV:2/A11
in disguise /ɪn dɪsˈɡaɪz/ verkleidet IV:3/B1
in English /ˌɪn‿ˈɪŋɡlɪʃ/ auf Englisch II:3/A8
in front /ɪn ˈfrʌnt/ vorn IV:5/A1
in front of /ˌɪn ˈfrʌnt‿əv/ vor I:4/B5
in German /ˌɪn ˈdʒɜːmən/ auf Deutsch I:2/B1
in my opinion /ɪn ˈmaɪ‿əˌpɪnjən/ meiner Meinung nach IV:1/A7
°in one's lifetime /ˌɪn wʌnz ˈlaɪfˌtaɪm/ im Laufe seines Lebens IV:BS/4
in order to /ˌɪn‿ˈɔːdə tʊ/ um zu IV:4/B7
in pairs /ˌɪn ˈpeəz/ paarweise IV:3/A11
°in return /ɪn rɪˈtɜːn/ im Gegenzug; dafür IV:3/O
in secret /ɪn ˈsiːkrət/ heimlich IV:3/B1
in the afternoon /ˌɪn ði‿ɑːftəˈnuːn/ am Nachmittag II:4/B8
in the end /ˌɪn ði‿ˈend/ schließlich III:6/B9
in the evening /ˌɪn ði‿ˈiːvnɪŋ/ am Abend IV:2/B2
in the middle of /ˌɪn ðə ˈmɪdl‿əv/ in der Mitte von I:4/A4
in the morning /ˌɪn ðə ˈmɔːnɪŋ/ am Morgen I:2/B7
in the street /ˌɪn ðə ˈstriːt/ auf der Straße I:3/A9
in time /ɪn ˈtaɪm/ rechtzeitig; pünktlich II:5/B9
include /ɪnˈkluːd/ beinhalten; einbeziehen IV:5/A11
°including /ɪnˈkluːdɪŋ/ einschließlich IV:1/O
inclusive /ɪnˈkluːsɪv/ allumfassend IV:3/A7
incredible /ɪnˈkredəbl/ unglaublich II:1/B7
indeed /ɪnˈdiːd/ wirklich; in der Tat IV:3/B8
Independence Day /ˌɪndɪˈpendəns deɪ/ Unabhängigkeitstag IV:Quiz
°independent /ˌɪndɪˈpendənt/ unabhängig IV:BS/1
India /ˈɪndiə/ Indien IV:6/Project C p. 130
individual /ˌɪndɪˈvɪdʒuəl/ individuell; einzeln IV:4/B7
Indonesia /ˌɪndəʊˈniːʒə/ Indonesien IV:6/Project C p. 130
indoors /ˌɪnˈdɔːz/ drinnen, im Haus IV:4/B1
industry /ˈɪndəstri/ Industrie III:5/A1
°influence /ˈɪnfluəns/ Einfluss IV:BS/9
°influential /ɪnfluˈenʃl/ einflussreich IV:BS/9
inform /ɪnˈfɔːm/ informieren IV:6/Project p. 118
information *(no pl)* /ˌɪnfəˈmeɪʃn/ Informationen II:6/B11
ingredient /ɪnˈɡriːdiənt/ Zutat III:1/B5
inhabitant /ɪnˈhæbɪtənt/ Einwohner/in, Bewohner/in IV:1/A10
take initiative /ˌteɪk‿ɪˈnɪʃətɪv/ die Initiative ergreifen IV:4/B7
injury /ˈɪndʒəri/ Verletzung IV:2/A8
insect /ˈɪnsekt/ Insekt IV:6/Project C p. 136
inside /ˈɪnˌsaɪd/ innen; drinnen; hinein II:2/A2
inspire /ɪnˈspaɪə/ inspirieren IV:1/B8
install /ɪnˈstɔːl/ installieren IV:4/A1
instead /ɪnˈsted/ stattdessen III:1/B1
instead of /ɪnˈsted‿əv/ anstatt IV:1/A2
institute /ˈɪnstɪˌtjuːt/ Institut IV:6/Project B p. 125
instruction /ɪnˈstrʌkʃn/ Anweisung; Instruktion III:1/B5
°instructor /ɪnˈstrʌktə/ Lehrer/in IV:BS/7
interest /ˈɪntrəst/ Interesse, Hobby II:1/B10
be interested in /ˌbi‿ˈɪntrəstɪd‿ɪn/ interessiert sein an III:2/A7
interesting /ˈɪntrəstɪŋ/ interessant I:3/B4
impression /ɪmˈpreʃn/ Eindruck IV:1/B1
internally displaced /ɪnˌtɜːnli dɪsˈpleɪst/ *intern vertrieben* IV:5/B3
surf the Internet /ˌsɜːf ˌði‿ˈɪntəˌnet/ im Internet surfen II:6/A6
interview /ˈɪntəˌvjuː/ Vorstellungsgespräch IV:4/B6; interviewen, befragen III:4/A3
into /ˈɪntuː/ in I:Welcome

introduction /ˌɪntrəˈdʌkʃn/ Einleitung IV:6/Project p.116
invent /ɪnˈvent/ erfinden III:5/I
invention /ɪnˈvenʃn/ Erfindung III:5/I
inventor /ɪnˈventə/ Erfinder/in III:5/A1
investigate /ɪnˈvestɪgeɪt/ untersuchen; recherchieren IV:6/Project p.132
invitation /ˌɪnvɪˈteɪʃn/ Einladung II:6/B11
invite /ɪnˈvaɪt/ einladen I:5/B2
involved /ɪnˈvɒlvd/ beteiligt IV:6/Project p.132
Ireland /ˈaɪələnd/ Irland II:4/A1
Irish /ˈaɪrɪʃ/ irisch IV:5/I
irresponsible /ˌɪrɪˈspɒnsəbl/ unverantworlich, verantwortungslos IV:6/Project B p.124
Is it …? /ˈɪz‿ɪt/ Ist es …? I:2/B7
Is there a …? /ˈɪz ðeər‿ə/ Gibt es ein/e …? I:1/B3
island /ˈaɪlənd/ Insel III:4/I
isle /aɪl/ (kleine) Insel IV:5/A2
isolated /ˈaɪsəˌleɪtɪd/ isoliert, einsam IV:2/A6
issue /ˈɪʃuː/ Frage; Thema; Problem IV:6/Project p.132
it /ɪt/ es I:Welcome
it's (= it is) /ɪts, ˈɪt‿ɪz/ *hier:* es kostet I:3/B1
Italian /ɪˈtæljən/ Italiener/in; italienisch IV:5/A1
Italy /ˈɪtəli/ Italien IV:1/A7
its /ɪts/ sein(e), ihr(e) *(sächlich)* II:2/B6

J

jacket /ˈdʒækɪt/ Jacke I:WB/1
jacket potato /ˌdʒækɪt pəˈteɪtəʊ/ Ofenkartoffel; Folienkartoffel III:1/A1
jam /dʒæm/ Marmelade I:2/A8
January /ˈdʒænjuəri/ Januar I:5/B7
jealous /ˈdʒeləs/ eifersüchtig, neidisch IV:1/B2
Jewish /ˈdʒuːɪʃ/ jüdisch IV:5/A1
job /dʒɒb/ Aufgabe I:4/A6; Stelle; Job; Beruf II:3/A1
join /dʒɔɪn/ mitmachen I:3/A1
join /dʒɔɪn/ *hier:* verbinden IV:5/P6; sich zu jdm gesellen IV:6/Project C p.130
joke /dʒəʊk/ Spaß; Witz II:6/A12
joke /dʒəʊk/ scherzen; Spaß machen IV:1/B2
You must be joking! *(informal)* /juː məs bi ˈdʒəʊkɪŋ/ Das meinst du doch nicht im Ernst!, Das soll wohl ein Witz sein! II:3/A1
Jordan /ˈdʒɔːdn/ Jordanien IV:5/B5
°journal /ˈdʒɜːnl/ Zeitschrift IV:BS/9
journey /ˈdʒɜːni/ Reise IV:5/A2
journey /ˈdʒɜːni/ reisen IV:5/A3
°joy /dʒɔɪ/ Freude IV:5/O
judge /dʒʌdʒ/ *(be)*urteilen, (ein)schätzen IV:1/A9
juice /dʒuːs/ Saft II:4/B5
orange juice /ˈɒrɪndʒ‿ˌdʒuːs/ Orangensaft I:Welcome
July /dʒʊˈlaɪ/ Juli I:5/B7
jump /dʒʌmp/ springen I:WB/1
jump off /ˌdʒʌmp‿ˈɒf/ herunterspringen IV:2/B2
jumper /ˈdʒʌmpə/ Pullover I:WB/1
June /dʒuːn/ Juni I:5/B7
just /dʒʌst/ gerade I:5/B3; nur; bloß II:1/A7; einfach; wirklich II:4/A1
just like me /ˌdʒʌst laɪk ˈmiː/ genau wie ich IV:5/B7

kayak /ˈkaɪæk/ Kajak IV:Quiz
keep *(irr)* /kiːp/ halten; behalten; aufbewahren III:2/B9
keep away /ˌkiːp‿əˈweɪ/ fernhalten IV:2/B7
keep doing sth /ˌkiːp ˈduːɪŋ sʌmθɪŋ/ etw weiter tun III:6/B2
keep fit /ˌkiːp ˈfɪt/ fit bleiben, (sich) fit halten III:3/A4
keep oneself busy /ˌkiːp wʌnˌself ˈbɪzi/ sich mit etw beschäftigen IV:2/A9
°ketchup /ˈketʃəp/ Ketschup IV:BS/5
key /kiː/ Schlüssel-; wesentliche(r, s) IV:5/A9
kick /kɪk/ treten III:3/B1
kid /kɪd/ Kind II:2/A2
kill /kɪl/ töten III:2/A9
kind /kaɪnd/ Art; Sorte I:4/B10
all kinds of /ˌɔːl ˈkaɪndz‿əv/ alle möglichen II:6/B11
king /kɪŋ/ König III:2/A9
kitchen /ˈkɪtʃən/ Küche I:2/A7
°kitchen staff /ˈkɪtʃən stɑːf/ Küchenpersonal IV:BS/8
kitchen utensils *(pl)* /ˈkɪtʃən‿juːˌtenslz/ Küchengeräte IV:6/Project B p.135
knee /niː/ Knie I:2/A1
knife (*pl* knives) /naɪf, naɪvz/ Messer I:2/A8
know *(irr)* /nəʊ/ wissen; kennen I:2/A8
I don't know. /ˌaɪ ˌdəʊnt ˈnəʊ/ Ich weiß es nicht. I:3/B6
knowledge /ˈnɒlɪdʒ/ Kenntnis; Wissen IV:6/Project p.119
known /nəʊn/ bekannt IV:1/P5

label /ˈleɪbl/ beschriften I:2/A13
label /ˈleɪbl/ Etikett, Schildchen IV:6/Project C p.128
labor *(AE)* = labour *(BE)* /ˈleɪbə/ Arbeit IV:6/Project C p.130
ladies and gentlemen /ˌleɪdiz‿ən‿ˈdʒentlmən/ (meine) Damen und Herren III:5/A2
lady /ˈleɪdi/ Frau; Dame III:1/A7
lake /leɪk/ See II:2/A2
°lamb /læm/ Lamm IV:BS/5
lamp /læmp/ Lampe I:4/A1
land diving /ˈlænd‿ˌdaɪvɪŋ/ *Lianenspringen* IV:2/I
language /ˈlæŋgwɪdʒ/ Sprache IV:Quiz
large /lɑːdʒ/ groß II:2/A2
last /lɑːst/ letzte(r, s) I:5/A2
last /lɑːst/ (an)dauern IV:2/B9
last night /ˌlɑːst ˈnaɪt/ gestern Abend II:4/A3
late /leɪt/ (zu) spät I:2/A2
later /ˈleɪtə/ später II:2/B6
latest /ˈleɪtɪst/ neueste(r, s) IV:1/B5
laugh /lɑːf/ lachen II:3/B1

laugh oneself silly *(informal)* /ˌlɑːf ˌwʌnself ˈsɪli/ sich kaputtlachen IV:1/A2
°laughter /ˈlɑːftə/ Gelächter, Lachen IV:BS/9
law /lɔː/ Gesetz; Recht IV:5/B3
lay *(irr)* /leɪ/ legen II:4/B5
lay hold of sb /ˌleɪ ˈhəʊld‿əv ˌsʌmbədi/ jdn bekommen IV:3/B8
lay the soil /ˌleɪ ðə ˈsɔɪl/ *hier:* den Boden vorbereiten IV:6/Project A p.123
lay the table /ˌleɪ ðə ˈteɪbl/ den Tisch decken II:4/B5
lead *(irr)* /liːd/ führen IV:3/A10
leader /ˈliːdə/ Leiter/in, Führer/in IV:3/P12
leaf (*pl* **leaves**) /liːf, liːvz/ Blatt III:1/B5
leaflet /ˈliːflət/ Prospekt; Broschüre IV:6/Project B p.133
learn *(irr)* /lɜːn/ lernen I:1/A6
learn *(irr)* /lɜːn/ *hier:* erfahren IV:5/A4
least /liːst/ am wenigsten IV:3/B6
at least /ət ˈliːst/ mindestens; wenigstens III:3/B1
leather /ˈleðə/ Leder IV:6/Project C p.131
leave *(irr)* /liːv/ zurücklassen; (übrig) lassen IV:2/A10; verlassen; abfahren I:2/B7
leave *(irr)* /liːv/ weggehen IV:3/B1
leave around /ˌliːv‿əˈraʊnd/ herumliegen lassen IV:2/B2
leave behind /ˌliːv bɪˈhaɪnd/ zurücklassen IV:2/A4
left /left/ (nach) links II:2/B7
be left /ˌbiː ˈleft/ übrig bleiben III:6/A2
have sth left /ˌhæv sʌmθɪŋ ˈleft/ etw übrig haben II:6/A3
on the left/on your left /ˌɒn ðə/jɔː ˈleft/ links, auf der/deiner linken Seite II:2/B7
on the left side /ɒn ðə ˌleft ˈsaɪd/ links II:1/B11
leg /leg/ Bein I:2/A1
lemonade /ˌleməˈneɪd/ Limonade II:1/B11
lesbian /ˈlezbiən/ lesbisch IV:2/A6
less /les/ weniger III:1/B1
lesson /ˈlesn/ Stunde; Unterricht I:5/A2
let *(irr)* /let/ lassen II:3/B3
let sb down /ˌlet ˌsʌmbədi ˈdaʊn/ jdn im Stich lassen IV:3/A8
let's (= let us) /lets, ˈlet‿əs/ lass(t) uns … I:Welcome
Let's go! /ˌlets ˈgəʊ/ Lass(t) uns gehen! I:1/A2
letter /ˈletə/ Brief; Buchstabe II:1/B10
liberty /ˈlɪbəti/ Freiheit IV:1/A9
library /ˈlaɪbrəri/ Bücherei I:3/A1
license plate *(AE)* /ˈlaɪsns pleɪt/ Nummernschild IV:1/A10
lie *(irr)* /laɪ/ liegen II:1/A7
lie down /ˌlaɪ ˈdaʊn/ sich hinlegen IV:5/A10
love life /ˈlʌv laɪf/ Liebesleben IV:3/A6
life (*pl* **lives**) /laɪf, laɪvz/ Leben II:3/A13
lifeguard /ˈlaɪfˌgɑːd/ Bademeister/in; Rettungsschwimmer/in IV:4/A1
°lifesaver /ˈlaɪfˌseɪvə/ Lebensretter/in IV:BS/10
lift /lɪft/ Aufzug IV:1/B5
light /laɪt/ Licht I:4/B1
light bulb /ˈlaɪt bʌlb/ Glühbirne IV:6/Project B p.125
lighter /ˈlaɪtə/ Feuerzeug IV:1/B8
like /laɪk/ mögen I:Welcome; wie I:4/A4
I don't like … /ˌaɪ ˈdəʊnt laɪk/ Ich mag … nicht. I:2/A7
like best /ˌlaɪk ˈbest/ am liebsten mögen I:5/B12
like better /ˌlaɪk ˈbetə/ lieber mögen IV:5/B7
like doing sth /laɪk ˈduːɪŋ ˌsʌmθɪŋ/ etw gern tun I:3/B11
like that /ˌlaɪk ˈðæt/ so IV:1/A7
like this /ˌlaɪk ˈðɪs/ so II:6/B11
likely /ˈlaɪkli/ wahrscheinlich IV:4/B6
line /laɪn/ Linie; Zeile I:4/B3
chat-up line /ˈtʃætʌp ˌlaɪn/ Anmache, Anmachspruch IV:3/A9
°line stander /ˈlaɪn ˌstændə/ Ansteher/in IV:BS/7
lion /ˈlaɪən/ Löwe I:WB/1
list /lɪst/ auflisten IV:4/B6; Liste I:2/A13
listen (to) /ˈlɪsn/ zuhören I:3/B6
literally /ˈlɪtrəli/ (wort)wörtlich IV:6/Project B p.127
°literature /ˈlɪtrətʃə/ Literatur IV:BS/9
litter /ˈlɪtə/ Abfall; Müll II:5/B2
little /ˈlɪtl/ klein I:Welcome
little /ˈlɪtl/ wenig IV:5/A2
live /lɪv/ leben; wohnen I:Welcome
°live /laɪv/ lebend IV:BS/4
living room /ˈlɪvɪŋ ˌruːm/ Wohnzimmer I:4/A6
local /ˈləʊkl/ örtlich; hiesig II:6/B11
°location /ləʊˈkeɪʃn/ Lage; Standort IV:1/O
lonely /ˈləʊnli/ einsam II:1/A7
long /lɒŋ/ lang I:2/A3
look /lʊk/ aussehen I:3/B4
take a look at /ˌteɪk‿ə ˈlʊk‿ət/ sich ansehen IV:2/I
look after /ˌlʊk‿ˈɑːftə/ sich kümmern um; aufpassen auf II:3/A8
look after sb /ˌlʊk‿ˈɑːftə ˌsʌmbədi/ sich um jdn kümmern I:4/A11
look (at) /ˈlʊk‿ət/ (an)sehen, (an)schauen I:1/A2
look for /ˈlʊk fə/ suchen nach I:3/A1
look out for /ˌlʊk‿ˈaʊt fɔː/ Ausschau halten nach IV:4/A7
look through /ˌlʊk ˈθruː/ durchsehen IV:6/Project p.118
look up /ˌlʊk‿ˈʌp/ nachschlagen IV:1/A6; nach oben sehen IV:3/O; hochschauen IV:BS/6
lorry /ˈlɒri/ Lastwagen IV:1/B5
lorry driver /ˈlɒri ˌdraɪvə/ Lastwagenfahrer/in II:3/A8
lose *(irr)* /luːz/ verlieren IV:3/A9
loser /ˈluːzə/ Verlierer/in IV:6/Project C p.129
get lost /ˌget ˈlɒst/ sich verirren II:1/B10
a lot (of) /ə ˈlɒt/ viel(e), jede Menge I:Welcome

lots /lɒts/ viel, jede Menge IV:Quiz
lots of /ˈlɒts‿əv/ viel, jede Menge I:Welcome
loud /laʊd/ laut I:2/B9
love /lʌv/ Liebe IV:3/I; lieben, sehr mögen I:Welcome
°be in love /ˌbi‿ɪn ˈlʌv/ verliebt sein IV:BS/6
love doing sth /lʌv ˈduːɪŋ ˌsʌmθɪŋ/ etw sehr gern tun II:Last year
love life /ˈlʌv laɪf/ Liebesleben IV:3/A6
°love poem /ˈlʌv ˌpəʊɪm/ Liebesgedicht IV:BS/5
love story /ˈlʌv ˌstɔːri/ Liebesgeschichte IV:3/B9
lovely /ˈlʌvli/ schön II:4/B7
lover /ˈlʌvə/ Liebende/r IV:3/B1
low /ləʊ/ niedrig III:1/B9
bad luck /ˌbæd ˈlʌk/ Pech II:1/B6
Good luck! /ˌɡʊd ˈlʌk/ Viel Glück! I:3/B6
luckily /ˈlʌkɪli/ zum Glück; glücklicherweise IV:1/A2
lucky /ˈlʌki/ glücklich II:3/A6
lunch /lʌntʃ/ Mittagessen I:5/A2
lunchbox /ˈlʌntʃbɒks/ Frühstücksdose IV:6/Project B p. 126
lunchtime /ˈlʌntʃtaɪm/ Mittagszeit, Mittagspause I:3/A1
lung cancer /ˈlʌŋ ˌkænsə/ Lungenkrebs IV:2/A8
lyrics *(pl)* /ˈlɪrɪks/ Liedtext IV:1/B8

M

machine /məˈʃiːn/ Maschine; Apparat I:4/A4
madam /ˈmædəm/ gnädige Frau IV:3/B8
madly /ˈmædli/ wie verrückt IV:3/A10
magazine /ˌmæɡəˈziːn/ Zeitschrift I:4/A11
magician /məˈdʒɪʃn/ Zauberkünstler/in IV:3/A9
main /meɪn/ Haupt- IV:3/B9
main clause /ˌmeɪn ˈklɔːz/ Hauptsatz IV:4/P4
main (course) /ˈmeɪn kɔːs/ Hauptgericht III:1/A3
majestic /məˈdʒestɪk/ majestätisch; erhaben IV:6/Project B p. 126
make *(irr)* /meɪk/ machen I:2/A7
make *(irr)* /meɪk/ *hier:* ergeben IV:Quiz; *hier:* schaffen IV:5/A9
make a break /ˌmeɪk‿ə ˈbreɪk/ ausbrechen IV:2/A4
make a living /ˌmeɪk‿ə ˈlɪvɪŋ/ seinen Lebensunterhalt verdienen IV:6/Project C p. 129
make friends (with) /ˌmeɪk ˈfrendz/ sich anfreunden (mit) II:3/A12
make (good) money /ˌmeɪk ˈmʌni/ (gut) verdienen; (viel) Geld verdienen II:3/A1
make notes /ˌmeɪk ˈnəʊts/ sich Notizen machen IV:2/A5
make sb do sth /ˌmeɪk ˌsʌmbədi ˈduː ˌsʌmθɪŋ/ jdn dazu bringen, etw zu tun IV:1/A3
make sth *(informal)* /ˈmeɪk ˌsʌmθɪŋ/ etw schaffen; *hier:* sich qualifizieren IV:1/A2
make sure /ˌmeɪk ˈʃɔː/ darauf achten, dass … III:5/A2
make up /ˌmeɪk‿ˈʌp/ erfinden, sich ausdenken III:1/A11
make up /ˌmeɪk‿ˈʌp/ *hier:* ausgleichen IV:4/B3
°male /meɪl/ männlich IV:4/O
°mall /mɔːl/ Einkaufszentrum IV:BS/8
man *(pl* **men)** /mæn, men/ Mann I:5/B7
man *(pl* men) /mæn, men/ Mensch IV:1/A9
manage /ˈmænɪdʒ/ schaffen IV:2/B6
how many /haʊ ˈmeni/ wie viele I:3/B5
many /ˈmeni/ viele I:5/B12
many times /ˌmeni ˈtaɪmz/ oft II:6/A2
map /mæp/ Karte I:2/B1
marble /ˈmɑːbl/ Murmel I:3/B5
March /mɑːtʃ/ März I:1/B2
°marinated /ˈmærɪneɪtɪd/ mariniert IV:BS/4
marine /məˈriːn/ Meeres-, See- IV:6/Project B p. 125
marine biologist /məˌriːn baɪˈɒlədʒɪst/ Meeresbiologe/in IV:6/Project B p. 125
mark /mɑːk/ Note; Zensur III:4/B9
mark /mɑːk/ markieren, kennzeichnen IV:3/A10
marked /mɑːkd/ markiert IV:1/P9
market /ˈmɑːkɪt/ Markt I:1/B2
marquee *(AE)* /mɑːˈkiː/ Markise, Vordach IV:1/B8
marriage /ˈmærɪdʒ/ Ehe; Heirat IV:3/B3
get married /ˌɡet ˈmærid/ heiraten IV:3/B1
marry /ˈmæri/ heiraten II:3/A1
marry *(veraltet)* /ˈmæri/ *hier etwa:* Ei nun! IV:3/B8
match /mætʃ/ Spiel I:3/A4; zuordnen; passen zu II:5/B1
match *(pl* **matches)** /mætʃ, ˈmætʃɪz/ Streichholz III:4/A11
matching /ˈmætʃɪŋ/ passend IV:1/P15
math *(AE, informal)* /mæθ/ Mathe *(Schulfach)* IV:1/A2
maths /mɑːθs/ Mathe I:5/A2
°matter /ˈmætə/ von Bedeutung sein; wichtig sein IV:BS/6
°as a matter of fact /əz‿ə ˌmætər‿əv‿ˈfækt/ übrigens IV:BS/8
maximize /ˈmæksɪmaɪz/ maximieren IV:1/A9
May /meɪ/ Mai I:5/B7
may /meɪ/ können; dürfen II:5/A3
maybe /ˈmeɪbi/ vielleicht II:1/B10
(to) me /miː/ mir; mich; ich I:Welcome
meal /miːl/ Mahlzeit; Essen II:1/A7
°mealworm /ˈmiːlwɜːm/ Mehlwurm IV:BS/4
°mealworm soup /ˈmiːlwɜːm suːp/ Mehlwurmsuppe IV:BS/4
mean /miːn/ gemein IV:2/A6
mean *(AE)* /miːn/ aggressiv, gefährlich IV:1/B8

mean *(irr)* /miːn/ meinen; bedeuten II:4/A3
meaning /ˈmiːnɪŋ/ Bedeutung III:1/A7
by any means /ˌbaɪ‿ˌeni ˈmiːnz/ auf jeden Fall IV:1/B8
meanwhile /ˈmiːnˌwaɪl/ inzwischen; unterdessen; mittlerweile IV:3/B3
measure /ˈmeʒə/ Maß, Maßeinheit IV:6/Project A p.134
meat /miːt/ Fleisch III:1/A7
meat loaf /ˌmiːt ˈləʊf/ Hackbraten IV:1/A7
mechanic /mɪˈkænɪk/ Mechaniker/in II:3/A8
°medal /ˈmedl/ Medaille IV:BS/9
medical /ˈmedɪkl/ medizinisch IV:4/A1
medicine *(no pl)* /ˈmedsn/ Medizin, Medikamente III:3/B4
meet *(irr)* /miːt/ treffen; sich treffen I:Welcome
Nice to meet you. /ˌnaɪs tə ˈmiːt jə/ Schön, dich/euch/Sie zu treffen. I:4/B9
°meet one's eye /ˌmiːt wʌnz‿ˈaɪ/ jdm in die Augen gucken IV:3/O
meet up /ˌmiːt‿ˈʌp/ (sich) treffen III:Last year
melting pot /ˈmeltɪŋ pɒt/ Schmelztiegel IV:1/B8
member /ˈmembə/ Mitglied II:4/A12
mention /ˈmenʃn/ erwähnen IV:3/A6
menu /ˈmenjuː/ Speisekarte; Menü III:1/A3
message /ˈmesɪdʒ/ Nachricht; Botschaft III:6/B3
method /ˈmeθəd/ Methode IV:6/Project C p.129
metre /ˈmiːtə/ Meter II:2/B11
metropolis /məˈtrɒpəlɪs/ Metropole IV:6/Project A p.134
Mexican /ˈmeksɪkən/ Mexikaner/in; mexikanisch IV:5/A9
Mexico /ˈmeksɪkəʊ/ Mexiko IV:2/B5
microbead /ˈmaɪkrəʊˌbiːd/ *winzige Plastikpartikel* IV:6/Project B p.126
in the middle of /ˌɪn ðə ˈmɪdl‿əv/ in der Mitte von I:4/A4
middle /ˈmɪdl/ Mitte II:2/A2
at midnight /æt ˈmɪdˌnaɪt/ um Mitternacht II:4/B8
might /maɪt/ könnte(st, n, t) IV:3/B1
migrant /ˈmaɪgrənt/ Zuwanderer/in IV:5/B3
°mile /maɪl/ Meile IV:BS/3
milk /mɪlk/ Milch I:2/A7
°milkshake /ˈmɪlkˌʃeɪk/ Milchshake IV:BS/5
mill around /ˌmɪl‿əˈraʊnd/ umherlaufen IV:4/B1
mime /maɪm/ mimen, pantomimisch darstellen IV:4/B1
mind /maɪnd/ Geist; Verstand IV:2/A4
mine /maɪn/ meine(r, s) III:1/A7
minimum wage /ˌmɪnɪməm ˈweɪdʒ/ Mindestlohn IV:1/A9
°mint sauce /ˈmɪnt sɔːs/ Minzsoße IV:BS/5
mirror /ˈmɪrə/ Spiegel IV:3/A4
miserable /ˈmɪzrəbl/ miserabel IV:3/B1
miss /mɪs/ verpassen; vermissen II:2/A10
missing /ˈmɪsɪŋ/ fehlend IV:5/P5
mistake /mɪˈsteɪk/ Fehler, Irrtum III:6/A1
mistake for /mɪˈsteɪk fɔː/ verwechseln mit IV:6/Project B p.125
mix /mɪks/ (ver)mischen III:1/B5
mixed /mɪkst/ gemischt IV:5/A4
mobile (phone) /ˈməʊbaɪl/ Handy I:Welcome
moccasin /ˈmɒkəsɪn/ Mokassin IV:Quiz
modal verb /ˈməʊdl vɜːb/ Modalverb IV:4/P6
°model /ˈmɒdl/ *hier:* Vorbild IV:5/O
mom *(AE)* /mɒm/ Mama IV:1/B5
at the moment /ˌæt‿ðə ˈməʊmənt/ im Moment I:3/B6
Monday /ˈmʌndeɪ/ Montag I:1/B2
money /ˈmʌni/ Geld II:2/B6
make (good) money /ˌmeɪk ˈmʌni/ (gut) verdienen; (viel) Geld verdienen II:3/A1
raise money /ˌreɪz ˈmʌni/ Geld aufbringen II:6/B11
spend money on /ˌspend ˈmʌni‿ɒn/ Geld ausgeben für II:4/A7
monkey /ˈmʌŋki/ Affe I:WB/1
month /mʌnθ/ Monat II:4/A3
moon /muːn/ Mond II:3/A1
more /mɔː/ mehr; weitere I:2/A7
morning /ˈmɔːnɪŋ/ Morgen I:4/A6
Good morning! /ˌgʊd ˈmɔːnɪŋ/ Guten Morgen! I:2/I
in the morning /ˌɪn ðə ˈmɔːnɪŋ/ am Morgen I:2/B7
this morning /ðɪs ˈmɔːnɪŋ/ heute Morgen II:4/A3
tomorrow morning /təˌmɒrəʊ ˈmɔːnɪŋ/ morgen Vormittag II:4/B5
mosque /mɒsk/ Moschee II:4/A1
most /məʊst/ die meisten; am meisten III:1/B1
most important /ˌməʊst‿ɪmˈpɔːtnt/ wichtigste(r, s) IV:Quiz
mostly /ˈməʊstli/ meistens IV:1/B5
mother /ˈmʌðə/ Mutter I:5/B7
motive /ˈməʊtɪv/ Motiv IV:5/A3
motorbike /ˈməʊtəˌbaɪk/ Motorrad II:6/B2
mountain /ˈmaʊntɪn/ Berg I:3/A9
mouse (*pl* **mice**) /maʊs, maɪs/ Maus I:1/A6
mouth /maʊθ/ Mund I:2/A2
move /muːv/ umziehen IV:5/B3; sich bewegen III:6/A3
move around /ˌmuːv‿əˈraʊnd/ umherreisen IV:5/B3
°movement /ˈmuːvmənt/ Bewegung IV:BS/9
movie *(AE)* /ˈmuːvi/ Film IV:1/B2
movie star /ˈmuːvi ˌstɑː/ Filmstar IV:3/A7
Mr /ˈmɪstə/ Herr *(Anrede)* I:2/A3
Mrs /ˈmɪsɪz/ Frau *(Anrede)* I:3/A1
much /mʌtʃ/ viel I:3/B4; sehr II:1/A7
how much /haʊ ˈmʌtʃ/ wie viel I:4/B6
How much is it? /ˌhaʊ mʌtʃ‿ˈɪz‿ɪt/ Wie viel kostet es? I:3/B4
mug /mʌg/ Becher I:3/B5
mum /mʌm/ Mama I:1/B2

munch /mʌntʃ/ mampfen IV:2/A9
music /ˈmjuːzɪk/ Musik II:Last year
musician /mjʊˈzɪʃn/ Musiker/in III:6/A3
must /mʌst/ müssen II:2/B2
mustn't (= must not) /ˈmʌsnt, mʌst ˈnɒt/ nicht dürfen II:5/A4
my /maɪ/ mein(e) I:Welcome ...
My name is ... /ˌmaɪ ˈneɪm‿ɪz/ Ich heiße ... I:Welcome ...
myself /maɪˈself/ mir/mich/ ich (selbst) III:2/A7

My name is ... /ˌmaɪ ˈneɪm‿ɪz/ Ich heiße ... I:Welcome ...
What's your name? /ˌwɒts jə ˈneɪm/ Wie heißt du? I:Welcome ...
call sb names /ˌkɔːl ˌsʌmbədi ˈneɪmz/ jdn beschimpfen II:5/B10
narrow /ˈnærəʊ/ eng; knapp III:2/B10
nasty /ˈnɑːsti/ gemein IV:3/A4
nation /ˈneɪʃn/ Land; Nation IV:5/A3
nationality /ˌnæʃəˈnæləti/ Nationalität IV:5/A1
Native American /ˌneɪtɪv‿əˈmerɪkən/ amerikanische/r Ureinwohner/in IV:Quiz
natural /ˈnætʃrəl/ natürlich IV:6/Project B p. 126
natural disaster /ˌnætʃrəl dɪˈzɑːstə/ Naturkatastrophe IV:5/B2
nature /ˈneɪtʃə/ Natur III:5/I
navigation bar /ˌnævɪˈgeɪʃn bɑː/ Navigationsleiste IV:6/I
near /nɪə/ nahe, in der Nähe von II:1/A2
nearly /ˈnɪəli/ fast; beinahe II:6/B4
necessary /ˈnesəsri/ notwendig, erforderlich IV:4/A3
neck /nek/ Hals; Nacken I:2/A1
need /niːd/ brauchen I:2/A8
need to /ˈniːd‿tʊ/ müssen II:4/A7
°negro *(pejorative)* /ˈniːgrəʊ/ Neger *(abwertend)* IV:BS/9
neighbor *(AE)* /ˈneɪbə/ Nachbar/in IV:4/B6
neighborhood *(AE)* /ˈneɪbəˌhʊd/ Viertel; Nachbarschaft IV:1/B5
neighbour /ˈneɪbə/ Nachbar/in I:1/B2
neighbourhood /ˈneɪbəˌhʊd/ Viertel; Nachbarschaft I:1/B2
nervous /ˈnɜːvəs/ nervös III:2/B1
net /net/ Netz IV:1/A6
never /ˈnevə/ nie, niemals I:4/A6
new /njuː/ neu I:1/A2
New Year /ˌnjuː ˈjɪə/ Neujahr II:4/A1
°newcomer /ˈnjuːˌkʌmə/ Neuankömmling IV:BS/8
news *(no pl)* /njuːz/ Neuigkeit; Nachrichten II:1/B6
news report /ˈnjuːz rɪˌpɔːt/ Nachrichtenmeldung IV:5/B2
newspaper /ˈnjuːzˌpeɪpə/ Zeitung III:4/B4
next /nekst/ nächste(r, s) I:3/B8; dann, als Nächstes III:5/A1
next to /ˈnekst‿tə/ neben I:4/A3
nice /naɪs/ schön; nett I:1/A6
Nice to meet you. /ˌnaɪs tə ˈmiːt jə/ Schön, dich/ euch/Sie zu treffen. I:4/B9
Nice to see you. /ˌnaɪs tə ˈsiː jə/ Schön, dich/euch/Sie zu sehen. I:5/B3
nicotine /ˈnɪkətiːn/ Nikotin IV:2/A7
night /naɪt/ Nacht; Abend III:2/B4
last night /ˌlɑːst ˈnaɪt/ gestern Abend II:4/A3
nightmare /ˈnaɪtˌmeə/ Albtraum IV:1/A9
no /nəʊ/ nein I:Welcome; kein(e) I:2/B1
no longer /ˌnəʊ ˈlɒŋgə/ nicht mehr IV:2/B7
no matter what /nəʊ ˌmætə ˈwɒt/ was auch (immer) passiert IV:3/B1
No trespassing! /ˌnəʊ ˈtrespəsɪŋ/ Kein Durchgang! IV:5/A8
no-one, no one /ˈnəʊ wʌn/ keiner II:5/A8
the Nobel Peace Prize /ðə nəʊˌbel ˈpiːs praɪz/ Friedensnobelpreis IV:Quiz
nobody /ˈnəʊbədi/ niemand; keiner I:5/B3
°nod /nɒd/ nicken IV:BS/6
noise /nɔɪz/ Geräusch II:2/B2
noisy /ˈnɔɪzi/ laut II:4/A7
non-fiction /ˌnɒn ˈfɪkʃn/ Sachliteratur IV:5/B9
non-natural /ˌnɒn‿ˈnætʃrəl/ nicht natürlich IV:6/Project C p. 136
non-profit /ˌnɒn ˈprɒfɪt/ gemeinnützig; nicht gewinnorientiert IV:6/Project C p. 131
non-smoking /ˌnɒn ˈsməʊkɪŋ/ Nichtraucher- IV:2/A9
none /nʌn/ keine(r, s); nichts IV:3/A4
normally /ˈnɔːmli/ normalerweise IV:2/A9
north /nɔːθ/ Norden III:5/A2
°Norwegian /nɔːˈwiːdʒn/ Norwegisch; norwegisch IV:BS/3
nose /nəʊz/ Nase I:2/A2
nosy /ˈnəʊzi/ neugierig IV:3/P11
not /nɒt/ nicht I:Welcome
not ... either /ˌnɒt‿ˈaɪðə/ auch nicht III:1/B1
not any /ˌnɒt‿ˈeni/ kein(e) III:Last year
not anymore /ˌnɒt‿ˌeni ˈmɔː/ nicht mehr III:3/A9
not anyone /ˌnɒt‿ˈeniwʌn/ niemand II:3/A1
not anything /ˌnɒt‿ˈeniˌθɪŋ/ nichts II:1/A7
not at all /ˌnɒt‿ət‿ˈɔːl/ überhaupt nicht III:3/A1
not even /ˈnɒt‿iːvn/ nicht einmal II:5/A8
not exactly /ˌnɒt‿ɪgˈzæktli/ eigentlich nicht; nicht gerade IV:6/Project C p. 130
not yet /nɒt ˈjet/ noch nicht II:2/B2
note /nəʊt/ Nachricht; Notiz II:1/B10
nothing /ˈnʌθɪŋ/ nichts III:2/B8
notice /ˈnəʊtɪs/ bemerken; wahrnehmen IV:3/A10
noun /naʊn/ Hauptwort; Substantiv; Nomen IV:5/P9
°novel /ˈnɒvl/ Roman IV:BS/9

November /nəʊˈvembə/ November I:5/B7
now /naʊ/ jetzt I:1/B2
°nowadays /ˈnaʊəˌdeɪz/ heutzutage; *hier:* in der letzten Zeit IV:BS/6
from nowhere /frəm ˈnəʊweə/ aus dem Nichts IV:4/B3
number /ˈnʌmbə/ Zahl; Nummer I:Welcome
nurse /nɜːs/ Krankenschwester; Krankenpfleger II:3/A8
nurse /nɜːs/ *hier:* Kindermädchen IV:3/B5; pflegen; stillen IV:3/B8
°nutritional value /njuːˌtrɪʃənl ˈvæljuː/ Nährwert IV:BS/7
°nutty /ˈnʌti/ nussig IV:BS/4
NYC (= New York City) /ˌen waɪ ˈsiː, ˌnjuː jɔːk ˈsɪti/ *die Stadt New York* IV:6/Project p. 118

O

o'clock /əˈklɒk/ Uhr I:2/A2
obvious, obviously /ˈɒbviəs, ˈɒbviəsli/ offensichtlich IV:4/A10
ocean /ˈəʊʃn/ Ozean; Meer IV:6/Project B p. 125
October /ɒkˈtəʊbə/ Oktober I:5/B7
of /əv/ von I:2/A7
Of course! /əv ˈkɔːs/ Natürlich! I:4/B6
of one's own /əv wʌnz‿ˈəʊn/ eigene(r, s) IV:2/B1
off /ɒf/ von; hinunter, herunter III:3/A1
offer /ˈɒfə/ anbieten IV:4/A10
office /ˈɒfɪs/ Büro II:2/B2
often /ˈɒfn/ oft; häufig I:4/A6
oil /ɔɪl/ Öl IV:6/Project A p. 134
old /əʊld/ alt I:Welcome …
How old are you? /haʊ‿ˈəʊld‿ɑː ˌjʊ/ Wie alt bist du? I:Welcome …
on /ɒn/ auf; an; in I:3/A9
on /ɒn/ weiter; vorwärts IV:5/A10; *hier:* mit IV:BS/10
What's on? /ˌwɒts‿ˈɒn/ Was ist los? I:3/A1
on average /ˌɒn‿ˈævərɪdʒ/ durchschnittlich IV:6/Project B p. 126
on foot /ˌɒn ˈfʊt/ zu Fuß II:6/B2
on its own /ˌɒn‿ɪts‿ˈəʊn/ von alleine II:5/B11
on one's own /ˌɒn ˌwʌnz‿ˈəʊn/ allein IV:4/B7
on the left/on your left /ˌɒn ðə / jɔː ˈleft/ links, auf der/deiner linken Seite II:2/B7
on the move /ˌɒn ðə ˈmuːv/ unterwegs IV:5/B1
on the phone /ˌɒn ðə ˈfəʊn/ am Telefon I:5/B3
on the right/on your right /ˌɒn ðə / jɔː ˈraɪt/ rechts, auf der/deiner rechten Seite II:2/B7
on time /ˌɒn ˈtaɪm/ pünktlich IV:4/B3
on top /ˌɒn ˈtɒp/ (oben) auf II:2/A2
once /wʌns/ früher IV:5/A2; einmal II:3/A1; sobald; wenn, als III:2/B4
°once again /ˌwʌns‿əˈgen/ abermals IV:BS/8
once more /ˌwʌns ˈmɔː/ noch einmal IV:5/A10
°once upon a time /ˌwʌns‿əˌpɒn‿ə ˈtaɪm/ es war einmal IV:4/O
the red one /ðə ˈred wʌn/ der/die/das rote III:2/A7
this one /ˈðɪs wʌn/ diese(r, s) hier III:2/A7
one day /ˌwʌn ˈdeɪ/ eines Tages II:1/B7
the green ones /ðə ˈgriːn wʌnz/ die grünen III:2/A7
only /ˈəʊnli/ nur; bloß I:2/A7
onwards /ˈɒnwədz/ von … an IV:3/O
open /ˈəʊpən/ öffnen; aufmachen I:2/B1; offen; geöffnet II:2/A8
opening hours *(pl)* /ˈəʊpənɪŋ‿ˌaʊəz/ Öffnungszeiten III:1/A9
in my opinion /ɪn ˈmaɪ‿əˌpɪnjən/ meiner Meinung nach IV:1/A7
opinion /əˈpɪnjən/ Meinung; Ansicht IV:5/B3
or /ɔː/ oder I:2/B7
orange /ˈɒrɪndʒ/ orange I:Welcome; Orange; Apfelsine III:1/A3
orange juice /ˈɒrɪndʒ‿ˌdʒuːs/ Orangensaft I:Welcome
order /ˈɔːdə/ bestellen III:1/A4
order /ˈɔːdə/ Reihenfolge IV:1/B3; Bestellung IV:BS/8
Are you ready to order? /ɑː juː ˌredi tʊ‿ˈɔːdə/ Möchten Sie bestellen? III:1/A4
the ordinary /ði‿ˈɔːdnri/ das Übliche; das Normale IV:2/A4
organic /ɔːˈgænɪk/ *hier:* aus biologischem Anbau IV:1/A7
organisational /ˌɔːgənaɪˈzeɪʃnəl/ organisatorisch IV:4/B7
organise /ˈɔːgənaɪz/ organisieren II:4/A7
organization *(AE)* = organisation *(BE)* /ˌɔːgənaɪˈzeɪʃn/ Organisation IV:6/Project A p. 123
organize *(AE)* = organise *(BE)* /ˈɔːgənaɪz/ organisieren IV:6/Project B p. 127
originally /əˈrɪdʒnəli/ ursprünglich IV:3/B6
other /ˈʌðə/ andere(r, s) I:3/B2
other than that … /ˌʌðə ðən ˈðæt/ abgesehen davon … IV:4/B8
our /aʊə/ unsere(r, s) I:1/B2
ourselves /aʊəˈselvz/ uns; wir selbst IV:1/A3
out /aʊt/ heraus, hinaus; aus II:1/B7
out of /ˈaʊt‿əv/ aus IV:4/B7
out of work /ˌaʊt‿əv ˈwɜːk/ arbeitslos III:4/B4
outdoor gear /aʊtˌdɔː ˈgɪə/ Outdoor-Ausrüstung IV:6/Project C p. 128
outdoors /ˌaʊtˈdɔːz/ draußen; im Freien IV:4/B1
outer space /ˌaʊtə ˈspeɪs/ Weltraum IV:3/A7
outside /ˌaʊtˈsaɪd/ außen; (nach) draußen II:1/A6; vor; außerhalb II:2/B2

over /ˈəʊvə/ über, hinüber; vorbei II:1/B3
over there /ˌəʊvə ˈðeə/ dort (drüben) I:4/B6
Over to you. /ˌəʊvə tə ˈjuː/ Jetzt bist du dran. I:3/B6
overcrowded /ˌəʊvəˈkraʊdɪd/ überfüllt IV:5/A2
on its own /ˌɒn‿ɪts‿ˈəʊn/ von alleine II:5/B11
own /əʊn/ eigene(r, s) I:3/A12
own /əʊn/ besitzen IV:2/A2

P

p (= penny, pence) /piː, ˈpeni, pens/ Pence I:4/B6
package /ˈpækɪdʒ/ verpacken IV:6/Project B p. 125
packaging /ˈpækɪdʒɪŋ/ Verpackung IV:6/Project B p. 124
packet /ˈpækɪt/ Packung III:4/A11
page /peɪdʒ/ Seite III:1/I
pain /peɪn/ Schmerz IV:5/A2
paint /peɪnt/ (an)malen III:Last year
painting /ˈpeɪntɪŋ/ Bild, Gemälde III:6/B2
pair /peə/ Paar IV:5/B5
a pair of /ə ˈpeər‿əv/ ein Paar II:4/B3
a pair of scissors /ə ˌpeər‿əv ˈsɪzəz/ Schere III:4/A11
palace /ˈpæləs/ Palast IV:3/B1
Pancake Day /ˈpænkeɪk deɪ/ Pfannkuchentag IV:Quiz
panel /ˈpænl/ Tafel IV:4/A7
pang /pæŋ/ (plötzliches) Schmerzgefühl IV:5/A10
panic /ˈpænɪk/ in Panik geraten IV:2/A10
paper /ˈpeɪpə/ Papier III:6/B9
°paper /ˈpeɪpə/ Zeitung IV:BS/8
paragraph /ˈpærəˌɡrɑːf/ Absatz; Abschnitt IV:4/A14
parents *(pl)* /ˈpeərənts/ Eltern I:1/A4
park /pɑːk/ parken IV:1/B5
parking lot *(AE)* /ˈpɑːkɪŋ lɒt/ Parkplatz IV:1/B5
parrot /ˈpærət/ Papagei I:1/A5
part /pɑːt/ Teil III:5/A6
°particularly /pəˈtɪkjʊləli/ besonders; vor allem IV:BS/7
partner /ˈpɑːtnə/ IV:1/B7
pass /pɑːs/ vorbeigehen an IV:3/A4
passenger /ˈpæsɪndʒə/ Fahrgast, Passagier/in IV:4/A1
passionately /ˈpæʃnətli/ leidenschaftlich IV:3/A10
past /pɑːst/ nach I:2/A7; vorbei; vorüber II:2/B7
past perfect /ˌpɑːst ˈpɜːfɪkt/ Plusquamperfekt, Vorvergangenheit IV:5/A5
pasta /ˈpæstə/ Nudeln IV:1/A7
patient /ˈpeɪʃnt/ geduldig IV:4/A13
pattern /ˈpætən/ Muster IV:1/A3
°pause /pɔːz/ innehalten, Pause machen IV:BS/2
pay *(irr)* /peɪ/ *(be)*zahlen III:1/A7
PE (= physical education) /ˌpiː ˈiː, ˌfɪzɪkl‿edjʊˈkeɪʃn/ Sport *(Schulfach)* I:5/A3
peace /piːs/ Frieden IV:Quiz
peanut /ˈpiːˌnʌt/ Erdnuss IV:2/B2
peer pressure /ˈpɪə ˌpreʃə/ Gruppenzwang IV:2/A7
pen /pen/ Stift I:2/B1
pencil /ˈpensl/ Bleistift I:2/B4
pencil case /ˈpensl ˌkeɪs/ Federmäppchen I:2/B4
penguin /ˈpeŋɡwɪn/ Pinguin I:WB/1
people /ˈpiːpl/ Leute; Menschen I:1/I
per /pɜː/ pro III:1/A9
perfect /ˈpɜːfɪkt/ perfekt IV:4/A10
perfectly /ˈpɜːfɪkli/ ganz genau IV:5/A10
perform /pəˈfɔːm/ aufführen IV:3/P12
performance /pəˈfɔːməns/ Aufführung; Darbietung II:6/B11
performance artist /pəˈfɔːməns‿ˌɑːtɪst/ Performancekünstler/in IV:4/A7
perfume /ˈpɜːfjuːm/ Parfüm, Duft II:4/B3
perhaps /pəˈhæps/ vielleicht II:2/B2
period *(AE)* /ˈpɪəriəd/ Stunde IV:1/A2
persecute /ˈpɜːsɪˌkjuːt/ verfolgen IV:5/B3
personal /ˈpɜːsnəl/ persönlich IV:2/A11
pesticide /ˈpestɪsaɪd/ Pestizid; Schädlingsbekämpfungsmittel IV:6/Project C p. 136
pet /pet/ Haustier I:WB/1
°pet food /ˈpet fuːd/ Tierfutter IV:BS/7
PG (= parental guidance) /ˌpiː ˈdʒiː, pəˌrentl ˈɡaɪdəns/ nicht jugendfrei IV:3/B6
Philippines /ˈfɪləpiːnz/ Philippinen IV:5/A7
phone /fəʊn/ Telefon II:4/A7; anrufen III:2/B10
answer the phone /ˌɑːnsə ðə ˈfəʊn/ ans Telefon gehen I:5/B3
on the phone /ˌɒn ðə ˈfəʊn/ am Telefon I:5/B3
What's your phone number? /ˌwɒts jə ˈfəʊn‿nʌmbə/ Was ist deine Telefonnummer? I:Welcome
photo /ˈfəʊtəʊ/ Foto II:1/A10
°photo shoot /ˈfəʊtəʊ ʃuːt/ Fotoshooting IV:5/O
take photos /ˌteɪk ˈfəʊtəʊz/ Bilder machen II:1/A10
phrase /freɪz/ Satz; Ausdruck II:6/B11
physical /ˈfɪzɪkl/ körperlich IV:1/B2
physiotherapist /ˌfɪziəʊˈθerəpɪst/ Physiotherapeut/in IV:4/A1
pianist /ˈpiːənɪst/ Pianist/in IV:3/A10
pick /pɪk/ aussuchen; pflücken, sammeln IV:3/A7
pick sb up /ˌpɪk ˌsʌmbədi‿ˈʌp/ jdn abholen I:4/B1
°pick up /ˌpɪk‿ˈʌp/ aufheben; *hier:* kaufen IV:BS/6
have a picnic /ˌhæv‿ə ˈpɪknɪk/ ein Picknick machen I:5/B11
picture /ˈpɪktʃə/ Bild I:3/A13
pie /paɪ/ Pastete; Kuchen IV:1/A7

piece /piːs/ Stück; Teil III:1/B5
piece of advice /ˌpiːs‿əv‿ədˈvaɪs/ Rat(schlag) IV:2/A9
piece of art /ˌpiːs‿əv‿ˈɑːt/ Kunstwerk III:6/B3
pig /pɪg/ Schwein I:Welcome
°pilgrim /ˈpɪlgrɪm/ Pilger/in IV:BS/2
pillow /ˈpɪləʊ/ Kissen I:4/A1
pin /pɪn/ *hier:* drücken IV:1/A6
°pine nut /ˈpaɪn‿nʌt/ Pinienkern IV:BS/4
place /pleɪs/ Ort; Platz I:Welcome
place /pleɪs/ *hier:* Wohnung IV:3/A4
place of birth /ˌpleɪs‿əv ˈbɜːθ/ Geburtsort IV:4/P10
placemat /ˈpleɪsmæt/ Platzdeckchen *(Methode)* IV:4/A13
placement /ˈpleɪsmənt/ Stelle; *hier:* Praktikumsstelle IV:4/B8
plain /pleɪn/ Ebene IV:5/A3
plan /plæn/ planen II:2/A10
plane /pleɪn/ Flugzeug II:1/A10
plant /plɑːnt/ Pflanze II:2/B11
plant /plɑːnt/ pflanzen IV:6/Project A p. 123
plastic /ˈplæstɪk/ Plastik III:4/A11
plastic bag /ˌplæstɪk ˈbæg/ Plastiktüte IV:6/Project p. 116
plate /pleɪt/ Teller I:2/A8
platform /ˈplætˌfɔːm/ Bahnsteig; Plattform II:2/A2
play /pleɪ/ spielen I:Welcome
play /pleɪ/ Spiel; (Theater) stück IV:3/B3
play the guitar /ˌpleɪ ðə gɪˈtɑː/ Gitarre spielen II:Last year
football player /ˈfʊtbɔːl ˌpleɪə/ Fußballspieler/in II:3/A6
player /ˈpleɪə/ Spieler/in III:3/A5
playground /ˈpleɪˌgraʊnd/ Spielplatz I:1/B3
playground /ˈpleɪˌgraʊnd/ *hier:* Schulhof IV:4/B7
please /pliːz/ bitte I:2/A7
plot /plɒt/ *hier:* Parzelle IV:6/Project A p. 123
plot of land /ˌplɒt‿əv ˈlænd/ ein Stück Land IV:6/Project A p. 123

plumber /ˈplʌmə/ Klempner/in IV:4/A1
pm (= post meridiem) /ˌpiːˈem, ˌpəʊst məˈrɪdiəm/ nachmittags; abends *(nur hinter Uhrzeit zwischen 12 Uhr mittags und Mitternacht)* I:3/A1
pocket /ˈpɒkɪt/ Tasche III:2/B5
pocket money /ˈpɒkɪt ˌmʌni/ Taschengeld II:6/A3
poem /ˈpəʊɪm/ Gedicht II:6/B11
°poet /ˈpəʊɪt/ Dichter/in IV:BS/9
point /pɔɪnt/ Punkt IV:1/A5
point (at/to) /pɔɪnt/ deuten (auf); zeigen (auf) III:4/A3
poison /ˈpɔɪzn/ Gift IV:3/B1
Poland /ˈpəʊlənd/ Polen IV:5/P2
polar bear /ˌpəʊlə ˈbeə/ Eisbär I:WB/1
pole /pəʊl/ Stange, Pfahl IV:2/B7; Pol IV:BS/3
police /pəˈliːs/ Polizei II:2/B2
police department /pəˈliːs dɪˌpɑːtmənt/ Polizeidienststelle IV:Quiz
police officer /pəˈliːs‿ˌɒfɪsə/ Polizeibeamte(r)/-beamtin II:3/A8
policeman (*pl* policemen) /pəˈliːsmən/ Polizist III:2/B1
°policewoman (*pl* policewomen) /pəˈliːsˌwʊmən, pəˈliːsˌwɪmɪn/ Polizistin IV:4/O
Polish /ˈpəʊlɪʃ/ Polnisch; polnisch IV:5/A1
°polite /pəˈlaɪt/ höflich IV:BS/8
politeness /pəˈlaɪtnəs/ Höflichkeit IV:4/B6
political /pəˈlɪtɪkl/ politisch IV:5/B2
pollute /pəˈluːt/ verschmutzen IV:6/Project p. 117
pollution /pəˈluːʃn/ Verschmutzung IV:6/Project B p. 124
swimming pool /ˈswɪmɪŋ puːl/ Schwimmbad I:1/B3
poor /pɔː/ arm II:1/B3
popular /ˈpɒpjʊlə/ beliebt IV:Quiz
population /ˌpɒpjʊˈleɪʃn/ Bevölkerung IV:2/B5
positive /ˈpɒzətɪv/ positiv IV:4/P9

possible /ˈpɒsəbl/ möglich II:6/B11
post /pəʊst/ posten; bekannt geben IV:1/B2
postcard /ˈpəʊstˌkɑːd/ Postkarte; Ansichtskarte I:3/B5
°postman (*pl* postmen) /ˈpəʊsmən, ˈpəʊsmən/ Postbote; Briefträger IV:4/O
°postwoman (*pl* postwomen) /ˈpəʊswʊmən, ˈpəʊsˌwɪmɪn/ Postbotin; Briefträgerin IV:4/O
potato (*pl* potatoes) /pəˈteɪtəʊ, pəˈteɪtəʊz/ Kartoffel II:4/B5
pound /paʊnd/ Pfund I:3/B1
pour /pɔː/ *hier:* schütten IV:3/A6
poverty /ˈpɒvəti/ Armut IV:2/B9
power /ˈpaʊə/ Strom; Kraft III:6/A3
power /ˈpaʊə/ antreiben IV:6/Project B p. 125
powerful /ˈpaʊəfl/ mächtig; stark III:6/A3
practical /ˈpræktɪkl/ praktisch IV:6/Project p. 132
practice *(AE)* /ˈpræktɪs/ üben IV:3/A4
practise /ˈpræktɪs/ üben I:3/A12
practise /ˈpræktɪs/ *hier:* machen; praktizieren IV:2/B7
pray /preɪ/ beten IV:1/B8
prayer /preə/ Gebet II:4/A1
preacher /ˈpriːtʃə/ Geistliche/r, Prediger/in IV:1/B8
precise /prɪˈsaɪs/ genau; präzise IV:4/A14
prefer /prɪˈfɜː/ vorziehen; bevorzugen III:3/A4
preferably /ˈprefrəbli/ vorzugsweise IV:6/Project B p. 126
pregnancy /ˈpregnənsi/ Schwangerschaft IV:2/A8
pregnant /ˈpregnənt/ schwanger IV:2/A8
premature /ˈprematʃə/ verfrüht, vorzeitig IV:2/A8
prepare /prɪˈpeə/ vorbereiten II:6/A12
present /ˈpreznt/ Geschenk I:5/B3

present (to) /prɪˈzent/ präsentieren I:3/A13
presentation /ˌprezn̩ˈteɪʃn/ Präsentation, Vortrag IV:1/A10
preserve /prɪˈzɜːv/ erhalten IV:6/Project B p. 127
president /ˈprezɪdənt/ Präsident/in; Vorsitzende/r IV:Quiz
peer pressure /ˈpɪə ˌpreʃə/ Gruppenzwang IV:2/A7
put pressure on /ˌpʊt ˈpreʃər‿ɒn/ Druck ausüben auf IV:6/Project C p. 129
pretend /prɪˈtend/ vorgeben; vortäuschen IV:3/A4
pretty /ˈprɪti/ hübsch II:4/B3; ziemlich II:6/B4
price /praɪs/ Preis II:2/A8
pride /praɪd/ Stolz IV:2/A3
primary school /ˈpraɪməri skuːl/ Grundschule IV:4/P10
prince /prɪns/ Prinz; Fürst IV:3/B3
principle /ˈprɪnsəpl/ Prinzip IV:6/Project B p. 135
prisoner /ˈprɪznə/ Gefangene/r III:4/A1
prize /praɪz/ Preis; Gewinn II:6/B6
probably /ˈprɒbəbli/ wahrscheinlich II:3/A6
produce /prəˈdjuːs/ herstellen III:5/B3
product /ˈprɒdʌkt/ Produkt IV:4/A7
°product launch /ˈprɒdʌkt lɔːntʃ/ Produkteinführung IV:BS/7
production /prəˈdʌkʃn/ Produktion IV:6/Project C p. 128
profession /prəˈfeʃn/ Beruf IV:4/A6
professional /prəˈfeʃnəl/ professionell; beruflich III:3/A7; Profi III:6/A2
profile /ˈprəʊfaɪl/ Profil, Porträt IV:2/B2
profit /ˈprɒfɪt/ Gewinn IV:6/Project C p. 130
program /ˈprəʊgræm/ Computerprogramm IV:4/B6
°program *(AE)* /ˈprəʊgræm/ Programm IV:BS/10
programme /ˈprəʊgræm/ Programm II:6/B11
programming /ˈprəʊˌgræmɪŋ/ Programmieren IV:4/B6
progress /ˈprəʊgres/ Fortschritt IV:6/Project p. 133
°progress /prəʊˈgres/ vorankommen IV:BS/3
project /ˈprɒdʒekt/ Projekt III:5/A2
°projection /prəˈdʒekʃn/ Projektion IV:1/O
projector /prəˈdʒektə/ Projektor, Vorführgerät IV:6/Project p. 133
promise /ˈprɒmɪs/ versprechen IV:3/B1
pronunciation /prəˌnʌnsiˈeɪʃn/ Aussprache IV:3/P10
properly /ˈprɒpəli/ richtig IV:3/A10
protect /prəˈtekt/ beschützen III:6/A3
proud /praʊd/ stolz III:4/A2
prove *(irr)* /pruːv/ beweisen III:1/A7
°public /ˈpʌblɪk/ öffentlich IV:1/O
°the public /ðə ˈpʌblɪk/ die Öffentlichkeit IV:1/O
public school *(AE)* /ˌpʌblɪk ˈskuːl/ staatliche Schule IV:5/A1
public transport /ˌpʌblɪk ˈtrænspɔːt/ öffentliche Verkehrsmittel IV:6/Project A p. 120
publish /ˈpʌblɪʃ/ veröffentlichen; herausgeben II:3/B9
puddle /ˈpʌdl/ Pfütze I:WB/1
pull /pʊl/ ziehen III:2/B10
°pull away /ˌpʊl‿əˈweɪ/ davon fahren IV:3/O
pull factor /ˈpʊl ˌfæktə/ Pull-Faktor IV:5/B3
pull out /ˈpʊl‿ˌaʊt/ herausziehen IV:4/B3
pumpkin /ˈpʌmpkɪn/ Kürbis IV:1/A7
pupil /ˈpjuːpl/ Schüler/in I:5/A7
purple /ˈpɜːpl/ violett; lila I:Welcome
purse /pɜːs/ Portmonee IV:6/Project C p. 129
°pursue /pəˈsjuː/ verfolgen IV:5/O
pursuit of /pəˈsjuːt‿əv/ Streben nach IV:1/A9
push /pʊʃ/ schieben; stoßen IV:5/B3
push factor /ˈpʊʃ ˌfæktə/ Push-Faktor IV:5/B3
put *(irr)* /pʊt/ setzen; stellen; legen I:2/A7
put into action /ˌpʊt‿ɪntʊ ˈækʃn/ in die Tat umsetzen IV:6/Project p. 119
put on /ˌpʊt‿ˈɒn/ anziehen; auflegen; auftragen III:3/B1
°put out /ˌpʊt‿ˈaʊt/ ausmachen IV:4/O
put pressure on /ˌpʊt ˈpreʃər‿ɒn/ Druck ausüben auf IV:6/Project C p. 129
put up /ˌpʊt‿ˈʌp/ aufhängen III:6/A3
put up /ˌpʊt‿ˈʌp/ errichten; bauen IV:6/Project A p. 123

Q

°quality /ˈkwɒləti/ Qualität IV:BS/7
quarter /ˈkwɔːtə/ Viertel I:2/B7
queen /kwiːn/ Königin III:2/A9
queer /kwɪə/ *hier:* homosexuell IV:2/A6
question /ˈkwestʃn/ Frage II:5/B1
questioning /ˈkwestʃnɪŋ/ *hier:* zweifelnd IV:2/A6
questionnaire /ˌkwestʃəˈneə/ Fragebogen IV:6/Project p. 119
°queue /kjuː/ Schlange, Reihe IV:BS/6
quick, quickly /kwɪk, ˈkwɪkli/ schnell II:1/B6
quiet /ˈkwaɪət/ leise; ruhig IV:1/B5
quit *(irr)* /kwɪt/ aufhören mit IV:2/A5
quite /kwaɪt/ ziemlich II:4/A7
°quite a lot /ˌkwaɪt‿ə ˈlɒt/ etliche(r, s) IV:BS/4
quiz /kwɪz/ IV:1/B7
quotation /kwəʊˈteɪʃn/ Zitat III:6/B1
quote /kwəʊt/ Zitat IV:3/A11
quote /kwəʊt/ zitieren IV:3/A6

R

rabbit /ˈræbɪt/ Kaninchen I:Welcome
race /reɪs/ Rasse IV:5/A1; Rennen II:1/B3
racist /ˈreɪsɪst/ Rassist/in; rassistisch IV:5/A1
railroad car *(AE)* /ˈreɪlˌrəʊd kɑː/ Eisenbahnwaggon IV:5/A3
railway station /ˈreɪlweɪ ˌsteɪʃn/ Bahnhof II:2/A2
rain /reɪn/ Regen I:Welcome
rain /reɪn/ regnen IV:1/B10
rainy /ˈreɪni/ regnerisch I:WB/1
°raise awareness /ˌreɪz‿əˈweənəz/ Bewusstsein schärfen IV:BS/10
raise money /ˌreɪz ˈmʌni/ Geld aufbringen II:6/B11
ranger /ˈreɪndʒə/ (Park)aufseher/in IV:Quiz
rat /ræt/ Ratte I:WB/1
I'd rather ... /ˌaɪd ˈrɑːðə/ Ich würde lieber ... I:5/A2
rather than /ˈrɑːðə ðæn/ anstatt IV:6/Project B p. 126
raw material /ˌrɔː məˈtɪəriəl/ Rohstoff IV:6/Project B p. 125
razor /ˈreɪzə/ Rasierer IV:6/Project B p. 127
RE (= religious education) /ˌɑːr‿ˈiː, reˌlɪdʒəs‿edjʊˈkeɪʃn/ Religion *(Schulfach)* I:5/A3
reach /riːtʃ/ erreichen IV:5/A4
reaction /riˈækʃn/ Reaktion IV:5/B4
read *(irr)* /riːd/ lesen I:4/A4
read along /ˌriːd‿əˈlɒŋ/ mitlesen IV:3/A6
read on /ˌriːd‿ˈɒn/ weiterlesen IV:5/I
read out /ˌriːd‿ˈaʊt/ (laut) vorlesen IV:3/A7
reading /ˈriːdɪŋ/ Lesen II:Last year
ready /ˈredi/ fertig, bereit III:1/A4
real /rɪəl/ wirklich; echt III:5/A1
realistic /ˌrɪəˈlɪstɪk/ realistisch III:5/B10
reality /riˈæləti/ Realität, Wirklichkeit IV:1/A9
realize (= realise) /ˈrɪəlaɪz/ sich bewusst sein, erkennen IV:4/A7
realize (= realise) /ˈrɪəlʌɪz/ *hier:* verwirklichen IV:1/A9
really /ˈrɪəli/ wirklich I:Welcome
reason /ˈriːzn/ Grund II:6/A9
give a reason /ˌɡɪv‿ə ˈriːzn/ einen Grund nennen IV:4/A4
rebuild /ˌriːˈbɪld/ wieder aufbauen IV:5/B5
receive /rɪˈsiːv/ erhalten; empfangen III:4/B2
receptionist /rɪˈsepʃnɪst/ Empfangsdame/Empfangschef IV:4/B2
recipe /ˈresəpi/ Rezept III:1/I
recognise /ˈrekəɡnaɪz/ erkennen II:3/B1
°recognition /ˌrekəɡˈnɪʃn/ Anerkennung IV:BS/9
recommend /ˌrekəˈmend/ empfehlen III:1/A7
record /riˈkɔːd/ aufnehmen III:3/B11
recyclable /riːˈsaɪkləbl/ recycelbar; wiederverwertbar IV:6/Project B p. 127
recycle /riːˈsaɪkl/ recyceln; wiederaufbereiten IV:6/Project p. 116
recycled /riːˈsaɪkld/ wiederverwertet; Recycling- IV:6/Project B p. 125
recycling bin /riːˈsaɪklɪŋ bɪn/ Wertstoffsammelbehälter IV:6/Project B p. 124
red /red/ rot I:Welcome
reduce /rɪˈdjuːs/ reduzieren IV:6/Project A p. 122
reflect /rɪˈflekt/ sich spiegeln in, zeigen, zum Ausdruck bringen IV:5/A1; reflektieren, nachdenken IV:6/Project p. 119
reflection /rɪˈflekʃn/ Reflexion IV:2/A4
reflexive /rɪˈfleksɪv/ reflexiv, rückbezüglich IV:1/P2
refugee /ˌrefjʊˈdʒiː/ Flüchtling IV:5/B3
refugee camp /ˈrefjʊˌdʒiː kæmp/ Flüchtlingslager IV:5/B5
registration /ˌredʒɪˈstreɪʃn/ *Überprüfung der Anwesenheit* I:5/A3
regular /ˈreɡjʊlə/ regelmäßig; üblich, normal IV:5/A1
°regularly /ˈreɡjʊləli/ regelmäßig IV:BS/9
relationship /rɪˈleɪʃnʃɪp/ Beziehung III:4/B1
relax /rɪˈlæks/ entspannen IV:2/B8
release /rɪˈliːs/ veröffentlichen; herausbringen IV:4/A7
release date /rɪˈliːs deɪt/ Erscheinungsdatum IV:3/A10
reliability /rɪˌlaɪəˈbɪlɪti/ Zuverlässigkeit IV:4/B6
reliable /rɪˈlaɪəbl/ verlässlich; zuverlässig IV:4/B6
°relief fund /rɪˈliːf‿fʌnd/ Hilfsfond IV:BS/10
°religious freedom /rəˌlɪdʒəs ˈfriːdəm/ Glaubensfreiheit IV:BS/2
rely on /rɪˈlaɪ‿ɒn/ sich verlassen auf IV:6/Project C p. 136
°remain /rɪˈmeɪn/ bleiben IV:BS/1
remember /rɪˈmembə/ sich erinnern an II:2/A8
remove /rɪˈmuːv/ entfernen IV:2/B7
°renaissance /rɪˈneɪsns/ Wiedergeburt, Renaissance IV:BS/9
renewable /rɪˈnjuːəbl/ erneuerbar IV:6/Project A p. 121
rent /rent/ Miete IV:5/B5
repair /rɪˈpeə/ reparieren II:3/A8
repeat /rɪˈpiːt/ wiederholen IV:1/P4
replace /rɪˈpleɪs/ ersetzen IV:1/P9
reply /rɪˈplaɪ/ antworten; erwidern II:1/B7
reply /rɪˈplaɪ/ Antwort IV:2/A10
report /rɪˈpɔːt/ Bericht IV:2/A7
report (to) /rɪˈpɔːt/ berichten; wiedergeben IV:2/A3
reported speech /ˌrɪ pɔːtɪd ˈspiːtʃ/ indirekte Rede IV:4/B8
reporter /rɪˈpɔːtə/ IV:1/B9
represent /ˌreprɪˈzent/ präsentieren, vertreten IV:1/A4
reputation /ˌrepjʊˈteɪʃn/ Ruf IV:1/B5

rescue /ˈreskjuː/ retten; befreien IV:3/B3; Rettungs- IV:5/O
research /rɪˈsɜːtʃ/ recherchieren IV:6/Project p. 119
research /rɪˈsɜːtʃ/ *hier:* Recherche IV:1/B10; *hier:* Untersuchungen IV:6/Project p. 132; Forschung IV:BS/3
resident /ˈrezɪdnt/ Bewohner/in IV:2/B2
resource /rɪˈzɔːs/ Quelle; Ressource IV:6/Project A p. 122
respect /rɪˈspekt/ respektieren IV:2/B7
response /rɪˈspɒns/ Antwort; Reaktion IV:5/B9
responsibility /rɪˌspɒnsəˈbɪləti/ Verantwortung; Pflicht IV:2/B3
responsible /rɪˈspɒnsəbl/ verantwortungsbewusst, verantwortlich IV:4/B6
restricted area /rɪˌstrɪktɪd‿ˈeəriə/ Sperrgebiet IV:5/A8
restyle /riːˈstaɪl/ neu entwerfen IV:6/Project C p. 129
result /rɪˈzʌlt/ Ergebnis IV:4/A11
result in /rɪˈzʌlt‿ɪn/ zur Folge haben; führen zu IV:2/A8
résumé *(AE)* /ˈrezjuːmeɪ/ Lebenslauf IV:4/B6
return /rɪˈtɜːn/ zurückkehren; zurückkommen IV:5/B5; zurückgeben II:5/A6
°in return /ɪn rɪˈtɜːn/ im Gegenzug; dafür IV:BS/6
returnable /rɪˈtɜːnəbl/ Mehrweg- IV:6/Project B p. 126
reusable /riːˈjuːzəbl/ wiederverwendbar IV:6/Project B p. 124
reuse /riːˈjuːz/ wiederverwenden IV:6/Project p. 116
review /rɪˈvjuː/ Kritik; Rezension IV:1/B10
reviewer /rɪˈvjuːə/ Kritiker/in IV:3/B6
°the Revolutionary War /ðə ˌrevəˌluːʃnri ˈwɔː/ Amerikanischer Revolutionskrieg IV:BS/1
rhyme /raɪm/ sich reimen IV:3/P3
rice /raɪs/ Reis III:1/A3
rich /rɪtʃ/ reich II:3/A1
ride /raɪd/ Fahrt IV:3/O
ride *(irr)* /raɪd/ fahren; reiten I:1/B4
ride a bike /ˌraɪd‿ə ˈbaɪk/ Fahrrad fahren I:1/A4
ride a horse /ˌraɪd‿ə ˈhɔːs/ reiten I:3/A8
right /raɪt/ Recht IV:2/B9; genau; direkt IV:4/A10; richtig I:2/B9; (nach) rechts II:2/B7
be right /ˌbiː ˈraɪt/ recht haben II:1/B7
on the right/on your right /ˌɒn ðə/jɔː ˈraɪt/ rechts, auf der/deiner rechten Seite II:2/B7
You're right. /ˌjɔː ˈraɪt/ Du hast recht. I:5/A2
right now /ˌraɪt ˈnaʊ/ im Moment IV:4/A10
ring *(irr)* /rɪŋ/ klingeln; läuten I:5/B3; anrufen III:6/A2
ringtone /ˈrɪŋˌtəʊn/ Klingelton IV:1/B5
rise *(irr)* /raɪz/ aufgehen; steigen II:1/B11
risk /rɪsk/ riskieren IV:3/P12
rival /ˈraɪvl/ rivalisierend IV:3/P12
°river /ˈrɪvə/ Fluss IV:BS/9
road /rəʊd/ Straße II:2/B7
°roast /rəʊst/ Braten IV:BS/5
°roast turkey /ˌrəʊst‿ˈtɜːki/ Putenbraten IV:BS/2
°roasted /ˈrəʊstɪd/ geröstet IV:BS/4
rock /rɒk/ Stein; Fels III:4/A1
rock *(informal)* /rɒk/ *hier:* Crack *(Rauschgift)* IV:1/B8
role /rəʊl/ Rolle IV:3/A4
°role model /ˈrəʊl ˌmɒdl/ Vorbild IV:BS/10
role play /ˈrəʊl pleɪ/ Rollenspiel IV:6/Project p. 133
romance /rəʊˈmæns/ Romanze IV:3/B6
romantic /rəʊˈmæntɪk/ romantisch IV:3/I
rooftop /ˈruːfˌtɒp/ Dach IV:6/Project p. 118
room /ruːm/ Raum; Zimmer I:Welcome
rope /rəʊp/ Seil III:4/A11
rot /rɒt/ verrotten, verfaulen IV:6/Project B p. 135
round /raʊnd/ um … herum III:2/A3
rub out /ˌrʌb‿ˈaʊt/ ausradieren IV:4/A7
rubbish /ˈrʌbɪʃ/ Müll I:4/A9
rude /ruːd/ unhöflich; primitiv IV:2/A6
ruin /ˈruːɪn/ zerstören; verderben IV:2/A7
rule /ruːl/ Regel II:5/A4
ruler /ˈruːlə/ Lineal I:2/B4
rumour /ˈruːmə/ Gerücht IV:2/A6
run *(irr)* /rʌn/ laufen; rennen I:3/A5
run *(irr)* /rʌn/ *hier:* in Betrieb sein IV:2/B2; *hier:* verlaufen IV:5/A9
°run around /ˌrʌn‿əˈraʊnd/ herumrennen IV:BS/8
run away /ˌrʌn‿əˈweɪ/ weglaufen III:2/B10
run out of /ˌrʌn‿ˈaʊt‿əv/ nicht mehr haben IV:6/Project A p. 134
running time /ˈrʌnɪŋ taɪm/ Laufzeit IV:3/A10
rush /rʌʃ/ eilen IV:3/B3
°be in a rush /ˌbi‿ɪn‿ə ˈrʌʃ/ in Eile sein IV:BS/6
Russia /ˈrʌʃə/ Russland IV:5/P2
Russian /ˈrʌʃn/ Russe, Russin; russisch IV:5/A1

sad /sæd/ traurig I:1/B2
safe /seɪf/ sicher; ungefährlich II:5/B11
safety /ˈseɪfti/ Sicherheit; Sicherheits- IV:2/B7
sail /seɪl/ Segel IV:4/A4; segeln IV:BS/2
sailmaker /ˈseɪlˌmeɪkə/ Segelmacher/in IV:4/I
salad /ˈsæləd/ Salat III:1/A1
sale /seɪl/ Verkauf III:2/I
salt /sɔːlt/ Salz III:1/B5
the same /ðə ˈseɪm/ der/die/das Gleiche; der-/die-/dasselbe III:1/A7

Saturday /ˈsætədeɪ/ Samstag I:1/B2
sauce /sɔːs/ Soße III:1/A3
sausage /ˈsɒsɪdʒ/ Wurst, Würstchen I:2/A7
save /seɪv/ sparen; aufheben IV:6/Project B p. 125; retten IV:BS/3
say *(irr)* /seɪ/ sagen I:1/B2
say goodbye /ˌseɪ gʊdˈbaɪ/ Abschied nehmen; Wiedersehen sagen IV:3/B1
scaffolding /ˈskæfəʊldɪŋ/ Gerüst IV:2/B7
scared /skeəd/ verängstigt III:4/A2
be scared (of) /ˌbiː ˈskeəd‿əv/ Angst haben (vor) II:1/B3
scarf (*pl* **scarfs** *or* **scarves**) /skɑːf, skɑːfs, skɑːvz/ Schal I:WB/1
scene /siːn/ Szene III:1/A11
schedule *(AE)* /ˈskeˌdʒul, ˈʃedjuːl/ *hier:* Stundenplan IV:1/A2
school /skuːl/ Schule I:Welcome
school day /ˈskuːl ˌdeɪ/ Schultag I:5/A8
school exchange /ˈskuːl‿ɪksˌtʃeɪndʒ/ Schüleraustausch IV:5/B1
school playground /ˌskuːl ˈpleɪˌgraʊnd/ Schulhof IV:6/Project p. 132
school report /ˌskuːl rɪˈpɔːt/ Schulzeugnis III:4/B4
school trip /ˈskuːl ˌtrɪp/ Schulausflug II:6/A10
school uniform /ˌskuːl ˈjuːnɪfɔːm/ Schuluniform II:5/B1
schoolbag /ˈskuːlˌbæg/ Schultasche I:2/B4
schoolwork /ˈskuːlˌwɜːk/ Schularbeiten IV:2/I
science /ˈsaɪəns/ Naturwissenschaft I:4/A11
°scientific /ˌsaɪənˈtɪfɪk/ naturwissenschaftlich IV:BS/3
scientist /ˈsaɪəntɪst/ Wissenschaftler/in III:5/A1
score /skɔː/ Punktestand IV:1/A2; einen Punkt machen IV:4/B7
score a goal /ˌskɔːr‿ə ˈgəʊl/ ein Tor schießen I:3/A6
Scotland /ˈskɒtlənd/ Schottland II:1/B1
scrambled /ˈskræmbld/ durcheinander gebracht IV:5/P3
sculptor /ˈskʌlptə/ Bildhauer/in IV:4/A7
°sculpture /ˈskʌlptʃə/ Skulptur IV:1/O
sea /siː/ Meer; See II:4/B8
seal /siːl/ Seehund; Robbe IV:6/Project B p. 125
search /sɜːtʃ/ Suche IV:6/Project A p. 122
search term /ˈsɜːtʃ tɜːm/ Suchbegriff IV:6/Project B p. 126
seashell /ˈsiːˌʃel/ Muschel I:3/B5
seat /siːt/ Sitz III:5/A1
second /ˈsekənd/ zweite(r, s) I:5/A3; Sekunde II:3/A1
secondary school /ˈsekəndri skuːl/ weiterführende Schule IV:1/A2
secret /ˈsiːkrət/ heimlich III:6/A3
in secret /ɪn ˈsiːkrət/ heimlich IV:3/B1
secretary /ˈsekrətri/ Sekretär/in IV:4/A1
section /ˈsekʃn/ Teil, Stück, Abschnitt IV:4/A13
see *(irr)* /siː/ sehen I:Welcome
Nice to see you. /ˌnaɪs tə ˈsiː jə/ Schön, dich/euch/Sie zu sehen. I:5/B3
°see you around *(informal)* /ˌsiː jʊ‿əˈraʊnd/ bis demnächst IV:3/O
See you (soon)! /ˌsiː juː ˈsuːn/ Bis bald! I:3/A5
seed /siːd/ Samen IV:6/Project p. 132
seem /siːm/ scheinen IV:2/A7
selection /sɪˈlekʃn/ Auswahl III:1/A9
°self (*pl* selves) /ˈself, selvz/ Selbst; Ich IV:5/O
sell *(irr)* /sel/ verkaufen II:6/B11
seller /ˈselə/ Verkäufer/in I:3/B4
°semi-autobiographical /ˌsemi‿ɔːtəʊbaɪəˈgræfɪkl/ halbautografisch IV:BS/9
send *(irr)* /send/ schicken II:1/B10
send off /ˌsend‿ˈɒf/ wegschicken IV:4/B3
senior school /ˈsiːniə skuːl/ Oberstufenschule IV:5/B5
sense /sens/ Sinn; Gefühl IV:5/B7
sentence /ˈsentəns/ Satz II:3/A1
separate /ˈseprət/ separat; gesondert IV:6/Project C p. 131
September /sepˈtembə/ September I:5/B7
serve /sɜːv/ servieren; bedienen III:1/A3
service /ˈsɜːvɪs/ Service; Dienst IV:4/P10
set a good example /ˌset‿ə gʊd‿ɪgˈzɑːmpl/ mit gutem Beispiel vorangehen IV:6/Project A p. 122
°set off /ˌset‿ˈɒf/ aufbrechen; auf den Weg machen IV:BS/3
set up /ˌset‿ˈʌp/ aufbauen III:6/A3
°set up /ˌset‿ˈʌp/ *hier:* gründen IV:BS/9
settler /ˈsetlə/ Siedler/in IV:1/A7
several /ˈsevrəl/ einige; verschiedene II:2/A2
severe /sɪˈvɪə/ schlimm, stark IV:1/B2
sewing machine /ˈsəʊɪŋ məˌʃiːn/ Nähmaschine IV:5/B5
shadow /ˈʃædəʊ/ Schatten IV:5/A3
°shake one's head /ˌʃeɪk wʌnz ˈhed/ den Kopf schütteln IV:BS/6
Shakespearean /ʃeɪkˈspɪəriən/ Shakespeare- IV:3/B8
shall /ʃæl/ sollen; werden III:2/A4
be a shame /ˌbi‿ə ˈʃeɪm/ schade sein IV:3/B6
share /ʃeə/ teilen II:3/B9
she /ʃiː/ sie I:Welcome
sheep (*pl* **sheep**) /ʃiːp/ Schaf I:WB/1
sheet /ʃiːt/ Blatt; Bogen IV:2/B5
shelf (*pl* **shelves**) /ʃelf, ʃelvz/ Regal I:4/A1
shell /ʃel/ Schale IV:5/B7
ship /ʃɪp/ Schiff II:2/A2
board a ship /ˌbɔːd‿ə ˈʃɪp/ ein Schiff besteigen IV:5/A4
shirt /ʃɜːt/ Hemd I:3/A12
°shiver /ˈʃɪvə/ zittern IV:3/O

shock /ʃɒk/ Schock IV:1/A2
shocked /'ʃɒkt/ schockiert, entsetzt IV:3/A5
°shocking /'ʃɒkɪŋ/ schockierend IV:BS/4
shoe /ʃu:/ Schuh I:WB/1
shoe shine boy /'ʃu:ʃaɪn bɔɪ/ Schuhputzer IV:2/B2
shoelace /'ʃu:ˌleɪs/ Schnürsenkel IV:4/B3
shoot *(irr)* /ʃu:t/ schießen II:6/B11
shoot *(irr)* /ʃu:t/ *hier:* filmen; drehen IV:3/B9
shop /ʃɒp/ Geschäft; Laden I:1/B2
shop /ʃɒp/ einkaufen IV:1/B5
do the shopping /ˌdu: ðə 'ʃɒpɪŋ/ einkaufen I:4/A6
go shopping /ˌgəʊ 'ʃɒpɪŋ/ Einkaufen gehen II:1/A2
shopping /'ʃɒpɪŋ/ Einkaufen; Einkaufs- I:2/A13
°shore /ʃɔ:/ Küste, Ufer IV:BS/10
short /ʃɔ:t/ kurz I:2/A3
short story /ʃɔ:t 'stɔ:ri/ Kurzgeschichte IV:3/B9
should /ʃʊd/ sollte(st, n, t) III:1/B1
shoulder /'ʃəʊldə/ Schulter I:2/A1
shout /ʃaʊt/ rufen; schreien II:1/B7
show *(irr)* /ʃəʊ/ zeigen II:1/B10
shy /ʃaɪ/ schüchtern III:4/B2
sibling /'sɪblɪŋ/ Geschwister IV:3/A7
sick /sɪk/ krank IV:5/A2
side /saɪd/ Seite IV:5/A9
side (dish) /'saɪd‿dɪʃ/ Beilage III:1/A3
sight /saɪt/ Sehenswürdigkeit II:1/A2
at first sight /ət ˌfɜ:st 'saɪt/ auf den ersten Blick IV:3/B1
°be out of sight /ˌbi‿ˌaʊt‿əv 'saɪt/ außer Sichtweite sein IV:3/O
sign /saɪn/ Zeichen; Schild III:2/B9
°significant /sɪg'nɪfɪkənt/ bedeutend IV:BS/9
silent /'saɪlənt/ still; *hier:* stumm IV:4/P3
silk /sɪlk/ Seide IV:6/Project C p. 131
silly /'sɪli/ albern; dumm II:1/B10
similar /'sɪmɪlə/ ähnlich IV:1/A4
simple present /ˌsɪmpl 'preznt/ einfache Gegenwart IV:4/P4
since /sɪns/ seit III:4/B2
sing *(irr)* /sɪŋ/ singen I:2/B9
°singalong /ˌsɪŋ‿ə'lɒŋ/ *gemeinsames Liedersingen* IV:BS/10
singer /'sɪŋə/ Sänger/in I:3/A1
single /'sɪŋgl/ einzige(r, s) IV:6/Project A p. 123
siren /'saɪrən/ Sirene IV:1/B8
sister /'sɪstə/ Schwester I:1/A4
sit *(irr)* /sɪt/ sitzen I:5/B3
sit around /ˌsɪt‿ə'raʊnd/ herumsitzen IV:4/B3
sit down /ˌsɪt‿'daʊn/ sich hinsetzen IV:4/B7
site /saɪt/ Stelle; Platz; Ort IV:2/B7
situated /'sɪtʃueɪtɪd/ gelegen IV:6/Project A p. 134
size /saɪz/ Größe III:6/B9
skate /skeɪt/ inlineskaten I:3/A8
skateboard /'skeɪtbɔ:d/ Skateboard fahren IV:4/B3
ski /ski:/ Ski fahren, Ski laufen I:3/A8
skilful /'skɪlfl/ geschickt III:3/A7
skill /skɪl/ Fähigkeit; Geschick IV:1/A4
skim /skɪm/ überfliegen IV:3/B6
skin /skɪn/ Haut IV:2/A7
skirt /skɜ:t/ Rock I:WB/1
sky /skaɪ/ Himmel II:3/A12
skyscraper /'skaɪˌskreɪpə/ Wolkenkratzer IV:1/B2
skywalker /'skaɪˌwɔ:kə/ *Bauarbeiter/in, der/die Wolkenkratzer baut bzw. auf diesen arbeitet* IV:4/I
°sledge /sledʒ/ Schlitten IV:BS/3
sleep *(irr)* /sli:p/ schlafen I:4/A4
sleepover /'sli:pˌəʊvə/ Übernachtung I:4/B1
slide /slaɪd/ *hier:* Folie IV:2/B9
slide show /'slaɪd ʃəʊ/ Diavortrag IV:6/Project p. 133
slim /slɪm/ schlank I:2/A3
slow, slowly /sləʊ, 'sləʊli/ langsam II:3/B2
small /smɔ:l/ klein I:1/B3
°smart /smɑ:t/ schlau IV:BS/6
smell *(irr)* /smel/ riechen II:4/B3
smell of /'smel‿əv/ nach etw riechen IV:2/A7
smile /smaɪl/ lächeln I:2/A6; Lächeln III:2/B9
smoke /sməʊk/ rauchen IV:2/A7
smoke /sməʊk/ Rauch IV:2/A7
smoke-free /ˌsməʊk 'fri:/ rauchfrei IV:2/A9
smoke-jumper /'sməʊkˌdʒʌmpə/ *Feuerspringer/in* IV:4/I
smoking /'sməʊkɪŋ/ Rauchen IV:2/A1
smuggle /'smʌgl/ schmuggeln IV:5/A8
snack bar /'snæk bɑ:/ Imbissbude IV:3/A4
snake-milker /'sneɪkˌmɪlkə/ Schlangenmelker/in IV:4/I
sneaker *(AE)* /'sni:kə/ Turnschuh IV:1/B5
snow /snəʊ/ Schnee I:Welcome
snowman (*pl* **snowmen**) /'snəʊmæn, 'snəʊmen/ Schneemann I:WB/1
snowy /'snəʊi/ verschneit, schneereich I:WB/1
so /səʊ/ deshalb; daher II:1/B7; *hier:* also II:2/B2
so far /'səʊ fɑ:/ bisher IV:3/A6
so that /'səʊ ðæt/ damit III:3/A9
soap /səʊp/ Seife I:2/A1
soccer /'sɒkə/ Fußball IV:1/A2
social /'səʊʃl/ gesellschaftlich; sozial IV:4/B1
social studies /'səʊʃl ˌstʌdiz/ *Schulfach, das unter anderem Erdkunde, Geschichte, Soziologie umfasst* IV:1/A2
social worker /'səʊʃl ˌwɜ:kə/ Sozialarbeiter/in IV:4/A1
sock /sɒk/ Socke I:WB/1
soft /sɒft/ weich IV:1/A6
soft skill /ˌsɒft 'skɪl/ *persönliche, soziale und methodische Kompetenzen* IV:4/B6

soften /ˈsɒfn/ weicher machen IV:2/B7
software developer /ˈsɒfˌweə dɪˌveləpə/ Softwareentwickler/in IV:4/A1
soil /sɔɪl/ Boden, Erde IV:2/B7
turn over the soil /ˌtɜ:n‿ˌəʊvə ðə ˈsɔɪl/ den Boden umgraben IV:2/B7
solution /səˈlu:ʃn/ Lösung IV:6/Project p. 119
solve /sɒlv/ lösen III:4/B2
some /sʌm/ einige, ein paar; etwas I:Welcome
somebody /ˈsʌmbədi/ jemand; irgendwer IV:1/B5
somehow /ˈsʌmhaʊ/ irgendwie IV:2/A7
someone /ˈsʌmwʌn/ jemand; irgendwer II:2/B2
something /ˈsʌmθɪŋ/ etwas I:3/B6
sometimes /ˈsʌmtaɪmz/ manchmal I:4/A6
somewhere /ˈsʌmweə/ irgendwo II:2/B2
son /sʌn/ Sohn I:5/B7
song /sɒŋ/ Lied III:6/A3
See you (soon)! /ˌsi: ju: ˈsu:n/ Bis bald! I:3/A5
soon /su:n/ bald II:6/A8
sore throat /ˌsɔ: ˈθrəʊt/ Halsschmerzen III:3/B4
Sorry. /ˈsɒri/ Es tut mir leid., Entschuldigung. I:Welcome
sort /sɔ:t/ sortieren; Sorte; Art IV:5/B3
soul /səʊl/ Seele III:2/B4
sound /saʊnd/ Geräusch; Klang II:2/A1; klingen, sich anhören II:4/A3
soup /su:p/ Suppe III:1/A1
south /saʊθ/ Süden IV:1/A1
South America /ˌsaʊθ‿əˈmerɪkə/ Südamerika IV:1/B5
°South Pole /ˌsaʊθ ˈpəʊl/ Südpol IV:BS/3
space /speɪs/ Raum; Platz IV:5/A4; Weltall III:5/A2
space /speɪs/ *hier:* Reklamefläche IV:4/A7
Spain /speɪn/ Spanien IV:5/P2
Spanish /ˈspænɪʃ/ Spanisch IV:1/A2
speak *(irr)* /spi:k/ sprechen; reden I:Welcome ...
speak out /ˌspi:k‿ˈaʊt/ seine Meinung deutlich vertreten IV:6/Project C p. 129
speaker /ˈspi:kə/ Sprecher/in IV:3/A7
special /ˈspeʃl/ besondere(r, s) II:4/A1
special /ˈspeʃl/ *hier:* besonders, speziell IV:1/B5
specialise in /ˈspeʃəlaɪz‿ɪn/ sich spezialisieren auf IV:4/A6
°species *(pl)* /ˈspi:ʃi:z/ Art; Spezies IV:BS/4
specific /spəˈsɪfɪk/ genau, bestimmte(r, s); spezifisch IV:4/B7
direct speech /daɪˌrekt ˈspi:tʃ/ direkte Rede, wörtliche Rede II:3/B9
speech bubble /ˈspi:tʃ ˌbʌbl/ Sprechblase IV:3/A8
spell *(irr)* /spel/ buchstabieren I:2/B1
spend *(irr)* /spend/ verbringen; ausgeben II:1/B11
spend money on /ˌspend ˈmʌni‿ɒn/ Geld ausgeben für II:4/A7
spice /spaɪs/ Gewürz III:1/A10
°spicy /ˈspaɪsi/ würzig; scharf IV:BS/4
°spider /ˈspaɪdə/ Spinne IV:BS/4
°spill /spɪl/ verschütten IV:BS/8
°spinach /ˈspɪnɪdʒ/ Spinat IV:BS/5
spirit /ˈspɪrɪt/ Geist; Stimmung IV:2/A4
team spirit /ˌti:m ˈspɪrɪt/ Teamgeist IV:1/A2
°spit out /ˌspɪt‿ˈaʊt/ ausspucken IV:BS/7
split /splɪt/ (ein)teilen IV:3/A4
split up /ˌsplɪt‿ˈʌp/ aufteilen IV:6/Project p. 118
°sponsor /ˈspɒnsə/ sponsern; als Sponsor finanzieren IV:BS/10
spooky /ˈspu:ki/ schaurig; unheimlich I:4/B1
spoon /spu:n/ Löffel I:2/A7
sport /spɔ:t/ Sport, Sportart I:3/I
sports centre /ˈspɔ:ts‿ˌsentə/ Sportcenter I:3/A9
sports field /ˈspɔ:ts fi:ld/ Sportplatz I:3/A1
sports hall /ˈspɔ:ts hɔ:l/ Sporthalle I:3/A1
sports shop /ˈspɔ:ts‿ʃɒp/ Sportgeschäft IV:4/B3
sportsmanship /ˈspɔ:tsmənʃɪp/ Fairness IV:1/A4
spotlight /ˈspɒtˌlaɪt/ Scheinwerfer; Aufmerksamkeit IV:6/Project p. 119
spray /spreɪ/ sprühen IV:2/A2
spread *(irr)* /spred/ verbreiten IV:2/A6; sich ausbreiten IV:5/A3
spring /sprɪŋ/ Frühling I:Welcome
squirrel /ˈskwɪrəl/ Eichhörnchen I:WB/1
stabilise (= stabilize) /ˈsteɪbəlaɪz/ stabilisieren IV:2/B7
stadium /ˈsteɪdiəm/ Stadion IV:1/B5
staff manager /ˈsta:f ˌmænɪdʒə/ Personalchef/in IV:4/B8
stage /steɪdʒ/ Bühne II:6/B11
stall /stɔ:l/ Stand III:2/A7
stamp /stæmp/ Briefmarke III:5/B1
stand *(irr)* /stænd/ stehen II:2/B11
stand for /ˈstænd fɔ:/ für etw stehen IV:Quiz
°stand in line /ˌstænd‿ɪn ˈlaɪn/ Schlange stehen IV:BS/7
°stand still /ˌstænd ˈstɪl/ stillstehen IV:BS/6
stand up paddleboarding /ˌstænd‿ʌp ˈpædlbɔ:dɪŋ/ Stehpaddeln IV:1/P6
stand up to sb /ˌstænd‿ˈʌp tə ˌsʌmbədi/ sich jdm widersetzen IV:2/A2
standard of living /ˌstændəd‿əv ˈlɪvɪŋ/ Lebensstandard IV:5/B3
stare at /ˈsteər‿æt/ anstarren IV:3/A4
start /sta:t/ anfangen; beginnen I:Welcome

°start /stɑːt/ Anfang; Beginn IV:BS/6
starter /ˈstɑːtə/ Vorspeise III:1/A3
starting point /ˈstɑːtɪŋ pɔɪnt/ Ausgangspunkt IV:1/A10
starve /stɑːv/ verhungern IV:5/A2
state /steɪt/ (Bundes)staat IV:Quiz
statement /ˈsteɪtmənt/ Äußerung, Stellungnahme; Aussage IV:1/A5
station /ˈsteɪʃn/ U-Bahn-Station; Bahnhof I:4/B1
railway station /ˈreɪlweɪ ˌsteɪʃn/ Bahnhof II:2/A2
statistics *(pl)* /stəˈtɪstɪks/ Statistik IV:5/A7
the Statue of Liberty /ðə ˌstætʃu‿əv ˈlɪbəti/ Freiheitsstatue IV:Quiz
stay /steɪ/ bleiben; wohnen II:1/A2
stay away from /ˌsteɪ‿əˈweɪ frɒm/ meiden; sich fernhalten von II:5/B11
°steak and kidney pie /ˌsteɪk‿ən ˌkɪdni ˈpaɪ/ Rindfleisch-Nieren-Pastete IV:BS/5
steal *(irr)* /stiːl/ stehlen III:2/B5
step /step/ Stufe; Schritt IV:1/B2; steigen; treten III:3/A1
°step off /ˌstep‿ˈɒf/ heraustreten aus IV:3/O
step out of /ˌstep‿ˈaʊt‿əv/ heraustreten aus IV:2/A4
stick /stɪk/ Schläger IV:1/A6
sticker /ˈstɪkə/ Aufkleber I:3/B5
still /stɪl/ (immer) noch II:1/B3
°stink bug /ˈstɪŋk bʌg/ Stinkwanze IV:BS/4
stomach /ˈstʌmək/ Magen; Bauch IV:5/A10
stomach ache /ˈstʌmək‿ˌeɪk/ Bauchschmerzen III:3/B2
stone /stəʊn/ Stein I:3/B5
stop /stɒp/ stehen bleiben; anhalten; aufhören II:1/B6
stop /stɒp/ stoppen; aufhalten IV:2/A4; *hier:* Haltestelle IV:3/O

store *(AE)* /stɔː/ Laden IV:2/B2
storeroom /ˈstɔːˌruːm/ Lagerraum, Abstellkammer IV:4/B3
storm /stɔːm/ Sturm III:4/A1
stormy /ˈstɔːmi/ stürmisch IV:5/A3
story /ˈstɔːri/ Geschichte I:3/B6
straight /streɪt/ *hier:* heterosexuell IV:3/A7; gerade(aus); direkt IV:6/Project p. 119
straight on /ˌstreɪt‿ˈɒn/ geradeaus II:2/B7
°strawberry /ˈstrɔːbri/ Erdbeere IV:BS/5
street /striːt/ Straße I:1/B3
in the street /ˌɪn ðə ˈstriːt/ auf der Straße I:3/A9
stressed /strest/ gestresst III:4/B1
stressful /ˈstresfl/ stressig; anstrengend IV:4/A1
strive for /ˈstraɪv‿fɔː/ streben nach IV:5/B7
strong /strɒŋ/ stark I:2/A3
student *(AE)* /ˈstjuːdnt/ Schüler/in; Student/in IV:1/A2
°studies *(pl)* /ˈstʌdis/ Studium IV:5/O
study /ˈstʌdi/ studieren; lernen IV:1/A2
study hall /ˈstʌdi hɔːl/ *Freistunde zur Stillbeschäftigung* IV:1/A2
stuff *(informal)* /stʌf/ Zeug III:5/A2
stupid /ˈstjuːpɪd/ dumm, blöd IV:3/A9
style /staɪl/ Stil IV:4/A7
subject /ˈsʌbdʒɪkt/ Schulfach I:5/A2
subject /ˈsʌbdʒɪkt/ *hier:* Betreff IV:1/A2
substance /ˈsʌbstəns/ Substanz; *hier:* Chemikalie IV:6/Project B p. 135
subway *(AE)* /ˈsʌbˌweɪ/ U-Bahn IV:4/A7
successful /səkˈsesfl/ erfolgreich III:3/A7
such /sʌtʃ/ so; solch II:2/B2
such as /ˈsʌtʃ‿æz/ wie III:6/A3
suddenly /ˈsʌdnli/ plötzlich II:1/B6

°suffer from /ˈsʌfə frəm/ leiden an IV:BS/3
sugar /ˈʃʊgə/ Zucker II:4/A1
suggest /səˈdʒest/ vorschlagen II:2/A10
sum up /ˌsʌm‿ˈʌp/ zusammenfassen IV:4/A4
summary /ˈsʌməri/ Zusammenfassung IV:2/P14
summer /ˈsʌmə/ Sommer I:Welcome
sun /sʌn/ Sonne I:Welcome
Sunday /ˈsʌndeɪ/ Sonntag I:1/B2
sunglasses *(pl)* /ˈsʌnˌglɑːsɪz/ Sonnenbrille I:WB/1
sunny /ˈsʌni/ sonnig I:WB/1
sunray /ˈsʌnreɪ/ Sonnenstrahl IV:5/B7
sunshine /ˈsʌnˌʃaɪn/ Sonnenschein II:6/A2
Super Bowl /ˈsuːpə bəʊl/ *Finale der US-amerikanischen American Football-Profiliga* IV:Quiz
supermarket /ˈsuːpəˌmɑːkɪt/ Supermarkt I:1/B3
support /səˈpɔːt/ (unter)stützen IV:1/A6
suppose /səˈpəʊz/ vermuten; annehmen II:4/A7
sure /ʃɔː/ sicher II:2/B6
°surf /sɜːf/ surfen IV:BS/7
surf the Internet /ˌsɜːf ˌði‿ˈɪntəˌnet/ im Internet surfen II:6/A6
surfing /ˈsɜːfɪŋ/ Surfen IV:1/P5
Surgeon General *(AE)* /ˌsɜːdʒn ˈdʒenrəl/ Gesundheitsminister/in IV:2/A8
surprise /səˈpraɪz/ Überraschung II:4/A7
surprised /səˈpraɪzd/ überrascht; erstaunt II:1/B7
survey /ˈsɜːveɪ/ Umfrage IV:4/A12
survival /səˈvaɪvl/ Überleben IV:5/A3
survive /səˈvaɪv/ überleben III:4/A11
sustainability /səˌsteɪnəˈbɪləti/ Nachhaltigkeit IV:6/Project A p. 123
sustainable /səˈsteɪnəbl/ nachhaltig IV:6/Project A p. 134

swap /swɒp/ tauschen IV:1/B7
swap shop /ˈswɒp ʃɒp/ Tauschbörse IV:6/Project C p.128
sweater /ˈswetə/ Pullover I:WB/1
sweatshop /ˈswetˌʃɒp/ Ausbeuterbetrieb IV:6/Project C p.128
sweaty /ˈsweti/ verschwitzt IV:5/B7
Sweden /ˈswiːdn/ Schweden IV:6/Project A p.121
sweep *(irr)* /swiːp/ fegen; kehren IV:4/B3
sweet /swiːt/ süß III:1/A1
swim *(irr)* /swɪm/ schwimmen I:1/A6
swimmer /ˈswɪmə/ Schwimmer/in III:3/A8
go swimming /ˌgəʊ ˈswɪmɪŋ/ Schwimmen gehen I:3/A9
swimming /ˈswɪmɪŋ/ Schwimmen I:3/B8
swimming pool /ˈswɪmɪŋ puːl/ Schwimmbad I:1/B3
switch off /ˌswɪtʃ‿ˈɒf/ ausschalten IV:6/Project p.116
switch on /ˌswɪtʃ‿ˈɒn/ einschalten I:4/B10
swollen /ˈswəʊlən/ geschwollen III:3/B1
syllable /ˈsɪləbl/ Silbe IV:3/P10
synthetic /sɪnˈθetɪk/ synthetisch IV:6/Project C p.130
Syria /ˈsɪriə/ Syrien IV:5/B5
Syrian /ˈsɪriən/ syrisch IV:5/B5

table /ˈteɪbl/ Tisch I:2/A7
table /ˈteɪbl/ Tabelle IV:1/A4
lay the table /ˌleɪ ðə ˈteɪbl/ den Tisch decken II:4/B5
table of contents /ˌteɪbl‿əv ˈkɒntents/ Inhaltsverzeichnis IV:2/A11
table tennis /ˈteɪbl ˌtenɪs/ Tischtennnis I:3/A1
tablespoon /ˈteɪblˌspuːn/ Esslöffel III:1/B5
take *(irr)* /teɪk/ erfordern; benötigen IV:4/B6; nehmen; bringen I:3/B4; *hier:* brauchen; dauern II:1/B1
take *(irr)* /teɪk/ *hier:* machen IV:6/I; *hier:* ertragen, verkraften IV:BS/5
I'll take it. /ˌaɪl ˈteɪk‿ɪt/ Ich nehme es. I:3/B4
take a course /ˌteɪk‿ə ˈkɔːs/ einen Kurs machen IV:4/B6
take a look at /ˌteɪk‿ə ˈlʊk‿ət/ sich ansehen IV:2/I
take a picture /ˌteɪk‿ə ˈpɪktʃə/ ein Bild machen IV:3/A9
take a seat /ˌteɪk‿ə ˈsiːt/ sich setzen IV:4/A10
take a test /ˌteɪk‿ə ˈtest/ einen Test machen III:3/I
take action /ˌteɪk‿ˈækʃn/ handeln IV:6/Project B p.126
°take ages *(informal)* /ˌteɪk‿ˈeɪdʒɪz/ ewig dauern IV:3/O
take away /ˌteɪk‿əˈweɪ/ wegnehmen; mitnehmen III:2/B8
take initiative /ˌteɪk‿ɪˈnɪʃətɪv/ die Initiative ergreifen IV:4/B7
take notes /ˌteɪk ˈnəʊts/ sich Notizen machen IV:1/A2
°take off /ˌteɪk‿ˈɒf/ abheben, starten IV:BS/9
°take on /ˌteɪk‿ˈɒn/ annehmen IV:BS/4
°take one's eyes off sth /ˌteɪk wʌnz‿ˈaɪz‿ɒf ˌsʌmθɪŋ/ sich von einem Anblick trennen IV:3/O
take out /ˌteɪk‿ˈaʊt/ hinausbringen I:4/A9
take part in /ˌteɪk ˈpɑːt‿ɪn/ teilnehmen an I:5/A7
take photos /ˌteɪk ˈfəʊtəʊz/ Bilder machen II:1/A10
take place /ˌteɪk ˈpleɪs/ stattfinden IV:1/A4
take sb on a tour /ˌteɪk ˌsʌmbədi‿ɒn‿ə ˈtʊə/ mit jdm einen Ausflug machen IV:1/B2
take the tube /ˌteɪk ðə ˈtjuːb/ die U-Bahn nehmen I:4/B3
take turns /ˌteɪk ˈtɜːnz/ sich abwechseln IV:1/P12
take up /ˌteɪk‿ˈʌp/ *hier:* annehmen IV:3/B3
talented /ˈtæləntɪd/ talentiert IV:4/I
talk about /ˈtɔːk‿əˌbaʊt/ sprechen über I:4/B1
talk (to) /tɔːk/ sprechen (mit); reden (mit) I:3/A4
tall /tɔːl/ groß I:2/A3
°tarantula /təˈræntjʊlə/ Tarantel IV:BS/4
task /tɑːsk/ Aufgabe IV:4/B3
target task /ˈtɑːgɪt ˌtɑːsk/ Zielaufgabe II:1/I
taste /teɪst/ schmecken II:4/B3
°taste /teɪst/ *hier:* probieren IV:BS/7
°taster /ˈteɪstə/ Vorkoster/in IV:BS/7
tasty /ˈteɪsti/ lecker III:1/A1
tea /tiː/ Tee I:2/A8
teach *(irr)* /tiːtʃ/ unterrichten I:3/A13
teacher /ˈtiːtʃə/ Lehrer/in I:3/A2
team spirit /ˌtiːm ˈspɪrɪt/ Teamgeist IV:1/A2
technician /tekˈnɪʃn/ Techniker/in III:6/A3
°technology /tekˈnɒlədʒi/ Technologie, Technik IV:BS/7
teen /tiːn/ jugendlich; Teenager- IV:2/A11
teenager /ˈtiːnˌeɪdʒə/ IV:2/A5
brush one's teeth /ˌbrʌʃ wʌnz ˈtiːθ/ sich die Zähne putzen I:2/A1
telephone call /ˈtelɪfəʊn kɔːl/ Telefonanruf IV:4/B4
tell *(irr)* /tel/ erzählen I:1/B2
tell *(irr)* /tel/ *hier:* sagen IV:1/A2
tell sb to do sth /ˌtel ˌsʌmbədi tə ˈduː ˌsʌmθɪŋ/ jdm sagen, dass er/sie etw tun soll IV:2/P5
temple /ˈtempl/ Tempel II:4/A1
tens of thousands /ˌtenz‿əv ˈθaʊzndz/ zehntausende IV:6/Project B p.125
tense /tens/ Zeitform; Tempus IV:5/P6
°tent /tent/ Zelt IV:BS/3
term /tɜːm/ Begriff III:6/B2
terrible /ˈterəbl/ schrecklich I:5/A2

test /test/ prüfen; testen IV:2/B7
take a test /ˌteɪk‿ə ˈtest/ einen Test machen III:3/I
text /tekst/ eine SMS schreiben IV:4/B3
text message /ˈtekst ˌmesɪdʒ/ SMS II:5/B10
textile /ˈtekstaɪl/ Textil IV:6/Project C p. 129
than /ðæn/ als II:4/A1
Thank you. /ˈθæŋk ju/ Danke. I:Welcome
I'm fine, thanks. /aɪm ˈfaɪn ˌθæŋks/ Es geht mir gut, danke. I:4/B9
thanks /θæŋks/ danke I:2/B1
°thanks to /ˈθæŋks tʊ/ dank; wegen IV:BS/2
Thanksgiving /ˈθæŋksˌɡɪvɪŋ/ Thanksgiving (amerikanisches Erntedankfest) IV:Quiz
that /ðæt/ das I:1/A2; dass II:1/B7; der, die, das; jene(r, s) III:2/A7
that /ðæt/ so IV:2/B2
that way /ˈðæt weɪ/ so, auf diese Weise IV:1/A7
that's (= that is) /ðæts, ˈðæt‿ɪz/ das ist I:Welcome; *hier:* das kostet I:3/B1
that's why /ˈðæts ˌwaɪ/ deshalb IV:2/B7
the /ðə/ der/die/das I:Welcome
theatre /ˈθɪətə/ Theater III:2/A3
their /ðeə/ ihr(e) I:1/A4
them /ðem/ sie; ihnen I:4/A11
theme /θiːm/ Thema; *hier:* Kapitel II:1/I
themselves /ðəmˈselvz/ sich; sie selbst IV:1/A3
then /ðen/ dann I:Welcome
there /ðeə/ dort; dahin I:4/A4
there are /ðeər‿ˈɑː/ dort sind; es gibt I:Welcome
there is /ðeər‿ˈɪz/ dort ist; es gibt I:Welcome
these (*pl* of this) /ðiːz/ diese; das I:1/A2
they /ðeɪ/ sie I:Welcome
thief (*pl* thieves) /θiːf, θiːvz/ Dieb IV:5/A10
thing /θɪŋ/ Ding; Gegenstand I:2/B4
think *(irr)* /θɪŋk/ denken; glauben I:1/A4
What do you think? /ˌwɒt‿də jə ˈθɪŋk/ Was hältst du davon? I:Welcome
think about /ˈθɪŋk‿əˌbaʊt/ nachdenken über I:4/B12
think about /ˈθɪŋk‿əˌbaʊt/ *hier:* halten von IV:4/A1
think of /ˈθɪŋk‿əv/ denken an, sich ausdenken II:2/A1
think up /ˌθɪŋk‿ˈʌp/ sich ausdenken; sich einfallen lassen IV:3/A4
third /θɜːd/ dritte(r, s) I:5/A3
thirst /θɜːst/ Durst IV:5/A9
this /ðɪs/ diese(r, s) I:Welcome
this morning /ðɪs ˈmɔːnɪŋ/ heute Morgen II:4/A3
those (*pl* of that) /ðəʊz/ diese, jene I:4/B6
though /ðəʊ/ obwohl II:2/B6
°though *(nachgestellt)* /ðəʊ/ jedoch IV:BS/6
thought /θɔːt/ Gedanke II:4/B3
thought bubble /ˈθɔːt ˌbʌbl/ Gedankenblase IV:3/A8
thousand /ˈθaʊznd/ tausend II:1/B11
threat /θret/ Drohung II:5/B10
threat /θret/ Bedrohung, Gefahr IV:6/Project B p. 125
threaten /ˈθretn/ *(be)*drohen II:5/B9
through /θruː/ durch II:3/A12
throughout /θruːˈaʊt/ im ganzen/in der ganzen IV:5/A3
throw *(irr)* /θrəʊ/ werfen III:2/B4
throw away /ˌθrəʊ‿əˈweɪ/ wegwerfen IV:6/Project B p. 126
Thursday /ˈθɜːzdeɪ/ Donnerstag I:1/B2
tidy /ˈtaɪdi/ ordentlich; aufgeräumt I:4/A2; aufräumen I:4/A6
tie /taɪ/ Krawatte I:5/A2
tie /taɪ/ binden IV:2/B7
tiger /ˈtaɪɡə/ Tiger I:WB/1
till /tɪl/ bis I:3/A5
time /taɪm/ Zeit I:2/A12; *hier:* Mal II:1/B1
all the time /ˌɔːl ðə ˈtaɪm/ die ganze Zeit II:4/B5
free time /friː ˈtaɪm/ Freizeit I:3/I
in time /ɪn ˈtaɪm/ rechtzeitig; pünktlich II:5/B9
What time is it? /wɒt‿ˈtaɪm‿ɪz‿ɪt/ Wie spät ist es? I:2/B1
at that time /æt ˈðæt‿taɪm/ zu jener Zeit IV:5/A2
running time /ˈrʌnɪŋ taɪm/ Laufzeit IV:3/A10
timeline /ˈtaɪmlaɪn/ Zeitachse IV:5/A11
many times /ˌmeni ˈtaɪmz/ oft II:6/A2
timetable /ˈtaɪmteɪbl/ Stundenplan I:5/A3
°tingling /ˈtɪŋɡlɪŋ/ Kribbeln IV:BS/6
tiny /ˈtaɪni/ winzig IV:1/B5
tip /tɪp/ Tipp IV:1/I
tired /ˈtaɪəd/ müde II:4/A3
title /ˈtaɪtl/ Titel; Überschrift II:3/B9
to /tʊ/ in; nach; zu I:Welcome; *hier:* vor I:2/B7; (um) zu II:3/A6
°to /tʊ/ *hier:* für IV:BS/10
to-do list /təˈduː ˌlɪst/ To-do-Liste IV:4/B4
today /təˈdeɪ/ heute I:3/B6
toe /təʊ/ Zeh II:6/B4
together /təˈɡeðə/ zusammen II:1/B1
toilet /ˈtɔɪlət/ Toilette II:4/A7
tomato (*pl* tomatoes) /təˈmɑːtəʊ, təˈmɑːtəʊz/ Tomate I:1/A4
tomorrow /təˈmɒrəʊ/ morgen II:3/A6
tomorrow morning /təˌmɒrəʊ ˈmɔːnɪŋ/ morgen Vormittag II:4/B5
ton /tʌn/ Tonne IV:6/Project B p. 126
tonight /təˈnaɪt/ heute Abend I:4/B9
too /tuː/ auch I:1/B2; zu II:1/B7
tool /tuːl/ Werkzeug IV:6/Project p. 132
tooth (*pl* teeth) /tuːθ, tiːθ/ Zahn I:2/A1
toothbrush /ˈtuːθbrʌʃ/ Zahnbürste I:WB/1
toothpaste /ˈtuːθpeɪst/ Zahnpasta I:2/A1

top /tɒp/ oberes Ende; Spitze IV:2/B7; beste(r, s) III:2/B8
top /tɒp/ oberste(r, s) IV:5/A7
on top /ˌɒn ˈtɒp/ (oben) auf II:2/A2
to the top /tʊ ðə ˈtɒp/ nach oben IV:1/B2
topic /ˈtɒpɪk/ Thema III:6/I
topping /ˈtɒpɪŋ/ *hier:* Belag IV:5/B7
torch (*pl* **torches**) /tɔːtʃ, ˈtɔːtʃɪz/ Taschenlampe I:4/B10
°torn /tɔːn/ hin- und hergerissen IV:BS/6
total /ˈtəʊtl/ Gesamtsumme IV:6/Project p. 132
total /ˈtəʊtl/ gesamt; völlig IV:5/A7
totally /ˈtəʊtli/ völlig, total IV:1/A7
touch /tʌtʃ/ berühren III:3/A1
touchdown /ˈtʌtʃˌdaʊn/ Versuch, Touchdown IV:1/A5
°tour /tʊə/ auf Tour gehen; besuchen IV:BS/10
take sb on a tour /ˌteɪk ˌsʌmbadi‿ɒn‿ə ˈtʊə/ mit jdm einen Ausflug machen IV:1/B2
°touring /ˈtʊərɪŋ/ Tournee- IV:BS/10
°toward(s) /təˈwɔːd(z)/ in Richtung, zu; gegenüber IV:3/O
tower /ˈtaʊə/ Turm II:2/A2
town /taʊn/ Stadt I:1/A9
toxic /ˈtɒksɪk/ giftig IV:6/I
toy /tɔɪ/ Spielzeug IV:6/Project B p. 125
cuddly toy /ˌkʌdli ˈtɔɪ/ Kuscheltier I:3/B5
toy car /ˌtɔɪ ˈkɑː/ Spielzeugauto I:3/B5
trace /treɪs/ Spur IV:6/Project C p. 128
trading company /ˈtreɪdɪŋ ˌkʌmpni/ Handelsgesellschaft IV:6/Project C p. 128
traditional /trəˈdɪʃnəl/ traditionell IV:1/A7
traffic /ˈtræfɪk/ Verkehr IV:6/Project p. 117
tragically /ˈtrædʒɪkli/ tragisch IV:3/B3
trailer /ˈtreɪlə/ Wohnwagen IV:2/B2
trailer park /ˈtreɪlə pɑːk/ Wohnwagenabstellplatz IV:2/B2
train /treɪn/ Zug I:3/B5
train /treɪn/ trainieren IV:2/A4
catch a train /ˌkætʃ‿ə ˈtreɪn/ einen Zug nehmen II:2/A2
trainers /ˈtreɪnəz/ Turnschuhe I:WB/1
training /ˈtreɪnɪŋ/ Ausbildung, Schulung IV:4/I
transgender /trænsˈdʒendə/ transsexuell IV:2/A6
public transport /ˌpʌblɪk ˈtrænspɔːt/ öffentliche Verkehrsmittel IV:6/Project A p. 120
transport /trænsˈpɔːt/ transportieren IV:6/Project B p. 125
transport /ˈtrænspɔːt/ Transport, Verkehrsmittel IV:6/Project A p. 134
trash *(AE)* /træʃ/ Müll, Abfall IV:2/B2
travel /ˈtrævl/ reisen II:1/A11
travel agency /ˈtrævl‿ˌeɪdʒnsi/ Reisebüro IV:4/P9
travel blog /ˈtrævl blɒg/ Reiseblog IV:1/I
travel caution /ˈtrævl ˌkɔːʃn/ *etwa:* Reisewarnung IV:5/A8
travel guide /ˈtrævl ˌgaɪd/ Reiseführer IV:1/B10
°treat /triːt/ behandeln IV:4/O
tree /triː/ Baum II:3/A8
No trespassing! /ˌnəʊ ˈtrespəsɪŋ/ Kein Durchgang! IV:5/A8
°tribe /traɪb/ Stamm IV:BS/1
trip /trɪp/ Reise; Fahrt III:2/A7
°trouble /ˈtrʌbl/ Ärger; Schwierigkeiten IV:4/O
get into trouble /ˌget‿ɪntʊ ˈtrʌbl/ in Schwierigkeiten geraten II:5/B11
(a pair of) trousers /ˈtraʊzəz/ Hose I:WB/1
truck /trʌk/ Lastwagen IV:1/B5
true /truː/ wahr II:1/B7
truly /ˈtruːli/ wirklich, wahrhaftig IV:3/A10
truth /truːθ/ Wahrheit II:4/A7
try /traɪ/ probieren; versuchen II:1/B1
try on /ˌtraɪ‿ˈɒn/ anprobieren III:2/A8
take the tube /ˌteɪk ðə ˈtjuːb/ die U-Bahn nehmen I:4/B3
Tuesday /ˈtjuːzdeɪ/ Dienstag I:1/B2
tummy *(informal)* /ˈtʌmi/ Bauch I:2/A1
turkey /ˈtɜːki/ Truthahn, Pute IV:1/A7
Turkey /ˈtɜːki/ Türkei IV:5/B5
Turkish /ˈtɜːkɪʃ/ Türkisch IV:5/B8
turn /tɜːn/ abbiegen II:2/B7
be one's turn /ˌbiː wʌnz ˈtɜːn/ an der Reihe sein I:4/B1
turn around /ˌtɜːn‿əˈraʊnd/ sich umdrehen II:1/B3
turn into /ˌtɜːn‿ˈɪntʊ/ umwandeln in IV:4/A14
turn off /ˌtɜːn‿ˈɒf/ ausschalten II:5/A6
turn on /ˌtɜːn‿ˈɒn/ einschalten I:3/B6
turn out /ˌtɜːn‿ˈaʊt/ ausschalten I:4/B1
turn over the soil /ˌtɜːn‿ˌəʊvə ðə ˈsɔɪl/ den Boden umgraben IV:2/B7
turtle /ˈtɜːtl/ Schildkröte IV:6/Project B p. 125
TV (= television) /ˌtiː ˈviː, ˈtelɪˌvɪʒn/ Fernseher; Fernsehen III:5/B1
watch TV /ˌwɒtʃ tiː ˈviː/ Fernsehen gucken I:3/B8
twice /twaɪs/ zweimal III:3/A4
type in /ˌtaɪp‿ˈɪn/ eingeben IV:6/Project p. 118
typical /ˈtɪpɪkl/ typisch III:1/B11
typing /ˈtaɪpɪŋ/ Maschineschreiben IV:4/B6

the UK (= United Kingdom) /ðə ˌjuː ˈkeɪ, juːˌnaɪtɪd ˈkɪŋdəm/ Vereinigtes Königreich IV:3/A10
uncle /ˈʌŋkl/ Onkel I:5/B3

under /ˈʌndə/ unter I:4/A3
underline /ˌʌndəˈlaɪn/ unterstreichen IV:4/A14
understand *(irr)* /ˌʌndəˈstænd/ verstehen I:3/A4
I don't understand. /ˌaɪ ˌdəʊnt‿ˌʌndəˈstænd/ Ich verstehe es nicht. I:3/A4
°unemployed /ˌʌnɪmˈplɔɪd/ arbeitslos IV:BS/8
unfriendly /ʌnˈfrenli/ unfreundlich III:4/B4
unhappy /ʌnˈhæpi/ unglücklich III:4/A2
unique /juːˈniːk/ einzigartig IV:6/Project B p. 127
the United Nations /ðə juːˌnaɪtɪd ˈneɪʃnz/ die Vereinten Nationen IV:2/B8
the United States /ðə juːˌnaɪtɪd ˈsteɪts/ die Vereinigten Staaten II:6/B2
university /ˌjuːnɪˈvɜːsəti/ Universität IV:5/B5
unsafe /ʌnˈseɪf/ unsicher; gefährlich IV:5/B3
unscramble /ʌnˈskræmbl/ wieder ordnen IV:1/P4
untidy /ʌnˈtaɪdi/ unordentlich; unaufgeräumt I:4/A2
until /ənˈtɪl/ bis II:1/B7
unused /ʌnˈjuːzd/ unbenutzt IV:6/Project A p. 123
unusual /ʌnˈjuːʒuəl/ ungewöhnlich IV:4/A6
up /ʌp/ nach oben; hinauf; oben III:3/A1
What's up? *(informal)* /ˌwɒts‿ˈʌp/ Was ist los? II:1/B7
up close /ʌp ˈkləʊs/ aus der Nähe IV:1/B2
up there /ˌʌp ˈðeə/ dort oben IV:1/B2
up to /ˈʌp tuː/ bis (zu) II:2/B11
upon /əˈpɒn/ auf; an IV:5/A3
upset /ʌpˈset/ aufgeregt; traurig III:4/B1
upstairs /ˌʌpˈsteəz/ (nach) oben II:6/A9
°uptown /ʌpˈtaʊn/ im Norden IV:BS/9
urban /ˈɜːrbən/ städtisch IV:6/Project p. 118

us /ʌs/ uns I:2/A8
(the) US (= United States) /ðə ˌju‿ˈes, juːˌnaɪtɪd ˈsteɪts/ US, Vereinigte Staaten (von Amerika); US- IV:Quiz
the USA (= United States of America) /ðə ˌju‿es‿ˈeɪ, juːˌnaɪtɪd ˌsteɪts‿əv‿əˈmerɪkə/ USA, Vereinigte Staaten von Amerika III:5/B3
use /juːz/ benutzen I:2/A13
use /juːs/ Verwendung; Einsatz IV:6/Project B p. 126
use up /ˌjuːz‿ˈʌp/ verbrauchen IV:6/Project C p. 131
useful /ˈjuːsfl/ nützlich II:3/A8
usually /ˈjuːʒuəli/ gewöhnlich; normalerweise I:4/A6

vacuum /ˈvækjuəm/ staubsaugen I:4/A6
valley /ˈvæli/ Tal IV:5/A10
variety /vəˈraɪəti/ Vielfalt IV:1/A4
vegetable /ˈvedʒtəbl/ Gemüse I:4/B5
vegetarian /ˌvedʒəˈteəriən/ Vegetarier/in; vegetarisch III:1/A3
veggie *(informal)* /ˈvedʒi, ˈvedʒtəbl/ Gemüse II:5/A6
version /ˈvɜːʃn/ Version, Fassung IV:3/B1
vertical /ˈvɜːtɪkl/ vertikal; senkrecht IV:6/Project p. 118
very /ˈveri/ sehr I:1/B2
the very first /ðə ˌveri ˈfɜːst/ der/die/das allererste IV:Quiz
vet /vet/ Tierarzt/-ärztin II:3/A8
°victim /ˈvɪktɪm/ Opfer IV:5/O
view /vjuː/ (Aus)sicht IV:1/B2
village /ˈvɪlɪdʒ/ Dorf II:1/B7
village elder /ˌvɪlɪdʒ‿ˈeldə/ Dorfälteste/r IV:2/B7
vine /vaɪn/ Rankengewächs IV:2/B7
violence /ˈvaɪələns/ Gewalt IV:5/A9
violin /ˌvaɪəˈlɪn/ Violine; Geige IV:4/A6
violinist /ˌvaɪəˈlɪnɪst/ Violinist/in; Geiger/in IV:4/A6

virtuous /ˈvɜːtʃʊəs/ tugendhaft; rechtschaffen IV:3/B8
°vision /ˈvɪʒn/ Vorstellung; Vision IV:5/O
visit /ˈvɪzɪt/ besuchen I:3/A1; Besuch I:4/B1
°visual /ˈvɪʒʊəl/ visuell, bildlich IV:1/O
°visualise /ˈvɪʒʊəlaɪz/ visualisieren; sichtbar machen IV:5/O
vocational /vəʊˈkeɪʃnəl/ beruflich IV:4/I
voice /vɔɪs/ Stimme IV:1/B8
volunteer /ˌvɒlənˈtɪə/ sich freiwillig melden; ehrenamtlich arbeiten IV:6/Project A p. 123
vote /vəʊt/ Stimme; Abstimmung, Wahl III:2/A11
voyage /ˈvɔɪɪdʒ/ Reise; Seereise IV:5/A3

W

wage /ˈweɪdʒ/ Lohn IV:6/Project C p. 130
wait /weɪt/ (er)warten III:3/A9
wait for /ˈweɪt fɔː/ warten auf I:4/A11
°wait in line /ˌweɪt‿ɪn ˈlaɪn/ in der Schlange stehen IV:BS/7
waiter/waitress /ˈweɪtə, ˈweɪtrəs/ Kellner/in II:1/B11
waiting room /ˈweɪtɪŋ ˌruːm/ Wartezimmer III:3/B1
wake sb up /ˌweɪk ˌsʌmbədi‿ˈʌp/ jdn aufwecken IV:3/B1
wake up /ˌweɪk‿ˈʌp/ aufwachen III:3/B7
walk /wɔːk/ gehen I:4/B3
°walk out /ˌwɔːk‿ˈaʊt/ gehen IV:BS/3
walk the dog /ˌwɔːk ðə ˈdɒg/ den Hund ausführen I:5/A4
wall /wɔːl/ Wand I:2/B1
wall painting /ˈwɔːl ˌpeɪntɪŋ/ Wandgemälde IV:4/A7
°wanna (= want to) *(informal)* /ˈwɒnə/ wollen IV:BS/6
want /wɒnt/ wollen I:1/B2
war /wɔː/ Krieg IV:5/B2
°war hero /ˈwɔː ˌhɪərəʊ/ Kriegsheld/in IV:BS/10

wardrobe /ˈwɔːdrəʊb/ Schrank I:Welcome
warm /wɔːm/ warm I:WB/1
warn /wɔːn/ warnen III:2/B9
warning /ˈwɔːnɪŋ/ Warnung IV:2/A8
health warning /ˈhelθ ˌwɔːnɪŋ/ Warnhinweis IV:2/A8
warrior /ˈwɒriə/ Krieger/in IV:5/B7
wash /wɒʃ/ waschen; sich waschen I:2/A1
do the washing up /ˌduː ðə ˌwɒʃɪŋ‿ˈʌp/ abspülen I:4/A6
washroom *(AE)* /ˈwɒʃˌruːm/ Toilette IV:1/B5
°wasp /wɒsp/ Wespe IV:BS/4
waste /weɪst/ verschwenden IV:2/B8; Abfall IV:6/Project A p. 122
watch /wɒtʃ/ beobachten; ansehen I:4/B1; Uhr III:2/B9
watch TV /ˌwɒtʃ tiː ˈviː/ Fernsehen gucken I:3/B8
water /ˈwɔːtə/ Wasser I:2/A2
water system /ˈwɔːtə ˌsɪstəm/ Wasseranlage IV:4/A1
way /weɪ/ Weg; Art; Weise I:4/B3
we /wiː/ wir I:Welcome
weak /wiːk/ schwach IV:5/A10
wealthy /ˈwelθi/ reich; wohlhabend IV:3/B8
wear *(irr)* /weə/ tragen I:Welcome
°weary /ˈwɪəri/ müde; erschöpft IV:BS/9
weather /ˈweðə/ Wetter I:Welcome
Wednesday /ˈwenzdeɪ/ Mittwoch I:1/B2
weed /wiːd/ Unkraut IV:6/Project C p. 136
week /wiːk/ Woche I:4/A11
all week /ˌɔːl ˈwiːk/ die ganze Woche lang II:6/A2
weekend /ˌwiːkˈend/ Wochenende I:4/B1
at the weekend /ˌæt‿ðə ˈwiːkend/ am Wochenende I:2/A12
weight /weɪt/ Gewicht III:4/B1
°weird /wɪəd/ merkwürdig; seltsam IV:BS/6

welcome /ˈwelkəm/ willkommen II:6/B11
well /wel/ nun I:3/A5; gut II:3/A12; gesund II:6/A12
Get well soon! /ˌget ˌwel ˈsuːn/ Gute Besserung! II:6/A12
well done /ˌwel ˈdʌn/ gut gemacht II:1/B3
°well-known /ˌwelˈnəʊn/ bekannt; berühmt IV:BS/9
well-organised /ˌwel‿ˈɔːgənaɪzd/ gut organisiert IV:4/A13
well-paid /ˌwel ˈpeɪd/ gut bezahlt IV:4/A1
wellie /ˈweli/ Gummistiefel I:WB/1
were /wɜː/ wäre(st, n, t) IV:3/A7
west /west/ Westen III:4/A9
wet /wet/ nass I:2/A2
wet season /ˌwet ˈsiːzn/ Regenzeit IV:2/B7
whale /weɪl/ Wal IV:6/Project B p. 125
what /wɒt/ was; welche(r, s) I:Welcome …
What about …? /ˌwɒt‿əˌbaʊt ˈ…/ Was ist mit …?/Wie wäre es mit …? I:Welcome
What do you think? /ˌwɒt‿də jə ˈθɪŋk/ Was hältst du davon? I:Welcome
what else /ˌwɒt‿ˈels/ was sonst I:2/A8
what makes sb tick /wɒt ˌmeɪks‿ˌsʌmbədi ˈtɪk/ was jdn bewegt IV:5/A1
What time is it? /wɒt‿ˈtaɪm‿ɪz‿ɪt/ Wie spät ist es? I:2/B1
What's on? /ˌwɒts‿ˈɒn/ Was ist los? I:3/A1
What's up? *(informal)* /ˌwɒts‿ˈʌp/ Was ist los? II:1/B7
What's your name? /ˌwɒts jə ˈneɪm/ Wie heißt du? I:Welcome …
What's your phone number? /ˌwɒts jə ˈfəʊn‿nʌmbə/ Was ist deine Telefonnummer? I:Welcome
whatever /wɒtˈevə/ was (auch immer) IV:3/A4

wheelchair /ˈwiːltʃeə/ Rollstuhl II:Last year
when /wen/ wann I:2/B7; wenn; als I:5/B11
whenever /wenˈevə/ wann auch immer IV:4/A7
where /weə/ wo; wohin I:1/A3
Where are you from? /ˌweər‿ə jʊ ˈfrɒm/ Woher kommst du? I:1/A3
whether /ˈweðə/ ob IV:3/A7
which /wɪtʃ/ welche(r, s); was I:3/A4
while /waɪl/ während II:2/B11
while /waɪl/ Weile IV:1/A2
whisper /ˈwɪspə/ flüstern; wispern IV:5/A10
white /waɪt/ weiß I:Welcome
who /huː/ wer; der/die/das I:1/A5
whoever /huːˈevə/ wer auch immer IV:3/A7
whole /həʊl/ ganz, gesamt IV:4/B3
whom /huːm/ wem; wen; der/die/das IV:3/B8
whose /huːz/ wessen I:5/B7
why /waɪ/ warum I:3/B7
wife (*pl* wives) /waɪf, waɪvz/ Ehefrau IV:3/B3
WiFi /ˈwaɪ faɪ/ WLAN III:1/A9
wildlife /ˈwaɪldˌlaɪf/ Tier- und Pflanzenwelt; Flora und Fauna IV:6/Project B p. 124
will /wɪl/ werden II:1/B7
win *(irr)* /wɪn/ gewinnen II:1/B3
wind /wɪnd/ Wind I:WB/1
windmill /ˈwɪnˌmɪl/ Windmühle IV:2/B6
window /ˈwɪndəʊ/ Fenster I:2/B1
windy /ˈwɪndi/ windig I:WB/1
wing /wɪŋ/ Flügel IV:3/B1
winner /ˈwɪnə/ Gewinner/in II:1/B3
winter /ˈwɪntə/ Winter I:Welcome
wise /waɪz/ weise IV:3/B8
wish /wɪʃ/ wünschen IV:5/B7; Wunsch IV:BS/5
°wishbone /ˈwɪʃˌbəʊn/ Gabelbein IV:BS/5
best wishes /ˌbest ˈwɪʃɪz/ viele Grüße II:6/A8

with /wɪð/ mit; bei I:Welcome
withal *(veraltet, nachgestellt)* /wɪð'ɔ:l/ mit IV:3/B8
within /wɪð'ɪn/ innerhalb IV:5/B3
without /wɪð'aʊt/ ohne II:1/B6
woman (*pl* **women**) /'wʊmən, 'wɪmɪn/ Frau I:5/B7
won't /wəʊnt/ nicht werden II:3/A1
wonder /'wʌndə/ sich fragen II:4/A7
wonderful /'wʌndəfl/ wunderbar, wundervoll II:1/A7
wood /wʊd/ Holz II:4/A7
wooden /'wʊdn/ Holz-, hölzern IV:2/B7
wool /wʊl/ Wolle IV:6/Project C p. 131
word /wɜ:d/ Wort I:2/B9
word web /'wɜ:d web/ Wortnetz IV:1/A8
wordbank /'wɜ:dbæŋk/ Wortfeld IV:6/Project p. 118
work /wɜ:k/ arbeiten I:5/A7; *hier:* funktionieren II:5/B2; Arbeit; Werk III:2/B4
work experience /'wɜ:k‿ɪkˌspɪəriəns/ Praktikum; Berufserfahrung IV:4/B3
work of art /ˌwɜ:k‿əv‿'ɑ:t/ Kunstwerk IV:4/A7
work out /ˌwɜ:k‿'aʊt/ errechnen; ausarbeiten IV:4/B7; *hier:* eine Lösung finden IV:BS/6
work placement /'wɜ:k ˌpleɪsmənt/ Praktikum, Praktikumsstelle IV:4/B6
workbook /'wɜ:kbʊk/ Arbeitsheft IV:2/B2
worker /'wɜ:kə/ Arbeiter/in IV:6/Project C p. 130
working day /'wɜ:kɪŋ deɪ/ Arbeitstag II:4/A1
world /wɜ:ld/ Welt I:5/A7
all over the world /ˌɔ:l‿ˌəʊvə ðə 'wɜ:ld/ auf der ganzen Welt IV:2/I
°all around the world /ˌɔ:l‿əˌraʊnd ðə 'wɜ:ld/ überall auf der Welt IV:1/O
worldwide /ˌwɜ:ld'waɪd/ weltweit IV:6/Project C p. 130
worry /'wʌri/ sich Sorgen machen III:4/B2
worried /'wʌrid/ beunruhigt; besorgt II:5/A1
Don't worry. /ˌdəʊnt 'wʌri/ Mach dir keine Sorgen. II:3/B1
worse /wɜ:s/ schlimmer III:5/A6
worst /wɜ:st/ schlimmste(r, s) III:2/B5
worth /wɜ:θ/ (lohnens)wert III:2/B5
worthless /'wɜ:θləs/ wertlos IV:2/A6
would /wʊd/ würde(st, n, t) II:2/A3
Would you like ...? /ˌwʊd ju: 'laɪk/ Hättest du gern ...?/Hättet ihr gern ...? I:4/B9
wrap /ræp/ einwickeln IV:6/Project B p. 126
wrestling /'reslɪŋ/ Ringkampf IV:1/A6
write *(irr)* /raɪt/ schreiben I:2/A13
write down /ˌraɪt‿'daʊn/ aufschreiben IV:1/A2
writer /'raɪtə/ Autor/in IV:5/A1
wrong /rɒŋ/ falsch II:3/A1

yard /jɑ:d/ *hier:* Yard *(Maßeinheit)* IV:1/A5
year /jɪə/ Jahr I:Welcome ...; Schuljahr, Klasse I:5/A3
yellow /'jeləʊ/ gelb I:Welcome
yellow cab *(AE)* /'jeləʊ kæb/ Taxi IV:1/B2
yes /jes/ ja I:Welcome
yesterday /'jestədeɪ/ gestern II:1/B6
yet /jet/ schon; noch IV:4/A10
°yet /jet/ *hier:* aber IV:5/O
not yet /nɒt 'jet/ noch nicht II:2/B2
you /ju:/ du; dich; dir; man; ihr; euch; Sie; Ihnen I:Welcome ...
You must be joking! *(informal)* /ju: məs bi 'dʒəʊkɪŋ/ Das meinst du doch nicht im Ernst!, Das soll wohl ein Witz sein! II:3/A1
You're right. /ˌjɔ: 'raɪt/ Du hast recht. I:5/A2
You're welcome. /ˌjɔ: 'welkəm/ Gern geschehen.; Keine Ursache. III:1/A7
young /jʌŋ/ jung II:4/A1
your /jɔ:/ dein(e); euer/eure I:Welcome ...
yours /jɔ:z/ deine(r, s); eure(r, s); Ihre(r, s) III:1/A7
yourself (*pl* **yourselves**) /jɔ:'self, jɔ:'selvz/ dich I:3/B6
youth /ju:θ/ Jugend; Jugendliche/r IV:2/I
youth club /'ju:θ ˌklʌb/ Jugendzentrum I:5/A7

Z

Zanzibar /'zænzɪbɑ:/ Sansibar IV:6/Project B p. 125
zoo /zu:/ Zoo I:WB/1
zoo-keeper /'zu:ˌki:pə/ Tierpfleger/in; Wärter/in II:2/B2

A

abbiegen turn
Abend evening
heute Abend tonight
gestern Abend last night
Abend night
Abendessen dinner
abends *(nur hinter Uhrzeit zwischen 12 Uhr mittags und Mitternacht)* pm (= post meridiem)
Abenteuer adventure
aber but
abfahren leave *(irr)*
Abfall litter
Abfalleimer bin
jdn abholen pick sb up
Absatz, Abschnitt paragraph
abspülen do the washing up
darauf achten, dass ... make sure
achten auf care
Affe monkey
Afroamerikaner/in; afroamerikanisch African American
AG; Klub club
Aktivität activity
albern silly
alle all; everybody; everyone
alle möglichen all kinds of
allein alone
von alleine on its own
alles everything; all
Alphabet alphabet
als than
als; wenn when
als; wie; während as
also so
alt old
Wie alt bist du? How old are you?
Alter age
am liebsten best
am liebsten mögen like best
am Morgen in the morning
am Nachmittag in the afternoon
am Telefon on the phone
am Wochenende at the weekend
Amerika America
Amerikaner/in; amerikanisch American
amerikanische/r Ureinwohner/in Native American
sich amüsieren enjoy oneself
an at; about; on
an der Reihe sein be one's turn
anbieten offer
andere(r, s) other
ein anderer/ein anderes/ eine andere another
ändern change
anders else
anders; andere(r, s) different
anfangen start; begin *(irr)*
sich anfreunden (mit) make friends (with)
angreifen attack
Angst fear
Angst haben (vor) be scared (of); be afraid (of)
anhalten stop
sich anhören, klingen sound
ankämpfen gegen fight *(irr)*
ankommen arrive
ankommen auf count
(an)malen paint
annehmen guess; suppose
anprobieren try on
Anruf call
anrufen call; phone; ring *(irr)*
ans Telefon gehen answer the phone
anschließend afterwards
(an)sehen, (an)schauen look (at); watch
Ansicht opinion
Ansichtskarte postcard
anstarren stare at
anstatt instead of
anstrengend hard
Antwort answer; response
(be)antworten answer; reply
Anweisung instruction
Anzeige advertisement (= advert)
anziehen put on
Apfel apple
Apfelsine orange
Apparat machine
April April
Arbeit; Werk work
arbeiten work
Arbeitgeber/in employer
arbeitslos out of work
arbeitsreich busy
Arbeitstag working day
arm poor
Art kind; way
Artikel article
Arzt/Ärztin doctor
außer Atem sein; atemlos sein be out of breath
attraktiv; reizvoll attractive
auch too; also; as well
auch nicht not ... either
auf on
(oben) auf on top
auf der Straße in the street
auf Deutsch in German
auf Englisch in English
Auf Wiedersehen. Goodbye.
aufbauen set up
aufbewahren keep *(irr)*
Geld aufbringen raise money
Aufführung performance
Aufgabe task; job
aufgeben give up
aufgehen; steigen rise *(irr)*
aufgeräumt tidy
aufgeregt excited, excitedly
aufgeregt; traurig upset
aufhängen put up
aufhören stop
Aufkleber sticker
aufladen charge
auflegen put on
auflisten list
aufmachen open
aufnehmen record
aufpassen auf look after
aufräumen tidy
aufregend exciting
aufstehen get up
auftragen put on
aufwachen wake up
jemanden aufwecken wake somebody up
Auge eye
August August
aus from; out of; out
Ausbildung education
Ausbildung, Schulung training
sich ausdenken, denken an think of
sich ausdenken, erfinden make up
Ausdruck; Satz phrase
den Hund ausführen walk the dog
ausgeben spend *(irr)*
Geld ausgeben für spend money on
ausgehen go out
im Ausland, ins Ausland abroad
ins Ausland fahren go abroad
ausleeren; ausräumen empty
(aus)leihen borrow
Ausrüstung equipment; gear
ausschalten switch off; turn out; turn off
aussehen look
gut aussehend good-looking; handsome
außen; (nach) draußen outside
außer except
außer Atem sein; atemlos sein be out of breath
außerhalb; vor outside
außerordentlich extremely
äußerst, höchst extremely
äußerste(r, s) extreme
Ausstattung equipment
nicht ausstehen können hate
aussteigen get out
Ausstellung exhibition
Auswahl selection
auswandern emigrate
auswärts essen eat out
Auto car
Autor/in writer

backen cook
Bäcker/in baker
Badezimmer bathroom
Bahnhof (railway) station
Bahnsteig platform
bald soon
Banane banana
Bauch tummy *(informal)*
Bauchschmerzen stomach ache
bauen build *(irr)*
Bauer/Bäuerin farmer
Bauernhof farm
Baum tree
Baumwolle; Baumwoll- cotton
(be)antworten answer
bearbeiten edit
Becher mug
bedecken cover
bedeckt cloudy
bedeuten; meinen mean *(irr)*
Bedeutung meaning
bedienen serve
(be)drohen threaten
sich beeilen hurry (up)
Beeil dich! Hurry up!
beeindruckend impressive; awesome
beenden end; finish
sich befassen mit deal with
beginnen start; begin *(irr)*
Begriff term
behalten keep *(irr)*
bei with; at
beide both
Beilage side (dish)
Bein leg
beinahe almost; nearly
Beispiel example
zum Beispiel for example
bekämpfen fight *(irr)*
bekannt geben announce
sich beklagen complain
bekommen get *(irr)*
belebt busy
beliebt popular
bemerken; wahrnehmen notice
benötigen take *(irr)*
benutzen use
beobachten watch
bequem comfortable
bereits already
Berg mountain
Beruf job
beruflich professional
Berufserfahrung work experience
berufstypische Qualifikationen hard skill
berühmt famous
berühren touch
beschädigen damage
beschäftigt busy
jemanden beschimpfen call somebody names
beschreiben describe
beschriften label
beschützen protect
besondere(r, s) special
besorgt worried
besprechen discuss
besser better
Gute Besserung! Get well soon!
bestellen order
Möchten Sie bestellen? Are you ready to order?
beste(r, s) best; top
Besuch visit
besuchen visit
Betrag amount
betreten enter
Betreuung care
Bett bed
beunruhigt worried
bevor before
bevorzugen prefer
sich bewegen move
Bewegung exercise
beweisen prove *(irr)*
sich bewerben um apply for
Bewohner/in resident
bewölkt cloudy
sich bewusst sein, erkennen realize (= realise)
sich einer Sache bewusst sein be aware of something
(be)zahlen pay *(irr)*
Beziehung relationship
Bild image; picture
Bild, Gemälde painting
Bilder machen take photos
Bildung education
Bildunterschrift caption
billig cheap
bis till; until
(spätestens) bis by
Bis bald! See you (soon)!
bis (zu) up to
ein (kleines) bisschen a (little) bit
bitte please
bitten ask
Blatt leaf (*pl* leaves); sheet *(Papier)*
blau blue
bleiben stay
Bleistift pencil
bloß only; just
Blume flower
Boden ground
Bogen sheet
Bohnen in Tomatensauce baked beans *(pl)*
Boot boat
Botschaft message
braten cook
brauchen need; take *(irr)*
braun brown
brechen break *(irr)*
Brief letter
Briefmarke stamp
Briefumschlag envelope
Brille glasses *(pl)*
bringen take *(irr)*
jemanden dazu bringen, etwas zu tun make somebody do something
britisch British
Brot bread
Brücke bridge
Bruder brother
Buch book
Bücherei library
Büchse can
Buchstabe letter
buchstabieren spell *(irr)*
Bühne stage
(Bundes)staat state
bunt colourful
Büro office
bürsten brush
mit dem Bus by bus
mit dem Bus fahren go by bus
Bushaltestelle bus stop

Chips crisps *(pl)*
Computerspielentwickler/in computer game designer
Cousin/e cousin
Creme; Salbe cream
Cupfinale, Pokalendspiel cup final

da because
daher so
dahin there
Dame; Frau lady
damit so that
danach after that
dankbar grateful
danke thank you, thanks
dann then
dann, als Nächstes next
darauf achten, dass ... make sure
Darbietung performance
das that
das ist, das kostet that's (= that is)
dass that
Datum date
dauern take *(irr)*
Daunendecke duvet
Debatte debate
den Tisch decken lay the table
dein(e) your
deine(r, s) yours
denken think *(irr)*
denken an, sich ausdenken think of
der/die/das the
der, die, das; jene(r, s) that
der/die/das; wer who
der/die/das Gleiche; der-/die-/dasselbe the same
der/die/das rote the red one
deshalb so

Detail, Einzelheit detail
deuten (auf) point (at/to)
Deutsch; deutsch German
auf Deutsch in German
Deutschland Germany
Dezember December
Diagramm chart
Dialog, Gespräch dialogue
dich yourself (*pl* yourselves); you
die grünen the green ones
die meisten; am meisten most
Dienstag Tuesday
diese(r, s) this
diese(r, s) hier this one
diese; das these (*pl* of this)
diese, jene those (*pl* of that)
Ding thing
dir you
direkt right
direkte Rede direct speech
Diskussion debate
diskutieren discuss
Doktor doctor
Donnerstag Thursday
Dorf village
dort there
dort (drüben) over there
dort ist; es gibt there is
dort sind; es gibt there are
Dose can
Jetzt bist du dran. Over to you.
(nach) drauβen outside
dreckig dirty
drinnen inside
dritte(r, s) third
(be)drohen threaten
Drohung threat
du you
Du hast recht. You're right.
nicht dürfen mustn't (= must not)
dumm silly; stupid
dunkel dark
durch through
durchfallen fail
durchschnittlich average
dürfen be allowed to; may

E

echt real
Ecke corner
Ei egg
Eichhörnchen squirrel
eigene(r, s) own; of one's own
eigentlich actually
ein Paar a pair of
ein(e) a/an
noch ein/e another
einander each other
Eindruck impression
eines Tages one day
einfach just; easy
einige some; several; few
einkaufen do the shopping
Einkaufen; Einkaufs- shopping
Einkaufen gehen go shopping
einladen invite
Einladung invitation
Einleitung introduction
einmal once
einsam lonely
einschalten turn on; switch on
einschlafen fall asleep
Einwanderer/in immigrant
Einwanderung immigration
Einwohner/in, Bewohner/in inhabitant
Eis ice cream
Eisbär polar bear
Elefant elephant
elektrisch electric
Elektrizität, Strom electricity
Elektro- electric
Eltern parents *(pl)*
empfehlen recommend
Ende end
enden end; finish
endlich at last; finally
Energie energy
eng narrow
Englisch; englisch English
auf Englisch in English
Enkel grandson
Enkelin granddaughter
entdecken discover
entfernen remove
entkommen escape
entscheiden; sich entscheiden decide
sich entscheiden; wählen choose *(irr)*
Entschuldigen Sie bitte!, Entschuldigung! Excuse me!
Entschuldigung., Es tut mir leid. I'm sorry.; Sorry.
entweder ... oder ... either ... or ...
entwerfen design
entwickeln develop
Entwicklung development
er he
erarbeiten develop
Erde earth
Erdkunde geography
Ereignis, Veranstaltung event
Erfahrung experience
erfinden invent
erfinden, sich ausdenken make up
Erfinder/in inventor
Erfindung invention
erfolgreich successful
erfordern take *(irr)*
erforschen explore
Ergebnis result
erhalten; empfangen receive
sich erinnern an remember
Erkältung cold
erkennen recognise
erkennen, sich bewusst sein realize (= realise)
erklären explain
erlauben allow
ernähren feed *(irr)*
Das meinst du doch nicht im Ernst! You must be joking! *(informal)*
(er)raten guess
erreichen reach
erschaffen create
erscheinen, auftauchen appear
erstaunt surprised
erste(r, s) first
erster Weihnachtsfeiertag Christmas Day
erwachsen sein, erwachsen werden grow up
Erwachsene/r adult
(er)warten wait
erwidern reply
erzählen tell *(irr)*
erzeugen create
es it
Es geht mir gut, danke. I'm fine, thanks.
es kostet it's (= it is)
Es tut mir leid., Entschuldigung. Sorry.; I'm sorry.
Essen food
essen eat *(irr)*, have *(irr)*
auswärts essen; im Restaurant essen eat out
Essen meal
Essgewohnheit eating habit
Esslöffel tablespoon
etwas something
etwas; einige, ein paar some
noch etwas anything else
etwas tun können be able to do something
etwas tun werden be going to do something
etwas übrig haben have something left
etwas weiter tun keep doing something
euch you
euer/eure your
eure(r, s) yours
Europa Europe
Europäer/in; europäisch European
Experiment, Versuch experiment
extrem extreme

Fabrik factory
Fähigkeit ability; skill
Fähre ferry
fahren drive *(irr)*
fahren; gehen go *(irr)*
fahren; reiten ride *(irr)*
Fahrrad fahren ride a bike
in Urlaub fahren go on holiday
ins Ausland fahren go abroad
Fahrgast, Passagier/in passenger
Fahrrad bike; bicycle
mit dem Fahrrad by bike
Fahrrad fahren ride a bike
Fahrt trip
Fakt fact
fallen fall *(irr)*
falls; wenn if
falsch wrong
Familie family
fangen catch *(irr)*
fantastisch fantastic
Farbe colour
farbenfroh colourful
fast almost; nearly
Februar February
Federmäppchen pencil case
Feedback, Rückmeldung feedback
Fehler, Irrtum mistake
Feier celebration
feiern celebrate
Feind/in enemy
Feld field
Fels rock
Fenster window
Ferien holiday(s)
fern far
sich fernhalten von stay away from
Fernsehen; Fernseher TV (= television)
Fernsehen gucken watch TV
fertig, bereit ready
Fest festival
(fest)halten hold *(irr)*
Festival festival
Feuer fire
Feuerwerk fireworks *(pl)*
Fieber haben have a temperature
finden find *(irr)*
Fisch fish (*pl* fish *or* fishes)
fit bleiben, (sich) fit halten keep fit
Flasche bottle
Fledermaus bat
Fleisch meat
Fliege fly
fliegen fly *(irr)*
fliehen escape
Flug flight
Flughafen airport
Flugzeug plane
folgen follow
folgende(r, s) following
Folienkartoffel jacket potato
Foto photo
Fotoapparat camera
Frage question
fragen ask
sich fragen wonder
Fragen stellen ask questions
Frau woman (*pl* women); Mrs *(Anrede)*
Frau; Dame lady
frei; kostenlos free
Freitag Friday
Freizeit free time
Freund/in friend
Freund *(Partner)* boyfriend
Freundin *(Partnerin)* girlfriend
freundlich friendly
Freundschaft friendship
Frieden peace
frisch fresh
Friseur/in hairdresser, hair stylist
Frohes Neues Jahr! Happy New Year!
Frosch frog
Frucht fruit *(no pl)*
früh early
früher once
Frühling spring
Frühstück breakfast
zum Frühstück for breakfast
frühstücken have breakfast
frustriert frustrated
Fuchs fox
(sich) fühlen feel *(irr)*
führen lead *(irr)*
Führer/in guide
fünfte(r, s) fifth
funktionieren work
für for
Fuß foot (*pl* feet)
zu Fuß on foot
Fußball football
Fußballspieler/in football player
Fußboden floor
füttern feed *(irr)*

Gabel fork
ganz all
ganz, gesamt whole
den ganzen Nachmittag lang all afternoon
die ganze Zeit all the time
die ganze Woche lang all week
Garten garden
Gärtner/in gardener
Gast guest
Gebäude building
geben give *(irr)*
Gebet prayer
Gebiet, Region area
geboren werden be born
gebrochen; kaputt broken
Geburtstag birthday
Herzlichen Glückwunsch zum Geburtstag! Happy birthday (to you)!
Gedanke thought
Gedicht poem
geduldig patient
gefährlich dangerous
Gefangene/r prisoner
Gefühl feeling
gegen against
Gegenstand thing
gegenüberstehen face
gehen walk
gehen; fahren go *(irr)*
Lass(t) uns gehen! Let's go!
Schwimmen gehen go swimming
Einkaufen gehen go shopping
Wie geht es dir? / Wie geht es Ihnen? How are you?
Es geht mir gut, danke. I'm fine, thanks.
gehören zu go with, belong to
Geist ghost
gelangen get *(irr)*
gelb yellow
Geld money
Geld aufbringen raise money
Geld ausgeben für spend money on
(viel) Geld verdienen make (good) money
gut gemacht well done
gemäß according to
Gemeinde, Gemeinschaft community
Gemüse vegetable; veggie *(informal)*
genannt called
genannt werden, heißen (be) called
genau right; exactly
genau, bestimmte(r, s); spezifisch specific
genial, klasse brilliant
genießen enjoy
genug enough
geöffnet open
geprellt bruised
gerade just
geradeaus straight on
Geräusch sound; noise
Gericht dish (*pl* dishes)
etw gern tun like doing sth
Hättest du gern …? / Hättet ihr gern …? Would you like …?
etw sehr gern tun love doing sth
Gern geschehen. You're welcome.
gerne certainly
Geschäft business; shop
geschehen happen
Geschenk gift; present
Geschichte story; history
Geschick skill
geschickt skilful

Geschwister brothers and sisters
geschwollen swollen
gesellschaftlich; sozial social
Gesicht face
Gespenst ghost
Gespräch conversation; call
Gespräch, Dialog dialogue
gestern yesterday
gestern Abend last night
gestresst stressed
gesund well; healthy
Gesundheit health
Getränk drink
Gewicht weight
Gewinn prize
gewinnen win *(irr)*
Gewinner/in winner
gewöhnlich usually
Gewürz spice
es gibt there is/there are
Gibt es ...? Is there ...?/ Are there ...?
Giraffe giraffe
Gitarre guitar
Gitarre spielen play the guitar
Glas glass
glauben think *(irr)*
glauben (an) believe (in)
der/die/das Gleiche; der-/die-/dasselbe the same
Viel Glück! Good luck!
glücklich happy; lucky
glücklich, froh glad
Glückwunsch! Congratulations!
Herzlichen Glückwunsch zum Geburtstag! Happy birthday (to you)!
Goldfisch goldfish (*pl* goldfish)
Gras grass
gratis for free
Gratuliere! Congratulations!
grau grey
groß big; tall; large
groß; großartig great
Großbritannien Great Britain; Britain
Größe size
Großeltern grandparents *(pl)*
Großelternteil grandparent
Großmutter grandmother
Großvater grandfather
grün green
die grünen the green ones
Grund reason
Gruppe group
Grüße greetings *(pl)*
viele Grüße best wishes
Fernsehen gucken watch TV
Gummistiefel wellie
gut good; well
Es geht mir gut, danke. I'm fine, thanks.
in Ordnung, gut fine
gut aussehend good-looking; handsome
gut gemacht well done
gut in etwas sein be good at something
(gut) verdienen make (good) money
Gute Besserung! Get well soon!
Guten Morgen! Good morning!

H

Haar hair
haben have *(irr)*; have got
halb half
hallo hello
Hals neck
Halsschmerzen sore throat
halten keep *(irr)*
halten für; betrachten consider
Was hältst du davon? What do you think?
Hamster hamster
Handel business
handeln act
Handlung action
Handschuh glove
Handy mobile (phone)
hart hard
hassen hate
Hättest du gern ...?/ Hättet ihr gern ...? Would you like ...?
häufig often
Hauptgericht main (course)
Hauptstadt capital
Haus house; home
zu Hause at home
nach Hause home
Hausaufgaben homework
Haustier pet
Haut skin
Heft exercise book
Heiligabend Christmas Eve
heimlich secret
heiraten marry
heiß hot
heißen, genannt werden (be) called
Wie heißt du? What's your name?
Ich heiße ... My name is ...; I'm (= I am) ...
(heißer) Kakao hot chocolate
Held hero (*pl* heroes)
helfen help
Kann ich dir/Ihnen helfen? Can I help you?
hell bright
Hemd shirt
heraus, hinaus out
herausbringen release
herausfinden find out
Herausforderung challenge
herausgeben publish
Herbst autumn
Herr *(Anrede)* Mr
herstellen produce
herum, umher around
(herunter)fallen fall off
Herz heart
Herzlichen Glückwunsch zum Geburtstag! Happy birthday (to you)!
heute today
heute Abend tonight
heute Morgen this morning
hier; hierher here
Hier, bitte! Here you are.; Here you go.
hiesig local
Hilfe help
nach Hilfe, als Hilfe for help
hilfreich helpful
Himmel sky
hinauf up
auf etwas (hinauf)steigen climb
hinausbringen take out
(hinaus)gehen go out
hinein inside
sich hinsetzen sit down
hinten behind
hinter behind
Hintergrund background
hinüber; vorbei over
hinunter; (nach) unten down
hinzufügen add
hoch high
hoffen hope
Hoffnung hope
Holz wood
hören hear *(irr)*
Hose (a pair of) trousers
hübsch pretty
Huhn chicken
Hund dog
den Hund ausführen walk the dog
hungrig hungry
Hut hat

ich I; me
Ich mag ... nicht. I don't like ...
Ich nehme es. I'll take it.
Ich verstehe es nicht. I don't understand.
Ich weiß es nicht. I don't know.
Ich würde lieber ... I'd rather ...
Idee idea
identifizieren identify
Igel hedgehog
ignorieren ignore
ihm, ihn him
ihnen them
Ihnen you
ihr you
ihr/ihre her
ihr(e) their
ihre(r, s) hers

Ihre(r, s) yours
im Ausland, ins Ausland abroad
im Internet surfen surf the Internet
im Moment at the moment
immer always
(immer) noch still
Immigrant/in immigrant
Immigration immigration
in in; into; to; at; on
in der Mitte von in the middle of
in Ordnung all right; fine
in Schwierigkeiten geraten get into trouble
in Urlaub fahren go on holiday
individuell; einzeln individual
Industrie industry
Informationen information *(no pl)*
Informationstechnologie, IT ICT (= Information and Communication Technology)
Ingenieur/in engineer
inlineskaten skate
innen inside
Innenstadt city
innerhalb within
ins Ausland fahren go abroad
Insel island
insgesamt altogether
Instruktion instruction
intelligent; hell bright
interessant interesting
Interesse, Hobby interest
interessiert sein an be interested in
im Internet surfen surf the Internet
interviewen, befragen interview
(irgend)ein(e) any
irgendetwas anything
irgendjemand; jede(r, s) anybody
irgendwer somebody; someone
irgendwo anywhere; somewhere
Irland Ireland
Ist es ...? Is it ...?

J

ja yes
Jacke jacket
Jahr year
Frohes Neues Jahr! Happy New Year!
Jahrhundert century
Januar January
jede(r, s) every; each
jeder; alle everybody; everyone
jede(r, s); irgendjemand anybody
jedenfalls anyway
jemals ever
jemand somebody; someone
jene(r, s); der, die, das that
jene, diese those (*pl* of that)
jetzt now
Jetzt bist du dran. Over to you.
Job job
Jugend; Jugendliche/r youth
Jugendzentrum youth club
Juli July
jung young
Junge boy
Juni June

K

Kaffee coffee
Käfig cage
(heißer) Kakao hot chocolate
Kalender calendar
kalt cold
Kamera camera
Kampf; Streit fight
kämpfen fight *(irr)*
Kaninchen rabbit
Kann ich dir/Ihnen helfen? Can I help you?
Kapitel; Thema theme
kaputt broken
kaputt machen break *(irr)*
Karneval carnival
Karte map; card
Kartoffel potato (*pl* potatoes)
Käse cheese
Kasten box
Katze cat
kaufen buy *(irr)*; get *(irr)*
Kaufhaus department store
kaum hardly
kein(e) no; not any
Keine Ursache. You're welcome.
keiner no-one, no one; nobody; none
Keks biscuit
Kellner/in waiter/waitress
kennen know *(irr)*
jemanden kennenlernen get to know somebody
Kerze candle
Kind child (*pl* children); kid
Kino cinema
Kirche church
Kissen pillow
Kiste box
Klang sound
Klasse class; year
Klassenkamerad/in classmate
Klassenzimmer classroom
Kleid dress
Kleider, Kleidung clothes *(pl)*; clothing
klein little; small
ein (kleines) bisschen a (little) bit
klettern climb
klingeln ring *(irr)*
klingen, sich anhören sound
Klub; AG club
klug clever
knapp narrow
Knie knee
Knochen bone
Koch/Köchin cook
kochen do the cooking; cook
kochen *(Flüssigkeit)* boil
etwas tun können be able to do something
komisch funny
kommen come *(irr)*; get *(irr)*
Woher kommst du? Where are you from?
Komm(t) herein! Come in.
Kommunikation communication
kommunizieren, sprechen communicate
König king
Königin queen
können may
können/nicht können can/can't
könnte(st, n, t) might; could
Kontrolle control
kontrollieren control; check
sich konzentrieren concentrate
Konzert concert
Kopf head
Kopfschmerzen headache
Körper body
kosten cost *(irr)*
kostenlos; frei free
es kostet it's (= it is)
Wie viel kostet es? How much is it?
köstlich, lecker delicious
Kostüm costume
Kraft energy
Kraft; Wucht force
krank sick; ill
Krankenpfleger nurse
Krankenschwester nurse
Krankheit disease
Krawatte tie
Kreide chalk
Kreis circle
Krieg war
Kritik review
Krokodil crocodile
Küche kitchen
Kuchen cake
sich kümmern um care
sich kümmern um; aufpassen auf look after
Kuh cow
Kühlschrank fridge
Kultur culture
Kunde/Kundin customer
Kunst art

Künstler/in artist
Kunstwerk piece of art
Kurs course
kurz short
Kuscheltier cuddly toy

L

lächeln smile
Lächeln smile
lachen laugh
Laden shop; store *(AE)*
Lampe lamp
Land country
lang long
... lang for *(+ Zeitraum)*
langsam slow, slowly
langweilig boring
lassen let *(irr)*
lass(t) uns ... let's (= let us)
Lass(t) uns gehen! Let's go!
Lastwagenfahrer/in lorry driver
laufen run *(irr)*
laut loud; noisy
läuten ring *(irr)*
leben live
Leben life (*pl* lives)
lecker delicious, tasty
leer (stehend) empty
legen lay *(irr)*; put *(irr)*
Lehrer/in teacher
leicht easy; easily
leid tun feel sorry for
Es tut mir leid., Entschuldigung. Sorry.
leise; ruhig quiet
sich leisten afford
lernen learn *(irr)*
lesen read *(irr)*
Lesen reading
letzte(r, s) last
Leute people
Lexikon dictionary
Licht light
Liebe love
liebe/r *(Anrede)* dear
lieben, sehr mögen love
Ich würde lieber ... I'd rather ...
Liebling; Lieblings- favourite
am liebsten mögen like best
Lied song
liegen lie *(irr)*
lila purple
Limonade lemonade
Lineal ruler
Linie; Zeile line
links left; on the left side
links, auf der/deiner linken Seite on the left/on your left
Liste list
Loch hole
Löffel spoon
(lohnens)wert worth
Was ist los? What's on?; What's up? *(informal)*
lösen solve
Lösung solution
Löwe lion
Luft air
Luftballon balloon
lustig funny; fun

M

machen do *(irr)*; make *(irr)*
Mach dir keine Sorgen. Don't worry.
ein Picknick machen have a picnic
einen Test machen take a test
mächtig powerful
Mädchen girl
Mahlzeit meal
Mai May
Mal time
Mama mum
man you
manchmal sometimes
Mann man (*pl* men)
Markt market
Marmelade jam
März March
Maschine machine
Mathe maths
Maurer/in bricklayer
Maus mouse (*pl* mice)
Mechaniker/in mechanic
Medizin, Medikamente medicine *(no pl)*
Meer sea
Meerschweinchen guinea pig
Mehl flour
mehr; weitere more
meiden; sich fernhalten von stay away from
mein(e) my
meine(r, s) mine
(meine) Damen und Herren ladies and gentlemen
meinen; bedeuten mean *(irr)*
Meinung opinion
meiner Meinung nach in my opinion
die meisten; am meisten most
Menge amount
viel, jede Menge a lot (of), lots of
Menschen people
Menschenmenge crowd
Menü menu
Messer knife (*pl* knives)
Meter metre
mich me
Miete rent
Milch milk
mindestens at least
mir (to) me
mir/mich/ich (selbst) myself
mit; bei with
mit; von by
mit dem Bus by bus
mit dem Bus fahren go by bus
mit dem Fahrrad by bike
mitbringen bring *(irr)*
Mitglied member
mitmachen join
mitnehmen take away
Mittagessen lunch
Mittagszeit, Mittagspause lunchtime
Mitte middle; centre
in der Mitte von in the middle of
um Mitternacht at midnight
Mittwoch Wednesday
Mobben bullying
mobben bully
Möchten Sie bestellen? Are you ready to order?
Mode fashion
mögen like
lieben, sehr mögen love
Ich mag ... nicht. I don't like ...
am liebsten mögen like best
alle möglichen all kinds of
möglich possible
im Moment at the moment
Monat month
Mond moon
Montag Monday
Morgen morning
morgen tomorrow
Guten Morgen! Good morning!
am Morgen in the morning
heute Morgen this morning
morgen Vormittag tomorrow morning
morgens, vormittags *(nur hinter Uhrzeit zwischen Mitternacht und 12 Uhr mittags)* am (= ante meridiem)
Moschee mosque
Motorrad motorbike
müde tired
mühelos easily
Müll rubbish; litter
Mund mouth
Münze coin
Murmel marble
Muschel seashell
Musik music
Musiker/in musician
müssen have to; must; need to
Mut courage
Mutter mother
Mütze cap

N

nach after; past; according to; to
nach Hause home
nach Hilfe, als Hilfe for help
(nach) links left
(nach) oben up, upstairs
(nach) rechts right
Nachbar/in neighbour

Nachbarschaft neighbourhood
nachdem after
nachdenken über think about
Nachmittag afternoon
am Nachmittag in the afternoon
den ganzen Nachmittag lang all afternoon
nachmittags pm (= post meridiem)
Nachricht message; note
Nachrichten; Neuigkeit news *(no pl)*
nachspielen act out
nächste(r, s) next
Nacht night
Nachtisch dessert
nachts at night
Nacken neck
als Nächstes, dann next
in der Nähe von, nahe near
namens called
Nase nose
nass wet
Natur nature
Natürlich! Of course!
Naturwissenschaft science
neben next to
nehmen take *(irr)*
Ich nehme es. I'll take it.
die U-Bahn nehmen take the tube
einen Zug nehmen catch a train
nein no
nervös nervous
nett; schön nice
neu new; fresh
Neuigkeit; Nachrichten news *(no pl)*
Neujahr New Year
nicht not
nicht dürfen mustn't (= must not)
nicht einmal not even
nicht mehr no longer; not anymore
nicht werden won't
nichts not anything; nothing
nie, niemals never
niedlich cute
niedrig low
niemand nobody; not anyone
noch; schon yet
(immer) noch still
noch ein/e another
noch einmal again
noch etwas anything else
Sonst noch etwas?, Darf es noch etwas sein? Anything else?
noch nicht not yet
Norden north
normalerweise normally; usually
Note mark
November November
Nummer number
nun well
nur only; just
nützlich useful; helpful

O

ob whether; if
(nach) oben up, upstairs
(oben) auf on top
oberes Ende top
Obst fruit *(no pl)*
obwohl though
oder or
Ofenkartoffel jacket potato
offen open
öffnen open
Öffnungszeiten opening hours *(pl)*
oft often; many times
ohne without
Ohr ear
Oktober October
Onkel uncle
orange orange
Orange orange
Orangensaft orange juice
ordentlich tidy
in Ordnung all right, fine
organisieren organise
Ort place; site
örtlich local
Osten east
Ostern Easter

P

Paar pair
ein Paar a pair of
ein paar, einige some
Packung packet
Papa dad
Papagei parrot
Papier paper
Parfüm, Duft perfume
Partner boyfriend
Partnerin girlfriend
passen zu go with; match
passieren happen; go on
Pause break
Pech bad luck
peinlich embarrassing
Pence p (= penny, pence)
persönlich personal
persönliche, soziale und methodische Kompetenzen soft skill
Pferd horse
Pflanze plant
Pflege; Sorgfalt care
Pflicht responsibility
Pfund pound
Pfütze puddle
ein Picknick machen have a picnic
Pinguin penguin
planen plan
Plastik plastic
Plattform platform
Platz place; site; space
plötzlich suddenly
Pokalendspiel cup final
politisch political
Polizei police
Polizeibeamte(r)/-beamtin police officer
Polizist policeman (*pl* policemen)
Pommes frites chips *(pl)*
Postkarte postcard
Praktikum work experience
Praktikum, Praktikumsstelle work placement
Präsentation, Vortrag presentation
präsentieren present (to)
Präsident/in; Vorsitzende/r president
Preis price; prize
pro per; a
probieren try
Produkt product
professionell professional
Profi professional
Programm programme
Projekt project
prüfen test
Prüfung exam
Publikum audience
Pullover jumper; sweater
pünktlich on time; in time
putzen brush
sich die Zähne putzen brush one's teeth

R

Rad fahren, radeln cycle
Rasse race
Rassist/in; rassistisch racist
raten, beraten; informieren advise
Rat(schlag) advice *(no pl)*
Ratte rat
rauchen smoke
Raum room; space
realistisch realistic
recherchieren research
Rechnung bill
Recht right
Du hast recht. You're right.
recht haben be right
(nach) rechts right
rechts, auf der/deiner rechten Seite on the right/on your right
rechtzeitig in time
recyceln recycle
direkte Rede, wörtliche Rede direct speech
reden speak *(irr)*
reden (mit) talk (to)
Regal shelf (*pl* shelves)
Regel rule
Regen rain
Regierung government
Region, Gebiet area
Regisseur/in director

regnerisch rainy
reich rich
an der Reihe sein be one's turn
Reis rice
Reise journey; trip
reisen travel
reiten ride a horse
Religion *(Schulfach)* RE (= religious education)
Rennen race
rennen run *(irr)*
reparieren repair
im Restaurant essen eat out
Rezension review
Rezept recipe
richtig right, correct; properly
riechen smell *(irr)*
riesig huge
Rock skirt
Rollstuhl wheelchair
rot red
Rücken back
Rückenschmerzen backache *(no pl)*
rufen shout; call

S

Saft juice
sagen say *(irr)*
Sahne cream
Salat salad
Salbe, Creme cream
Salz salt
sammeln collect
Sammlung collection
Samstag Saturday
Sänger/in singer
satt full
Satz sentence; phrase
sauber clean
sauber machen clean; clean up
schaden, beschädigen damage
Schaf sheep (*pl* sheep)
Schal scarf (*pl* scarfs *or* scarves)
scharf hot
schaurig spooky
Schauspieler/in actor/actress
scheinen seem
Schere a pair of scissors
schicken send *(irr)*
schieben push
schießen shoot *(irr)*
ein Tor schießen score a goal
Schiff ship
Schild sign
Schinkenspeck bacon
schlafen sleep *(irr)*
schlagen beat *(irr)*; hit *(irr)*
schlank slim
schlau clever
schlecht; schlimm bad
schließlich finally; in the end; at last
schlimmer worse
schlimmste(r, s) worst
Schluss end
schmecken taste
Schmerz pain
Schmetterling butterfly
schmutzig dirty
Schnee snow
Schneemann snowman (*pl* snowmen)
schneereich snowy
schneiden cut *(irr)*
schnell fast; quick, quickly
Schokolade chocolate
schon already
schön beautiful; lovely; nice
Schön, dich/euch/Sie zu sehen/treffen. Nice to see/meet you.
schon; noch yet
Schottland Scotland
Schrank wardrobe; cupboard
schrecklich awful; terrible
schreiben write *(irr)*
Schreibtisch desk
schreien shout; cry
schüchtern shy
Schuh shoe
Schulausflug school trip
Schuld fault
Schule school
Schüler/in pupil
(Schüler)versammlung assembly
Schulfach subject
Schuljahr, Klasse year
Schultag school day
Schultasche schoolbag
Schulter shoulder
Schuluniform school uniform
Schulzeugnis school report
Schüssel, Schale bowl
schwarz black
Schwein pig
schwer heavy; difficult
Schwester sister
schwierig difficult
in Schwierigkeiten geraten get into trouble
Schwimmbad swimming pool
schwimmen swim *(irr)*
Schwimmen swimming
Schwimmen gehen go swimming
Schwimmer/in swimmer
See lake; sea
Seele soul
sehen see *(irr)*
(an)sehen, (an)schauen look (at)
Schön, dich/euch/Sie zu sehen. Nice to see you.
Sehenswürdigkeit sight
sehr very; much
Seife soap
Seil rope
sein be *(irr)*
sein; seine(r, s) his
sein(e), ihr(e) *(sächlich)* its
seit since
Seite page
auf der/deiner linken Seite on the left/ on your left
auf der/deiner rechten Seite on the right/ on your right
Sekunde second
der-/die-/dasselbe the same
selbst even
September September
servieren serve
setzen put *(irr)*
sich setzen take a seat
sich mit jemandem in Verbindung setzen contact somebody
sich amüsieren enjoy oneself
sich anfreunden (mit) make friends (with)
sich beeilen hurry (up)
sich befassen mit deal with
sich beklagen complain
sich bewegen move
sich bewerben um apply for
sich bewusst sein, erkennen realize (= realise)
sich die Zähne putzen brush one's teeth
sich einer Sache bewusst sein be aware of something
sich erinnern an remember
sich etwas vorstellen imagine
sich fragen wonder
(sich) fühlen feel *(irr)*
sich hinsetzen sit down
sich konzentrieren concentrate
sich kümmern um look after; care
sich leisten afford
sich Sorgen machen worry
(sich) treffen meet up
sich umdrehen turn around
sich verirren get lost
sich verlieben fall in love
sich; sich selbst herself; himself
sich; sie selbst themselves
sicher sure; safe; certainly
sie she; they; them; her
Sie you
Siedler/in settler
singen sing *(irr)*
Sitz seat
sitzen sit *(irr)*
Ski fahren, Ski laufen ski
SMS text message
so such; like this
so ... wie as ... as
sobald; wenn, als once
Socke sock
sogar even

Sohn son
solch such
sollen; werden shall
sollte(st, n, t) should
Sommer summer
Sonne sun
Sonnenbrille sunglasses *(pl)*
Sonnenschein sunshine
sonnig sunny
Sonntag Sunday
sonst else
Sonst noch etwas?, Darf es noch etwas sein? Anything else?
was sonst what else
sich Sorgen machen worry
Mach dir keine Sorgen. Don't worry.
Sorte kind
Soße sauce
sowieso anyway
spät; zu spät late
Wie spät ist es? What time is it?
Spaß fun; joke
(viel) Spaß haben have (a lot of) fun
(viel) Spaß machen be (good/great) fun
später later; afterwards
(spätestens) bis by
Speisekarte; Menü menu
Spiegelei fried egg
Spiel match; game
spielen play; act
Gitarre spielen play the guitar
Spieler/in player
Spielplatz playground
Spielzeugauto toy car
spitze awesome
Spitze top
Sport *(Schulfach)* PE (= physical education)
Sport, Sportart sport
Sportcenter sports centre
Sporthalle sports hall
Sportplatz sports field
Sprache language
sprechen speak *(irr)*
sprechen (mit) talk (to)
sprechen über talk about
springen jump
Stadt city; town
städtisch urban
Stand stall
stark strong; powerful
stattdessen instead
stattfinden take place
staubsaugen vacuum
Steckbrief fact file
stehen stand *(irr)*
stehen bleiben stop
stehlen steal *(irr)*
steigen step
steigen; aufgehen rise *(irr)*
auf etwas (hinauf)steigen climb
Stein stone; rock
Stelle site; job
stellen put *(irr)*
Steppdecke duvet
sterben die
Stiefel boot
Stift pen
Stil style
Stimme; Abstimmung, Wahl vote
Stockwerk floor
stolz proud
stoßen push
stoßen gegen, treffen hit *(irr)*
schlagen hit *(irr)*
strahlend, hell bright
Strand beach
Straße street; road
auf der Straße in the street
Streichholz match (*pl* matches)
Streit; Kampf fight
Strom, Elektrizität electricity
Strom; Kraft power
Stück piece
studieren; lernen study
Stufe; Schritt step
Stuhl chair
Stunde lesson; hour
Stundenplan timetable
Sturm storm
suchen nach look for
Süden south
super fantastic; awesome
Supermarkt supermarket
Suppe soup
im Internet surfen surf the Internet
süß cute; sweet
Szene scene

Tafel blackboard
Tag day
Tagebuch diary
eines Tages one day
Tante aunt
Tanz dance
tanzen dance
Tanzen dancing
Tasche bag; pocket
Taschengeld pocket money
Taschenlampe torch (*pl* torches)
Taschentuch handkerchief (*pl* handkerchiefs/handkerchieves)
Tasse cup
Tatsache fact
tausend thousand
Techniker/in technician
Tee tea
Teil part; piece
teilen share
teilnehmen an take part in
Telefon phone
am Telefon on the phone
ans Telefon gehen answer the phone
Was ist deine Telefonnummer? What's your phone number?
Teller plate
Tempel temple
Termin date
einen Test machen take a test
testen test
teuer expensive
Theater theatre
Thema topic; theme
Tier animal
Tierarzt/-ärztin vet
Tierpfleger/in zoo-keeper
Tiger tiger
Tisch table
den Tisch decken lay the table
Tischtennnis table tennis
Titel title
Tochter daughter
Tod death
Toilette toilet
toll amazing *(informal)*
Tomate tomato (*pl* tomatoes)
ein Tor schießen score a goal
töten kill
traditionell traditional
tragen wear *(irr)*; carry
Traum dream
träumen dream *(irr)*
traurig sad
treffen; sich treffen meet *(irr)*; meet up
treffen, stoßen gegen hit *(irr)*
Schön, dich/euch/Sie zu treffen. Nice to meet you.
treten kick; step
trinken drink *(irr)*; have *(irr)*
Trinken; Getränk drink
tschüs(s) bye
tun do *(irr)*
etw gern tun like doing sth
etw sehr gern tun love doing sth
etwas tun können be able to do something
etwas tun werden be going to do something
etwas weiter tun keep doing something
jemanden dazu bringen, etwas zu tun make somebody do something
Tür door
Turm tower
Turnen do gymnastics
Turnhalle gym (= gymnasium)
Turnschuhe trainers
typisch typical

die U-Bahn nehmen take the tube
U-Bahn-Station station
üben practise
über about; across; over
überhaupt at all; anyway

überhaupt nicht not at all
überleben survive
Übernachtung sleepover
überprüfen check
Überprüfung der Anwesenheit registration
überqueren cross
überrascht surprised
Überraschung surprise
Überschrift heading; title
übrig bleiben be left
etwas übrig haben have something left
übrigens by the way; actually
Übung exercise
Uhr o'clock *(bei Nennung der Uhrzeit)*; clock; watch
um at
um; herum, umher around
um ... herum round
um Mitternacht at midnight
um zu in order to; to
sich umdrehen turn around
Umgebung, Umfeld; Umwelt environment
umsteigen; wechseln change
umweltbewusst green
umweltbewusst werden go green
umziehen move
unangenehm embarrassing
unaufgeräumt untidy
unbewohnt empty
und and
Unfall accident
unfreundlich unfriendly
ungefähr about
ungefährlich safe
ungewöhnlich unusual
unglaublich incredible
unglücklich unhappy
unheimlich spooky
Universität university
unmöglich impossible
unordentlich untidy
uns us
uns; wir selbst ourselves
unsere(r, s) our
(nach) unten down
unten, unter below
unter beneath; under
unter; zwischen among
Unterhaltung conversation
Unterricht lesson
unterrichten teach *(irr)*
unterstreichen underline
(unter)stützen support
untersuchen explore
Urlaub holiday(s)
in Urlaub fahren go on holiday
US, Vereinigte Staaten (von Amerika); US- (the) US (= United States)
USA, Vereinigte Staaten von Amerika the USA (= United States of America)

V

Vater father
Vati dad
Vegetarier/in; vegetarisch vegetarian
Verabredung date
verändern change
verängstigt frightened; scared
Veranstaltung event
Verantwortung responsibility
verantwortungsbewusst, verantwortlich responsible
verärgert angry, angrily; annoyed
Verband bandage
Verbandskasten first aid kit
verbessern improve
(ver)brennen burn *(irr)*
verbringen spend *(irr)*
verdienen earn
(gut) verdienen; (viel) Geld verdienen make (good) money
Vereinigte Staaten von Amerika the USA (= United States of America)
die Vereinigten Staaten the United States
Vereinigtes Königreich the UK (= United Kingdom)
verfolgen follow
verfügbar available
vergessen forget *(irr)*
sich verirren get lost
Verkauf sale
verkaufen sell *(irr)*
Verkäufer/in seller
Verkehr traffic
verlassen; abfahren leave *(irr)*
verlässlich reliable
sich verlieben fall in love
verlieren lose *(irr)*
(ver)mischen mix
vermissen; verpassen miss
vermuten suppose; guess
veröffentlichen release; publish
verrückt crazy
(Schüler)versammlung assembly
verschiedene different; several
verschmutzen pollute
verschneit snowy
verschwinden disappear
Verständigung communication
verstehen understand *(irr)*
Ich verstehe es nicht. I don't understand.
Versuch experiment
versuchen try
viel much; lots of, a lot (of)
wie viel how much
Viel Glück! Good luck!
(viel) Spaß haben have (a lot of) fun
(viel) Spaß machen be (good/great) fun
viele many, a lot (of)
wie viele how many
viele Grüße best wishes
vielleicht maybe; perhaps
Viertel neighbourhood; quarter
vierte(r, s) fourth
violett purple
Vogel bird
voll full
völlig all
von from; of
von; mit by
von alleine on its own
von; hinunter, herunter off
vor before; to; in front of; ago
vor; außerhalb outside
vorbei past
vorbei; über, hinüber over
vorbeigehen an pass
vorbereiten prepare
Vorderseite front
vorher before
morgen Vormittag tomorrow morning
morgens, vormittags *(nur hinter Uhrzeit zwischen Mitternacht und 12 Uhr mittags)* am (= ante meridiem)
vorn in front
vorschlagen suggest
vorsichtig carefully
Vorspeise starter
vorspielen act out
sich etwas vorstellen imagine
Vorstellung idea
Vorstellungsgespräch interview
vorüber past
vorziehen prefer

W

wachsen; werden; anbauen grow *(irr)*
Wahl choice
wählen; sich entscheiden choose *(irr)*
wahnsinnig crazy
wahr true
während while; during
während; als; wie as
Wahrheit truth
wahrscheinlich likely; probably
Wald forest

Wand wall
wann when
warm warm
warnen warn
warten auf wait for
Wärter/in zoo-keeper
Wartezimmer waiting room
warum why
was; welche(r, s) what; which
was (auch immer) whatever
Was hältst du davon? What do you think?
Was ist deine Telefonnummer? What's your phone number?
Was ist los? What's on?; What's up? *(informal)*
Was ist mit …? / Wie wäre es mit …? What about …?
was sonst what else
waschen; sich waschen wash
Wasser water
Wechselgeld change
wechseln; umsteigen change
Wecker alarm clock
Weg way
weg away
wegen because of; due to
weglaufen run away
wegnehmen take away
wehtun, schmerzen hurt *(irr)*
weich soft
erster Weihnachtsfeiertag Christmas Day
zweiter Weihnachtsfeiertag Boxing Day
weil because
weinen cry
Weise way
weiß white
weit far
weit weg far away
weiter further
etwas weiter tun keep doing something
weitere; mehr more
weitergehen, weiterfahren; weiterreden go on
weiterlesen read on
weitermachen carry on
welche(r, s); was what; which
Wellensittich budgie
Welt world
Weltall space
wenige few
weniger less
wenigstens at least
wenn; als when
wenn; falls if
wer; der / die / das who
Werbung advertisement (= advert)
werden get *(irr)*; become *(irr)*; will
nicht werden won't
etwas tun werden be going to do something
werfen throw *(irr)*
wessen whose
Westen west
Wettbewerb competition
Wetter weather
wichtig important
wichtig sein count
widerlich disgusting
wie how; like; such as
wie; als; während as
Wie alt bist du? How old are you?
Wie geht es dir? / Wie geht es Ihnen? How are you?
Wie heißt du? What's your name?
wie man how to
Wie spät ist es? What time is it?
wie viel how much
Wie viel kostet es? How much is it?
wie viele how many
Wie wäre es mit …? How about …?
wieder again
wiederaufbereiten recycle
Auf Wiedersehen. Goodbye.
wiederverwenden reuse
Wiese grass
willkommen welcome
Wind wind
windig windy
Winter winter
wir we
wirklich really; real; just
wirksam, effektiv effective
wissen know *(irr)*
Ich weiß es nicht. I don't know.
Wissenschaftler/in scientist
Witz joke
Das soll wohl ein Witz sein! You must be joking! *(informal)*
witzig fun
WLAN WiFi
wo; wohin where
Woche week
die ganze Woche lang all week
Wochenende weekend
am Wochenende at the weekend
Woher kommst du? Where are you from?
Wohltätigkeitsorganisation charity
wohnen live; stay
Wohnzimmer living room
Wolke cloud
wollen want
Wort word
Wörterbuch dictionary
wunderbar, wundervoll wonderful
würde(st, n, t) would
Wurst, Würstchen sausage

Z

Zahl number
zählen count
Zahn tooth (*pl* teeth)
Zahnbürste toothbrush
Zahnpasta toothpaste
sich die Zähne putzen brush one's teeth
Zeh toe
Zeichen sign
zeichnen draw *(irr)*
Zeichnung drawing
zeigen show *(irr)*
zeigen (auf) point (at/to)
zeigen, vorführen demonstrate
Zeile line
Zeit time
die ganze Zeit all the time
Zeitachse timeline
Zeitschrift magazine
Zeitung newspaper
Zensur mark
Zentrum centre
zerbrechen break *(irr)*
zerbrochen; kaputt broken
zerstören destroy
Zeug stuff *(informal)*
ziehen pull
Zielaufgabe target task
ziemlich quite; pretty
Zigarette cigarette
Zimmer room
Zitat quote; quotation
Zoo zoo
zu too; to
zu Fuß on foot
zu Hause at home
(zu) spät late
Zucker sugar
zuerst first
Zug train
einen Zug nehmen catch a train
zugeben admit
Zuhause home
zuhören listen (to)
Zukunft future
zum Beispiel for example
zum Frühstück for breakfast
Zuneigung fühlen care
zuordnen match
zurück back
zurückgeben return
zurückkehren return
zurückkommen return
zurücklassen; (übrig) lassen leave *(irr)*
zusammen together
zustimmen agree
Zutat ingredient
zuverlässig reliable
zuvor before
Zweig, Ast; Zweigstelle branch
zweimal twice
zweiter Weihnachtsfeiertag Boxing Day
zweite(r, s) second
zwischen between

Names

Girls/Women
Alicia /əˈlɪʃə/
Amanda /əˈmændə/
Amani /əˈmɑːni/
Amy /ˈeɪmi/
Angela /ˈændʒələ/
Angie /ˈændʒi/
Anna, Annie /ˈænə, ˈæni/
Betty /ˈbeti/
Bev /bev/
Briana /briˈænə/
Carrie /ˈkæri/
Cheryl /ˈtʃerəl/
Claire /kleə/
Cristina /krɪˈstiːnə/
Ellie /ˈeli/
Emma /ˈemə/
Eyonna /aɪˈɒnə/
Fatima /ˈfætɪmə/
Frances /ˈfrɑːnsɪs/
Gabrielle /ˌgæbriˈel/
Gemma /ˈdʒemə/
Gwyneth /ˈgwɪnəθ/
Hailee /ˌheɪˈliː/
Hannah /ˈhænə/
Heather /ˈheðə/
Jane /dʒeɪn/
Janet /ˈdʒænɪt/
Jean /dʒiːn/
Jenny /ˈdʒeni/
Jessica /ˈdʒesɪkə/
Julia /ˈdʒuːliə/
Juliet /ˈdʒuːliət/
Karen /ˈkærən/
Katie /ˈkeɪti/
Katrina /kəˈtriːnə/
Lena /ˈliːnə/
Lindsay /ˈlɪndzi/
Lisa /ˈliːsə/
Maria /məˈriːə/
Marian /ˈmæriən/
Maya /ˈmeɪə/
Megan /ˈmegən/
Melanie /ˈmeləni/
Miriam /ˈmɪriəm/
Muzoon /mʌˈzuːn/
Natalie /ˈnætəli/
Nina /ˈniːnə/
Rosa /ˈrəʊzə, ˈrɒsə/
Sandy /ˈsændi/
Savannah /səˈvænə/
Serena /səˈriːnə/
Sonia /ˈsɒniə/
Sue /suː/
Sylvia /ˈsɪlviə/
Zoe /ˈzəʊi/

Boys/Men
Aaron /ˈeərən/
Akash /əˈkɑːʃ/
Alan /ˈælən/
Alex /ˈælɪks/
Alexander /ˌælɪgˈzɑːndə/
Anthony /ˈæntəni/
Arne /ɑːn/
Arnold /ˈɑːnld/
Benjamin /ˈbendʒəmɪn/
Bernie /ˈbɜːni/
Bert /bɜːt/
Beymer /ˈbiːmə/
Bilal /ˌbiˈlɑːl/
Bill, Billy /bɪl, ˈbɪli/
Bob /bɒb/
Brad /bræd/
Bruce /bruːs/
Carl /kɑːl/
Carlo /ˈkɑːləʊ/
Chris /krɪs/
Christy /ˈkrɪsti/
Danny /ˈdæni/
Douglas /ˈdʌgləs/
Faisal /ˈfaɪsl/
Falcon /ˈfɔːlkən/
George /dʒɔːdʒ/
Harry /ˈhæri/
Hassan /həˈsɑːn/
Henry /ˈhenri, ˌɒnˈriː/
Jack /dʒæk/
Jake /dʒeɪk/
Jamie /ˈdʒeɪmi/
Jean-Michel /ʒɑːnmɪˈʃel/
Jerome /dʒəˈrəʊm/
Joe /dʒəʊ/
John, Johnny /dʒɒn, ˈdʒɒni/
Joseph /ˈdʒəʊzɪf/
Josh /dʒɒʃ/
Joshua /ˈdʒɒʃjuə/
Keith /kiːθ/
Kiam /ˈkiːəm/
Langston /ˈlæŋstən/
Larry /ˈlæri/
Laurence, Lawrence /ˈlɒrəns/
Leonardo /ˌliːəʊˈnɑːdəʊ/
Levi /ˈliːvaɪ/
Lucas /ˈluːkəs/
Luther /ˈluːθə/
Malcolm /ˈmælkəm/
Mark /mɑːk/
Martin /ˈmɑːtɪn/
Max /mæks/
Mercutio /mɜːˈkjuːʃiəʊ/
Mike /maɪk/
Nick /nɪk/
Noah /ˈnəʊə/
Oliver /ˈɒlɪvə/
Oscar /ˈɒskə/
Paris /ˈpærɪs/
Pete /piːt/
Peter /ˈpiːtə/
Peter-John /ˈpiːtəˌdʒɒn/
Phil /fɪl/
Pierre /piˈeə/
Popeye /ˈpɒpaɪ/
Raoul /raʊˈuːl/
Richard /ˈrɪtʃəd/
Roald /ˈrəʊəld/
Robbie /ˈrɒbi/
Robert /ˈrɒbət/
Robinson /ˈrɒbɪnsən/
Romeo /ˈrəʊmiəʊ/
Samoset /ˈsɑːməzet/
Seb /seb/
Shawn /ʃɔːn/
Simon /ˈsaɪmən/
Squanto /ˈskwɒntəʊ/
Steven /ˈstiːvn/
Tamal /ˈtæmɪl/
Thomas /ˈtɒməs/
Tim /tɪm/
Todd /tɒd/
Tom /tɒm/
Tony /ˈtəʊni/
Tybalt /ˈtaɪbɔːlt/
Tyler /ˈtaɪlə/
William /ˈwɪljəm/
Zach /ˈzæk/

Families
Almellehan /ælˌmeleɪˈhɑːn/
Amundsen /ˈæməndsən/
Basquiat /ˌbæskiˈɑː/
Black /blæk/
Blue /bluː/
Booth /buːð/
Bradley /ˈbrædli/
Cameron /ˈkæmrən/
Capulet /ˈkæpjulet/
Carlei /ˈkɑːleɪ/
Carter /ˈkɑːtə/
Carulli /kəˈruli/
Fiennes /faɪnz/
Ford /fɔːd/
Giles /dʒaɪlz/
Gilmour /ˈgɪlmɔː/
Hall /hɔːl/
Hambleton /ˈhæmbltn/
Haring /ˈheərɪŋ/
Hinawy /ˌhiˈnɑːwi/
Hogan /ˈhəʊgən/
Hudson /ˈhʌdsn/
Hughes /hjuːz/
Hunte /ˈhʌnti/
Huxley /ˈhʌksli/
Jealous /ˈdʒeləs/
Jean /dʒiːn/
Johnson /ˈdʒɒnsn/
Jones /dʒəʊnz/
Kamkwamba /kæmˈkwɑːmbə/
Kennedy /ˈkenədi/
Keyes, Keys /kiːz/
King /kɪŋ/
Koerner /ˈkɜːnə/
Lemkey /ˈlemki/
Madden /ˈmædn/
Michael /ˈmaɪkl/
Miller /ˈmɪlə/
Minghella /mɪŋˈgelə/
Montague /ˈmɒntəgjuː/
Moore /mʊə/
O'Grady /əʊˈgreɪdi/
O'Hara /əʊ ˈhɑːrə/
Paltrow /ˈpæltrəʊ/
Penn /pen/
Potter /ˈpɒtə/
Rickman /ˈrɪkmən/
Robbins /ˈrɒbɪnz/
Rodriguez /rɒˈdriːgez/
Sanders /ˈsændəz/
Saralegui /ˌsærəˈlegi/
Schwarzenegger /ˈʃwɔːtsənegə/
Scott /skɒt/
Sewell /ˈsjuːəl/
Shakespeare /ˈʃeɪkspɪə/
Shuckburgh /ˈʃʌkbərə/
Small /smɔːl/
Solem /ˈsɒləm/
Springsteen /ˈsprɪŋstiːn/
Steinfeld /ˈstaɪnfeld/
Stevenson /ˈstiːvnsən/
Strauss /straʊs/
Straw /strɔː/
Vettese /vəˈtesi/
Washington /ˈwɒʃɪŋtən/
Wigand /ˈwɪgənd/
Wilde /waɪld/
Wise /waɪz/
Wood /wʊd/

Other Names
AIDS /eɪdz/
aloha /əˈləʊhə/
American football /əˌmerɪkən ˈfʊtˌbɔːl/
Banksy /ˈbæŋksi/
Bendys /ˈbendiz/

Names

Big Apple /ˌbɪɡ‿ˈæpl/
Bishopston /ˈbɪʃəpstən/
Briarwood Mall /ˌbraɪərwʊd ˈmɔːl/
Broadway /ˈbrɔːdˌweɪ/
the Brooklyn Bridge /ðə ˌbrʊklɪn ˈbrɪdʒ/
caps-on /ˌkæps‿ˈɒn/
Central Park /ˈsentrəl pɑːk/
Chicago Defender /ʃɪˌkɑːɡəʊ dɪˈfendə/
Columbia /kəˈlʌmbiə/
Crisis /ˈkraɪsɪs/
the Declaration of Independence /ðə ˌdekləˌreɪʃn‿əv ‿ˌɪndɪˈpendəns/
Empire State Building /ˌempaɪə ˈsteɪt ˌbɪldɪŋ/
Empire State of Mind /ˌempaɪə ˌsteɪt‿ əv ˈmaɪnd/
Fairtrade /ˈfeətreɪd/
5Pointz /ˌfaɪv ˈpɔɪnts/
Flatiron Building /ˈflætˌaɪən ˌbɪldɪŋ/
Fleet /fliːt/
Ford /fɔːd/
Globe /ɡləʊb/
Greenpeace /ˈɡriːnˌpiːs/
Ground Zero /ˌɡraʊnd ˈzɪərəʊ/
Harley Davidson Motor Company /ˌhɑːli ˌdeɪvɪdsn ˈməʊtə ˌkʌmpni/
Harmon /ˈhɑːmən/
Haverstock /ˈhævəstɒk/
hip hop /ˈhɪp hɒp/
Hurricane Katrina Relief Fund /ˌhʌrɪkeɪn kəˌtriːnə rɪˈliːf‿fʌnd/
Independence Day /ˌɪndɪˈpendəns deɪ/
International Rescue Committee /ɪntəˌnæʃnəl ˈreskjuː kəˌmɪti/
Jet /dʒet/
Jets /dʒets/
Kokua /kəˈkua/
Kokua Festival /kəˌkua ˈfestɪvl/
LGBTQ /ˌel dʒiː biː tiː ˈkjuː/
Los Angeles Lakers /lɒs‿ˌændʒəliːz ˈleɪkəz/
Major League Baseball, MLB /ˌmeɪdʒə ˌliːɡ ˈbeɪsbɔːl, ˌem‿el ˈbiː/
Manhattan Island /mænˌhætn‿ˈaɪlənd/
Mayflower /ˈmeɪˌflaʊə/
McDonalds /mək ˈdɒnəldz/
MetLife Stadium /ˌmetlaɪf ˈsteɪdiəm/
the National Basketball Association, NBA /ðə ˌnæʃnəl ˈbɑːskɪtbɔːl ‿əˌsəʊsiˌeɪʃn, ˌen biː‿ˈeɪ/
the National Football League, NFL /ðə ˌnæʃnəl ˈfʊtbɔːl‿ˌliːɡ, ˌen‿ef‿ˈel/
New York City Police Department /ˌnjuː jɔːk ˌsɪti pəˈliːs dɪˌpɑːtmənt/
the Nobel Peace Prize /ðə nəʊˌbel ˈpiːs praɪz/
One World Trade Center /ˌwʌn ˌwɜːld‿ˈtreɪd ˌsentə/
Pancake Day /ˈpænkeɪk deɪ/
Panthers /ˈpænθəz/
Pilgrim Fathers /ˌpɪlɡrɪm ˈfɑːðəz/
Plymouth High /ˌplɪməθ ˈhaɪ/
Pop Shop /ˈpɒp ʃɒp/
pull factor /ˈpʊl ˌfæktə/
push factor /ˈpʊʃ ˌfæktə/
Red Cross /ˌred ˈkrɒs/
the Revolutionary War /ðə ˌrevəˌluːʃnri ˈwɔː/
Rockefeller Center /ˈrɒkəˌfelə ˌsentə/
San Francisco 49ers /ˌsæn frənˌsɪskəʊ ˌfɔːtiˈnaɪnəz/
Scott's Last Expedition /ˌskɒts ˌlɑːst‿ekspəˈdɪʃn/
Shark /ʃɑːk/
Spiderman /ˈspaɪdəmæn/
Spingarn /ˈspɪŋɡɑːn/
the Statue of Liberty /ðə ˌstætʃu‿əv ˈlɪbəti/
Super Bowl /ˈsuːpə bəʊl/
Terra Nova /ˌterə ˈnəʊvə/
Terra Nova Expedition /ˌterə ˈnəʊvə‿ˌekspəˌdɪʃn/
Tex-Mex /ˌteks ˈmeks/
Times Square /ˈtaɪmz‿ˌskweə/
UNICEF /ˈjuːnɪsef/
the United Nations /ðə juːˌnaɪtɪd ˈneɪʃnz/
West Side Story /ˌwest saɪd ˈstɔːri/
World Trade Center /ˌwɜːld‿ˈtreɪd ˌsentə/
Yankees /ˈjæŋkiz/
Youth Helpline /ˌjuːθ ˈhelplaɪn/

Geographical Names

Afghanistan /æfˈɡænɪstɑːn/
Africa /ˈæfrɪkə/
America /əˈmerɪkə/
the Antarctic /ði‿æntˈɑːktɪk/
Arizona /ˌærɪˈzəʊnə/
Asia /ˈeɪʒə/
Atlantic Ocean /ətˌlæntɪk‿ˈəʊʃn/
Australia /ɒˈstreɪliə/
Bangladesh /ˌbæŋɡləˈdeʃ/
Birmingham /ˈbɜːmɪŋəm/
Bolton /ˈbəʊltən/
Boston /ˈbɒstən/
the Bronx /ðə ˈbrɒŋks/
Brooklyn /ˈbrʊklɪn/
California /ˌkæləˈfɔːniə/
Canada /ˈkænədə/
the Caribbean /ðə ˌkærɪˈbiən/
Chicago /ʃɪˈkɑːɡəʊ/
China /ˈtʃaɪnə/
Cobh /kəʊv/
Columbia /kəˈlʌmbiə/
Coney Island /ˌkəʊni‿ˈaɪlənd/
Detroit /dɪˈtrɔɪt/
Donegal /ˌdɒnɪˈɡɔːl/
Ellis Island /ˌelɪs‿ˈaɪlənd/
England /ˈɪŋɡlənd/
Florida /ˈflɒrɪdə/
Frankfort /ˈfræŋkfət/
Georgia /ˈdʒɔːdʒə/
Ghana /ˈɡɑːnə/
Greater New York /ˌɡreɪtə ˌnjuː ˈjɔːk/
Greece /ɡriːs/
Harlem /ˈhɑːləm/
Hawaii /həˈwaii/
Hollywood /ˈhɒliwʊd/
Honolulu /ˌhɒnəˈluːluː/
Iceland /ˈaɪslənd/
India /ˈɪndiə/
Indonesia /ˌɪndəʊˈniːʒə/
Italy /ˈɪtəli/
Japan /dʒəˈpæn/
Joplin /ˈdʒɒplɪn/
Jordan /ˈdʒɔːdn/
Lebanon /ˈlebənən/
Lenape /ləˈnɑːpe/
London /ˈlʌndən/
Los Angeles /lɒs‿ˈændʒəliːz/
Madison /ˈmædɪsən/
Malawi /məˈlɑːwi/
Malmö /ˈmælməʊ/
Manhattan /mænˈhætn/
Massachusetts /ˌmæsəˈtʃuːsɪts/
Mexico /ˈmeksɪkəʊ/
Mexico City /ˌmeksɪkəʊ ˈsɪti/
Michigan /ˈmɪʃɪɡən/
Milwaukee /mɪlˈwɔːki/
Missouri /mɪˈzʊəri/
New York /ˌnjuː ˈjɔːk/
New York City /ˌnjuː jɔːk ˈsɪti/
Newcastle /ˈnjuːˌkɑːsl/
NYC (= New York City) /ˌen waɪ ˈsiː, ˌnjuː jɔːk ˈsɪti/
Oahu /əʊˈɑːhuː/
Oxfordshire /ˈɒksfədʃə/
Paris /ˈpærɪs/
Pennsylvania /ˌpentsəlˈveɪniə/
Plymouth /ˈplɪməθ/
Poland /ˈpəʊlənd/
Portland /ˈpɔːtlənd/
Puerto Rico /ˌpwɜːtəʊ ˈriːkəʊ/
Queens /kwiːnz/
Reading /ˈredɪŋ/
Reykjavik /ˈreɪkjəvɪk/
Richmond /ˈrɪtʃmənd/
Russia /ˈrʌʃə/
Sacramento /ˌsækrəˈmentəʊ/
San Francisco /ˌsæn frənˈsɪskəʊ/
Silicon Valley /ˌsɪlɪkən ˈvæli/
South America /ˌsaʊθ‿əˈmerɪkə/
South Pole /ˌsaʊθ ˈpəʊl/
Spain /speɪn/
Staten Island /ˌstætn‿ˈaɪlənd/
Sweden /ˈswiːdn/
Syria /ˈsɪriə/
Texas /ˈteksəs/
Turkey /ˈtɜːki/
the UK (= United Kingdom) /ðə ˌjuː ˈkeɪ, juːˌnaɪtɪd ˈkɪŋdəm/
Vancouver /vænˈkuːvə/
Vanuatu /ˌvænuˈɑːtuː/
Verona /vəˈrəʊnə/
Washington, D.C. /ˌwɒʃɪŋtən diː ˈsiː/
Wisconsin /wɪˈskɒnsɪn/
Zaatari /ˈzɑtɑri/
Zanzibar /ˈzænzɪbɑː/

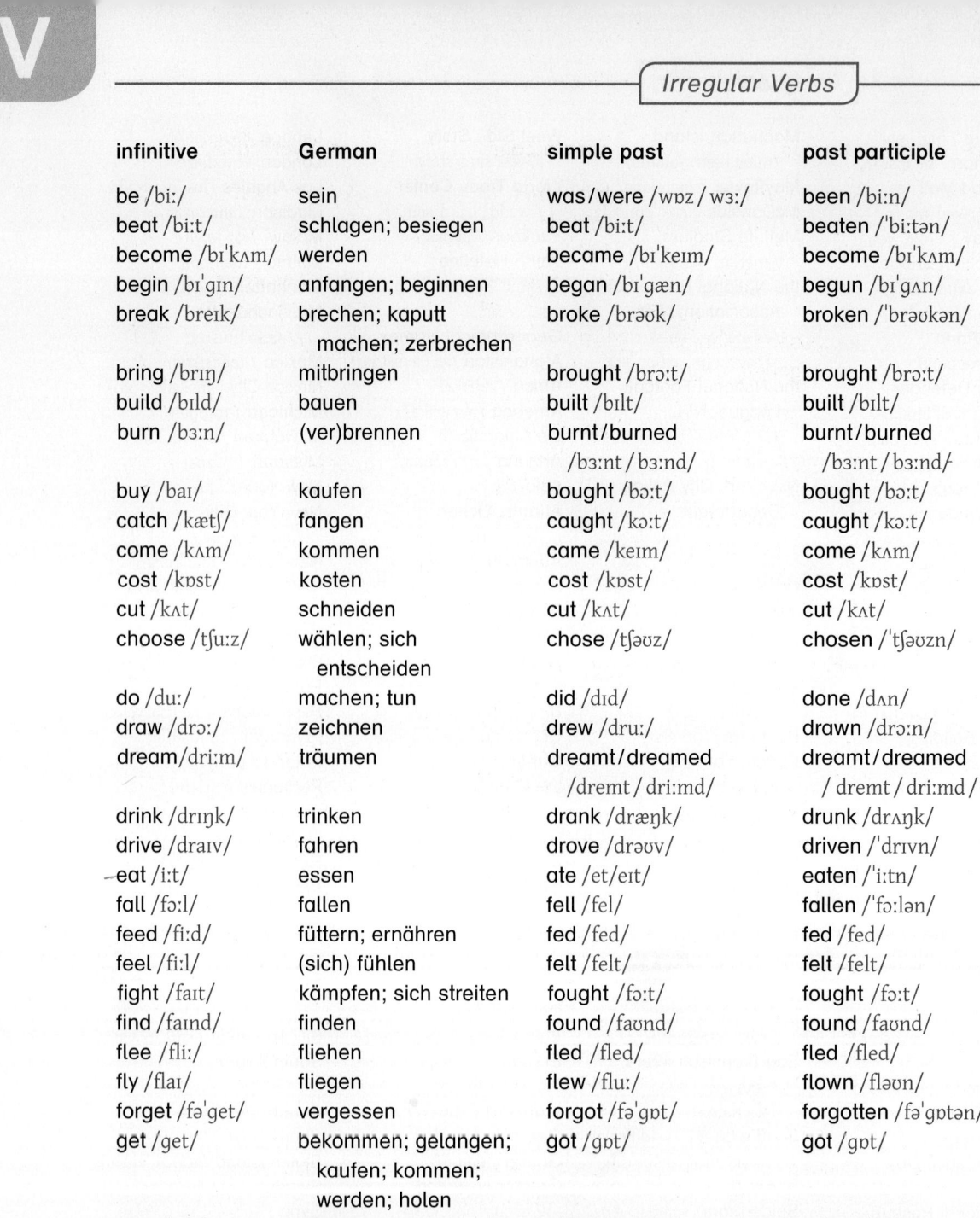

infinitive	German	simple past	past participle
be /biː/	sein	was/were /wɒz/wɜː/	been /biːn/
beat /biːt/	schlagen; besiegen	beat /biːt/	beaten /ˈbiːtən/
become /bɪˈkʌm/	werden	became /bɪˈkeɪm/	become /bɪˈkʌm/
begin /bɪˈgɪn/	anfangen; beginnen	began /bɪˈgæn/	begun /bɪˈgʌn/
break /breɪk/	brechen; kaputt machen; zerbrechen	broke /brəʊk/	broken /ˈbrəʊkən/
bring /brɪŋ/	mitbringen	brought /brɔːt/	brought /brɔːt/
build /bɪld/	bauen	built /bɪlt/	built /bɪlt/
burn /bɜːn/	(ver)brennen	burnt/burned /bɜːnt/bɜːnd/	burnt/burned /bɜːnt/bɜːnd/
buy /baɪ/	kaufen	bought /bɔːt/	bought /bɔːt/
catch /kætʃ/	fangen	caught /kɔːt/	caught /kɔːt/
come /kʌm/	kommen	came /keɪm/	come /kʌm/
cost /kɒst/	kosten	cost /kɒst/	cost /kɒst/
cut /kʌt/	schneiden	cut /kʌt/	cut /kʌt/
choose /tʃuːz/	wählen; sich entscheiden	chose /tʃəʊz/	chosen /ˈtʃəʊzn/
do /duː/	machen; tun	did /dɪd/	done /dʌn/
draw /drɔː/	zeichnen	drew /druː/	drawn /drɔːn/
dream /driːm/	träumen	dreamt/dreamed /dremt/driːmd/	dreamt/dreamed / dremt/driːmd /
drink /drɪŋk/	trinken	drank /dræŋk/	drunk /drʌŋk/
drive /draɪv/	fahren	drove /drəʊv/	driven /ˈdrɪvn/
eat /iːt/	essen	ate /et/eɪt/	eaten /ˈiːtn/
fall /fɔːl/	fallen	fell /fel/	fallen /ˈfɔːlən/
feed /fiːd/	füttern; ernähren	fed /fed/	fed /fed/
feel /fiːl/	(sich) fühlen	felt /felt/	felt /felt/
fight /faɪt/	kämpfen; sich streiten	fought /fɔːt/	fought /fɔːt/
find /faɪnd/	finden	found /faʊnd/	found /faʊnd/
flee /fliː/	fliehen	fled /fled/	fled /fled/
fly /flaɪ/	fliegen	flew /fluː/	flown /fləʊn/
forget /fəˈget/	vergessen	forgot /fəˈgɒt/	forgotten /fəˈgɒtən/
get /get/	bekommen; gelangen; kaufen; kommen; werden; holen	got /gɒt/	got /gɒt/
give /gɪv/	geben	gave /geɪv/	given /ˈgɪvn/
go /gəʊ/	gehen; fahren	went /went/	gone /gɒn/
grow /grəʊ/	wachsen	grew /gru/	grown /grəʊn/
have /hæv/	haben; essen, trinken	had /hæd/	had /hæd/
hear /hɪə/	hören	heard /hɜːd/	heard /hɜːd/
hide /haɪd/	verstecken	hid /hɪd/	hidden /ˈhɪdn/
hit /hɪt/	schlagen; treffen, stoßen gegen	hit /hɪt/	hit /hɪt/
hold /həʊld/	(fest)halten	held /held/	held /held/
hurt /hɜːt/	wehtun, schmerzen	hurt /hɜːt/	hurt /hɜːt/
keep /kiːp/	(be)halten	kept /kept/	kept /kept/

Irregular Verbs

infinitive	German	simple past	past participle
know /nəʊ/	kennen; wissen	knew /nju:/	known /nəʊn/
lay /leɪ/	legen	laid /leɪd/	laid /leɪd/
lead /li:d/	führen	led /led/	led /led/
learn /lɜ:n/	lernen	learnt / learned /lɜ:nt / lɜ:nd/	learnt / learned /lɜ:nt / lɜ:nd/
leave /li:v/	verlassen; abfahren; weggehen	left /left/	left /left/
let /let/	lassen	let /let/	let /let/
lie /laɪ/	liegen	lay /leɪ/	lain /leɪn/
lose /lu:z/	verlieren	lost /lɒst/	lost /lɒst/
make /meɪk/	machen	made /meɪd/	made /meɪd/
mean /mi:n/	meinen; bedeuten	meant /ment/	meant /ment/
meet /mi:t/	treffen; sich treffen	met /met/	met /met/
pay /peɪ/	(be)zahlen	paid /peɪd/	paid /peɪd/
prove /pru:v/	beweisen	proved /pru:vd/	proved / proven /pru:vd / 'pru:vn/
put /pʊt/	legen; setzen; stellen	put /pʊt/	put /pʊt/
quit /kwɪt/	aufhören mit	quit / quitted /kwɪt / 'kwɪtɪd/	quit / quitted /kwɪt / 'kwɪtɪd/
read /ri:d/	lesen	read /red/	read /red/
ride /raɪd/	fahren; reiten	rode /rəʊd/	ridden /'rɪdn/
ring /rɪŋ/	anrufen; klingeln; läuten	rang /ræŋ/	rung /rʌŋ/
rise /raɪz/	aufgehen; steigen	rose /rəʊz/	risen /'rɪzn/
run /rʌn/	laufen; rennen	ran /ræn/	run /rʌn/
say /seɪ/	sagen	said /sed/	said /sed/
see /si:/	sehen	saw /sɔ:/	seen /si:n/
sell /sel/	verkaufen	sold /səʊld/	sold /səʊld/
send /send/	schicken	sent /sent/	sent /sent/
shoot /ʃu:t/	schießen; filmen	shot /ʃɒt/	shot /ʃɒt/
show /ʃəʊ/	zeigen	showed /ʃəʊd/	shown /ʃəʊn/
sing /sɪŋ/	singen	sang /sæŋ/	sung /sʌŋ/
sit /sɪt/	sitzen	sat /sæt/	sat /sæt/
sleep /sli:p/	schlafen	slept /slept/	slept /slept/
smell /smel/	riechen	smelt / smelled /smelt / smeld/	smelt / smelled /smelt / smeld/
speak /spi:k/	reden; sprechen	spoke /spəʊk/	spoken /'spəʊkən/
spell /spel/	buchstabieren	spelt / spelled /spelt / speld/	spelt / spelled /spelt / speld/
spend /spend/	ausgeben; verbringen	spent /spent/	spent /spent/
spread /spred/	verbreiten	spread /spred/	spread /spred/
stand /stænd/	stehen	stood /stʊd/	stood /stʊd/
steal /sti:l/	stehlen	stole /stəʊl/	stolen /'stəʊlən/
sweep /swi:p/	fegen; kehren	swept /swept/	swept /swept/
swim /swɪm/	schwimmen	swam /swæm/	swum /swʌm/
take /teɪk/	bringen; dauern; brauchen; nehmen	took /tʊk/	taken /'teɪkən/

Irregular Verbs

infinitive	German	simple past	past participle
teach /tiːtʃ/	unterrichten	taught /tɔːt/	taught /tɔːt/
tell /tel/	erzählen; sagen	told /təʊld/	told /təʊld/
think /θɪŋk/	denken; glauben	thought /θɔːt/	thought /θɔːt/
throw /θrəʊ/	werfen	threw /θruː/	thrown /θrəʊn/
understand /ˌʌndəˈstænd/	verstehen	understood /ˌʌndəˈstʊd/	understood /ˌʌndəˈstʊd/
wear /weə/	tragen	wore /wɔː/	worn /wɔːn/
win /wɪn/	gewinnen	won /wʌn/	won /wʌn/
write /raɪt/	schreiben	wrote /rəʊt/	written /ˈrɪtn/

Tipp:
Einige Verben bilden das *simple past* und das *past participle* nach einem ähnlichen Muster. Wenn du sie dir in Gruppen sortierst, kannst du dir die Formen vielleicht besser merken.

bring – brought – brought
buy – bought – bought
fight – fought – fought
think – thought – thought
catch – caught – caught
teach – taught – taught

ring – rang – rung
sing – sang – sung
swim – swam – swum

draw – drew – drawn
fly – flew – flown
grow – grew – grown
know – knew – known
throw – threw – thrown

cut – cut – cut
hit – hit – hit
hurt – hurt – hurt
let – let – let
put – put – put

Bildquellen
Umschlag außen: Dirk Schmidt/dsphotos.de
Innenumschlag vorn: Joachim Zwick, Gießen (Karte USA)

adpic Bildagentur, Köln: 19 (M. Baumann); akg-images GmbH, Berlin: 4; alamy images, Abingdon/ Oxfordshire: 3 (Art Kowalsky), 4, 5 (grzegorz knec), 5 (D. Hurst), 13, 17, 18 (Vanity License Plate Wisconsin), 19 (© OJO Images Ltd), 25 (© Michael Dwyer / Alamy), 27 (BeeJay Images), 28 (Steve Skjold), 28 (dalekhelen), 34 (derek webb), 34 (© EmmePi Travel), 34 (© Batchelder), 39 (© Cultura RM), 39 (© Frank Sanchez), 55 (© Juice Images), 56 (© Jane Williams), 57 (Freddie Jones), 58 (Varie), 75 (© Jim Parkin), 76 (Gianni Muratore), 78 (NatPar Collection), 78 (© Michael Doolittle), 94 (Rob Walls), 99, 101 (© Mike Goldwater), 102, 106 (© Trinity Mirror / Mirrorpix), 106 (© ZUMA Press, Inc.), 108 (© Ron Buskirk), 108 (© FEMA), 108 (© Danita Delimont), 108 (© Danita Delimont), 109, 111 (© imageBROKER), 111 (© PACIFIC PRESS), 111 (© Paula Solloway), 120 (© David Grossman), 123, 124 (DBURKE), 128 (Alex Serge), 128 (Carolyn Jenkins), 128 (Realimage), 128 (Ronald Karpilo), 130 (Stefan Sollfors), 130 (Neil McAllister), 137 (Mary Evans Picture Library), 139 (Archive Pics), 139 (Archive Pics), 139 (Archive Pics), 140, 146 (World History Archive), 168 (Wolfgang Kunz), 168 (© Jim Parkin), 172 (Ronald Karpilo); Bildagentur Schapowalow, Hamburg: 31 (Robert Harding); Bildagentur Schuster GmbH, Oberursel: 24 (Liaison); bildunion GmbH, Ladenburg: 18 (Jan-Dirk Hansen); British Columbia Lung Association, Vancouver: 54; Caro Fotoagentur, Berlin: 169 (Hoffmann); Centers for Disease Control and Prevention, Atlanta: 54; Colourbox.com, Odense: 31 (Giovanni), 116, 166; Courtesy of Maya`s Ideas, LLC, Georgia: 131 (Janice Flander), 131 (Phil Skinner); Courtesy of Woodward Gallery, NYC, NYC: 34 (Richard Hambleton: Untitled, shadow head portrait 2005, acryl on paper, 24 x 18,87 inches/61 x 47,9 cm, signed and dated lower right, WGRH1198); Daniel Harnett, Frankfurt: 41; dreamstime.com, Brentwood: 102 (Patrick Poendl); Druwe & Polastri, Cremlingen/Weddel: 46, 46, 96; F1online digitale Bildagentur GmbH, Frankfurt/M.: 46 (Aflo); fotolia.com, New York: 4 (B. Wylezich), 18, 19 (Mila Supynska), 19 (Daniel Ernst), 20 (Gordana Sermek), 20 (Aaron Amat), 20 (mshch), 20 (tuja66), 23 (Barry Barnes), 25 (vivalapenler), 37 (rh2010), 39 (Edyta Pawlowska), 41 (Constantinos), 42 (Marco Scisetti), 46 (siempreverde22), 47 (Rafael Ben-Ari), 60, 76 (Christoph Hänel), 83 (Andres Rodriguez), 86 (kasto), 89 (endostock), 94 (apops), 94 (contrastwerkstatt), 116 (eugenesergeev), 116 (rdnzl), 116 (M.Rosenwirth), 117 (Narong Jongsirikul), 117 (mangostock), 118 (alisonhancock), 118 (Kara), 118 (bluedesign), 119 (Thomas Söllner), 120 (alisonhancock), 120 (Kara), 120 (bluedesign), 121 (guy), 124 (nmann77), 124 (Maxim Malevich), 124 (trainman11), 124 (BillonPhotos.com), 124 (Jens Metschurat), 125 (ferhaterdem), 126 (Monkey Business), 126 (Richard Carey), 128 (zhu difeng), 129 (Paul Hill), 140, 165 (Constantinos), 167 (© jorisvo), 167 (f9photos), 168 (highwaystarz), 172 (Maxim Malevich), 172 (BillonPhotos.com); Getty Images, München: 4, 5, 17 (Chaz Niell/Icon SMI), 29, 49, 101 (John Moore), 123, 124, 145 (Randy Faris), 147 (Tim Mosenfelder), 147 (Kristian Dowling); Greenpeace Deutschland e.V., Hamburg: 128 (Leaving Traces); Hannelore Debus, Mörfelden-Walldorf: 82, 82; Harald Thumser, Frankfurt am Main: 118, 120, 171; International Rescue Committee, New York: 114 (Meredith Hutchison), 114 (Meredith Hutchison); iStockphoto.com, Calgary: 5 (freerangestock), 17 (ActionPics), 17 (ActionPics), 18 (Missing35mm), 20 (dny3d), 20 (spaxiax), 20 (Joao Virissimo), 24 (pr3m-5ingh), 24 (AndreyKrav), 24 (© Anthony Brown), 25 (ferenz), 27 (peeterv), 27 (Terraxplorer), 39 (Todor Tsvetkov), 47 (vicente fernandez), 49, 52 (vicente fernandez), 76 (Abasolutum), 76 (Andrey Popov), 78 (lestor27), 96 (© DragonImages), 97, 101 (stellalevi), 101 (Shelley Dennis), 105 (AndreyKrav), 108 (Pattie Steib), 109 (dinosmichail), 113 (dinosmichail), 113 (EdStock), 144, 144 (TommL), 144, 168 (Alen Popov), 168 (Ana Abejon), 169 (shapecharge), 170, 170; JOKER: Fotojournalismus, Bonn: 168 (Marcus Gloger); laif, Köln: 30 (Sasse), 123; Leemage, Berlin: 80; mauritius images GmbH, Mittenwald: 21, 43 (Uwe Umstätter), 47, 125; Miguel Amortegui, Rottingdean: 40, 56, 78; Muna Tseng Dance Projects Inc., New York, New York: 79 (Keith Haring: New York subway, ca. 1983, Photo: Tseng Kwong Chi © artwork The Keith Haring Foundation), 79 (Keith Haring: Pisa/Italy 1989, Photo: Tseng Kwong Chi ©artwork The Keith Haring Foundation); OKAPIA KG - Michael Grzimek & Co., Frankfurt/M.: 76 (Klaus Rose); Panther Media GmbH (panthermedia.net), München: 76 (123branex), 94 (Bernd Geller); Picture-Alliance GmbH, Frankfurt/M.: 19, 53, 67 (Photoshot), 76 (dpa), 83 (PhotoAlto/Frédéric Cirou), 86 (ZB / Patrick Pleul), 94 (ZB/Hendrik Schmidt), 106 (epa Morrison), 108 (dpa epa/Vincent Laforet/New York Times), 113 (dpa/ANSA), 113 (epa/Azmitia), 117 (Paul Hilton), 128 (ZUMA Wire), 165 (EPA/Soohoo), 166 (Bildagentur-online), 172 (ZUMA Wire); pixabay.com, Neu-Ulm: 16, 21 (CCC Creative Commons),

31 (skezze/CC0 Creative Commons), 31 (CCC Creative Commons); pixelio media GmbH, München: 25 (Cornerstone), 76 (Tim Reckmann); Polyp Cartoons, Manchester: 118, 121; Preserve, Waltham: 127; PREVOST Vincent/hemis.fr, Berlin: 50; Shutterstock.com, New York: 19 (Charlotte Purdy), 19 (Diego Cervo), 23 (Ahturner), 25 (Stuart Monk), 25, 28 (AJR_photo), 31 (T photography), 32, 39 (goodluz), 39 (kostudio), 45 (XarisStudio), 76 (Dragon Images), 95 (Lightspring), 96 (Odua Images), 96 (Monkey Business Images), 96 (Samuel Borges Photography), 96 (Dragon Images), 98, 98 (alexilena), 99, 101 (Gila Photography), 107 (Chris Loneragan), 116 (Dudarev Mikhail), 116 (lzf), 117 (Take Photo), 117 (Alison Hancock), 118 (Anmarin Nantasen), 120 (Anmarin Nantasen), 120 (PomInOz), 128 (paul prescott), 129, 129, 167 (T photography), 171 (lzf); stock.adobe.com, Dublin: 124; terre des hommes Deutschland e.V., Osnabrück: 47 (Theo Dom); Thomson Reuters (Markets) Deutschland GmbH, Berlin: 17 (Enrique Marcaria), 46 (Finbarr O'Reilly); ullstein bild, Berlin: 4, 66 (Lombard), 99 (Granger Collection), 112 (Lineair); Visum Foto GmbH, Hannover: 89 (Staudt); wikimedia. commons: 117 (gemeinfrei); © Terreform Center for Advanced Urban Research, New York: 122.

Textquellen

30 „Empire State of Mind", Text: Carter, Shawn/Hunte, Angela/Keyes, Bert/Keys, Alicia/Robinson, Sylvia/Sewell, Janet/Shuckburgh, Alexander; Copyright: Carter Boys Music/EMI April Music/Foray Music/Gambi Music Inc/Global Talent Publishing/J Sewell Publishing/Lellow Productions Inc/Masani El Shabazz, EMI Music Publishing Germany GmbH, Berlin/Rolf Budde Musikverlag GmbH, Berlin/Neue Welt Musikverlag GmbH, Hamburg

38 „Proud", Text: Small, Heather Marquerita/Vettese, Peter John; Copyright: EMI Music Publishing Ltd./Universal Music Publishing MGB Ltd., EMI Music Publishing Germany GmbH & Co. KG, Hamburg, Musik Edition Discoton GmbH, Berlin

41 „Butt out I quit" adaptiert von Spot on (3/2008) „I quit"

51 „Children's Rights and Responsibilities" adaptiert von http://cyc-net.org/cyc-online/cycol-0101-rights.html

58 „I'll be there for you", Text: Crane, David L/Kaufmann, Marta Fran/Skloff, Michael Jay/Solem, Philip Ronald/Wilde, Danny C/Willis, Allee; Copyright: W B MUSIC CORP/WARNER-TAMERLANE PUBLISHING CO, Neue Welt Musikverlag GmbH, Hamburg

59 „Love is inclusive", Amy Frances Koerner, Portsmouth

70 Auszug aus „Romeo and Juliet", Act 1, Scene 5, Page 6, used with permission from SparkNotes, LLC, SparkNotes and the SparkNotes logo are trademarks owned and/or controlled by SparkNotes, LLC or its affiliates. All rights reserved.
http://nfs.sparknotes.com/romeojuliet/page_68.html

96 „The kids in school with me", Langston Hughes, © 1994 by The Estate of Langston Hughes, published by permission of Harold Ober Associates, New York

98 „City of Chicago", Luka Bloom

100 1850: Table 4. Region and Country or Area of Birth of the Foreign-Born Population, With Geographic Detail Shown in Decennial Census Publications of 1930 or Earlier: 1850 to 1930 and 1960 to 1990, U.S. Census Bureau:
https://www.census.gov/population/www/documentation/twps0029/tab04.html,
https://www.census.gov/history/www/through_the_decades/fast_facts/1850_fast_facts.html
2000: U.S. Census Bureau, Census 2000, Summary File 3:
https://www.census.gov/prod/2003pubs/c2kbr-34.pdf,
https://www.census.gov/history/www/through_the_decades/fast_facts/2000_new.html

107 „People on the move" adaptiert von Amnesty International:
https://www.amnesty.org/en/what-we-do/people-on-the-move/

110 „Growing Strong" von Eyonna Martinez und „I've arrived" von Kiam Hayes, aus: *Through the Fire – Original Poems of the Universal Refugee Experience*, edited by Carl McClendon

114 „Never give up on your dream", adaptiert von *Vision not Victim Programme*,
http://www.ibtimes.co.uk/when-i-grow-syrian-refugee-girls-dreams-future-realised-beautiful-photoshoots-1541775

125 „Plastic – it's all around us" adaptiert von Surfrider,
http://www.surfrider.org.au/rise_above_plastics

125 „Reducing pollution – and saving energy“ adaptiert von BW Recycling,
http://www.bwrecycling.co.uk/environment/

126 „Here are ten easy ways …“ adaptiert von Surfrider
http://www.surfrider.org.au/rise_above_plastics

127 „Preserve Gimme 5“ adaptiert von Preserve
https://www.preserveproducts.com/recycle/programs/gimme-5-caps-recycling-4569

147 „Jack Johnson“, written by Savannah in Hawaii for The MY HERO Project. Reprint permission from The MY HERO Project (myhero.com), http://myhero.com/hero.asp?hero=JJohnson_Aikahi_es_07

Yonkers
Bronxville
Dumont
Bergenfield
Tenafly
Mont Vernon
New Rochelle
Pelham Manor
Englewood
Teanock
Long Island Sound
Bronx
NEW
Teterbord Airport
Fort Lee
NEW YORK
JERSEY
Hudson River
Harlem
East River
Great Neck
NEW YORK
Central Park
La Guardia Airport
Long Island City
Flushing
Central Station
Jackson Heights
Flushing Meadows
Manhattan
East River
Queens
JERSEY CITY
Williamsburg
Bushwick
Long Island
See detail map
Liberty I.
Statue of Liberty
Woodhaven
Upper New York Bay
East New York
J.F.Kennedy Airport
Flatbush
Jamaica Bay
Bay Ridge
Staten Island
Brooklyn
Jamaica Bay Wildlife Refuge
(Richmond)
Far Rockaway
Sheepshead Bay
Floyd Bennett Field
Lower New York Bay
Coney Island
Rockaway Inlet
Rockaway Park
Rockaway Point
Atlantic Ocean
0 mile 1 1/4 2 1/2
0 km 2,5 5